Patriotism to the Earth

Patriotism to the Earth

The Quest for Humane Global Governance

Richard A. Falk
Professor Emeritus, Princeton University

With Sasha Milonova

ROWMAN & LITTLEFIELD
Lanham • Boulder • New York • London

Executive Acquisitions Editor: Michael Kerns
Associate Editor: Elizabeth Von Buhr
Sales and Marketing Inquiries: textbooks@rowman.com

Credits and acknowledgments for material borrowed from other sources, and reproduced with permission, appear on the appropriate pages within the text.

Rowman & Littlefield
Bloomsbury Publishing Inc, 1385 Broadway, New York, NY 10018, USA
Bloomsbury Publishing Plc, 50 Bedford Square, London, WC1B 3DP, UK
Bloomsbury Publishing Ireland, 29 Earlsfort Terrace, Dublin 2, D02 AY28, Ireland
www.rowman.com

British Library Cataloguing in Publication Information Available

Library of Congress Cataloging-in-Publication Data
Names: Falk, Richard A., author. | Milonova, Sasha, author.
Title: Patriotism to the Earth : a quest for humane global governance /
Richard A. Falk, with Sasha Milonova.
Description: Lanham, Maryland : Rowman & Littlefield, 2025. |
Includes bibliographical references and index.
Identifiers: LCCN 2024053919 (print) | LCCN 2024053920 (ebook) | ISBN 9781538196878
(cloth) | ISBN 9781538196885 (paperback) | ISBN 9781538196892 (ebook)
Subjects: LCSH: Patriotism. | International relations—Environmental aspects. |
Globalization—Environmental aspects. | Environmentalism—
International cooperation. | Internationalism.
Classification: LCC JC329 .F25 2025 (print) | LCC JC329 (ebook) |
DDC 327.1/7—dc23/eng/20250228
LC record available at https://lccn.loc.gov/2024053919
LC ebook record available at https://lccn.loc.gov/2024053920

For product safety related questions contact productsafety@bloomsbury.com.

*For love of earth and its guardians, human and others,
dreaming of justice and peace, and an eco-resilient future
for all*

CONTENTS

Acknowledgments xiv

Introduction 1

Knowledge and Activism Without Adaptation or Justice 1

Historical Circumstances 2

Dysfunctional Structures, Norms, and Ideologies 4

Evolutionary Relevance 5

Notes 6

References 6

Part One A Frame for Inquiry 9

1 Toward a Global Imaginary for the Twenty-First Century 11

Explaining the Gaps 14

Four Fundamental Features of the Westphalian World Order 17

Modifying Expectations 21

Notes 24

References 25

2 Nonviolent Geopolitics: Law, Politics, and Twenty-First-Century Security 27

The UN Charter and a Legalistic Approach to Nonviolent Geopolitics 28

The Political/Ethical Argument for Nonviolent Geopolitics 32

Opportunities, Challenges, and Tendencies 37

Notes 38

References 39

3   Failures of Legitimacy: Global Governance and
     International Relations 41

     Global Governance and Legitimacy After World War I 47

     Global Governance and Legitimacy Crises After World War II 49

     Global Governance and Legitimacy Crises During the Cold War 52

     Global Governance and Political Legitimacy in the Era of Neoliberal
        Globalization 54

     Failures of Global Governance in the Twenty-First Century 55

     Conclusion 57

     Notes 59

     References 60

4   A Pluralist Cosmopolitanism 63

     Preliminary Considerations 64

     A Framework for Assessment 68

     Why and Which Cosmopolitanism? 69

     Conclusion 73

     Notes 75

     References 75

5   Global Contexts of Power 77

     Decolonization and the Decline of Hard Power 78

     International Intervention 80

     Post-9/11 Forms of Power 82

     Consequences 83

     Conclusion 85

6   Constitutional Guidelines for Global Governance 87

     Old Realism Versus New Realism 94

     Rethinking the Westphalian Structure of World Order 97

     Reform Proposals Within a Westphalian Framing: An Independently
        Funded UN Emergency Peace Force, Global Parliament, and
        Peoples' Tribunals 98

Toward an International Rule of Law 100

Subverting Westphalia 101

Notes 109

References 111

Part Two Pillars of Order: Horizons of Aspiration 115

7   International Law: Overcoming War and Collective Violence 117

International Law as It Emerged in Europe 121

  The Westphalian System 121

  Just War Tradition 122

  Primacy of Geopolitics 123

  Outlawing War 123

  Paradigm Shift 126

Reimagining Law and War 127

  Reclaiming Realism 127

  Envisioning Structural Reform 129

Avenues of Endeavor 131

  The Archetypal Struggle Against Nuclearism 131

  The Non-Proliferation Treaty (NPT) and Geopolitical Enforcement Regime 132

  Treaty of Prohibition of Nuclear Weapons (TPNW): Abolition Aspirations 133

  No First Use (NFU) of Nuclear Weapons 134

  Managing the Global Ecosystem 134

  Challenging Informal Censorship 135

  Revisioning Citizenship 137

Notes 139

References 139

8 Appropriating Normative Geopolitics: Civil Society, International Law, and the Future of the United Nations 141

Points of Departure 141

Global North Critical Expositions of International Law 143

The Question of Agency: Military and Political Ascendancy 144

The UN Fits In 145

Note on the UN and the Israel/Palestine Conflict 149

Conclusion 155

Notes 156

References 156

9 Global Inequality and Human Rights: An Odd Couple 159

Inequality Discourse in the United States and the Global South 161

Explaining the Disconnect 163

A Reframing of Human Rights and Inequality 164

Toward a "Universal Declaration on Human Rights and Inequalities of Income and Wealth" 169

Conclusion 171

Notes 173

References 176

10 International Law and Transformative Innovations: The Case of Criminal Accountability 179

Point of Departure 179

A Conceptual Prologue 180

For and Against Normative Determinism 183

The Nuremberg Judgment 190

Beyond Nuremberg 194

Notes 201

References 206

11 Peoples' Tribunals and the Peace Movement's Quest for Justice 209

The Judicial Dimension of Global Governance 209

Civil Society Justice 211

Investigating State Criminality 212

Note 215

References 215

12 Reparations, International Law, and Global (In)Justice: Extensions of Reparations to Global Governance 217

A New Frontier 218

Points of Departure 218

International Law: Authority and Instruments 222

Shadows of Misunderstanding 226

Some Limiting Conditions 232

Unevenness of Material Circumstances 233

Remoteness in Time 234

Absence of Individuation 236

Generality of Obligation 237

Extreme Selectivity 238

What International Law Can Do 238

Notes 240

References 244

13 Transformational Justice in a Neoliberal and Statist World Order 249

Transitional and Transformational Justice: Conceptual Points of Departure 249

The Transformational Option After World War II 252

World Order Constraints on Transitional and Transformational Justice 254

The Failures of Transition in the Arab Spring 256

The Iranian/Islamic Revolution: A Sustained Transition and a
Successful Transformation 259

Applying the Lessons of Transition and Transformation to the
Palestine/Israel Struggle 263

The Liberal Bias Toward Transition Without Transformation 265

Conclusion 268

Notes 270

References 271

14 Revisiting the Earth Charter 273

Note 279

References 279

Part Three Varieties of Cosmopolitanism 281

15 Fred Dallmayr's Visionary Cosmopolitanism 283

Sources of Inspiration 285

Choosing the Road of Spiritual Cosmopolitanism 288

Conclusion 290

Notes 292

References 292

16 Father Miguel d'Escoto's *The Spiritual Sources of Legal
Creativity* 295

Notes 303

References 303

17 David Ray Griffin's Postmodern Politics and Spirituality:
Do We Need (or Want) World Government? 305

Why a Democratic World Government Is Necessary 307

Why a Democratic World Government Is Possible 309

Why the Advocacy of a Democratic Global Government Is Not
Desirable 313

Notes 315

References 315

18 Edward Demenchonok's Visionary Cosmopolitanism 317

A Cosmopolitan Visionary for Our Time 317

Notes 322

References 323

19 Global Solidarity: Toward a Politics of Impossibility 325

The Imprisoned Imagination 325

On What Is Possible 327

References 330

20 Global Solidarity as the Vital Precondition to Cosmopolitan Transition 331

Do We Have the Time? 333

Index 335
About the Author 354

ACKNOWLEDGMENTS

We hope this book is read as a testament of faith as well as a work of scholarship. It is in this respect an alternative paradigm to the prevailing attachment of foreign policy advisers of political leaders to an outmoded 'political realism.' Its endeavor is to elevate the influence of law, morality, and ecological wisdom in relation to the conduct of foreign policy orientations of the governments of sovereign states.

In this spirit, Richard Falk wants to take this opportunity to express the deepest thanks to Sasha Milonova, who joined this project late, but contributed in so many ways to produce a manuscript that was genuinely collaborative in spirit and commitment. It was my great pleasure to have the immense benefit of Sasha's skill, enlivened by her warm manner and our intellectual rapport. Hopefully, we will find the occasion to repeat this collaborative experience in the future.

Falk also wants to acknowledge his deep friendship with David Ray Griffin, Fred Dallmayr, and Father Miguel d'Escoto, three recently deceased extraordinary persons who exemplified the worldview that we have been developing to achieve ecologically informed and politically reformed structures and operational realities of global governance. Their influence extends far beyond the chapters in Part Three dedicated to their work and is reinforced by the final chapter celebrating Edward Demenchnok's cosmopolitan vision of a just world.

Sasha Milonova wishes to thank Richard Falk for his generous mentorship over the years on what it means to live a meaningful scholar-activist life. This collaboration was a source of unprecedented intellectual growth and camaraderie. She is also grateful to Sonya, Chris, Irina, and Pavel for their unwavering support, and to all those who offered a couch, a ride to the airport, or a word of wisdom over a warm meal during the particularly nomadic years that corresponded with the writing of this book - it would not have been possible without you.

It is also our pleasure to acknowledge Michael Kerns, a senior editor of Rowman & Littlefield, who encouraged the submission of this book proposal, and has been steadfast in his support for our editorial efforts ever since, working with Samuel Withers and Jacqueline Plante Wilson on readying the manuscript for production by expert copy editing and overall guidance.

We are also grateful to Anne Hunt as Project Manager on behalf of Integra Software Services, who has offered us guidance throughout and much welcome encouragement.

Introduction

Knowledge and Activism Without Adaptation or Justice

Modernity prides itself on its core achievement—basing political order and economic advancement on the tools of reason and an unwavering trust in science-based knowledge and technologically driven progress. Yet when it comes to grappling with the large problems of our time, it is obvious that there exist wide and dangerous gaps between what we as a species know, what we believe, and what we do, both individually and collectively.

Organized governance structures have only selectively integrated this Enlightenment ethos into ethically framed formulations and implementation by way of policy choices. This explains part of the pathos of modernity, which, despite the technological wonders it continues to achieve, has led to the first bio-ethical-ecological crisis of global scope in the whole of planetary history. To address responsibly such a crisis in relation to climate change or comparable problems requires an adequate diagnosis, together with new strategies for bringing our knowledge and collective wisdom to bear synergistically. Additionally, there exists a discrediting, and likely paralyzing, normative gap between what we do and should be doing in relation to the ethical, social, and political dimensions of ecological resilience.

The severe threats to present and, even more manifestly, to future human generations and habitat well-being have long been convincingly confirmed by a consensus among climate experts drawn from all parts of the planet (Oreskes 2014; IPCC 2021). Civil society activists have been sounding the alarm, raising public awareness and anger throughout the world, increasingly vindicated by the unprecedented frequency of extreme weather events. The Swedish activist, Greta Thunberg, speaking a few years ago to an audience composed of United Nations (UN) diplomatic representatives of member governments, gave the issue an embittered intergenerational memorable twist: "You will die of old age. I will die from climate change."

Not only do we know and increasingly experience the multiple harms due to global warming but we are also receiving dire and reliable warnings that, unless the underlying situation is corrected within a narrow temporal window of diminishing opportunity, the effects of climate change will cause an ascending series of worsening events and impacts. These include extreme weather causing flooding, drought, heat waves, wildfires, famine, and superstorms; sea levels rising; destruction of river systems and lakes; glacial melting and polar warming; unmanageable migratory flows; polarized and frightened citizenries drawn to extremist and denialist politics; demagogic styles of political leadership; and a deteriorating quality of democratic governance. Many persons occupying positions of leadership have possessed this knowledge for several decades, yet most governmental and private sector responses remain deeply disappointing and, worse, objectively menacing.

Helen Camakaris (2021), in a perceptive article, writes: "The existential risks we now face are largely the consequence of neoliberal capitalism and partisan politics, super-charging growth, greed, and short-term self-interest." She sensibly concludes that the time has come to rethink the fundamentals of democracy and the economy and act "to quiet the partisan rage that is currently tearing the US apart." It is our view that this partisan rage, together with the greed-fueled preoccupation with maximizing the efficiencies of capital at the expense of human well-being and the natural habitat, is additional to the causal explanation Camakaris provides—a product of historical circumstances, nationalism, spreading consumerism, demographic pressures, and the fragmented form of *world order* that has been evolving since the middle of the seventeenth century, when it began to take its current shape and dynamics in Europe.[1]

Historical Circumstances

Two elements of the historical circumstances bear heavily on why the present context fails to take rational account of the scientific consensus and its evidence-based warnings about the future. The first of these circumstances relates to the outcome of the Cold War, which induced a triumphal and escapist mood in the West about the superiority of what was touted at the time as "market-based constitutionalism" that resulted in privileging capital flows at the expense of people. This in turn gave rise to "neoliberal globalization" as guided by market-oriented ideologies of growth and minimum regulation. As long as the Soviet Union was associated with a socialist alternative on national stages, the political class in the West, including its economic elites, felt obliged to supply a measure of social protection to their citizenry and to place some limits on the accumulation of wealth by the ultrarich. With the Soviet collapse, countervailing ideological forces no longer existed to exert a restraining impact on rapacious economic and social policies, and the result was to appraise economic well-being almost exclusively reliance on aggregate gross domestic product (GDP) growth statistics and corporate profitability. In other words, humanity and natural habitat are paying this enduring price for a distorted and short-sighted response by the political classes in the West, led by the United States, to the Soviet collapse and the related discrediting of socialism as an alternative. As well, the soft power influence of the West also has led most elites throughout the world to crave uncritically for higher life standards of living as potentially delivered by steady economic growth.

The second historical circumstance of particular relevance to the difficulties associated with mobilizing a political consensus on climate change at a global level that adequately complements the scientific or expert consensus relates to the postcolonial character of intergovernmental relations at the UN and elsewhere. Newly independent countries in Asia and Africa either refused to be distracted in their efforts to give the highest policy priorities to rapid economic and social development and often challenged whether their relationship to industrialization deserved to be burdened by constraints designed to keep global warming within tolerable limits. After all, the West evolved economically with the help of technological innovations without heeding environmental limits until late in the prior century.

This was not an idle and self-serving claim by the Global South. The buildup of greenhouse gasses in the atmosphere was predominantly a consequence of industrialization in the West, yet the countries currently suffering most from climate change are in Africa and the Middle East, including significant destruction of the agricultural foundations of their economic viability, prompting millions of climate refugees to flee their countries and seek entry elsewhere to improve their livelihood prospects. The countries in the West refuse responsibility for current global conditions, and if they do accept migrants, it is not because of an acknowledgment of causal connections of their behavior with migration flows. It is more in the spirit of hypocritical and purely discretionary humanitarian gestures to display to the world the high moral standards that exist in the West. Accordingly, a certain effort is made by affluent countries to convey a willingness to apportion fairly the burdens of adjusting to global warming. Yet analyzing and negotiating safe limits on carbon emissions has largely ignored the underlying injustices arising from the historical antecedents of colonial governance, an aspect of which was the adoption of policies designed to keep colonized peoples backward so as to retain a predominant role for the West in the colonial era, which depended upon the raw materials and agricultural goods sought by the factories and lifestyles of the West.[2]

Dysfunctional Structures, Norms, and Ideologies

The failures of rational response to climate change—and similarly to pandemics, migration flows, and ongoing political conflict—also reflect the impacts of the deeply engrained and generally legitimated fragmentation of world order, even as built into the structures of the United Nations. There are many references to the efforts of "the global community" to act and perform cooperatively, but behavioral patterns do not vindicate such rhetoric of solidarity. International institutions are overwhelmingly controlled by governments of sovereign states, whose representatives are beholden to *national* interests rather than either *human* or *global* interests. It could not be otherwise given the ideology of nationalism, "political realism," and geopolitical ambition that orients behavior toward the well-being and ambitions of individual sovereign states—in other words, maximizing what is good for the part rather than taking into account the well-being of the whole, creating a situation of what system theorists call "sub-system dominance" and "zero-sum" policymaking and problem-solving.

It may be that the process of evolution, which has demonstrated that natural selection privileges cooperation, is in the early stages of manifesting an evolutionary jump ahead by the human species. Global cooperative potential may be on the verge of breakthroughs, which, if they occur, will only be adequately explained retrospectively as they are hidden from view until after their unexpected occurrence. As matters now stand, there are not sufficient shared values at the global level to constitute community, and the cooperative alignments that are most robust in terms of commitment and funding are alliances formed to confront adversary states, a pattern responsive to the recent resurgence of transactionally oriented nationalism. This is partially a reaction against the homogenizing impacts of economic globalization on human identity that for many generations has nurtured a sense that true patriotism involves maximizing national interest, even at the expense of others.

This pattern was exemplified during the COVID-19 pandemic by the kind of vaccine diplomacy that illustrated the primary international realities of geopolitics, nationalism, and statism. It also illustrated the secondary reality of multistate, mutually antagonistic clusters and the tertiary reality of special interest private sector actors, especially the large vaccine manufacturers. Some civil society transnational actors are oriented toward holistic perspectives but exert minimal influence in settings where important global challenges are regressively addressed, for example, in relation to climate change, the COVID-19 pandemic, regulation of markets, migrant rights, strategic security interests, and nuclear weapons.

Evolutionary Relevance

At first glance, the timelines of both biological and cultural evolution seem much too long to be relevant to unraveling prospects for immediate, effective, and just responses to the multiple challenges posed by climate change. And yet we cannot be certain that there has not been taking place, over the course of antecedent decades and centuries, natural selection processes that cumulatively incline toward the emergence of *species identity*, along with an appreciation of the mutual benefits of collective cooperation on a global scale. In effect, humanity in various contexts seems increasingly aware that the tepid responses to climate change, and perhaps other apocalyptic threats to the future of humanity, are indeed dire news.

It is possible that the Paris Climate Agreement of 2015, although falling short of what the scientific consensus prescribed with respect to reductions of carbon emissions necessary for assurances that a safe ceiling for global warming will be achieved, was a preliminary breakthrough for collective action to address climate change at a global level. It seemed a dramatic recognition by 196 governments of sovereign entities that collective action in the form of global cooperation was indispensable in view of the dangers confronting humanity, and if necessary levels of cooperation are to be achieved, it must take account of diverse capabilities, vulnerabilities, and experience of these state actors. Such an event constituted a global moment of universal recognition and even celebration. It was a political victory limited by the voluntary nature of participation and implementation, as well as subject to withdrawal. As suggested, it could be understood as a manifestation of an emergent evolutionary trend. The withdrawal of the United States from the Agreement by the Trump presidency in 2018, followed by the return to full participation in 2021 by the Biden presidency, can be interpreted in contradictory ways or as the ebb and flow of the underlying evolutionary reality. It may be best understood as revealing the opaqueness of evolution as to its unfolding character. In this instance, in relation to the fragility and weakness of moves toward global cooperative problem-solving or as signifying the super-difficult tasks of modifying the behavior of the principal political actors in the prevailing fragmented world order.

Because intergovernmental behavior continues to be driven by short-termism as well as nationalism, sovereign rights, and geopolitical ambition, it would seem that transnational civil society activism is faced with the main evolutionary responsibility and opportunity to act more forcibly in support of a transition from statism to regionalism/globalism. This must be accompanied by a corresponding appreciation at the state level for deference to international law and other mechanisms to contain militarism, recourse to war, and capitalism, and so serve a drastically revised view of "political realism" and "geopolitical ambition" (Falk 2017; Brecher 2017, 2020; Davutoglu 2021; Johansen 2021).

If there is to be a positive outcome to the bio-ethical-ecological crisis, it will necessarily be more comprehensive than bridging the current gap between knowledge and action as reflected in the polarized politics within and among sovereign states that misdirects the popular imagination toward subsidiary concerns of national egoism, pop culture, and hyped security threats obscuring the unprecedented challenge to human well-being and species survival. Also of crucial importance is the parallel normative gap between neoliberal capital-driven ethics and eco-humanistic ethics expressive of an inclusive practice of justice responsive both to human rights and the rights of nature (UDME 2010). If bold action begins to be taken to bridge or transcend these gaps, we can begin to feel less discouraged about prospects for overcoming the current "evolutionary mismatch," but not until then.

Notes

1   These positions are analyzed in compelling detail in Rifkin (2022).
2   See Nayyar (2019) on the de-development of Asia during the period of European colonialization.

References

Brecher, Jeremy. 2017. *Against Doom: A Climate Insurgency Manual*. Binghamton, NY: PM Press.

Brecher, Jeremy. 2020. *Common Preservation in a Time of Mutual Destruction*. Binghamton, NY: PM Press.

Camakaris, Helen. 2021. "Evolutionary Mismatch, Partisan Politics, and Climate Change: A Tragedy in Three Acts." *This View of Life*, March 9.

Davutoglu, Ahmet. 2021. *Systemic Earthquake and the Struggle for World Order*. Cambridge: Cambridge University Press.

Falk, Richard. 2017. *Power Shift: On the New Global Order*. London: Zed Books.

Intergovernmental Panel on Climate Change (PCC). 2021. *Climate Change 2021: The Physical Science Basis. Contribution of Working Group I to the Sixth Assessment Report of the Intergovernmental Panel on Climate Change* (Masson-Delmotte, V., P. Zhai, A. Pirani, S. L. Connors, C. Péan, S. Berger, N. Caud, Y. Chen, L. Goldfarb, M. I. Gomis, M. Huang, K. Leitzell, E. Lonnoy, J. B. R. Matthews, T. K. Maycock, T. Waterfield, O. Yelekçi, R. Yu, and B. Zhou [eds.]). Cambridge, UK, and New York: Cambridge University Press. DOI:10.1017/9781009157896.

Johansen, Robert C. 2021. *Where the Evidence Leads: A Realistic Strategy for Peace and Human Security*. Oxford: Oxford University Press.

Nayyar, Deepak. 2019. *Resurgent Asia: Diversity in Development.* Oxford: Oxford University Press.

Oreskes, Naomi, 2014. "Scaling Up Our Vision." *Isis* 105 (2): 379–91. https://doi.org/10.1086/676574.

Rifkin, Jeremy. 2022. *The Age of Resilience: Reimagining Existence on a Rewilding Earth.* New York: St. Martin's Press.

Universal Declaration of the Rights of Mother Earth (UDME). 2010. World People's Conference on Climate Change and the Rights of Mother Earth. Cochabamba, Bolivia, April 22. https://www.rightsofnaturetribunal.org/wp-content/uploads/2018/04/ENG-Universal-Declaration-of-the-Rights-of-Mother-Earth.pdf (accessed September 19, 2024).

PART ONE

A Frame for Inquiry

1

Toward a Global Imaginary for the Twenty-First Century

Mark Mazower ends his synoptic book devoted to Western approaches to global governance with the following mystifying words: "The idea of governing the world is becoming yesterday's dream" (2012, 427). What Mazower appears to mean is that grand alternatives to the Westphalian framework of world order—whether based on political integration, global law, world government, supranationalism at the regional level, or functionalist visions of a networked world—were at one time *political projects* of practical interest but have, one by one, been put aside after reaching some kind of dead end of limited achievement, or have produced a sense of disillusionment. As a result, such ambitious ideas of post-Westphalian global governance now have only "historical" relevance as examples of "yesterday's dream." There is a counterintuitive dimension of this skeptical conclusion, as never before has the need for structural, ideological, and substantive modifications of the Westphalian framework seemed more practical if human security, ecological resilience, and political viability are used as criteria of appraisal.

The Westphalian framework—the state-centric/Western system of world order that has been globalized in the aftermath of the collapse of colonialism—started out as an essentially regional system in seventeenth-century Europe. It came to be conveniently, if somewhat misleadingly, associated with the Peace of Westphalia (1648). The basic structural innovation in 1648 was to postulate an international society constituted by territorial sovereign states. This structure has evolved over time, although the constituent elements of sovereignty and territoriality have retained their status as dominant descriptive features, a persistence juridically expressed by the universally accepted norm affirming "the equality of states." This image of a world of sovereign states expresses a somewhat misleading image of a horizontal (state-to-state) distribution of authority, and thus overlooks the unevenness of states associated with their varying size, population, resource endowment, political independence, military capability, geographical location, climate, civilizational base, and geopolitical acumen (a "Great Power" or geopolitical actor, as compared to a normal state).

This unevenness produces a condition of gross geopolitical inequality that can be understood as the vertical, hierarchical, and hegemonic dimensions of the Westphalian structure in which the strong impose their will on the weak, especially by means of war and threats, as well as diplomatic, economic, and cultural leverage. The legitimating logic of the Westphalian paradigm was exclusively statist in nature, allocating political authority on the basis of territorial sovereignty, which gave a new salience to the ordering roles of fixed international boundaries. In extending their control beyond Europe, colonialism legalized European expansionism to Asia and Africa, as well as Latin America, which was augmented by settler colonialism in North America. In fundamental respects, the state-centric image of world order exhibits tensions between status based on the formal equality of states, the operative impact of political inequality, and European colonial expansionism and exploitation of non-Western societies denied the benefits of statehood. In grasping the innovative character of the Westphalian framework, reference to the pre-Westphalian prevalence of empire and city-states, especially in Europe, as antecedent forms of political arrangements devoted to the maintenance of order understood as authority, security, and shared belief, as well as the establishment of community.

Reverting to Mazower's metaphor, yesterday's dream has become today's necessity, yet depressingly, he is rather convincing in his pessimistic assessment of present horizons of expectation for several reasons, especially if "the world" is conflated with "the West": post–Cold War disillusionment with any proposals that are perceived to be utopian; dramatic weakening of American leadership in the pursuit of global public goods as compared to the period following World War II; and the overall decline of West-centric civilizational authority and self-confidence, combined with a corresponding rise to geopolitical prominence of non-Western political actors. These factors are reinforced by such situational developments as the prolonged global economic recession, the financial crisis and loss of confidence in the European Union, the ironic post-Marxist materialist worldview that subordinates politics to economics in the priorities of democratic electorates, as well as the complexities of the digital age and related technological innovations that revolutionize the interaction of people and also of the connections linking information, knowledge, and wisdom. Undoubtedly, these contextual developments are altering the style of political leadership when it comes to different levels of problem-solving in relation to various global challenges.

Such skepticism is further reinforced by recent experiences in a number of critical policy-shaping arenas. A central one has been the failure to reform the composition of the UN Security Council despite widespread agreement that the geopolitical landscape has shifted significantly since the organization was established in 1945. Another is the failure to make credible efforts to implement Barack Obama's 2009 vision of a world without nuclear weapons and the lack of any sustained political excitement about such denuclearizing prospects in civil society. Another, though this list is far from exhaustive, has been the disappointments associated with the results of annual climate change negotiations at the global level that seem incapable of translating the warnings by climate scientists into an appropriate regulatory framework responsive to the challenge of global warming.

These illustrations are abetted by more concrete disappointments, including the failure of the UN to establish some kind of emergency peace force to address humanitarian and natural catastrophes, and the refusal of the International Criminal Court (ICC) to consider allegations of criminality that involve the behavior of major state actors, especially the United States. The ICC is probably the most "utopian" undertaking since World War II, at least in its presumed mission of imposing standards of criminal accountability upon those who act on behalf of sovereign states, but in its first decades of operation it has mainly deferred to the geopolitical constraints of a state-centric world, what we describe as the vertical dimension of Westphalian world order reflecting the inequality of states. This deference has been shown in a number of ways: by the refusal of the main states to become parties, by the unwillingness of the ICC or the UN to challenge the impunity of those who act on behalf of these states, and by the UN's unwillingness to carry out the recommendations of the UN's Gold Report, which addressed a clear instance of fundamental violations of international law arising from Israel's Operation Cast Lead 2008–9 attack on Gaza.

We would like to put this discouraging picture in a framework delimited by the interaction of three horizons of expectation to bring some clarity into this inquiry:

1. *politics of possibility:* what constitutes a political project with attainable goals;

2. *politics of necessity*: what is needed to reach certain goals that constitute urgent global public goods (e.g., nuclear disarmament, regulation of greenhouse gas emissions, poverty eradication, and humane treatment of migrants); and

3. *politics of desirability and spirituality*: what would both close the gaps between feasibility and necessity and provide a transcendent perspective that encompasses religious and cosmic levels of understanding of worldly issues. Such normativity also accords with widely endorsed human values beyond the boundaries associated with the Peace of Westphalia (1648).

It is the overall argument that present gaps between feasibility and necessity are unsustainable, although precise assessments of the timing, forms of tension, and possible collapse remain uncertain, obscure, and are essentially indeterminate. For reasons of convenience, we label this domain as *extraordinary politics*, that is, politics as the art of the *impossible* or *the politics of impossibility*. Further, reverting to history, the extraordinary happens in relation to many unanticipated jumps in the domain of political behavior.

Prominent examples include the end of the Cold War and the implosion of the Soviet Union, the generally peaceful transformation of apartheid South Africa into a constitutional democracy, and the Arab Spring as an unexpected series of societal eruptions. Such a pattern, theorized by Charles Jencks (1995) as "the jumping universe" and Nassim Taleb (2007) as "the black swan" phenomenon, suggests that what seems impossible does occasionally happen. It also should be understood that as a result of intrusions of the unanticipated, drastic regressions are also part of human experience, including catastrophic events, such as the rise of Nazism, followed by the Holocaust, the wartime use of atomic bombs and the post-1945 development of nuclear weaponry, and, more recently, the Gaza and Rohingya genocides.

From this perspective, in the face of such perceived gaps between feasibility and necessity on matters of collective survival, it is also likely that extremist movements with bizarre solutions to global challenges will attract significant followings. Such "solutions" include divine intervention or apocalyptic design, paranoid politics, and scapegoating, which blames the systemic dangers on some fraction of humanity, such as a religious or ethnic minorities and immigrants. The tendency for society to be attracted to such pathological extremes seems to be what Antonio Gramsci (1977) had in mind when he warned about the appearance of "morbid symptoms" during periods of fundamental societal transition during which the old is not yet dead and the new is yet be born. The embrace of techno-geopolitics during a period when the limits of planetary carrying capacity are being tested makes ours a period of unprecedented danger. The rise of fundamentalist religion and politics is to be expected under such conditions, making it particularly important for those who are dedicated to the politics of desirability/spirituality, as conceived within broad eco-humanist and cosmopolitan traditions of rationality, to articulate and promote their understanding of how best to close the gaps between feasibility and necessity. Such articulations must liberate reason from its Enlightenment moorings by enlargements of several kinds: incorporating the wisdom and ethics of native peoples, Asian civilizations, and world religions and by encompassing what Upendra Baxi (2012) has in mind when he refers to "insurgent reason."

Explaining the Gaps

What justifies the label of "necessity" is a matter of interpretation and judgment. We are associating necessity positively with the improvement of the human condition as measured by widely accepted human rights standards and negatively by the goal of avoiding catastrophic damage to human well-being, most dramatically in relation to threats mounted against the survival of the human species and its world civilizations, as well as the avoidance and mitigation of humanitarian and natural catastrophes (e.g., respect for the carrying capacity of the earth). As far as "desirability/ spirituality" is concerned, it is related to supplementing what is necessary. The desirable can be understood in relation to the promotion of health, security, nonviolence, longevity, and happiness as ends to be sought beyond the domain of mere necessity. The spiritual dimension of human existence addresses the inner extensions of experience that nurture expansions of human consciousness and outer inclusiveness in relation to the species and habitat, as well as appreciation for the relevance of the cosmos.

While necessity might require constraints on aggregate economic growth that impose heavy burdens on individuals, society, and ecological stability, desirability can move in different directions by promoting fairness as a guide to achieve more equitable distribution of the benefits and burdens of economic activity or through education that moves toward substituting cultural and spiritual engagement, as well as a love of nature and its habitats for the gratifications provided by consumerism, pleasure hunting, activities associated with heavy carbon footprints, and in gross inequities of the current phase of capitalism.

For several centuries, the Westphalian foundation of world order achieved tolerable results, at least for the countries comprising the West, including exhibiting a capacity for cooperation among sovereign states and a flexibility regarding the participation of independent states. Among the most notable achievements were the management of the global commons in a manner that accommodated many diverse interests, the establishment of international institutions to facilitate cooperation among states, and the expansion of membership in these institutions to accommodate internationalism after the collapse of European colonialism. Of course, such a plural order was problematic if viewed from various historical standpoints in relation to horizons of desire. War, colonialism, exploitation, and oppression persisted, and notions of territorial sovereignty shielded states and their leaders from accountability in the event of severe violations of standards of natural justice. Even here, Westphalian adaptation was evident in the development of international criminal law, including the establishment in 2002 of the International Criminal Court, war crimes tribunals, and the overall rise of international human rights discourses. These achievements are diminished to a significant extent by the realization that double standards in implementation produce a very uneven and geopolitically tainted record of compliance and enforcement. Impunity for the powerful and accountability for the weak underscores this morally and legally deficient application of norms. This is especially so as these norms and procedures were designed to establish and implement universal standards of behavior rather than shields for geopolitical actors and their friends and swords for use against enemies.

Arguably widening the gaps between horizons of feasibility and horizons of necessity occurred on the battlefields of World War I, and especially World War II, highlighted by the use of atomic bombs against Japanese cities in 1945. In theory, such a gap could be closed by reaching a verified and enforced agreement to destroy existing nuclear weapons arsenals and a monitored and enforced pledge never to develop or possess them in the future. Despite giving lip service to such laudable goals, a credible commitment never came into existence. Instead, what has taken place is the limited spread of these weapons to a series of leading states, codified in a Non-Proliferation Treaty (NPT) that establishes a legal/political regime based on a two-tiered hierarchical management of nuclear weaponry. One dangerous feature of global security in the nuclear age is the unregulated discretion of the nine nuclear states with the respect to the size, development, and nature of their arsenals of these weapons of mass destruction as well as the secrecy of war plans to have recourse to threats and uses of nuclear weapons. Over time this approach to nuclearism heightens risks of an apocalyptic future for humanity.

The NPT provisions seek to avoid such hegemonic structures by obligating the nuclear weapons states to pursue nuclear disarmament in good faith and to share technology helpful for nuclear energy with nonnuclear weapons states. But after more than fifty years, it is evident that the regime that emerged from the NPT is an oligarchy among nuclear weapons states determined to retain sovereign control over the weaponry, reinforced by refusals to implement the disarmament provision contained in Article VI of the NPT.[1] This tension between the language of the NPT and the behavior of the leading nuclear weapons states has become harder to obscure since the Treaty of Prohibition of Nuclear Weapons, entered into force in 2021.

An ironic feature of this evasion of the challenge of necessity in relation to nuclear weapons is to make the United States and its North Atlantic Treaty Organization (NATO) allies (United Kingdom, France) self-appointed managers of the non-proliferation regime. Such a geopolitical role, the full extension of the vertical side of the Westphalian logic, has eroded the broader legal effort to criminalize nondefensive international warfare by creating a new pretext for aggressive war. The Iraq War of 2003 was undertaken allegedly to address the prospect of an emergent Iraqi nuclear weapons program, and the ongoing threats directed at Iran are based on its alleged quest for nuclear weaponry, all while omitting any mention of Israel's existing nuclear weapons arsenal enveloped in an ambiguous formal rationale.

In effect, Westphalian efforts to address the gap between feasibility and necessity have so far avoided catastrophic consequences since Nagasaki but without removing unsustainable risks over time. There are several mutually reinforcing explanations for why this gap cannot be closed by the problem-solving mechanisms and cooperative arrangements normally relied upon within the Westphalian framework. This can be best illustrated by reference to four fundamental features of the current phase of Westphalian world order and by two aggravating situational considerations.

Four Fundamental Features of the Westphalian World Order

The four fundamental features of the Westphalian world order are as follows:

1. Prioritization of national over human/global interests and the public good: The absence of strong, centralized decision-making mechanisms diminishes capacity to address challenges that can only be met by giving primacy to the realization of *global interests* and the production of *global public goods*. The state-centric/geopolitical structures of world order are organized on the basis of the promotion of *national interests* with global public goods an incidental consideration. Robert Johansen (1980) made an important academic and normative contribution by encouraging American foreign policy to be shaped by the enlightened reconciliation of national and global or human interests.[2]

In this regard, the failure to arrange for nuclear disarmament and for the control of greenhouse gas emissions is illustrative of definite and critical global challenges that are acknowledged but not addressed. To adequately deal with such global challenges requires a major reform of present structures and processes comprising global governance, with a sufficient capability to realize the global interests that are visible on horizons of necessity. Such reforms need also to be sensitive to aspirations associated with horizons of desirability/spirituality, like the prohibition of nuclear energy facilities or reduction of greenhouse gas emissions in conformity with agreed criteria of climate justice.

To some extent, over the course of the Westphalian era, less demanding global interests have been promoted effectively either because of overlap with the national interests of major states or due to hegemonic leadership that includes some sense of responsibility for protecting global interests. Among the many examples are public order of the oceans, protection of Antarctica, control of ozone depletion, mitigation of conflict in outer space, and articulation of international humanitarian law.

The failure in relation to nuclear weapons and climate change can be partly explained because, in both settings, national interests did not coincide sufficiently with global interests, and hegemonic leadership was not at issue. In these two substantive contexts, the issues raised challenge the core concerns of the nation-state: security by means of hard power as measured by destructive capabilities and economic growth and profitability of capital. In both instances, entrenched bureaucratic and private sector resistance to achieving global interests was a further complicating factor. These gaps can only be closed by the emergence of a robust politics of desirability/ spirituality, which is deliberately situated outside of the domain of *normal politics*.

2. Territorial borders: Westphalian structures of authority are preoccupied with *borders* in the sense of territorial limits on the exercise of national sovereignty, while the policy agenda of the twenty-first century requires a focus on other kinds of *limits*—on population growth, greenhouse gas emissions, and overextraction of nonrenewable resources—to ensure equitable and sustainable uses of the global commons, such as space, the oceans, financial instruments, technological innovation, and medical innovations.

The Westphalian approach is premised on sovereignty over enclosed territory and internationally recognized boundaries, as well as shared use in the global commons, with autonomy the basic condition within state, and freedom and reciprocity the fundamental basis of mutually beneficial use outside of states. This allocation of regulatory logics works reasonably well for short-term behavior and has been abetted by numerous networks dedicated to promoting cooperative linkages among states and non-states, but it is not adapted to address non-territorial concerns or to deal with severe pressures on various aspects of equitable and sustainable behavior in the global commons or, for that matter, as with respect to genocide or ecocide within sovereign states.

When dealing with limits rather than borders, time as well as space become crucial elements in devising and implementing an effective and humane approach. The leadership of sovereign states is preoccupied with very short timeframes and is therefore not inclined to be receptive to curtailing security or economic growth if the alleged harm is situated far in the future or if the locus of harm is remote from the territorial community. For instance, global warming is unevenly distributed in such a way that the areas where the temperature rise has been greatest and most damaging is far removed from the areas of greatest per capita and aggregate greenhouse gas emissions.

A preoccupation with limits, for instance, with deference to carrying capacity of the earth, is not congenial with either the structure or ideology of the current world order when considering its nationalist and territorial characteristics. The United States, which to a significant extent is both a normal state and a non-territorial *global state* due to its force projection on a global scale (e.g., its network of hundreds of foreign bases, military dominance of space and oceans, Central Intelligence Agency (CIA) covert penetration and surveillance of foreign sovereign spaces, and globalization of capital and finance) lacks the leadership orientation now to address the challenges associated with limits. This lack contrasts with its historic success in restoring security and prosperity to a world of sovereign borders in the period shortly after World War II, although the colonialist extension of several European states cast a shadow of illegitimacy over the then-prevailing world order. The point being argued is that this current incapacity and unwillingness of the United States to exert benevolent leadership is partly conceptual (unaccustomed to thinking in relation to "the world" as distinct from specific countries *in the* world) and partly situational (the substitution of neoliberal for Keynesian economics, the polarization of domestic politics, and the rise of ultra-nationalist and chauvinistic political forces, e.g., in relation to resisting gun control).

3. The exclusion of non-state civil society actors from policy-forming arenas: Civil society actors, especially those organized on a transnational basis, have a natural inclination and strong motivation to reflect commitments to global interests and global public goods. Their orientation is more often shaped by ideas of the *human interest*, transcending the national interest, backed up by informal commitments to the present reality of "world citizenship" and "global civil society" (Kaldor 2003). In this respect, the aggregate of civil society actors function as, in effect, "the conscience of humanity" in relation to global policy, despite acknowledging divisions and tensions in their ranks. The most evident expression of this role has been in the context of global policy conferences on such themes as poverty, climate change, human rights, war, nuclear weapons, and population policy. Initiatives undertaken in the face of geopolitical resistance at various stages include the movements that built support for the Anti-Personnel Landmines Treaty, the establishment of the International Criminal Court (ICC), and the negotiation of the UN Treaty on the Prohibition of Nuclear Weapons—a set of developments that could be identified as a "new internationalism."

To date, the institutions of world order, including the United Nations, have given lip service to the relevance of global civil society but have not been willing to alter membership and participation rules and procedures to accommodate the spectacular quantitative and qualitative development of this dimension of world order. Similarly, proposals to move in more inclusive and democratizing directions, for instance, by establishing a global peoples' parliament, has not met with a positive response from within the UN and elsewhere (Falk and Strauss 2011).

4. The re-articulation of territoriality as the defining feature of the Westphalian conception of world order: The multiple impacts of globalization, drone warfare and surveillance, space satellites, nuclear radiation, cybersecurity and warfare, global media, transnational crime, non-state political movements, and transnational political violence have diminished sovereign authority over territorial space. In effect, the last half century has witnessed an extraordinarily robust trend toward the *de-territorializing* of world order. This trend is evident in the fundamental reconfiguration of conflict, which replicates the shift from conflict between territorial entities and the present period in which the central conflict ("The Long War") is between a non-territorial network of radical revisionist political actors and their affiliates and a global state representing the West that projects its hard power to the far corners of the planet.[3] To act to uphold the authority of territorial states in relation to unwanted flows of information and people, *re-territorializing* countermoves have been made, such as blacklisting and blocking internet sites and building walls along borders to discourage illegal crossings by migrants. In an opposite direction is the encroachment of territorial claims on spheres of activity previously classified as belonging to "the global commons": the extension of coastal claims of states, for security and resource reasons, from three- to twelve-mile territorial limits, complemented by the establishment of exclusive economic zones that extend for two hundred miles offshore, and by continental shelf claims of the same extent, or further depending on geological configurations. These expansions of territoriality reflect the growing importance of living and nonliving resources of the seas, including the energy reserves situated beneath the continental shelf. Such a pattern has given rise to a dramatic increase in maritime disputes, including several involving overlapping claims to uninhabited islands whose value is associated with offshore resources and strategic locations.

In effect, the cosmopolitan perspectives that are dominant in the civil society archipelago of actors operate in zones of advocacy that bridge the gaps both between feasibility and necessity, as well as necessity and desirability/spirituality, demanding what is necessary while seeking what is desirable, and even spiritual. Whether their influence and impact will grow in the years ahead may well determine the degree to which the global/human interest outlook gains traction.

It is necessary also to acknowledge that the Ukraine War, commencing with the Russian attack on February 24, 2022, and continuing in a form that highlights the geopolitical conflict between Russia and the United States/NATO, indirectly called attention to the dangerously escalating rivalry for global preeminence between China and the United States. These developments revived widespread concerns about a new era of "Great Power" rivalry in the nuclear age. In such a setting, the preoccupations since 2001 with transnational terrorism and internal war seem to be superseded, at least temporarily, by geopolitical alignment struggles that are determined whether or not the unipolarity of the post–Cold War decades is ending.

Modifying Expectations

The above analysis imparts a rather gloomy set of expectations. Perhaps the most disheartening feature is the weak commitment to civilizational and species survival in the face of unacceptable risks associated with weaponry of mass destruction and projections of disastrous levels of average global temperature rise, as well as the dangers embedded in the heightening within the global setting of geopolitical conflict. Short-term, narrowly conceived special interests and traditional national security ambitions have so far decisively disregarded the wisdom of prudence. At the same time, as distinct from premodern civilizational challenges, as depicted by Jared Diamond (2011, 2019), the contemporary challenges are primarily a result of human activities and, in principle, can be altered by human intervention. It is for this reason that sage observers have described this period as "the Anthropocene age."

The structural, ideological, and situational context seems to work against timely adjustments to horizons of necessity, much less attentiveness to horizons of desire/spirituality. The rational mind can only cope with such prospects by denial, escapism, or indulging some kind of bizarre reading of human destiny in the form of various end-time scenarios. Yet we know that human experience cannot be fully explained without taking account of radical uncertainty and hidden forces. When Tolstoy poses the question as to why historians always get the story of the future wrong, he contends that their gaze is on the surface of things, while change is a product of the fermenting of underground forces that erupt from below societal surfaces. These eruptions cannot be predicted, but their occurrence can be made more likely by working on behalf of a future that we believe to be necessary and desirable, and a refusal to be convinced by a dysfunctional understanding of what is feasible. We have to hope that the gradual heating of the global crucible will lead the mythical frog to jump to safety before it is scalded to death.

In this sense, defying conventional wisdom and rational assessment about the future is an indispensable precondition for constructive thought and action with respect to prospects for what we identify as "humane global governance." Such an outlook also reflects the spirit underlying the slogan of the World Social Forum: "Another World is Possible," which contradicts the feelings of closure brought on by the "there is no alternative" (TINA) prescription of neoliberalism so influentially inflected in the international influence exerted by Margaret Thatcher during the 1980s. More broadly, such a path follows David Graeber's (2004) admonition to overcome the anti-utopian cultural disposition that followed from the false labeling of Nazism and Stalinism as "utopian."

The utopian quest can be articulated in rather different ways. The strongest conventional view of promoting a positive world order transition from a Westphalian plural world order is to perceive world government in some form as necessary to manage the disarmament process and thereby overcome the menace of catastrophic war. It is also posited by some as functionally beneficial because it enables a concentration of energy and resources on productive activities. Over the course of time, and with faith in the power of human rationality, the project of establishing a world government is conceived of as feasible because long-term trends suggest centralization of authority and political integration, as well as a fundamental human drive toward unity.

A modification of this vision that falls short of addressing the deficiencies of the present arrangements of power and authority contends that the world is already the beneficiary of a benevolent world government in the form of the American role in providing stability and supplying the ingredients of humane governance.

The best arguments for world government are set forth in a federalist form by Clark and Sohn (1966) or a quasi-imperial form by Michael Mandelbaum (2005). Both formulations are premised on an assessment of necessity. Clark and Sohn suggest a radical reform of the UN Charter primarily motivated by war prevention goals that would effectively centralize peacekeeping authority in the UN, while trying to entice the participation of the non-Western world through its promise of promoting greater material equity and poverty reduction through reforms of the world economy. Such a position supposes that through the intervention of reason in developing the federalist case, and a leadership role assigned to the United States in the Mandelbaum approach, the gap associated with feasibility can be overcome.

In our terminology, Mandelbaum's "utopian" project is dystopian and should be rejected from the perspectives of horizons of desire/spirituality. It is dystopian on several grounds: a tendency to freeze the existing structures of inequity and to create a rigid hierarchy of power, privilege, and status; an ensured dynamic of resistance on the part of those sovereign entities and popular forces that fear authoritarianism and the likelihood that a globally centralized governmental structure would overcome opposition by relying on oppressive means, which would undoubtedly include high levels of surveillance and reliance on drones to patrol the world and establish totalistic forms of surveillance. To a degree, the Mandelbaum model is descriptive of the manner in which global security has been managed since the end of the Cold War, which is by United States as the sole globally engaged governmental authority, acting sometimes alone and other times in concert with its Western allies, leaving most states to exercise self-determined self-government so long as they accept the basic discipline of neoliberal globalization.[4]

Such embodiments of world government are rejected for two principal reasons: first, non-responsiveness to the agenda of global interests as set forth above and, second, inconsistency with the values associated with global justice and embodied in the overlapping zones of agreement contained in the Universal Declaration of Human Rights and the two major covenants on human rights.[5] A more tolerable variant of world government for the future is the idea of regionalization as a halfway house. This perspective looked more promising a few years ago before the European Union hit major bumps in the road to establishing a regional federation that could serve as a model for other regions.[6]

These post-Westphalian conceptions are essentially top-down conceptions, both in their origins in the minds of thinkers and strategists and in their image of historical agency, which relies on the persuasive effects of reason and self-interest, including a collective will to survive. Another orientation is bottom-up, democratic in conception and agency, a result of movement for "governance-from-below," a confidence in local empowerment and its global potentialities ("act locally, think globally"). David Graeber offers the following prescription for those he calls "radical intellectuals": "to look to those who are creating viable alternatives, try to figure out what would be the larger implications of what they are (already) doing, and then offer those ideas back, not as prescriptions but as contributions, possibilities—as gifts" (2004, 1).

The attractiveness of such an approach relates to the assurance that the transformation will challenge existing hierarchies and will exert its influence by the weight of popular demands.[7] The shape of the Arab upheavals in 2011 exhibited this orientation toward political action on a national scale, challenging existing governance structures without offering an alternative ideology or even program and avoiding any impression of vanguardism, that is, a small elite guiding the masses. Such a "new" politics inspired the worldwide, yet short-lived, Occupy movement. The enduring impact of these once-hopeful developments has been disappointing. The Arab upheavals have not led to more humane national governance. On the contrary, they have produced massive collective violence and established even more severe forms of oppression, and the Occupy movement displayed no capacity to sustain itself in the face of distractions and resistance.

In reaction, we favor some combination of elements as providing the foundation for an approach to humane and responsive commitments to the challenges of global governance in the twenty-first century. The nature of the global interest clearly requires stronger central institutions of authority to handle such concerns as weaponry of mass destruction and climate change. At the same time, worries about further entrenching injustices and antidemocratic modes of collective administration suggest the importance of having changes in global governance come about as responsive to pressures from below, democratizing in process and result. What will give rise to such populist capabilities cannot be currently discerned. This is a period of waiting, and hopefully not for the sort of large-scale catastrophe that would effectively discredit the existing structure and ideology of world order through the resumption of a full-scale cold war, or worse, a plunge into a geopolitically driven hot war.

A period of waiting should not be seen as a period of inactivity. Local struggles for justice and for ecologically sustainable means to provide food, water, energy, and cleaner air to communities can be considered an outcome of ecologically informed world order pedagogy. Also, broader issues ranging from identification with the symbolic struggle of the Palestinian people against the last major remnant of colonialism to the grassroots advocacy of nuclear disarmament can help define the tenor of public opinion and, by so doing, influence the political options of governmental leaders. In effect, there is no credible blueprint for humane global governance, but there are attitudes, actions, and aspirations that can set the stage in such a way as to heighten the prospect that historical opportunities as presented will be acted upon in positive ways.

Perhaps this recommended engagement with present and future challenges can be best expressed enigmatically: "it shouldn't be such a task to live in the present conscious of *futureness*" (De Piero 2013, 585–92). Or more prosaically, we cannot close the gaps between feasibility and necessity in humane and sustainable ways without activating and affirming the normative imagination, whose role it is to clarify, agitate, inspire, and give societal credibility to "horizons of desire and spirituality."

Notes

1   For further consideration, see Falk and Krieger (2012). Given the apocalyptic scale of the risks, reliance on this structure is reckless in the extreme. The classic statement on the apocalyptic risks can be found in Schell (1982); for an effort to overcome the gap, see the trenchant analysis and proposal set forth by Deudney (2007, 244–64).

2   We prefer "global interest" to "human interest," if a choice is made, to avoid the impression of anthropocentrism and a recognition that other aspects of global reality deserve protection, and not just for the sake of human enhancement or pleasure. There exists in Europe and South America a robust "rights of nature" movement.

3   For a conservative assessment along these lines, see Bobbitt (2008).

4   For opposing prescriptions relating to such a vision, see Gill (2008) and Barnett (2005).

5   The two covenants are the UN International Covenant on Civil and Political Rights and the International Covenant on Economic, Social, and Cultural Rights, both passed in 1966.

6   The positive potentials of world order regionalism are best explicated in Paupp (2009).

7   For broader assessment from such an outlook, see Hardt and Negri (2004).

References

Barnett, Thomas P. M. 2005. *Blueprint for Action: A Future Worth Creating*. New York: G. P. Putnam's.

Baxi, Upendra. 2012. "Public and Insurgent Reason: Adjudicatory Leadership in a Hyper-globalizing World." In *Global Crises and the Crisis of Global Leadership*, edited by Stephen Gill, 161–78. Cambridge: Cambridge University Press.

Bobbitt, Philip. 2008. *Terror and Consent: The Wars for the Twenty-first Century*. New York: Knopf.

Clark, Grenville, and Louis B. Sohn, 1966. *World Peace Through World Law*, 3rd ed. Cambridge, MA: Harvard University Press.

De Piero, W. S. 2013. "Mickey Rourke and the Bluebird of Happiness: A Notebook." *Poetry*, February.

Deudney, Daniel. 2007. *Bounding Power: Republican Security Theory from the Polis to the Global Village*. Princeton, NJ: Princeton University Press.

Diamond, Jared. 2011. *Collapse: How Societies Choose to Fail or Succeed*. New York: Penguin.

Diamond, Jared. 2019. *Upheaval: How Nations Cope with Change and Crisis*. London: Allen Lane.

Falk, Richard, and David Krieger. 2012. *Path to Zero: Dialogues on Nuclear Danger*. London: Routledge.

Falk, Richard, and Andrew Strauss. 2011. *A Global Parliament: Essays and Articles*. Berlin, Germany: Committee for a Democratic UN.

Gill, Stephen. 2008. *Power and Resistance in the New World Order*, 2nd rev. ed. New York: Palgrave Macmillan.

Graeber, David. 2004. *Fragments of an Anarchist Anthropology*. Chicago: Prickly Paradigm Press.

Gramsci, Antonio. 1977. *Quaderni del Carcere*, vol. 1, Quaderni 1–5. Turin: Giulio Einaudi.

Hardt, Michael, and Antonio Negri. 2004. *Multitude: War and Democracy in the Age of Empire*. New York: Penguin.

Jencks, Charles. 1995. *The Architecture of the Jumping Universe: A Polemic: How Complexity Science Is Changing Architecture and Culture*. Hoboken, NJ: Wiley & Sons.

Johansen, Robert. 1980. *The National Interest and the Human Interest: An Analysis of US Foreign Policy*. Princeton, NJ: Princeton University Press.

Kaldor, Mary. 2003. *Global Civil Society: An Answer to War*. Cambridge, UK: Polity.

Mandelbaum, Michael. 2005. *The Case for Goliath: How America Acts as the World's Government in the Twenty-First Century*. New York: Public Affairs.

Mazower, Mark. 2012. *Governing the World: The History of an Idea*. New York: Penguin.

Paupp, Terrence. 2009. *The Future of Global Relations: Crumbling Walls, Rising Regions*. New York: Palgrave.

Schell, Jonathan. 1982. *The Fate of the Earth*. New York: Random House.

Taleb, Nassim. 2007. *Black Swan: The Impact of the Highly Improbable*. New York: Random House.

2

Nonviolent Geopolitics:

Law, Politics, and Twenty-First-Century Security

Our aim in this chapter is to set forth a practical appreciation of real-world conditions as interpreted by reliance on a humanistic optic. This perspective privileges the enhancement of the security capabilities of a hybrid statist/geopolitical system of world order. The focus will be placed on the contributions of international law to the stabilization of relations and a more ambitious realization of the ethical potential of organized society, while not losing sight of persisting patterns of behavior that reflect the continuing dominance of sovereign territorial states.

We sketch here a conception of a world order premised on nonviolent geopolitics, as well as consider some obstacles to its realization. We believe such a futurist scenario is compatible with realistic hopes, if not a sense of what is currently attainable. By focusing on the interplay of "law" and "geopolitics," the intention is to consider the role played both by normative traditions of law and morality and the "geopolitical" traditions based on political will and ambition that continue to exert decisive influences on the dominant political actors occupying the global stage. A nonviolent geopolitics challenges the major premise of realism that security, leadership, stability, and influence in the twenty-first century continue to rest primarily on military power backing coercive diplomacy. Sophisticated versions of realist conceptions of world politics are recently expressed by referencing the mixture of hard and soft power capabilities, with the latter referring to reliance on persuasion and positive incentives rather than threats and force.[1]

From such perspectives, international law plays a marginal role in relation to war/peace and global security issues. Nevertheless, international law is useful as a policy instrument for denouncing the behavior of adversaries. It is not to be relied upon in objectively calculating the interest of one's own country within the spheres of national, regional, and global security, where old-style realism continues to hold sway. As such, the principal contribution of international law, aside from its underestimated utility in facilitating cooperation, is where adherence to legal norms consistently upholds mutual interests.

This chapter has three objectives:

1. to show the degree to which the victors in World War II essentially crafted, via the United Nations (UN) Charter, a world order which, if fully implemented, might have effectively marginalized war and encoded by indirection a system of nonviolent geopolitics; in other words, the constitutional and institutional foundations for humane global governance already exist but in inchoate and somewhat contradictory forms;[2]

2. to critique the realist paradigm that has never actually relinquished its hold over the imagination of dominant political elites, an approach that refuses to this day to acknowledge the obsolescence, costs, and dangers associated with the war system, and has recourse to force when geopolitical interests dictate despite UN Charter core prohibitions; and

3. consider some of the trends in international life that make it rational, despite the continued prevalence of realism among foreign policy advisers, to work toward the acceptance and practice of nonviolent geopolitics in practice and belief, as explicated by the formalities and rules of international law. In one sense, nonviolent geopolitics can be thought of as a shift in emphasis from a hard power approach to nation and global security and foreign policy to a soft power approach.

The UN Charter and a Legalistic Approach to Nonviolent Geopolitics

In the immediate aftermath of World War II, particularly in light of the horrendous atomic bombings of Japanese cities and the strategic bombings of German cities, even many foreign policy specialists of realist disposition were deeply worried by what it might portend for the future. Without much hesitation, a constitutional framing of world politics that contained crucial elements of nonviolent geopolitics was agreed upon. In one respect, this was a continuation of a trend that started after World War I with the establishment of the League of Nations, reflecting the then halfhearted governmental endorsements of Woodrow Wilson's sentiment that the terrible conflagration amounted to "a war to end all wars."

Yet while the European colonial governments *rhetorically* accommodated Wilson's worldview, they continued to believe and act as if the war system was viable and integral to maintaining Western hegemony, especially given the consensus that conflict with the Soviet Union would dominate the next phase of international relations. The League of Nations proved to be irrelevant in avoiding the onset of World War II, although its functional contributions exceeded expectations as a new feature of world order. Their acceptance was confirmed by their adoption and expansion after 1945 in relation to the UN.

World War II was different from prior wars because it offered political leaders a grim warning that a future war among major states would likely entail the use of nuclear weapons. It ended up entrusting the future to an institutionalized coalition of victorious powers, dominated by the West, that had cooperated against the menace posed by fascism. This anti-fascist coalition had, in the view of the American wartime leader Franklin Roosevelt, a capacity to cooperate to maintain the peace for the sake of common security that had been effectively demonstrated in waging war. Beyond this, the memories of the Great Depression and the realization that the punitive peace imposed on Germany in the Versailles Treaty had encouraged the rise of Hitler, gave the leadership in the world at that time strong incentives to facilitate cooperation in trade and investment with the defeated enemy states. US-led commitments to restoring the economies of defeated Germany, Italy, and Japan were justified as the preferred way to avoid the recurrence of another cataclysmic depression. Additionally, these defeated enemies were soon recast as potential allies in the new preoccupying struggle to contain Soviet expansion and weaken its missionary advocacy of socialism seen as a direct challenge to the hegemonic aspirations of a market-driven international economic order shaped by the practices and priorities of the Global West.

It was in this atmosphere that the UN Charter was agreed upon with its cardinal principles based on the following:

1. the unconditional prohibition of recourse to force in international relations except in self-defense against a prior armed attack, which was interpreted to mean the outlawry of war as an instrument of national policy. This amounted to a legalistic push in the direction of nonviolent geopolitics, which did not correspond with the behavior of many states, above all the Permanent Five (P5) UN conception of Great Powers;

2. the reinforcement of this prohibition with a collective commitment of the UN membership to support any state that was the target of nondefensive force, including acting forcibly under UN auspices to restore the territorial integrity and political independence of such

a violated state. Furthermore, it was widely accepted *legally* that under no conditions was it to be acceptable for a state to acquire territory by recourse to force. This second principle also did not correspond with dominant patterns of political behavior of a variety of states;

3. by "the Nuremberg promise," which pledged that in the future *all* political leaders who engage in aggressive warfare (not only those who lost wars) and other international crimes would be held criminally responsible on an individual basis; and

4. a nonintervention commitment to respect the internal sovereignty of all states, whether large or small, via the acceptance of an unconditional obligation to refrain from any interference in matters essentially within its domestic jurisdiction, including civil strife or insurgent challenge.

Such a legal framework, if implemented by self-restraint, prudence, habits of compliance, and enforcement, would have effectively eliminated international warfare and military intervention, preserved the statist structure of world order, and created a robust set of collective security mechanisms to inhibit and respond to aggression as needed, as well as defeat and punish political leaders who engaged in aggressive warfare or severe deprivations of human rights (i.e., Crimes Against Peace). It is important to realize that this *legalistic* vision of world order assumed that it was *politically* possible to establish such a warless world and that *rationality* would prevail in the nuclear age to redefine the hard power approaches to security policy as conceived by "political realists" over the centuries and carried into practice by leaders with similar views. It is also relevant to observe that the nonviolent geopolitics embedded in the UN Charter never involved an overt embrace of nonviolence as a precondition of political life. It was understood, perhaps wrongly, that *within* states violent insurgent politics and various forms of civil strife would occur and would not violate *international* norms, nor in most instances endanger international peace and security. By the Charter scheme, internal wars were beyond the writ of the social contract made by states to renounce recourse to *international* violence. In this respect, an internal war, unless it spilled over boundaries to become a species of international warfare, was not to be addressed by the UN. International law although somewhat ambiguously configured to favor established government over internal opponents. A central characteristic of this bias toward political stability rendered military assistance to governments "legal" while treating as unlawful similar support for its internal opponents.

Even within this legalistic conception of nonviolent geopolitics there are significant difficulties. First of all, the conferral of a right of veto on the five permanent members of the Security Council (P5) meant that no decision adverse to the vital interests of most of the most dangerous political actors in the world could be reached. This amounted to a de facto exemption from the commitment to nonviolent geopolitics that greatly compromised the value of the legal framing in the UN Charter, making the optimistic assumption of an enduring alliance for peace absolutely crucial if the security claims being posited by the UN were to be taken seriously.

Second, the acceptance of internal sovereignty as legally absolute meant that there would be no legal basis for effectively challenging the recurrence of genocide, severe crimes against humanity, and other catastrophic circumstances confronting a society caught in civil strife of the sort that occurred in Syria over the course of more than a decade starting in 2011. Even more so, hampering any effective response to Israeli unlawful actions in Occupied Palestine that were not even regarded from an international perspective as taking place within Israel's sovereign territory.

Of course, these *legal* shortcomings seem almost irrelevant in view of the lack of political will to implement the Charter vision of nonviolent geopolitics. In retrospect, it seems clear that before the Charter had even been ratified, governing elites in the United States and the Soviet Union reaffirmed their reliance on national military capabilities, political alliances, and deterrent doctrines. These nuclear superpowers grounded their main security concerns on the logic of countervailing hard power, known more technically as doctrines of "deterrence." Also, the anti-fascist alliance, so effective in wartime, collapsed quickly afterward in the absence of a common enemy, and the long Cold War ensued, which underscored a strategic conflict that doomed the collective security dimensions of the Charter vision. This failure of global peace diplomacy strengthened Westphalian statism in both its horizontal (equal state sovereignty) and vertical (geopolitical) dimensions.

These legal gaps could have been overcome if the worldview of the leading political actors truly embraced nonviolent geopolitics as more than a kind of vague aspirational framing of security that must not be allowed to interfere with realist faith in deterrence, weapons development, war planning, military strength, and secret war plans once the initial shock and awe of the dawning of the nuclear age subsided. What this meant in relation to the positions advocated here is that violent or war-prone geopolitics was fully restored and justified, arguably universalized, and restrained only by a quality of enhanced prudence in relation to great power confrontations, as during the various Berlin crises of the 1950s[3] and the Cuban Missile Crisis of 1962. Prudence had always been a cardinal political feature of the classical realist approach, but was not until the advent of nuclear weapons was it elevated to a central role in balancing the pursuit of vital interests against the risks of catastrophic warfare.[4]

The Political/Ethical Argument
for Nonviolent Geopolitics

The contrasting argument presented here is that political outcomes in wars, whether international or internal, since the end of World War II have been primarily shaped by soft power ingenuity that has rather consistently overcome conditions of military inferiority to achieve its desired political outcomes. The United States completely controlled land, air, and sea throughout the Vietnam War, winning every battle and, yet, eventually lost the war and killed as many as five million Vietnamese on the road to the failure of its military intervention. Ironically, the US government went on after a long pause to engage the victorious Vietnam government. It currently enjoys a friendly and productive diplomatic and economic relationship. In this sense, the strategic difference between defeat and victory is almost unnoticeable, making the wartime casualties and devastation even more tragic, seemingly worse than pointless, even from a strategic perspective.

Nevertheless, US militarists refused to learn from such outcomes, treating the impact of its own defeat in Vietnam as a kind of geopolitical disease, the "Vietnam syndrome." The Vietnam experience was a strong reflection of a historical trend supportive of the legitimate claims of self-determination despite the seeming military vulnerability of such nationalist movements in the face of motivated and overwhelming intervention. Mainstream realists drew the wrong lessons from Vietnam, insisting that the outcome was an exception rather than the rule, a case where domestic demoralization within the United States undermined support for the war rather than being a case of losing to a stronger adversary. In effect, overcoming the Vietnam syndrome meant restoring confidence in hard power geopolitics and thereby neutralizing selective domestic opposition to nondefensive war making. This militarist spin given to the Vietnam outcome revived explicit control over the shaping of American foreign policy in the aftermath of the Gulf War in 1991, which revealingly prompted the American president at the time, George H. W. Bush, to proclaim immediately after achieving military victory on a desert battlefield, to utter these memorable words: "We finally kicked the Vietnam syndrome."[5] What Bush meant by his words was that the United States demonstrated once more that it could wage and win wars quickly and at acceptable costs. The American president did not bother to notice that such victories were obtained only where the terrain was suited for a purely conventional military encounter or the capability and the will of the enemy to resist was minimal or nonexistent.

It is not that hard power is obsolete but, rather, that it is not able to shape the outcomes in the most characteristic violent political conflicts of the period since 1945, namely the political struggle to expel oppressive forces that represent a foreign imperial power or to resist military intervention.

Hard power is still decisive in encounters with hard power, or in situations where the weaker side is rather defenseless and the stronger side is prepared to carry its military dominance to genocidal extremes. It is hardly surprising, then, that the excessive and anachronistic reliance on hard power solutions in situations of conflict has led to a series of failures, both acknowledged (Iraq, Afghanistan), unacknowledged (Syria, Libya), and horrifying in its execution (Israel 2023–24).

As long as the United States invests so much more heavily in military capabilities than any other state, it is bound to exaggerate security threats or pursue its interests along a hard power path. By refusing to reckon with clear historical trends favoring soft power dominance in the most characteristic conflict situations it has also situated the United States on the wrong side of history. Israel also exemplifies such an approach culminating with its ill-conceived genocidal campaign against Hamas in 2023–24, relying on its military superiority to destroy and kill but not being able to control the adverse political results of this massive military operation. One other cost of hard power or violent geopolitics is undermining whatever lingering respect exists for either the rule of law in global politics or the authority of the United Nations.

A second demonstration of the anachronistic reliance on a violence-based system of security was associated with the response to the 9/11 attacks on the Twin Towers and the Pentagon, dual symbols of US imperium. A feature of this event was the exposure of the extreme vulnerability of the most militarily dominant state in the whole of human history to attack by a non-state actor without access to advanced weaponry, lacking major resources and a secure territorial base. In the aftermath of 9/11, it became clear that the enormous US investment in achieving "full spectrum dominance" had not brought enhanced security but, on the contrary, had produced the most acute sense of insecurity in the history of the country.

Once again, the wrong lesson was drawn, namely that the way to restore security was to wage war against terror regardless of the distinctive nature of this new kind of threat. Counterterrorism relied on the mindless use of the military machine abroad and restraints on liberties at home, despite the absence of a territorial adversary or any plausible means/ends relationship between recourse to war and reduction of the threat (Cole and Lobel 2007; Falk 2003). The appropriate lesson, borne out by experience, is that such a security threat can best be addressed by a combination of transnational law enforcement and through addressing the *legitimate* grievances of the political extremists who launched the attacks. The Spanish response to the Madrid terrorist attacks of March 11, 2004, seemed sensitive to these new realities: withdrawal from involvement in the Iraq War while enhancing police efforts to identify and arrest violent political activists, and joining in the dialogic attempts to lessen tension between Islam and the West.[6]

In another setting, former British prime minister John Major has observed that he only began to make progress in ending the violence in Northern Ireland when he stopped thinking of the IRA (Irish Republican Army) as a terrorist organization and began treating it a political actor with real grievances and its own motivations in reaching accommodation and peace. Israeli leaders could learn from this British shift to diplomacy in addressing their "Irish Problem."

The right lesson is to recognize the extremely limited utility of military power in conflict situations within the postcolonial world, grasping the extent to which popular struggle fully engaging people has exerted historical agency during the last seventy-plus years. It has shaped numerous outcomes of conflicts that could not be understood if assessed only through a hard power lens, which interprets history as almost always determined by wars being won by the stronger military side earning it the authority to shape the peace.[7] Every anti-colonial war in the latter half of the twentieth century was won by the militarily weaker side, which prevailed in the end despite suffering disproportionate losses along its way to victory. It won because the people were mobilized on behalf of independence against foreign colonial forces, and their resistance included gaining complete control of the high moral ground that shapes legitimacy wars. It won because of a political truth embodied in the Afghan saying: "You have the watches, we have the time." Gaining the high moral ground both delegitimized colonial rule and legitimized anti-colonial struggle; in the end, even the state-centric and initially empire-friendly UN was induced to endorse anti-colonial struggles by reference to the right of self-determination and rights of resistance, which were proclaimed to be rights of all oppressed peoples. The Palestinian struggle against Israeli settler colonialism continues at the time of publication and is hampered by the presence of several unique problematic aspects.

Of course, it is true that this ascendancy of soft power capabilities in political struggles was not always the case. Throughout the colonial era, and until the mid-twentieth century, hard power was generally effective and efficient, as demonstrated by the colonial conquests of the Western Hemisphere with small numbers of well-armed troops: for example, British control of India with a few thousand soldiers and the success of "gunboat diplomacy" in supporting US economic imperialism in Central America and the Caribbean. What turned the historical tide against militarism was the rise of national and cultural self-consciousness in the countries of the South, most dramatically in India under the inspired leadership of Gandhi, where coercive nonviolent forms of soft power first revealed their potency.

More recently, abetted by the communications revolution, resistance to oppressive regimes based on human rights has been illustrating the limits of hard power governance in a globalized world. The anti-apartheid campaign extended the struggle against the racist regime that governed South Africa to a symbolic global battlefield where the weapons relied upon were coercive nonviolent reliance on boycotts, divestment, and sanctions. The collapse of apartheid in South Africa was partially achieved by developments outside of its sovereign territory, a pattern that is now being repeated in the Palestinian "legitimacy war" being waged against Israel. The outcome is not assured, and it is possible for the legitimacy war to be won and yet the oppressive conditions sustained, as seems to be currently the case with respect to Tibet, Chechnya, and Puerto Rico.

Against this background, it is notable, and even bewildering, that geopolitics continues to be driven by a realist consensus that ahistorically believes that history continues to be determined by the grand strategy of hard power dominant state actors.[8] In effect, realists have lost touch with reality. It seems correct to acknowledge that there remains a rational role for hard power, as a defensive hedge against residual statist and geopolitical militarism, but even here the economic and political gains of demilitarization would seem to far outweigh the benefits of an anachronistic dependence on hard power forms of self-defense, especially those that risk wars fought with weaponry of mass destruction. With respect to non-state political violence, hard power capabilities are of little or no relevance, and security can be best achieved by accommodation, intelligence, and transnational law enforcement. The US recourse to war in addressing the al-Qaeda threat, as in Iraq and Afghanistan, has proved to be costly, ineffectual, and misdirected.[9] Just as the US defeat in Vietnam reproduced the French defeats in their colonial wars waged in Indochina and Algeria, the cycle of failure is being renewed in the post-9/11 global setting. Why do such lessons bearing on the changing balance between hard and soft power remain unlearned in the imperial centers of geopolitical maneuver?

It is of great importance to pose this question even if no definitive answer is now available. There are some suggestive leads that relate to both material and ideological explanations. On the materialist side, there are deeply embedded governmental and societal structures whose identity and narrow self-interests are bound up with a maximal reliance upon and projection of hard power. These structures have been identified in various ways in the US setting: "national security state," "military-industrial complex," "military Keynesianism," and "the war system." It was the famed former general, President Dwight Eisenhower, who in 1961 famously warned of the military-industrial complex in a farewell speech, notably making the observation after he was no longer able to exert influence on military spending.[10]

In the interval since Eisenhower's warning, a more deeply rooted domestic structure of support for militarism has evolved that extends to mainstream media, conservative think tanks, a vast array of highly paid lobbyists, a budget-hungry Pentagon, and a deeply compromised Congress whose majority of members have substituted campaign support for conscience. This politically entrenched paradigm linking realism and militarism makes it virtually impossible to challenge a military budget even at a time of fiscal deficits that are acknowledged by conservative observers to endanger fiscal stability, including the viability of the dollar-based US empire (Ferguson 2010). The scale of the military budget, combined with navies in every ocean, more than seven hundred foreign military bases, and a huge investment in the militarization of space exhibit the self-fulfilling inability to acknowledge the dysfunctionality of such a global posture.[11] The United States spends more than what the next ten leading states spend, without reaping benefits for either the national or global interest.

The most that can be expected by way of adjustment of the realist consensus under these conditions is a certain softening of the hard power emphasis. In this respect, one notes that several influential adherents of the realist consensus have recently called attention to the rising importance of nonmilitary elements of power in the rational pursuit of a grand strategy that continues to frame geopolitics by reference to presumed hard power "realities," but are at the same time critical of arch militarism attributed to neoconservatives (Nye 1990; Walt 2005; Gelb 2009).[12] This same tone pervades the speech of Barack Obama at the 2009 Nobel Peace Prize ceremony. This realist refusal to comprehend a *largely* post-militarist global setting is exceedingly dangerous given the continuing hold of realism on the shaping of policy by governmental and market/finance forces.[13] Such an outmoded realism not only engages in imprudent military undertakings but also tends to overlook a range of deeper issues bearing on security, survival, and human well-being, including climate change, peak oil, water scarcities, fiscal fragility and market freefall, poverty, and social and physical infrastructure. As such, this kind of policy orientation is incapable of formulating the priorities associated with sustainable and benevolent forms of global governance.

In addition to the structural rigidity that results from the entrenched militarist paradigm, there arises a systemic learning disability that is incapable of accurately explaining the main causes of past policy failures. As a practical matter, this leads policy options to be too often shaped by unimaginative thinking trapped within a militarist box. In recent international experience, thinking about security led the Obama administration to escalate US involvement in an internal struggle for the future of Afghanistan and to leave the so-called military option on the table for dealing with the prospect of Iran's acquisition of nuclear weapons.

An attractive alternative policy approach in Afghanistan would have been based on the recognition that the Taliban is a movement seeking nationalist objectives amid raging ethnic conflict. As a result, it would tend toward a conclusion that US security interests would benefit from ending combat operations, followed by the phased withdrawal of all NATO (North Atlantic Treaty Organization) forces, a major increase in developmental assistance that avoids channeling funds through a corrupted Kabul government, and a genuine shift in US foreign policy toward respect for the politics of self-determination. Similarly, in relation to Iran, instead of threatening a military strike and advocating punitive measures, a call for regional denuclearization, which insists on the inclusion of Israel, would be expressive of both thinking outside the militarist box and the existence of more hopeful, nonmilitary responses to admittedly genuine security concerns.

Opportunities, Challenges, and Tendencies

Some form of geopolitics is almost bound to occur given the gross inequality of states and the weakness of the United Nations as the institutional expression of unified governance for the planet. Especially since the collapse of the Soviet Union, the primacy of the United States has resulted inevitably in its geopolitical ascendancy. Unfortunately, this position has been premised upon an unreconstructed confidence in the hard power paradigm, which combines militarism and realism, producing violent geopolitics in relation to critical unresolved conflicts. The experience of the past decades shows clearly that this paradigm is untenable from both pragmatic and principled perspectives. It fails to achieve its goals at acceptable costs, if at all. It relies on immoral practices that involve the mass killing of innocent persons, widespread devastation, and an enormous waste of resources.

Perhaps the leading test of the thesis outlined here is the ongoing struggle for self-determination of the Palestinian people, whether in the form of a single secular state encompassing the whole of historic Palestine or an independent, equal, and viable sovereign state of its own, coexisting alongside the existing Israeli state. As matters now stand, after decades of occupation, the Palestinian struggle is relying mainly on a legitimacy war, using an array of soft power instruments, including diplomacy and lawfare, a nonviolent coercive boycott and divestment campaign, and a variety of civil society initiatives challenging Israeli policies. Uncertainty exists as to the future outcome. The whole soft power orientation has taken a giant leap forward following the Arab Spring, in which unarmed popular movements challenged dictatorial and oppressive regimes with some notable successes (though unfortunately temporary, especially in Egypt and Tunisia). Elsewhere among Arab countries, the upheavals at least achieved promises of extensive reforms. Increasingly, the potentialities of constructing a world order based on soft power principles is gaining support, moving the idea of nonviolent geopolitics from the domain of utopianism to being on the verge of becoming a genuine political project. Of course, there is resistance and pushback, especially from the hard power holdouts led by the United States and Israel.

Those political forces relying on the alternative of nonviolent practices and principles have, in contrast, shown a capacity to achieve political goals and a willingness to pursue their goals by ethical means, sometimes at great personal risk. The Gandhi movement resulting in Indian independence, the Mandela-led transformation of apartheid South Africa, people power in the Philippines, and the soft revolutions of Eastern Europe in the late 1980s are exemplary instances of domestic transformations based on nonviolent struggle that entailed dangers for militants and resulted in some high-profile bloody sacrifices. None of these soft power victories has produced just societies or addressed the entire agenda of social and political concerns, often leaving untouched exploitative class relations and bitter societal tensions, but they have managed to overcome immediate situations of oppressive state/society relations without significant reliance on large-scale violence.

Turning to the global setting, there exist analogous opportunities for the application of nonviolent geopolitics. There is a widespread recognition that war between large states is not a rational option as it is almost certain to involve huge costs in blood and treasure, and reach mutually destructive results rather than, as in former times, producing a clear winner and loser. The opportunities for nonviolent geopolitics are also grounded in the willingness of governments to accept the increasingly practical self-constraining discipline of international law as reinforced by widely endorsed moral principles embodied in the great world religions and leading active civilizations. A further step in this direction would be a repudiation by the nine nuclear states of weaponry of mass destruction, starting with an announced declaration of no first use of nuclear weaponry and moving on to an immediate and urgent negotiation of a nuclear disarmament treaty that posits as a *non-utopian* goal "a world without nuclear weapons" (Krieger 2009). The essential second step is liberating the moral and political imagination from the confines of militarism, and consequent thinking within that dysfunctional tool kit that remains a staple component of the realist mindset in control of the leading countries in the West, especially the United States. This psycho-political challenge to move away from reliance on war-making capabilities as the cornerstone of security is made more difficult by the bureaucratic and private sector deeply entrenched tendencies to rely upon militarist framings of security policy.

Notes

1   A mainstream exception is Rosecrance (2002).

2   There is an ambiguity. The UN Charter can be interpreted as ensuring the winning countries in World War II a legal framework that lent legitimacy to militarized forms of Western-dominated geopolitics, as made evident by the design of the Security Council—P5 veto.

3   Berlin as a divided city brought US and Soviet troops into direct contact early in the Cold War, generating tensions that could have easily produced World War III.

4   This realist approach was influentially articulated in Aron (1966).

5   The issue did not entirely disappear, as shown in the reports of the Project for a New American Century, bringing together leading foreign policy neoconservatives who lamented the reluctance of the American people to project international force more readily in the aftermath of the Cold War. Linking this impulse to the rush to war by the presidency of George W. Bush in the wake of the 9/11 attack to skepticism about the official version of the 9/11 attacks was the centerpiece of David Ray Griffin's many books on the subject—see his original book (2004) bearing the title *The New Pearl Harbor: Disturbing Questions about the Bush Administration and 9/11.*

6   This comparison is analyzed in a similar manner by Galtung (2008).

7   Significantly documented in Schell (2003).

8   It is notable that the changes in the global geopolitical landscape associated with the rise of China, India, Brazil, and Russia are largely to do with their economic rise and not at all with their military capabilities, which remain trivial compared to those of the United States.

9   As interventionary struggles go on year after year with inconclusive results, but mounting costs in lives and resources, the intervening sides contradict their own war rationale, searching for compromises, and even inviting the participation of the enemy in the governing process. This has been attempted in both Iraq and Afghanistan, but only after inflicting huge damage on the people and the societal infrastructure, as well as often enduring major loss of life among their own troops and incurring great expense.

10 Among the valuable studies are Barnet (1972) and Lewin (1968).

11 Most convincingly demonstrated in a series of books by Chalmers Johnson—see especially the first of his three books on the theme (2004).

12 For a progressive critique of American imperial militarism, see Kolko (2006).

13 Several leading scholars have long been sensitive to the disconnect that separates even relatively prudent realists from reality. For a still relevant major work, see Galtung (1980). For other recent perceptive studies along these lines: Booth (2007), especially the section on "emancipatory realism" (87–91); Camilleri and Falk (2009); and Mittelman (2010).

References

Aron, Raymond. 1966. *Peace and War: A Theory of International Relations.* Garden City, NY: Doubleday.

Barnet, Richard J. 1972. *The Roots of War.* New York: Atheneum.

Booth, Ken. 2007. *Theory of World Security.* Cambridge: Cambridge University Press.

Camilleri, Joe, and Jim Falk. 2009. *Worlds in Transition: Evolving Governance Across a Stressed Planet.* Cheltenham, UK: Edward Elgar.

Cole, David, and Julius Lobel, eds. 2007. *Less Safe, Less Free: Why America is Losing the War on Terror.* New York: New Press.

Falk, Richard. 2003. *The Great Terror War*. Northampton, MA: Olive Branch Press.

Ferguson, Niall. 2010. "The Fragile Empire: Here Today, Gone Tomorrow—Could the United States Fall Fast?" *LA Times*, February 28.

Galtung, Johan. 1980. *The True Worlds: A Transnational Perspective*. New York: Free Press.

Galtung, Johan. 2008. "Searching for Peace in a World of Terrorism and State Terrorism." In *Peace Movements and Pacifism after September 11*, edited by Shin Chiba and Thomas J. Schoenbaum, 32–48. Cheltenham, UK: Edward Elgar.

Griffin, David Ray. 2004. *The New Pearl Harbor: Disturbing Questions About the Bush Administration and 9/11*, 2nd ed. Northampton, MA: Olive Branch Press.

Gelb, Leslie H. 2009. *Power Rules: How Common Sense Can Rescue American Foreign Policy*. New York: Harper-Collins.

Johnson, Chalmers. 2004. *The Sorrows of Empire: Militarism, Secrecy, and the End of the Republic*. New York: Metropolitan.

Kolko, Gabriel. 2006. *The Age of War: The United States Confronts the World*. Boulder, CO: Lynne Rienner.

Krieger, David, ed. 2009. *The Challenge of Abolishing Nuclear Weapons*. New Brunswick, NJ: Transaction.

Lewin, Leonard C. 1968. *Report from Iron Mountain on the Possibility and Desirability of Peace*. London: Macdonald.

Mittelman, James H. 2010. *Hyperconflict: Globalization and Insecurity*. Stanford, CA: Stanford University Press.

Nye, Joseph S. 1990. *Bound to Lead: The Changing Nature of American Power*. New York: Basic Books.

Rosecrance, Richard. 2002. *The Rise of the Virtual State: Wealth and Power in the Coming Century*. New York: Basic Books.

Schell, Jonathan. 2003. *The Unconquerable World: Power, Nonviolence, and the Will of the People*. New York: Henry Holt.

Walt, Stephen M. 2005. *Taming American Power: The Global Response to American Power*. New York: Norton.

3

Failures of Legitimacy:

Global Governance and International Relations

The idea of legitimacy in international relations possesses three interrelated dimensions: legal notions of rule-governed behavior by states and international institutions, ethical and cultural notions of humanitarianism ("the good" and the prudent), and an overall political emphasis on effectiveness and global problem-solving. Global governance stresses how minimum international order is managed given the distribution of authority and control operative in international relations. It is necessary to take account of the essentially state-centric character of world order as modified at various stages by the behavior of states pursuing extraterritorial goals of various kinds.

Geopolitics modifies purely statist conceptions of global governance by the imposition of the strategic priorities of a state pursuing an extraterritorial policy agenda, reflecting the ambitions and objectives of regional and global states that perform leadership and hegemonic roles in international political life that may or may not conform to legal, moral, and prudential guidelines. In these geopolitical settings, *legitimacy* is often invoked as a justification of a course of action that exceeds the constraints of *legality*, and for that reason alone is controversial.

Legitimation should be distinguished from legitimacy. It refers to the procedures and means by which legitimacy is achieved or diminished, and may involve adherence to relevant legal norms, and in rare instances, their deliberate avoidance.[1] For instance, Palestine gained a limited form of legitimacy as a state in 2012 by being accepted as a non-voting member of the UN through adherence to international treaties, membership in international institutions, including UNESCO (United Nations Educational, Scientific, and Cultural Organization), and being accepted as a party to the International Criminal Court, as well as by receiving diplomatic recognition from more than 130 countries (UNGA 2012). By way of comparison, Myanmar has lost legitimacy by being discredited in world public opinion and human rights nongovernmental organizations (NGOs). The government is widely perceived as guilty of crimes against humanity in the treatment of the Rohingya people, leading to the filing of a legal complaint by Gambia of genocide at the International Court of Justice in a case awaiting decision. In other words, legitimation refers to a dynamic element that raises or lowers the quality, and even the acquisition and entitlements, of legitimacy. Legitimacy is significant in part because it sets rules for participation in the structures of global governance, but it also strongly influences the reputation of political actors and political discourse. The reputational role of a state is not purely normative as it reflects considerations of effectiveness, capabilities, and benevolent cooperative relationships with other political actors. The UN loses legitimacy when it fails to address global crises within its remit in an equitable and effective manner accords with the letter and spirit of its Charter.

The international system is currently viewed as legitimate to the extent that the territorial sovereignty and rights of self-determination of all states are respected most of the time, robust economic development is facilitated, gross violations of human rights are opposed, and effective responses to ecological problems of global scope are forthcoming. The legitimacy of global governance within a given historical period continues to be dependent on the leadership roles played by global states (influential states with extraterritorial engagements, previously referred to as "Great Powers," and more recently as "geopolitical actors") and the degree to which these actors behave in conformity with the normative order constituted by prevailing ideas of international law and morality, as well as manage to achieve both effective and desirable results from the perspective of the regional and global common good (Bull 2012).

Ideas informing legitimacy shift over time as the legal status of established practices loses or gains political and ethical acceptance. International slave trade, colonialism, aggressive war making, genocide, apartheid, and ecocide are illustrative of such delegitimizing trends, while self-determination, resistance, rights, and transnational criminal law enforcement are examples of legitimizing trends (Falk et al. 2012).

In some instances, tensions are present between adherence to legal norms and upholding humanitarian values. For example, the precedent set by NATO (North Atlantic Treaty Organization) embarking upon the Kosovo War justified recourse to a nondefensive war despite its illegality (violating the UN Charter) by giving an overriding priority to legitimacy factors, including the anticipation of massive ethnic cleansing of the ethnic Albanian majority. This apprehension seemed reasonable to many informed observers at the time given the genocidal assault by Serbian forces on Muslim captives a few years earlier in Srebrenica (1995). But the legitimacy claims remained controversial, seen by adversaries of NATO as a rationalization for undisclosed strategic motivations, including demonstrating that NATO retained relevance after the end of the Cold War, and avoiding a Russian foothold in the Balkans by way of solidarity with Serbia.

Legitimacy as a justification for an otherwise unlawful recourse to war became even more controversial when relied upon a few years later by backers of the military attack and regime-changing occupation of Iraq in 2003. Even when UN authorization was obtained from the Security Council, as was the case in 2011, with respect to establishing a no-fly zone in Libya to protect the endangered citizenry of Benghazi facing the prospect of mass slaughter by troops dispatched by the Tripoli government (headed by Qhadaffi), issues of legitimacy and legality remain relevant (UNSC 2011). The loss of legitimacy occurred when the limited humanitarian authorization of the use of force in Libya was unilaterally extended by NATO forces supposedly implementing the limited UN mandate by engaging in an unauthorized regime-changing intervention that deposed the leader of the Libyan government, leading to his extra-legal execution, a coercive transfer of power to opposition forces, and sustained internal strife causing chaos. This loss of legitimacy due to an unauthorized expansion of the Libyan mission led to distrust on the part of the members of the Security Council that had abstained, allowing a no-fly zone to be established.

This loss of trust was partly responsible for disabling the UN from playing an effective conflict resolution role in Syria after the uprising of 2011. The Syrian struggle evolved further until it became a sustained and multipronged struggle of internal and external political forces to gain control of the Syrian governance structures. In this instance, a policy dilemma of global governance is exposed between adhering to strictly *legal* criteria or endorsing extra-legal considerations of international crime prevention and the protection of vulnerable peoples. By its membership in the UN, the Syrian government retained its formal legitimacy status, which included a preferential position with respect to the receipt of foreign military assistance. This status was definitely eroded over time by evidence of widespread reliance by Damascus on tactics and practices that violated international criminal law, creating a case for UN action under the authority of the "responsibility to protect" (R2P) norm that accepted potential UN responsibilities to act, not necessarily violently, in ways that sidestep the supremacy of territorial sovereignty of a state (Falk 2019a). These somewhat legalistic considerations were overridden by opposing geopolitical alignments with either the Damascus regime or various insurgent groups in what increasingly was described as "a proxy war" between external pro- and anti-Damascus countries.

We rely on an analytical/historical approach to grasp the diverse and multiple questions of legitimacy and global governance. These concerns have been implicit ever since the mid-seventeenth-century Peace of Westphalia but have only become internationally important for a little over a century because of antiwar and global security management concerns. Earlier, when the Westphalian framework was basically a European regional arrangement with a global reach by way of colonial empires, the French Revolution created successive waves of political activity that reshaped the nature of legitimacy, pitting the legitimacy claims of a religiously based monarchy at violent odds with secular based republicanism (Kissinger 1957). Such ideological confrontations were also present throughout most of the twentieth century, involving warfare to overcome fascist challenges to Westphalian ideas of legitimacy, as well as to regional and international stability, which included normative values of domestic inclusiveness toward minority ethnicities and religions, and the prohibition of aggressive force (General Treaty 1928). Then, after 1945, the intensity of ideological/imperial confrontations in a post-Hiroshima world order inclined ideological and geopolitical rivalry to be carried on without being consistently resolved in the traditional manner by recourse to war, yet giving rise to arms races and peripheral wars that were destructive, although contained by fears of escalation.

Global governance also emerged slowly from its Westphalian roots, which had initially repudiated the non-territorial authority of the Holy Roman Empire, and both legitimating and delegitimating roles long played by the pope and the Catholic Church. Despite these initiatives, the formal resilience of Westphalia, the operative character of world order, continues to reflect, especially with respect to war and peace and world economy issues, the primacy of geopolitical managers. In this fundamental sense, state-centrism provides the everyday framework of international relations, but when national security and major economic interests are at stake, geopolitics continues to guide global policy after the collapse of empires and colonialist patterns of rule and the geopolitical decline of Europe.

This Western-oriented structure endured more successfully with respect to the second aspect of global governance, which concerned the world economy and was preoccupied with the avoidance of any recurrence of the Great Depression that had been responsible for so much chaos, conflict, and distress in the West during the 1930s. The Bretton Woods institutions (the World Bank and International Monetary Fund) were seen as fostering global economic growth and offering a measure of crisis stability in the decades after 1945. This was interpreted in ways that gave economic global governance a generally positive image among Western elites until gradually challenged by China's spectacular emergence, as well as by the rise of East Asia generally, from its enforced decline during the period of European colonial dominance. Post-1945 neoliberal economic governance began to be more critically viewed by anti-imperialist civil society activism in the Global South. Trade, investment, and monetary policy was widely perceived as unfairly weighted to maximize Western economic interests by affirming market ideology. Criticism was led by progressive individuals from newly independent former colonial states.

Worldwide progressive forces persuaded governments in the Global South to put forward a collective call for a New International Economic Order (NIEO) in the 1970s by a fervent appeal to the UN. This anti-capitalist tide of opinion and action frightened the West at the height of the Cold War and led to strong Western reactions that withdrew earlier efforts embodied in General Assembly Resolution 377 to empower the UN General Assembly for coercive authority. The idea was to ensure that the UN could be an effective Western-controlled policy instrument in future Cold War crisis situations, and not employed by adversaries. This South-inspired initiative to establish an NIEO-oriented UN, in our assessment, explains the enduring Western reluctance to give the UN any greater authority, particularly the General Assembly, the most democratic political organ of the UN.

These developments also stimulated the emergence of overtly pro-capitalist private sector groupings such as the Trilateral Commission and the Davos World Economic Forum. Such organizations became very effective in securing the status quo as far as world economic structures and policies were concerned. Capitalist agenda items were promoted under misleading banners of serving the economic public good by these well-funded private initiatives that became very instrumental in building public support for neoliberal globalization.

The idea of crises in global governance can be most clearly understood by reference to a significant gap or loss of legitimacy in addressing the agenda of global problems confronting humanity. Such a generalization is especially revealing in relation to issues stemming from extreme vulnerabilities of marginalized and repressed ethnic, religious, and economic minorities. From a normative perspective, this was a worse governance deficiency than the inadequacies of war prevention efforts and the failures to uphold commitments to seek nuclear disarmament. These are admittedly controversial comparisons.

The *systemic* problem of preventing major wars posed overriding challenges to leading governments after both world wars of the last century. The use of atomic bombs in 1945 and the later development and retention of nuclear weaponry by a small group of states, as well as being a major setback from the perspective of war prevention, exposed the inability of existing structures and processes of global governance to uphold the global public good.

This inability pertained to the spectrum of global problems. Illustrative of failures to meet situational challenges include major instances of ethnic cleansing, genocide, apartheid, ecocide, natural disasters, and ecological imbalances. For a variety of contextual reasons, the challenges posed did not give rise to problem-solving motivations, capabilities, or political will on the part of the sovereign states acting on their own or collectively. At this historical moment, when global concerns are causing unrest and growing frustration with respect to climate change, nuclear weaponry, biodiversity, migration, pandemics, forever wars (Franklin 2018), cyber warfare, and poverty, the deficiencies of global governance are finally being widely acknowledged. This is at least a first step. The growing awareness of these deficiencies help explain the severe decline in the overall legitimacy of state-centric world order and the weakness of the arenas of cooperative problem-solving as centrally provided by the UN. This occasions pessimism as no alternative framework seems either emergent or feasible and, hence, prompts political escapism in various forms and recourse to "a politics of impossibility" that, under the circumstances, seems almost rational.

This contemporary decline of world order confidence is particularly associated with the unacceptability and ineffectiveness of sovereign control over ecological global public goods, such as the Amazon Rainforest, energy policy, the weakness of the regulatory framework based on international law when it comes to enforcement, and the inability of the United Nations to provide strong enough mechanisms for global cooperation in matters of serious concern to the whole world.

These structural drawbacks were dramatized by the failures to foster robust cooperation at the global level in response to the COVID-19 pandemic of the early 2020s. Changing attitudes and values at different historical moments alter perceptions of the deficiencies in global governance. The present mood of desperate concern is accentuated by the decline of "liberal internationalism," which underpinned, although always accompanied by activist enclaves of ideological dissent, earlier phases of more constructive American global leadership. This decline is reinforced by and related to the rise of ultranationalist one-eyed leaders in many countries that weakens, even further, existing mechanisms for the shared promotion of the global common good. The COVID-19 pandemic contrasted the globally anemic and toxically nationalistic and market-driven responses of global governance structures and procedures to a health crisis of the greatest magnitude. At the same time, the pandemic gave rise to a sense of the underutilized potential of and need for a stronger UN to enhance the quality of global governance.

This UN response to the pandemic is meaningfully relevant in several respects. The World Health Organization (WHO), as a specialized agency addressing health, demonstrated its role as a source of trustworthy information that was perceived as relatively free from political manipulation (although this assessment was contested, mainly by the United States during the Trump presidency) and as capable of issuing a widely invoked and authoritative declaration on March 11, 2020, that the COVID-19 disease warranted treatment as a "pandemic."

Additionally, the UN secretary general asserted himself in a manner that reminded the world of his status as a leading moral authority figure by urging the suspension of sanctions during the pandemic and by calling for "a global ceasefire" with respect to ongoing international conflicts. The mere encouragement of such initiatives temporarily increased the legitimacy of the UN as a vital component of global governance and, to some extent, enhanced UN relevance as a political actor.

At the same time, the silence of the geopolitically attuned Security Council exerted an opposite impact, underscoring the ineffectiveness of the political organs of the UN when it comes to managing a response in a political atmosphere dominated by the rivalry between China and the United States. Trump's defunding of the WHO had more of a delegitimizing effect on the US world leadership role than it did on harming the reputation of this UN health agency, as did the refusal by Washington to heed the humanitarian call by the UN secretary general for a suspension of sanctions until the world health crisis was resolved (Franklin 2018).

Global Governance and Legitimacy After World War I

Although crises of global governance have periodically occurred ever since feudal Europe was gradually superseded by somewhat more centralized Westphalian forms of governance, the mentality of modernity increasingly, although unevenly, guided policy formation and patterns of global leadership after 1648. The immense loss of life in World War I, combined with the emergence of a communist adversary in the Soviet Union, the rise of anti-colonialist nationalism in non-Western regions and anti-imperial nationalism in Latin America, and the decline of European control over the world system were elements of this crisis of global governance. Both the emergence of the Soviet Union and the United States as dominant political actors fractured the prior more consolidated administration of global governance by the Western European colonial powers. This led to tensions between populist antiwar activism throughout civil society and the previously established hegemonic imperial order in international relations.

This legitimacy crisis was intensified by the consequences of the punitive approach taken toward Germany as the main loser in the world war of 1914–18. As mentioned, this approach contributed to the rise of an extreme form of nationalism that included a resumption of German revisionist efforts to assert its dominance over continental Europe, including the European portions of the Soviet Union. Beyond this, the colonial ambitions of the United Kingdom and France led to the imposition of artificially delimited and constituted territorial states in the collapsed Ottoman Empire throughout the Middle East. Efforts to challenge this unstable, inhumane, and increasingly anachronistic form of global governance did meet some opposition from leaders in the United States and the Soviet Union, but it proved ineffectual at the time (Mayer 1968).

The United States pressed the norm of ethnic self-determination as applicable to the political future of the ethnic communities formerly governed by the Ottoman Empire at the Versailles Peace Conference. US diplomatic leverage also managed to give the League of Nations a mission to promote the peaceful settlement of disputes and to oppose, or at least weaken, colonialist maneuvers by the United Kingdom and France.

The League's main tool for muting European colonialism was a political compromise in the form of the imposition of mandatory administrative regimes in the entities that were formerly components of the fallen empires. Instead of colonial rule, the mandates in the Middle East (and Africa) were supposedly being administered by colonial power as a "sacred trust of civilization." The mandates system was seen as a halfway house between colonial subjugation and self-determination. In practice, these mandates, ranked in relation to their degree of readiness for political independence, were often administered as if occupied territories subject to colonial authority.

The League was too weak in several of its dimensions, as was the mandates system formally operating under an international regime, to overcome the deficiencies of statism (as manipulated by geopolitics) with respect to war/peace issues or colonialism. This became especially clear in the Middle East, most disastrously in Palestine, which was subject to British mandatory authority between the two wars. Furthermore, the German time bomb was not identified as a dangerous feature of World War I peace diplomacy until after it began exploding as a result of the rise of Nazism.

The imposition of artificial political communities on the Middle East and the punitive peace imposed on Germany (through reparations and demilitarization) not only aggravated the deficiencies of global governance as gauged by standards of legitimacy, both as to values and effectiveness. It also constituted "geopolitical crimes" whose negative impacts continue to be experienced throughout the Middle East in the forms of denials of self-determination and genocidal warfare (Falk 2019b).

The essence of these crimes was the imposition of territorial multiethnic European states, with artificially imposed boundaries, that reflected both the background of Westphalian nationalism and the foreground of the colonial ambitions of Britain and France rather than respecting ethnic identities and the politics of traditional tribalized communities as the basis of state formation. This political arrangement for a region accustomed to Ottoman reliance on ethnically and tribally constituted communities as supplemented by Islamic civilizational-territorial identities (caliphate, umma) was disruptive. It seemingly required coercive and repressive ethnic or religious patterns of state governance to avoid strife and chaos among tribes and distinct ethnicities. Minorities and subjugated identities have suffered until now from these post–World War arrangements fashioned to serve European colonial interests.

A second dimension of diplomatic criminality at the peace conference after World War I was the international acceptance of the pledge of the British Foreign Office to look with favor on the establishment of a Jewish homeland in Palestine, without the consent of the resident population and at a time when the Jewish minority in Palestine was estimated at no more than 8 percent of the population (Schneer 2012). In effect, the twilight of British colonialism was handled in ways that facilitated the rise and success of Zionist settler–colonial militarism, leading by stages to genocidal patterns of ethnic cleansing of the majority resident Arab population.

From the perspective of global governance, these elements of peace diplomacy possessed a high degree of legitimacy at the time given the prevailing *political* norms, which gave victors in wars discretion to impose their will on postwar arrangements, including colonialist political configurations. There were many subsequent geopolitical crimes committed in the Middle East, including by states external to the region taking intrusive steps, such as arming and supporting compliant dynastic elites, to maintain influence over the pricing and supplying of oil and natural gas to world markets.[2]

Global Governance and Legitimacy Crises After World War II

World War II ended in an atmosphere that combined contradictory sentiments with respect to past and emergent legitimacy crises. The defeat of Germany and Japan in the war overcame the legitimacy crises associated with aggressive warfare that involved the conquest and occupation of a series of sovereign states by liberating the peoples of these countries, restoring their sovereign authority, and punishing the perpetrators in war crimes trials. The ending of the war overcame for several decades the legitimacy crisis associated with the rise of fascist ideology, as well as its policies and practices, which flagrantly assaulted the conscience of humanity, especially genocidal behavior and numerous specific crimes of the Axis powers.

The war crimes trials in Nuremberg and Tokyo, although flawed by "victors' justice," did help document the criminality of the defeated countries and establish future guidelines for all governments with respect to individual responsibility for adhering to international criminal law (Taylor 1992; Minear 1971). The documentation of genocide also challenged the major premise of Westphalian world order by its linkage of severely abusive human rights practices within the domain of sovereign authority as connected with territorial expansionism. In effect, the internal politics of states was drawn into the orbit of geopolitics although without directly repudiating the legitimacy long associated in the West with statism.[3] In this respect, unconditional statism could be regarded as posing a new legitimacy crisis, at least with respect to genocide, and later in relation to apartheid and ecocide, especially large-scale ecocide under conditions of either war or peace.

At the same time, despite the end of the war and the formal repudiation of aggressive uses of force, there were emerging legitimacy crises that related to concerns about global governance. Above all was the ultimate concern about the recurrence of a major war, especially given the retention, development, and use of atomic bombs and missile technology and sovereign control over permissibly secret war plans. This concern was reinforced by the uncontested awareness that the League of Nations offered little reason to be hopeful about maintaining peace and security. The establishment of the United Nations within a framework that was supposedly designed to overcome selective deficiencies of the League, principle among which was the non-participation of several leading states and the absence of an outright condemnation of any prohibited recourse to international force (UNGA 1945).

A high cost by way of operational effectiveness was paid to create an institutional structure that would encourage continuing participation by leading states. The organization was headquartered in the United States, which was partly chosen as a hedge against any renewal of American non-participation via a revival of its traditional posture of isolationism. It also gave the Soviet Union assured protection against the Security Council becoming a polity tool of a presumed pro-Western majority. More fundamentally, built into the constitutional structure was a tactical accommodation of the realities of geopolitics. In a decisive retreat from universalism, the UN Charter accorded the five winners in World War II (really the four winners, plus China) permanent membership in the Security Council and a right of veto.

This trade-off between accepting geopolitical inclusion and achieving universal participation has had uneven and offsetting impacts on solving the legitimacy crisis of global governance associated with the institutional absence of effective mechanisms to protect global interests and uphold respect for international law. It was essential that the UN serve as an effective venue for promoting national interests, including eventually constructing an effective global rule of law. The UN as a political actor was weakened to a significant degree by this trade-off, although its membership was successfully universalized when it came to participation, and furthermore, no state has dropped out over the course of its existence, except Indonesia briefly.[4]

The UN role, once established and operative, departed from what had been originally envisioned and promised to the public. The actual UN left the most militarized states unregulated with respect to war prevention. It posed no security limitations on the residual responsibility of traditional geopolitical mechanisms (deterrence, militarism, alliances) to maintain peace and security. This marginalization of the UN with respect to war prevention left the leaders of the organization and its members free to rethink its role and their own future. Rather than giving up on the UN, the organization polished its image by shifting priorities and enlarging the range of their activities. This resulted in significant contributions in such other areas of international life as development, human rights, global lawmaking, culture, health, and environment.

As contended here, the most acute legitimacy crisis in 1945 involved the possible use, retention, deployment, and continuing development of weapons of mass destruction, especially the atomic bomb, followed by the advent nuclear weaponry. Against the background of the destruction of Japanese cities, the fear was widespread, highlighted by growing signs of an acute geopolitical rivalry between a US-led Western global alliance network and the Soviet-led alliance of Eastern Europe, China, North Vietnam, and North Korea. Under these conflict-generating conditions, preventing major warfare became the highest governance priority, but few leaders of governments were comfortable about relying, for their security, on legal prohibitions and UN authority, including its general claim to sustain world peace and effectively get rid of the nuclear menace (Barnet 1960). The state-centric system, faced with deepening conflict among the permanent members of the Security Council, relied as earlier on countervailing alliances backed up by formidable peacetime military capabilities to prevent war from breaking out among geopolitical adversaries and their close allies. This reliance on weapons to keep the peace was later supplemented by deployments and doctrines of deterrence, thus basing nuclear age security on credible threats by rivals to retaliate massively against civilian targets if attacked or unduly provoked. As war-fighting plans were highly guarded state secrets, no attempt was made to develop restrictions on the actual use of nuclear weapons.

Did this solve the legitimacy crisis of the nuclear age in relation to either peace or security? These arrangements were touted by political realists in and out of government as the best possible solution given the challenging circumstances. More objectively viewed, entrusting the peace of the world, and human destiny itself, to these geopolitical actors may have been, in retrospect, the least bad solution, but it was all along fraught with catastrophic risks and uncertainties, as well as being morally and legally problematic.[5]

In addition to peace and security concerns in 1944–45, there were acute worries in the West about the world economy that had been lifted from the doldrums of the Great Depression only by the onset of World War II. National economies and the world economy were believed to be vulnerable to relapses with the resumption of peace. The challenges associated with ensuring economic stability and material progress were seen as crucially bearing on whether global governance processes and structures could achieve legitimacy in Western eyes.

The approach adopted rested on a combination of the Bretton Woods institutions and the unilateral American effort to facilitate a rapid economic recovery of Europe from the ravages of war. The central governance idea was to construct a rules-governed liberal international order given institutional direction by the establishment the World Bank and International Monetary Fund (IMF), and later augmented by the World Trade Organization. Although relatively successful in producing sustained growth and avoiding severe, prolonged recessions, the liberal international order was dominated by United States economic policy, the NATO alliance with Western Europe, and its version of capitalism. It failed to achieve global inclusiveness except on Western terms. This was principally due to ideological cleavages with Marxist versions of socialism as practiced and advocated by Soviet and Chinese developmental economics, the troubled political relationships underpinning the Cold War. The ideological rivalry with socialism in Europe and persisting political leverage of organized labor, together with the legacy of the New Deal in the United States, led post-1945 capitalism to avoid predatory extremes. Gross inequalities, a squeezed middle class, and pockets of sustained poverty have resulted in such extremes during the aftermath of the Cold War, accentuated by ecological entropy, and resulting in a new, barely discernible legitimacy crisis. This current crisis can be framed as the distortions accompanying the transition from industrial age to digital age capitalism.

Global Governance and Legitimacy Crises During the Cold War

An underlying question bearing on global governance is whether the intense geopolitical and ideological rivalries of the Cold War era should, by its degree of war-proneness, be viewed as a legitimacy crisis that was never overcome until the collapse of the Soviet Union and the incorporation of China as a dynamic participant in the world economy. It was obvious that the avoidance of catastrophic warfare depended on the self-restraint and rationality by the main Cold War antagonists rather than respect for international law or the authority of the UN.

It was a decentralized mode of global governance that depended on the good judgment of the political elites of these two opposed nuclear superpowers. Despite some close calls and tense confrontations, the more than four decades of the Cold War did not produce any instances of strategic warfare or use of nuclear weaponry. Some international relations scholars have insisted that the exchange of deterrent nuclear threats should be credited with solving the legitimacy crisis associated with nuclear weaponry. This is because it deserved major credit for avoiding a major war during the Cold War (Mearsheimer 2014). The implication of this realist claim is that without the perceived severity of mutual devastation associated with a war fought with nuclear weapons, the intensity of conflict between the United States and the Soviet Union would have produced a massive war fought with conventional weapons, likely producing tens of millions of deaths and widespread destruction. Such a line of interpretation suggests that not only was the legitimacy crisis arising from the deployment of nuclear weapons overcome but also an innovative state-centered security system achieved a form of global governance that maintained a prolonged and almost unprecedented "geopolitical peace."

As might be expected, such analysis is contested on several grounds. First, that it was morally and legally unacceptable to base world peace on such genocidal threats that involved the indiscriminate targeting of millions of civilians, including spreading death and disease by radiation to societies not directly engaged in the conflict (Thompson 1982; Lifton 1987). Second, the maintenance of credible deterrent threats was accompanied by dangers of accidental use or miscalculations that, on several occasions, almost led to the launch of nuclear weapons against an adversary, suggesting that "geopolitical peace" was more a matter of luck than rationality and, as such, is not acceptable as a long-term solution to the legitimacy crisis created by the deployment, continuing development, and proliferation of the weaponry (Schell 1984; Sherwin 2020). Indeed, in the post–Cold War period, the legitimacy crisis of "nuclear apartheid" remains unresolved (Falk 2020).

Third, a side effect of avoiding direct warfare between the two superpowers was to magnify violent rivalries on the periphery of international relations, leading to limited, yet devastating, wars in the geopolitically divided countries of Korea and Vietnam (and almost Germany), as well as countless interventions and the militarization of many postcolonial non-Western countries.

Of course, we are unable to assess the achievements and disappointments of the roads not taken. A stronger UN and a less intense rivalry between East and West might have emerged if a successful nuclear disarmament process had been implemented, having secondary effects of moderating geopolitical tensions. Yet, hypothetically, the removal of nuclear inhibitions might have resulted in the outbreak of a nonnuclear war causing far greater casualties than even World War II, estimated at fifty million deaths. Or, given the high levels of distrust, a breakdown of nuclear disarmament might have occurred, producing an accelerated rearmament race that led to nuclear war. Such contrary to fact conjectures can be illuminating but are inconclusive as non-confirmable.

A second feature of the Cold War period, with lasting transformative effects on global governance, was the collapse of European colonialism in

Africa and Asia, and the weakening of US imperialism in Latin America. This globalization of the Westphalia model ended the governance hybridity of colonial empires and states that existed in 1945 when the UN was established, but not the meta-legal role of geopolitics. Despite the American defeat in Vietnam (and elsewhere) and the Soviet defeat in Afghanistan (and subsequent collapse), the political elites of neither country adjusted to the declining agency of military superiority.

Global Governance and Political Legitimacy in the Era of Neoliberal Globalization

In the years after the Soviet collapse, China's surge, and the absence of any serious ideological or geopolitical clashes, the capitalist West became preoccupied with the promise of economic globalization and an image of legitimacy shaped by what establishment circles called "market-oriented constitutionalism." As long as economic growth continued, an uncritical approach was adopted in the West to globalization, overlooking the subsequent perils arising from capital flows that privileged cheap labor, outsourcing, and minimal environmental and safety regulation.[6]

This onset of predatory globalization on a global scale is causing a twenty-first-century backlash by way of reactionary populism that includes a global swing toward ultranationalism and autocratic governance, hostility to immigrants, and widespread alienation of workers who seek scapegoats and autocrats rather than struggling to achieve a emancipatory revolution.

In this context, a temporary de-securitization of international relations occurred. The Gulf War of 1992 manifested a consensus among the Security Council members that seemed to suggest that the UN could lend its legitimation to geopolitical undertakings involving the use of force, and that this convergence was in accord with basic Charter norms. US global leadership after the Cold War was economistic and ideological, stressing efficiencies of capital, low tariffs, and open markets for trade and investment along with the virtues of procedural democracy. American leadership faltered when it came to safeguarding global interests or taking advantage of the end of the Cold War to strengthen mechanisms for global cooperation and win/win approaches to global problem-solving. It overlooked looming global threats and failed to seize available opportunities to strengthen world order in a variety of ways, including more independence and better funding for the UN, as well as tabling a proposal for phased and verified nuclear disarmament. This weakness of global leadership contributed to the glaring deficiencies of global governance that became all too evident in subsequent decades.

Furthermore, concerns were growing about environmental issues, particularly the increasing menace of global warming. The Earth Summit of 1992 displayed both a rising global consciousness and a determined resistance to encroaching upon economic growth or consumerist lifestyles. The American president at the time, George H. W. Bush, signaled this kind of capitalist materialism with a nationalist flourish by sending a terse message to the delegates attending the UN Earth Summit in Brazil: "The American way of life is non-negotiable." Decoded, this message was expressing the prevalent view that environmental protection, in this case involving obligatory reductions in releasing greenhouse gasses, must yield to the efficiency of capital if the goals conflict. By refusing to apply the precautionary principle to the dangers of global warming that have long been confirmed by a consensus of climate scientists, the legitimacy crisis that has beset the world in the last decade with respect to ecologically responsive global governance, was postponed at the cost of an intensification of present ecological damage and the prospect of far higher future adjustment costs.[7]

In all respects, the period immediately after the end of the Cold War seemed, on the surface, to be free of legitimacy crises pertaining to global governance, yet these appearances were soon exposed as deceptive and misleading. In retrospect, it seems conclusive that there was a subtle, almost hidden, crisis of global leadership that failed to mobilize the world for emergent challenges to global governance that became evident, even ominous, in the first decades of the twenty-first century. This developing awareness casts doubt on whether the outcome of the Cold War was as positive as treated in the West. Not only were opportunities lost but a neoliberal approach to trade and investment led to destabilizing inflationary trends and large increases in inequalities domestically and internationally that in turn produced a reinvigoration of right-wing politics of exclusion and anti-internationalism.

Failures of Global Governance in the Twenty-First Century

Although globalization survived the deep recession of 2008–9, societal critiques arose on both the left and right. Complaints on the left centered on the human and societal consequences of global inequality, denial of human rights, and ecological irresponsibility. Complaints from the right concentrated on failures to protect national economies against deindustrialization, dependencies on cheap foreign migrant labor, and outsourcing, on one side, and excessive internationalism, on the other.

In the United States, a bipartisan consensus continued its unquestioned willingness to overinvest in militarism without weighing the costs and benefits of doing so, and in the process encouraged reactive militarism throughout the world. This inflated a threat environment even from the viewpoint of traditional ideas of "national security" without even taking account of the demilitarizing advantages of a "human security" approach.

With respect to security issues, the 9/11 attacks in 2001 on the World Trade Center and Pentagon instantly produced a re-securitization of international relations as it was traditionally conceived with a focus on "enemies" and "warfare." This also entailed a gradual shift of attention away from the economistic agenda of the 1990s to a somewhat more traditional geopolitical agenda after 9/11, although what was novel about this new conflict paradigm was that neither adversary was a traditional territorial sovereign state. In this sense it became obvious that 9/12 had a bigger and longer impact on international relations than 9/11 due to the American choice of a response strategy based on "war" rather than "crime," a choice partly motivated by the neoconservative push for a more proactive foreign policy, especially in the Middle East, after the Soviet collapse. Such a response both converted the world into a global battlefield between terrorists and counterterrorism efforts, with an inevitable erosion of state-centric world order, without any legitimating alternative put in its place. This also created a new cluster of political justifications for geopolitical militarism. Terrorists chose their targets without regard to sovereign rights, and so did counterterrorist governments. In this atmosphere regime-changing interventions became more frequent. Also, a greater emphasis was placed on technological fixes to increase the precision of military tactics while reducing casualties on the intervening side. In practice this meant an increasing reliance on drones and special forces, targeting terrorist suspects and training sites wherever they were suspected of being located. These adaptations reaffirmed the old thinking that political order in international relations rested on hard power rather than formalities of law and respect for territorial sovereignty. The overall impact of the "war on terror" was to erode still further Westphalian statist traditions under the looming threat of what might be described as "geopolitical globalization." This process was effective in superseding sovereignty as the prime basis of organizing political community in the modern world (Falk 2003).

This response to the 9/11 attacks, which showed the acute vulnerability of even highly militarized countries to a determined low-technology adversary, provided further evidence that there were very significant limits on the capacity of traditional preparedness for war and even military superiority to provide homeland security to national populations, but rather than recast security, the political leaders of major states doubled down on outmoded militarist approaches to security. To underscore the learning disabilities of the West, instead of drawing lessons from the remarkable rise of China to a position of formidable rival global leader, China was increasingly cast in the role of a new grave threat to the West. It became popular in the West to provoke China so as to vindicate NATO-led Asian containment responses by way of coercive diplomacy and militarist confrontations. Such a familiar recourse to confrontation tactics to address a rising geopolitical rival was dangerous and dysfunctional. The alternative of viewing China as constituting a healthy competitive challenge to the economically complacent West was never seriously considered by Western foreign policy elites.

The other failures of global governance posing legitimacy crises concern the diversion of energy and resources from non-terrorist threats to security, including climate change, loss of biodiversity, and nuclear weaponry. These failures were abetted by the absence of global leadership to plan for and encourage cooperative problem-solving of global-scale challenges and anticipatory responses to warnings about intensifying threats of great magnitude as confirmed by relevant experts. The lack of preparedness for the 2020 pandemic was, as argued, a spectacular instance of this world order weakness from the perspective of human security that exposes the system to collapse if not corrected.

The backlash culminated from 2015 onward, epitomized by the rise of democratically elected autocrats who were ultranationalists. As a result, a triple legitimacy crisis has emerged: a vacuum of global leadership related to threats and cooperative solutions; a mismatch between a regressive global security paradigm in response to terrorist challenges and statist principles of world order; and a normative decline in relation to the authority of human rights norms, international law generally, and UN authority.

Conclusion

The nature of legitimacy crises has varied over time due to the perception of global challenges, the character of moral sensitivity among political leaders, and the degree to which existing mechanisms for problem-solving are available and effective. An important variable relating to global governance is the attunement of major governments to cooperative solutions, which includes taking account of diverse and unequal capabilities and needs, as well as the common good, and can be interpreted by reference to the rubric of "global leadership."

Since 1945, this role has been predominantly played by the United States, but with ups and downs depending on the viewpoint of particular leaders and the political mood prevailing in the country. The inward, transactional turn adopted in 2017, when Donald Trump became president, gave rise to an unfortunate repudiation by the US government of many of the positive contributions associated with liberal internationalist leadership, which themselves had fallen far short of optimal accommodation to emergent global governance challenges. It was US leadership that led to cooperative outcomes with respect to the public order of the oceans and administration of Antarctica, or more recently to the Nuclear Arms Agreement with Iran

(JCPOA) or the Paris Climate Change Agreement. Trump withdrew US participation from these treaty frameworks and encouraged untimely and disruptive retreats from all forms of internationalism. Biden took some halting steps to restore the traditionally more international stance of the United States, but did so by giving priority to a revival of Cold War style geopolitics, as in Ukraine, an extremely fragile and inflammable global historical context, and even more so by acting so pronouncedly in support of the globally repudiated Israeli approach to governing occupied Palestinian territories as heightened by the 2023–24 genocide.

Transnational civil society activism can, to an extent, provide some pressure to overcome the consequences of dysfunctional global leadership, encouraging reforms in global governance responsive to resolving the legitimacy crises of the time. The extraordinary mobilizing impact of the young Swedish activist, Greta Thunberg, is illustrative. She was more effective in delivering a message of urgency about climate change than were political leaders, influential media platforms, and even climate experts.

As with 9/11, the COVID-19 pandemic created opportunities to choose more constructive paths of action. The aftermath of the crisis is testing what was learned, which has not given grounds for much hope. As publics and their political representatives tend to correct *past* mistakes while averting their eyes from *future* threats, we can be reasonably optimistic that when the next pandemic strikes, the world will be better prepared, including possessing far more efficient warning and guidance capabilities, but only with respect to what has occurred in the past, without being responsive to future threats of a related, but distinct, character that is likely to accompany the disease threats posed by new viruses with different properties, points of origin, and modes of contagion.

Substantive legitimacy crises have been previously discussed in relation to policy shifts in the priorities of order and justice in international relations at major historic junctures. With respect to procedural dimensions, the issues posed may be more controversial and deserve more extended discussion, but the stress placed here is as follows: precautionary principle, cautionary respect for evidence and consensus among qualified experts; mechanisms for protecting global, human interests, and the common good; and taking account of economic, gender, ethnic vulnerabilities, capabilities, and fairness.

There have been international legitimacy crises as long as there has been political rivalry between independent actors, but it is only in the past one hundred years or so that the issues of global governance have become salient, and only since the advent of nuclear weaponry that the limitations of global governance are seen as presenting issues of grave concern about the viability of civilization and even the survival of the human species.

Although antecedent pandemics were so alarmingly regarded, there was insufficient medical knowledge and real time interconnectedness during their unfolding to believe that human effort could have a preventive or mitigating impact by way of advance preparation, and recourse was had to religious explanatory perspectives. The world was without alternatives to reactive responses, although not altogether. Ancient civilizations fearing famines leaned to store food essential for resilience in the face of agricultural crises brought about by natural causes or human incompetence.

In facing the interconnected challenges of the present period, there is enough understanding of many impending threats and their feared consequences to arouse widespread despair about prospects for fashioning responses with the ability to overcome the most dangerous legitimacy crises unless a transformative politics in the form of "green politics" and "climate justice" emerges from civic activism. We know much of what needs to be done to protect the common good, but the political will that is required to confront entrenched special interests benefiting from the short-sighted status quo remains absent. And up to now, civil society is not sufficiently mobilized, lacking the leverage to exert sufficient pressure on political elites to overcome dysfunctional mixtures of inertia, special interests, and resistance to change.

Notes

1   There are instances when legality and legitimacy are in tension, for instance, an authorization to use force to avoid genocide or ethnic cleansing is blocked by a veto at the UN Security Council, and a state or coalition of states acts on its own without being able to claim self-defense in accordance with Article 51 of the UN Charter. The Kosovo War of 1999 is a clear example.

2   It is important to differentiate "geopolitical crimes" from international crimes that are so designated by international law. The concept of geopolitical crime is intended to highlight the wrongdoings of diplomats and diplomacy. An ambiguous current example is the complicity of states in relation to the Gaza genocide, which can be interpreted either as breaking the law prohibiting genocide or outside of its orbit of prohibition.

3   The overwhelming assumption of international law is that a state deserves "a margin of appreciation" in the form of an opportunity to address international crimes through national procedures, and only after failing to do so is it appropriate to invoke international procedures.

4   Indonesia withdrew from the UN over criticism of its "Crush Malaysia" campaign in the mid-1960s, proposing to form an alternate organization, but soon returned to the UN and gave up its ambitious plans.

5   Critics of nuclearism include Schell (1982), Lifton and Falk (1982), Falk and Krieger (2012), Nye (1986), and Thompson (1982).

6   Among critical exceptions are Mittelman (2000), Sassen (1998), and Falk (1999).

7   The precautionary principle first gained international endorsement by its
     inclusion in the final declaration of the UN Conference on Environment and
     Development held in Stockholm in 1972, formulated as follows: "In order to
     protect the environment, the precautionary approach shall be widely applied
     by States according to their capabilities. Where there are threats of serious
     or irreversible damage, lack of full scientific certainty shall not be used as
     a reason for postponing cost-effective measures to prevent environmental
     degradation." The stronger formulation of the precautionary idea is to
     "require" its application, and to disallow balancing benefits and burdens if the
     risk threatens irreparable ecological harm.

References

Barnet, R. J. 1960. *Who Wants Disarmament?* Boston: Beacon Press.

Bull, Hedley. 2012. *The Anarchic Society: A Study of Order in World Politics*,
    4th ed. London: Red Globe Press.

Falk, Richard. 1999. *Predatory Globalization: A Critique.* Cambridge, UK: Polity
    Press.

Falk, Richard. 2003. "Reviving Global Civil Society After September 11." In
    Traditions, Values, and Humanitarian Action, edited by Kevin M. Cahill,
    344–67. Fordham: Fordham University Press.

Falk, Richard. 2017. "Challenging Nuclearism: The Nuclear Ban Treaty Assessed."
    Asia-Pacific Journal 15 (14): article 2.

Falk, Richard. 2019a. "R2P and the Palestinian Ordeal." *Global Justice in the
    Twenty-First Century*, May 23. richardfalk.wordpress.com.

Falk, Richard. 2019b. "Geopolitical Crimes: A Preliminary Jurisprudential
    Proposal." *State Crime Journal* 8 (1): 5–18.

Falk, Richard. 2020. "Contesting Nuclearism: Management or Transformation?
    An Urgent Challenge." *Global Justice in the Twenty-First Century*, January 1.
    richardfalk.wordpress.com.

Falk, Richard, and David Krieger. 2012. *Path to Zero: Dialogues on Nuclear
    Dangers.* New York: Routledge.

Falk, Richard, Mark Juergensmeyer, and Vesselin Pospovski, eds. 2012. *Legality
    and Legitimacy in Global Affairs.* New York: Oxford University Press.

Franklin, H. Bruce. 2018. *Crash Course: From the Good War to the Forever War.*
    New Brunswick: Rutgers University Press.

Kissinger, Henry A. 1957. *A World Restored: Metternich, Castlereagh, and the
    Problems of Peace, 1812–1822.* Boston: Houghton Mifflin.

Lifton, Robert Jay. 1987. *The Future of Immortality and Other Essays for a
    Nuclear Age.* New York: Basic Books.

Lifton, Robert Jay, and Richard Falk, 1982. *Indefensible Weapons: The Political
    and Psychological Case Against Nuclearism.* New York: Basic Books.

Mayer, Arno J. 1968. *Political Origins of the New Diplomacy, 1917–1918.*
    New Haven, CT: Yale University Press.

Mearsheimer, John J. 2014. *The Tragedy of Great Power Politics*. New York: W. W. Norton.

Minear, Richard H. 1971. *Victors' Justice: Tokyo War Crimes Trial*. Princeton, NJ: Princeton University Press.

Mittelman, James H. 2000. *The Globalization Syndrome: Transformation and Resistance*. Princeton, NJ: Princeton University Press.

Nye, Joseph S. 1986. *Nuclear Ethics*. New York: The Free Press.

Sassen, Saskia. 1998. *Globalization and Its Discontents*. New York: The New Press.

Schell, Jonathan. 1982. *The Fate of the Earth*. New York: Random House.

Schell, Jonathan. 1984. *The Abolition*. New York: Knopf.

Schneer, Jonathan. 2012. *The Balfour Declaration: The Origins of the Arab–Israeli Conflict*. New York: Random House.

Sherwin, Martin. 2020. *Gambling with Armageddon: Nuclear Roulette from Hiroshima to the Cuban Missile Crisis*. New York: Knopf.

Taylor, Telford. 1992. *The Anatomy of the Nuremberg Trials: A Personal Memoir*. New York: Knopf.

Thompson, E. P. 1982. *Beyond the Cold War*. London: Merlin.

United Nations General Assembly (UNGA). 1945. *United Nations Charter*. Article 2 (4): 51.

UNGA. 1948. UNGA Res. 217A. "The Universal Declaration of Human Rights." Paris, December 10.

UNGA. 2012. UNGA Res. 67/19. "Palestinian Membership in the UN." New York, November 29.

United Nations Security Council (UNSC). 2011. March 17.

4

A Pluralist Cosmopolitanism

A peaceful world involves more than the absence of war or political violence, either direct or structural. War prevention is a laudable and necessary goal and increasingly accepted as practical and beneficial, yet even for political actors with dominant military capabilities, it does not constitute an adequate conception of peace. Arguably, in this sense, the preamble of the United Nations (UN) Charter, by identifying peace so exclusively with war prevention, offers the world an insufficiently comprehensive understanding of peace, although there is interpretative space due to the ambiguities of language. The touchstone words: "We, the peoples of the United Nations determined to save succeeding generations from the scourge of war" can be read either in the narrow sense of war prevention or more broadly as organically linked to human rights, global justice, and social progress, which are affirmed in the following lines of the preamble.

The historical context informing the founding of the UN was dominated by fresh memories of the carnage of World War II and the growing anxiety about the apocalyptic horrors that might accompany a third world war. For this reason, a sense of peace as the opposition of war, rather than as the opposite of injustice, was to be expected at the time, but no longer at *this* time, given the development priorities associated with the policy atmosphere of the postcolonial world.

In what follows, we first address some preliminary considerations surrounding different notions of "peace" and peacebuilding and the appropriate methodologies to study them. In so doing, we compare competing international relations paradigms—including realist, liberal, and other approaches—concluding that cosmopolitanism is the one most concerned with reconciling unity with difference, through mutual understanding of otherness, maintaining creative tensions among rootedness in particularity, and respect for and a celebration of diversity, as well as an embrace of universal values and identity. Rather than relying on one standard definition of "cosmopolitanism," we urge the adoption of a moral epistemology that is overtly value-oriented and normatively ambitious, without being oblivious to the structural characteristics of collective political behavior that tend to privilege the personal and national self at the expense of the other. We provide a framework for peacebuilding assessments that frames inquiry around different "horizons" of aspiration (feasibility, necessity, desirability/ spirituality) and lay out a new version of cosmopolitanism, which centers on the importance of peacebuilding objectives that are necessary and desirable.[1] This latter position requires hybridity because finding ways to strengthen the promotion of human or species interest cannot occur without an appreciation of local, concrete, and ecological forms of embeddedness.

Preliminary Considerations

For peace to be sustainable and valuable to sustain implies the absence, or at least the minimization of, exploitation and oppression, as well as a maximum effort to avoid warfare and other forms of political violence. Peace in this more maximal sense remains utopian, although peacebuilding of national, regional, and global scope can be situated within the realm of the political as it aspires to achieve an improved world order that is beneficial for everyone, rests on evolutionary processes and degrees of achievement, and refrains from positing as a goal the realization of the unrealizable.[2]

An intriguing proposal in the peacebuilding mode was put forward by William vanden Heuvel, former US representative to the United Nations (UN), who suggested designating 2020, the seventy-fifth anniversary of the UN, as the year to "confront" the scourge of war. The intervening years could then demonstrate bringing peace on earth by mobilizing the public and private sectors, by organizing the new energy of social media, by recognizing the extraordinary groups that have carried the struggle for peace against the seeming inevitability of violence, and by inviting "the peoples of the United Nations," in whose name the Charter was adopted, to find their voice by expressive support for what is to be done to enhance future life prospects (Heuvel 2016).

It may be clarifying to treat avoidance of war, whether international, transnational, or internal, as *minimal* peace, and the inclusion of justice and human rights as constitutive of *maximal* peace. Of course, there exists a spectrum of opinion as shaped by different gradations and combinations, reflective of distinct angles of civilizational vision and variations in class consciousness. Whether America is a peaceful country or not seems quite different from the perspective of affluent suburbs and gated communities than from the inner cities of Baltimore, Chicago, or Detroit. Minimal peace for "Black Lives Matter" contrasts with how internal peace and security is understood at the Pentagon, border security, and the police. Similarly, is

America a peacekeeper or war maker in its global role and identity, or is it an amalgam that often acts regressively but not always?

In approaching this kind of subject matter, it is important to acknowledge the interpretative perspective that guides inquiry. All pretensions of knowledge bearing on policy and practice is "situated knowledge" reflecting place, class, ethnicity, race, gender, sexual orientation, spoken language, and so forth. Such an insistence is especially important in the United States, given its character as a global state possessing the largest and most globally active war machine in human history as supplemented by its global "soft power influence" by way of lifestyle, media influence, and popular culture. There are at least two reasons to classify the United States as a global state in-the-making and -unmaking: (1) its rejection of the concept of the defense of its territorial homeland as the essence of its "national security" and (2) the presence of extensive military capabilities deployed beyond its territorial boundaries, as operationalized by hundreds of overseas bases and national intelligence and prison sites in forty-five countries, special forces operating covertly in more than one hundred countries, separate navies stationed in every ocean, as well as being the leading arms supplier and seeking control of outer space for purposes of networking, surveillance, and military operations.

Of course, empires in the past had complex presences beyond their homeland, but this generally involved an extension of territorial sovereign claims and formal empire, and not the kind of presence that pretends to reconcile respect for the sovereign pretensions of Westphalian statehood of foreign countries with intrusive assertions of hegemonic *global* statehood. These intrusions have become more characteristic of the re-securitization of international politics after 9/11, further intensified by the renewal of Cold War geopolitics due to the Ukraine War, epitomized by the emergence of a global battlefield, where both anti-state extremists and the global state choose their targets without deference to foreign sovereign rights while being ultra-protective of all aspects of national sovereignty. While counterterrorist operations have abated somewhat, recent years have witnessed an intensification of Great Power rivalry, especially between the United States and Russia and the United States and China, with an increasing likelihood that this second incipient Cold War will turn hot at some point in the not so distant future.

At stake, also, is what might be called "situated methodology" and "situated epistemology." There has been a growing professional consensus in the West that for knowledge to be useful, it should be as "scientific" as possible, which is interpreted to mean both subject to empirical or cognitive validation and repudiating the embrace of an avowedly prescriptive, religious, or normative agenda. We find unsatisfactory and misleading the recent well-received attempts to show that war and extreme poverty are diminishing aspects of human experience (Pinker 2011; Goldstein 2012;

World Bank Group 2018). It may not be that such quantitative measures lie or deceive, but they divert our attention from the real unresolved challenges of peacebuilding—the subverting of "peace" by way of technological and tactical innovation in the form of attack drones and suicide bombing, as well as alarming complacency about the risks and probable magnitude of a nuclear war, whether initiated by accident, miscalculation, or geopolitical tensions. In this respect, we favor the adoption of a moral epistemology that is overtly value-oriented, normatively ambitious, and behaviorally prudent without being oblivious to the structural characteristics of *collective* political behavior that tends to privilege the self, and especially the national self, at the expense of the external other.

The World Order Models Project (WOMP) relied upon this kind of normative framework during the 1970s and 1980s in carrying out its peacebuilding explorations. This endeavor, which began in the mid-1960s, invited representative scholars from around the world to contribute coherent ideas in book-length studies of "feasible utopias" to be realized by the 1990s. The proposals were intended to become political projects with transitional scenarios depicting paths from here to there. It was a transnational undertaking illustrative of relying on a moral epistemology (posited in the form of four values agreed upon by participants), while indulging political, ethical, and ideological pluralism with respect to policy priorities and implementation. The four values agreed upon, and varied in interpretation during the project, were *minimization of violence, maximization of economic well-being, social and environmental justice*, and *search for ecological equilibrium*.

This orientation implies a shared normative platform, but with the expectation of a diversity of priorities and interpretative perspectives by those who accepted this framework of inquiry. For instance, during the development of WOMP, those from the Global South were preoccupied with maximizing development, cultural autonomy, and participation, while those in the North or West focused their attention on the mitigation of geopolitical rivalry, the avoidance of a World War III, and the establishment of stronger international institutions with a global orientation (Kothari 1974; Falk 1975).

A more civilizational approach to moral epistemology has been developed by Tu Weiming, affirming the Confucian normative landscape for its emphasis on empathy and virtuous living, and for its disregard for the epistemological paradigms that are most debated in social science venues. Tu posits his point of departure in Confucian terms: "As we become aware of our earth's vulnerability and increasingly wary of our own fate as an 'endangered species,' what are the critical spiritual questions we must ask?" The response to his own question is partially conveyed by these characteristic words: "As exploration of Confucian spirituality must take the following into consideration: the self as creative transformation; the community as a necessary vehicle for human flourishing; nature as the proper home for our form of life; and Heaven as the source of ultimate self-realization" (Tu 2010, 209–10).

It might be instructive to point out that during the second stage of WOMP, when the goal became to find among the participants common substantive grounds for addressing the challenge of norm creation and institution building in accord with WOMP values, the collaborative venture disintegrated; neither diagnosis nor prescriptions could be agreed upon. Differences in outlook and understanding were too fundamental to overcome, despite repeated meetings and efforts and the amiable underpinnings of friendship of leading participants in the project. The nature of these differences was not primarily epistemological but, rather, the way in which tactics and strategies were prioritized with respect to a global policy agenda. The sharpest tension was perhaps between the adoption of a counter-hegemonic agenda that concentrated on economic development (based on drastic de-Westernizing reforms of global trade and investment regimes) and according priority to a security agenda preoccupied with diminishing geopolitical rivalry and political violence, especially war and militarism, responding to the withering attention to the Cold War.

Prescriptive common ground can sometimes exist within a given paradigm or between paradigms for contradictory reasons. Kenneth Waltz, the main architect of *structural realism*, at times seemed to favor, although never quite advocate, the spread of nuclear weapons, as he believed that only deterrence can sustain peace among geopolitically ambitious sovereign states, and that no better deterrent exists than nuclear weaponry (Art and Jervis 2013). Differing in emphasis, others believed that it was only a further proliferation of nuclear weapons that might sufficiently shock the nuclear weapons states and their publics about the risks of nuclearism, especially in the United States, so that the cosmopolitan option of a world without nuclear weapons could become more plausible to political leaders. In effect, Waltz believed that global security based on reliable deterrence was the best solution to nuclear danger, I and others believed such a world order was itself unacceptably risky and insisted on privileging the goal of nuclear disarmament, treating proliferation as a dangerous but perhaps effective way of building support among foreign policy elites for the denuclearization of international life. From a *classical realist* perspective, Henry Kissinger and his prominent coauthors seemed to adopt a nuclear abolitionist position, but for prudential reasons of security combined with the optimal geopolitical assurance of continued American military dominance given its superiority in conventional warfare (Kissinger 1957).

There is also a consideration of what kind of label is best adapted to the sort of discourse that is being encouraged by this focus on peace and peacebuilding. Although we aspire to an Archimedean point that transcends the local, national, and regional, we are not comfortable with a purely universalist, humanist, and secular orientation and, therefore, would opt for a conception of "cosmopolitanism" that is dialectical and inclusive, as well as ethically sensitive to the framing of thought and action by reference to international human rights standards and is, at the same time, sensitive to the political and cultural rootedness of situated knowledge.[3] It might be helpful to acknowledge "cosmopolitanisms," that is, the plural renderings of the paradigm based on a variety of center/periphery normative and institutional arrangements. For instance, a cosmopolitanism presupposing the global monopoly of legitimate force under UN auspices or a world government structure contrasts with a grassroots cosmopolitanism that is expressive of Gandhian nonviolence and the agency of people so mobilized.

There is also a question whether the privileging of species identity should be associated with cosmopolitanism, especially in view of the dire future scenarios associated with global warming, biodiversity loss, and nuclear dangers. Our experience is that cosmopolitanism, as least if presented as a world order terminology, does not have a deep intellectual or cultural resonance for non-Western civilizational traditions and hence lacks ethical and political traction. Perhaps the terminology of global or cosmic humanism might be more acceptable across cultural boundaries, especially if understood dialectically and as encompassing diverse worldviews and civilizational orientations. It is vital to diverge from realist and liberal structural determinism associated with the assumption that useful knowledge about international political life must take for granted the primacy and permanence of state-centric forms of world order, dependent on a war-security nexus as evolved through the seventeenth-century invention and universalization of "the Westphalian state."[4] Constructivism is more noncommittal about the nature of international reality and views what is "real" as the product of "social construction" (and deconstruction), and not derivative from or frozen on the basis of an immutable cerebral hypothesis of an embedded structure reflecting the interaction and mentality of foreign policy elites in leading Westphalian states.

A Framework for Assessment

Our main framework for assessment was earlier set forth by reference to horizons of feasibility, necessity, and desirability/spirituality, and there is no reason to repeat here.[5]

A short dialogue among paradigm advocates would go as follows:

Cosmopolitan: Nuclear disarmament is the only acceptable policy.
Realist: You are distracting us by positing the unattainable.
    Deterrence and the non-proliferation regime have avoided any use of nuclear weapons since 1945.

Liberal: We can do many things to make the control of nuclear weapons safer and less accident-prone without hampering American global engagements. Those who advocate nuclear disarmament should appreciate the adage: "The best is the enemy of the good." Arms control tasked with management of nuclear dangers is what we should be thinking about.

Cosmopolitan: I have a better adage: "The good is the enemy of perfect." Arms control is content with the management of nuclear weapons that overlooks their fundamental moral defects of threatening the quality of life to be experienced by future generations, of the ethical deformations associated with relying on threats to kill millions of innocent persons, and of accepting a hegemonic world order in which the few nuclear weapons states have the capabilities to determine the fate of humanity. Phased, verifiable nuclear disarmament is indispensable for long-term security and the realization of humane forms of global governance.

Critical Realist: Those peoples without nuclear weapons are utterly vulnerable to the irrationalities and ambitions of the nuclear weapons states. This is intolerable and must be transformed either by the availability of the weaponry to all states, or preferably, its total prohibition along with other weapons of mass destruction.

Liberal: Let's get real.

Realist: I've heard enough of this bullshit. I am leaving. So long as the earth is a sphere rotating around the sun, states will continue to act to preserve, if not expand, their influence and wealth, as well as do their best to reduce prospects of attacks by enemies. Living with risk is integral to the human condition and pertains to all nonhuman life forms. Only the spiritual can claim in certain respect an *eternal* life span.

Why and Which Cosmopolitanism?

The type of cosmopolitanism supported here is rooted in an affirmation of species identity as organically linked to other conventional modalities of identity. It is given precedence with respect to policies and practices bearing on survival, sustainability, resilience, and atrocity avoidance and prevention, as well as peace and peacebuilding. As such, it is conscious of and aspiring toward peacebuilding goals that are perceived as necessary, desirable, and spiritually fulfilling.

In this respect, it takes time and space in seriously comprehending the future, which is conceived in terms of *process*, that is, an unfolding that contains multiple realities. We express the engagement of individuals against this background as "citizen pilgrims," participating in the life of polities of varying scope from the perspectives of necessity, desire, and spiritual attentiveness, while being mindful of their place-holding role due to a multitude of sensible efforts to reduce menacing risks in the immediate settings of policy choice. For instance, taking nuclear weapons off hair-alert status would qualify as feasible, and certainly seems necessary and desirable, or avoiding the election of political leaders, especially in nuclear weapons states, who seem mentally unstable or insensitive to the importance of upholding and reinforcing the nuclear taboo and, more generally, exhibiting respect for international law, multilateral problem-solving, and the UN.

With this in mind, there are insights and emphases from other methodological perspectives that can be encompassed by a "responsible cosmopolitanism." In distinguishing between the "feasible" and the "necessary," it is helpful to take into account the most instructive and critical forms of "realism" and their relationship to scientific consensus and available knowledge, while allowing room for dissent. In this regard, we find the emphases of some scholarly treatments of international relations on the societal aspects of state-centric world order as possessing common ground with cosmopolitan thought. In this regard, we share with Hedley Bull and Martin Wight, founders of the English School of International Relations, a strong distaste for the geopolitics of military intervention (Bull 1968).

At the same time, Bull's degree of attachment to a Hobbesian view of statism led him to reject all efforts to extend the rule of law by imposing criminal accountability on those who act on behalf of sovereign states. In this mode, Bull vigorously rejected the idea of the Nuremberg assessment of German war crimes after World War II, not on the familiar grounds that it was flawed because it represented "victors' justice" but because it overrode the idea that states were truly sovereign, that is, the last word when it came to law, justice, and order (Bull 1968). Bull did not intend a moral endorsement of the behavior of Nazi leaders, but it was his belief that, given the state structure of world order, the idea of an international criminal law procedure represented both moral hypocrisy and normative overreaching or hubris.

Liberalism is itself far less interesting and important than realism in conceiving of its beneficial relevance. We conceive of liberalism as essentially a normative add-on to most forms of realism and often somewhat insensitive to the structural underpinnings of world order that it is endorsing. This interpretation of liberalism as a derivative of realism is elaborated very convincingly by Michael Doyle (1997). In this regard, liberalism generally seeks to operate at the outer edge of the feasible and is most notable in its support for the elaboration of human rights and the strengthening of international institutions without shaking the foundations of state-centric, geopolitically managed, and market-oriented world order, a view most definitively and fluently championed by John Ikenberry.

There is a minority among liberal thinkers who advocate some form of world government without directly challenging either Western hegemony, statism, or capitalism. Clark and Sohn proceeded by way of a radical reform of the UN Charter that would effectively centralize peacekeeping authority in the UN, while trying to entice participation by the non-Western world through efforts to promote economic growth, greater equity, and poverty reduction (Clark and Sohn 1966; Holcombe 1967). Other conceptions of world government are more comfortable with a constitution-building process, often generalizing the formation of the American republic in the late eighteenth century, especially imposing limitations of the authority of global governance via checks and balances of various kinds.

In other words, liberalism is normatively helpful in softening the jagged edges of realism, but it accepts as embedded in the reality of international relations both the hierarchical character of world order, the persistence of the war system, and the legitimacy of neoliberal globalization. These features are unacceptable from cosmopolitan perspectives, being treated as three of the main deficiencies in the current global setting. In our period of history, although with a greater sense of urgency than in earlier periods, the *structures* and *procedures* of the world economy and the geopolitically defined, ecologically fragile, and entropic state system need to be transformed if fundamental survival and well-being challenges are to be met and a new ecological equilibrium established.

Critical theory attempts to examine global issues from a perspective that is sensitive to the philosophical or ontological nature of world order as it is informed by evolving historical context. Critical theory develops its views from an outlook that is responsive to "common humanity" without abandoning the state-centric and hegemonic character of contemporary world order, giving special attention to "the promotion of emancipatory politics" as expressed through "the normative dimensions of radical traditions in international relations proposed by world society thinking, feminist theorizing, social idealism, and third world security specialists" (Falk 2020, 148). This tension between affirming a common humanity and acknowledging the relevance of radical traditions of emancipatory thought is what I have been identifying as "situated knowledge." It is essential to the shaping of a responsible cosmopolitanism, and gives content to an appropriate moral epistemology.

This degree of compatibility between critical theory and cosmopolitanism is brought out clearly by Stephen Gill in his introduction to *Critical Perspectives on the Crisis of Global Governance*. The critical character of the analysis is

based on the assumption that any definition of global governance needs to be premised upon the changing ontology of world order in a period of global transformation, allied to a critical epistemology that is applied not only to analyse global governance but also to identify strategic alternatives open to progressive social and political forces.

(Gill 2015, 14)

Gill's outlook adopts a negative view of neoliberal globalization because of its incompatibility with the formation of the sort of community attitudes of ecologically responsible and compassionate governance that correspond to the interests of *people* rather than *market* drivers of human progress such as economic growth, corporate earnings, and trade and investment figures that tend to ignore the existential plight of people as living, often suffering, beings.

Cosmopolitanism can be greatly enriched by incorporating these main ideas from critical theory, giving its view on a unified destiny greater normative resonance throughout the world (Williams 2005). This grounding of cosmopolitan thinking would help overcome tendencies and temptations to engage in abstract theorizing and would also ensure a more secure platform for engaging in the diverse thinking and experience of peoples in the here and now struggles against oppressive conditions of various kinds, ecological encroachments, and in pursuit of emancipatory political goals. Among the sites of struggle that are particularly relevant with the present historical period are climate change, nuclear weapons and power policy, refugee and asylum policies, global health, and sustainable, resilient development.

Constructivism is also quite compatible with the form of cosmopolitanism advocated here and is an indispensable tool for its elaboration, thereby providing a broad platform of potential academic collaboration. In our understanding, constructivism, as such, is noncommittal about goals and values, and is not avowedly normative. In contrast, cosmopolitanism, by privileging that which benefits humanity as a species, is holistic in outlook, rejecting various political standpoints that privilege the part (e.g., state, religion, civilization, ethnicity) over the whole. Constructivist disregard of structures and skepticism about meta-narratives is helpful when it comes to deconstructing exploitative hierarchies, in its critical mode, but as an epistemology, it goes too far in these directions. For both diagnostic and prescriptive purposes, it is crucial to articulate structures and procedures, and even meta-narratives, that either take advantage of or block appropriate responses to policy and behavioral challenges that develop within the domains of necessity and desire.

To be more concrete, it is impossible to appreciate the imprudent responses to the advent of nuclear weapons, climate change, and migrant flows without an awareness of the distorting impacts of embedded economic, political, environmental, and psychological structures of world order within and among sovereign states and governing elites. In this regard, cosmopolitanism is better conceived of as a holistic response to realist modes of thought, although methodologically it can gain understanding from both critical theory's consideration of context and projection of emancipatory futures and the constructivist emphases on heeding the long-excluded voices of the marginalized.

Conclusion

Realism, liberalism, critical theory, constructivism, and cosmopolitanism are all in their own distinctive ways substantively concerned with peace and peacebuilding, although not unconditionally or exclusively. The realist paradigm tends to equate peace with stability and the defense of the established order but also with the avoidance of imprudent adventures, the rejection of normative constraints on the pursuit of vital national interests, and hostility toward utopian projects, whether from a left or right revolutionary orientation (Marxist/Fascist traditions) or liberal character (world federalism/world government).[6] What is often called "classical realism" tends toward moderation and structural conservatism in its most characteristic embodiments.[7] The structural features predominate in structural realism that derive behavioral patterns based on the distribution of power and authority among leading state actors. With Kissinger and Raymond Aron, there is an appreciation that "power" is incapable of promoting stability unless resting on widely shared notions of prudence and legitimacy at the main power/authority centers in the world. Neither of these prominent international relations figures was concerned about whether these qualities were combined with imperial, hegemonic, and exploitative features or had much respect for international law or the UN when it came to promoting peace and stability.

Liberalism promotes reforms that give a greater role to international arrangements, including the networking potentialities of the digital age. It also welcomes the advent of human rights and is favorably inclined toward international and transnational cooperation that is facilitated by respect for international law and entry into cooperative international arrangements, including the UN and the Bretton Woods institutions. It views peacebuilding mainly through a functional lens of thickening interactivity to the extent possible, with these linkages based on mutual benefit to state bureaucracies and their operative transnational constituent parts (e.g., relations based on transnational cooperation between finance ministers or defense ministers rather than with governments as a whole) (Slaughter 2004).

Cosmopolitanism is currently preoccupied with how to actualize the implications of species identity in concrete policy contexts. Because of the fragmenting impact of statism and nationalism, geopolitics, and the exploitative effects of global market forces, cosmopolitanism is concerned with transforming these constitutive structures of world order as essential preconditions to its peacebuilding and ecological endeavors. It is not averse to such liberal initiatives as "Alliance of Civilizations" (the Spanish–Turkish UN-sponsored project countering Samuel Huntington's thesis of a post–Cold War "clash of civilizations") as a way of affirming *human identity* while embracing cultural and other forms of diversity. Cosmopolitanism more than other perspectives is concerned with reconciling unity with difference, through mutual understanding of otherness, a celebration of diversity, and an embrace of universal values and identity. In this regard realism disavows unity as attainable or desirable (except in certain imperial formations or geopolitical hierarchies), while liberalism tends to affirm tolerance and hospitality as ways to humanize the operations of state-centric world order.

Without losing this focus on what is *globally* required to serve the human interest, it is important for cosmopolitan traditions of thought to learn from critical theorists, especially with regard to the importance of context, ontological changes, ecological challenges, and the multiplicity of strategies and conceptions of emancipatory political thought and action. Learning from realists is also important to convey the relevance of structure and power to the formation of policy.

Whether "cosmopolitanism" is a sufficiently "cosmopolitan" name remains an open question. An alternative way of describing the approach, which retains the normative affirmation of a species/ecological/spiritual orientation, would be "global humanism" or "global justice movement" or, simply, "the unity of humanity." In any event, this orientation is dependent on developing both an appropriate moral epistemology and an improved theorizing of practice that achieves a more persuasive blending of abstraction and concreteness. In the end, cosmopolitan's intellectual and political advantage is to encourage holistic thinking about the global nature of current world crises and the importance of finding ways to strengthen the promotion of human or species interest without losing an appreciation of local, concrete, and ecological embeddedness. Whether this kind of approach can combine a governmental approach, involving institutional building with a reorientation of normative thinking that is more inclusive and affirming of local initiatives, while still giving preferential treatment to those who are marginalized and vulnerable, is uncertain.

What is more evident is that these approaches to the study and praxis of peace and peacebuilding can each benefit from a hybrid model that incorporates central insights of alternative worldviews, while not losing sight of the impacts that policymaking has on target populations. The normative element is prominent in different ways in critical thinking, liberalism, and cosmopolitanism; the analytical feature of realism and constructivism contributes a practical awareness of the difficulties that await those who seek change. The most appropriate knowledge to advance peace and peacebuilding, as well as fashioning the contours of what might be called "an ecological civilization," would combine normative and analytic perspectives, and aspiring to a creative synergism. If one considers such issues as designing a program to handle the refugee challenge or to preserve biodiversity, it seems evident that normative goals of ethical behavior, species sustainability, and spiritual sensitivity depend on synthesizing an analytic appreciation of state sovereignty with a commitment to the exploration of transformative potentialities.

Notes

1   This framework is previously used in Falk (2017).

2   Peacebuilding can also perform as a sequel to regime-changing interventions, as in Afghanistan and Iraq, and result in internal strife, resistance, prolonged conflict, and repressive ethnic, gender, and religious relations, as these instances illustrate.

3   The writing of Kwame Anthony Appiah (2006) is suggestive along these lines.

4   See, for example, the work of Hedley Bull (1977) on the English School.

5   See "Explaining the Gaps" in chapter 1.

6   See, for example, Raymond Aron's argument about prudence as the cardinal virtue of realist statecraft (1966).

7   Falk (2015) assesses Kissinger along similar, more critical, lines.

References

Appiah, Kwame Anthony. 2006. *Cosmopolitanisms: Ethics in a World of Strangers*. New York: W. W. Norton.

Aron, Raymond. 1966. *Peace and War: A Theory of International Relations*. Garden City, NY: Doubleday.

Art, Robert, and Robert Jervis. 2013. "Kenneth Waltz and His Legacy: The Man and the State of War." *Foreign Affairs*, May 22. www.foreignaffairs.com/articles/united-states/2013-05-22/kenneth-waltz-and-his-legacy.

Bull, Hedley. 1968. "The Grotian Conception of International Society." In *Diplomatic Investigations: Essays in the Theory of International Politics*, edited by Herbert Butterfield and Martin Wight, 51–73. Cambridge, MA: Harvard University Press.

Bull, Hedley. 1977. *The Anarchical Society: A Study of Order in World Politics*. New York: Macmillan.

Clark, Grenville, and Louis B. Sohn. 1966. *World Peace Through World Law*, 3rd ed. Cambridge, MA: Harvard University Press.

Doyle, Michael. 1997. *Ways of War and Peace: Realism, Liberalism, and Socialism*. New York: W. W. Norton.

Falk, Richard. 1975. *A Study of Future Worlds*. New York: The Free Press.

Falk, Richard. 2015. "Henry Kissinger: Hero of our Time." *Millennium* 44 (1): 155–64. https://doi.org/10.1177/0305829815594038.

Falk, Richard. 2017. *Power Shift*. London: Zed.

Falk, Richard. 2020. "A Pluralist Cosmopolitanism for the Twenty-First Century." In *Peacebuilding Paradigms: The Impact of Theoretical Diversity on Implementing Sustainable Peace*, edited by Henry F. Carey, 147–59. Cambridge: Cambridge University Press.

Gill, Stephen, ed. 2015. *Critical Perspectives of the Crisis of Global Governance: Reimagining the Future*. London: Palgrave.

Goldstein, Joshua. 2012. *Winning the War on War: The Decline of Armed Conflict Worldwide*. New York: PLUME/Penguin.

Heuvel, William vanden. 2016. "Letters." *The Nation*, February 16.

Holcombe, Arthur Norman. 1967. *A Strategy of Peace in a Changing World.* Boston: Harvard University Press.

Ikenberry, John. 2011. *Liberal Leviathan: The Origins, Crisis, and Transformation of the American World Order.* Princeton, NJ: Princeton University Press.

Kissinger, Henry A. 1957. *A World Restored: Metternich, Castlereagh, and the Problems of Peace, 1812–1822.* Boston: Houghton Mifflin.

Kothari, Rajni. 1974. *Footsteps into the Future: Diagnosis of the Present World and a Design for an Alternative.* New York: The Free Press.

Lifton, Robert Jay. 2017. *The Climate Swerve: Reflections on Mind, Hope, and Survival.* New York: The New Press.

Pinker, Steven. 2011. *The Better Angels of Our Nature.* New York: Penguin.

Slaughter, Anne-Marie. 2004. *The New World Order.* Princeton, NJ: Princeton University Press.

Tu, Weiming. 2010. *The Global Significance of Concrete Humanity.* New Delhi: Center for Studies in Civilization.

Williams, Paul. 2005. "Critical Security Studies." In *International Society and Its Critics*, edited by Alex J. Bellamy, 135–50. Online: Oxford University Press.

World Bank Group. 2018. *Poverty and Shared Prosperity 2018: Piecing Together the Poverty Puzzle.* October 17. https://openknowledge.worldbank.org/server/api/core/bitstreams/34b63a7c-7c89-5474-b9d3-f4f35085fe83/content.

5

Global Contexts of Power

For most students and practitioners of international relations, dominant modes of thinking about world politics derive from several traditions stressing the role of force and the management of military power. Thucydides, Niccolò Machiavelli, Thomas Hobbes, and Carl von Clausewitz provide canonical interpretations of this understanding of international relations as a domain of pure power that shapes the interplay of autonomous political actors. In modern times, this interplay has become more complex but continues to involve the role and use of instruments of coercion, especially in the conduct of conflictual relations among sovereign territorial states. This is obvious in situations of warfare and the design of war prevention strategies.

The modern versions of realist thought have been influentially related to the contemporary world by a series of commentators, including Raymond Aron, Hans Morgenthau, George F. Kennan, Hedley Bull, Henry Kissinger, Kenneth Waltz, John Mearsheimer, and Stephen Walt, who were alive to the ideological dimensions of world politics. The operative practices of leading governments were guided by deep state mechanisms and think tanks. After the Cold War, the more academic literature in the West associated realism with a less ideological, more economistic approach to international relations. This emphasis on economic policy gained prominence as the main driver of conflict and of foreign policy ambitions. The international management of global security under these changed conditions was reinforced by constitutionalism at the state level that became accepted in the West as the touchstone of political legitimacy, although the management of international relations generally was more pragmatic substantively.

This realist consensus is deeply skeptical about the relevance of either morality or international law with respect to both waging war and keeping the peace, particularly with respect to the strategic interests of geopolitical actors. Such a perspective is also not well adapted to addressing urgent current concerns about global public goods in the face of such challenges as climate change or the menace of weaponry of mass destruction. Unfortunately, global policymaking by most political leaders throughout the world continues to be based on an increasingly outmoded, zero-sum view of political reality, which is strongly biased toward win/lose strategies of problem-solving and unduly dismissive of win/win strategies of cooperation and accommodation. This criticism seems particularly applicable to the leadership of the most important countries, and to the United States more than others. The result is an exaggerated reliance by such actors on the historical agency of relative military capabilities for the achievement of a wide spectrum of national goals. The dysfunctions of realism are increasingly evident in political settings, as by being often antagonistic to the more cooperative approaches essential for successful problem-solving of such varied systemic challenges of global scope as pandemics, climate change, and migration flows.

Decolonization and the Decline of Hard Power

What realism has failed to act upon in the twenty-first century is the declining relevance of hard power to the resolution of international conflicts, maintenance of regional and global security, and the compensatory rise in significance of soft power, whether or not linked to an actor possessing inferior hard power. Even a superficial consideration of the history of internationally relevant conflicts since the end of World War II validates this generalization. The decolonization movement as it unfolded in one country after another illustrated the potency of a historical trend that linked the soft power benefits of legitimacy (for instance, the legitimacy of self-determination struggles as contrasted with the illegitimacy of colonial claims) as overcoming shortcoming associated with military inferiority (as measured by weaponry and battlefield outcomes). Overall, yet with some exceptions, the trend has favored political victories for actors successfully combining legitimacy advantages of a struggle with strong normatively informed grievances as understood through optics of law and morality underpinning a soft power approach to conflict resolution. This repatterning of influence has produced outcomes in colonial wars leading to a decolonizing form of sovereign independence in the aftermath of more or less bloody conflicts, overall, a vindication of resurgent nationalism. At the same time, this shift should not be exaggerated as "colonialism after colonialism" is manifest in a multitude of imperial arrangements that have impaired the dynamics of self-determination in many countries throughout the Global South.

Reviewing this pattern of results in colonial wars strengthens the opinion that the impact of legitimacy and dynamics of agency shifted the relation of political forces in anti-colonial wars in manner that contradicted realist expectations. At one extreme, decolonization struggles were bloody, as in Indochina and Algeria, while at the other extreme the violence was minimal, as with the ending of British colonial rule in India thanks to the Gandhian movement based on massively mobilized nonviolent militancy. But in almost every case, the outcome was the same: a victory for the militarily weaker, yet politically and normatively more legitimate, side.

Part of the argument here is that power has been transformed by altered historical conditions, especially the spread of a nationalist ethos to the non-Western world, and the degree to which exemplary soft power victories by the weaker side encouraged the commitment of oppressed peoples to accept the high costs of liberation. The demonstration effect of victorious outcomes over Western colonial powers was considerable. Challenges to colonial rule a half-century earlier in essentially similar circumstances were not undertaken. This reflected the prevailing belief that anti-colonialism was regarded as hopeless by the leadership of native populations. All in all, this shift deserves a better understanding, rooted in historical experience and leading to a single overwhelming explanation—*ideas matter*.

This same pattern has also prevailed in situations of settler colonialism, at least where the native population was not effectively neutralized, or at least marginalized, by ethnic cleansing or outright recourse to genocide. Colonial forces with their own nationalist priorities prevailed in the western hemisphere, Australia, and New Zealand. The most notable exception is South Africa, where the struggle of the majority African population managed eventually to dismantle the apartheid regime peacefully by its successful blending of occupying the legitimacy high ground, with effective reliance upon the instruments of soft power, including support of transnational solidarity politics. These consisted of governmental and civic boycotts, divestment, and sanctions initiatives.

The Palestinian struggle for self-determination is finally appearing to gain the upper hand in the legitimacy war by mobilizing coercive soft power around the world in a manner that increasingly resembles the earlier victorious anti-apartheid movement in South Africa, but this may be deceptive. The hardline dominance of Israel as a Jewish apartheid state, bolstered by the deep historical rootedness of Jews in historic Palestine and the contemporary linkage to the geopolitics of the Global West, has clouded the outcome of this most recent experience of settler colonialism. Israel's genocidal assault against the population of Gaza in 2023–25 underscores the uncertainty that surrounds the future of Palestinian aspirations and Israeli resolve to establish Greater Israel.

Depending on circumstances, state power will not easily give in to challenges from below and without: The "battlefield" for control of the symbols of legitimacy (mainly, ideas and norms relating to morality and law) and the deployment of soft power instruments of coercion and persuasion are *global* in scope and *non-territorial* in character. As Tibet's failed efforts even to achieve autonomy, much less self-determination, teach us: sometimes success in the legitimacy war does not control political outcomes. Such disappointment occurs where there are insufficient soft power capabilities to overcome hard power superiority and political will. In such instances hard power tactics are often accompanied by a soft power dismissal of national resistance as "terrorism."

International Intervention

Another critical pattern of conflict involves intervention in foreign societies via military force. Here again, contemporary reliance on military power is often misguided in terms of costs and results. In many respects, the American experience in Vietnam is paradigmatic. The United States had complete military dominance in all dimensions of the conflict as compared with the indigenous forces of resistance. The United States could destroy at will and inflict much higher casualty rates than it endured. And yet it lost the war! The soft power/legitimacy dimensions turned out to be decisive in the end, which were combined in sophisticated ways with innovative resistance tactics to hard power. This meant that, despite the unquestionable military inferiority on the Vietnamese side, the native population was so strongly motivated that it could absorb huge losses without eroding its political will to resist foreign intervention.

Additionally, the Vietnamese resistance inflicted enough losses on its powerful American adversary as to eventually erode the political will and domestic base of support of the intervener in what was viewed as "a war of choice" and not convincingly connected with national security interests. As the war went on year after year, an increasing number of Americans pondered the question, "Is it worth it?" and answered with a resounding, "No." The anti-colonial idea of self-determination was also a factor, weakening the American resolve based on a farfetched Cold War rationale.

This Vietnamese experience is not an isolated instance. The Soviet Union had a similar experience of hard power frustration in Afghanistan during the 1980s, as did Iraq in Iran after launching an attack based on its hard power edge. There are many more examples in the period since 1945, and almost no substantial counterexamples.

The United States, so heavily invested in hard power approaches to its global security vision, has tried to explain the outcome in Vietnam as a matter of *doctrinal* failure (that is, an inability both to make effective use of its hard power dominance and to wage the legitimacy war more intelligently). So far, doctrinal fixes have been attempted to overcome past failures, but they have yet to enable the side with hard power superiority with improved prospects of political victory at an acceptable cost in lives and resources. The recent test cases for the United States are the abysmal extended counterinsurgency and state-building experiences in Iraq and Afghanistan, which suggest strongly that the foreign intervener, even if prepared to bear exorbitant costs and despite a wide margin of hard power advantages, might still lose out in the end to a determined national resistance, combined with political fatigue on the intervening side, who has so much less at stake with respect to the outcome of such a struggle.

This persisting refusal to acknowledge the limits of hard power in counterinsurgency situations and counterterrorist operations has damaged the credibility of American world leadership, as well as contributed to its overall economic and political decline, including with respect to the quality of life in its own country. The reinvention of counterinsurgency doctrine—its extension to counterterrorist contexts and being made somewhat more sensitive to the nationalist and developmental concerns of indigenous populations—seems unable to alter the fundamental *illegitimacy* of foreign military intervention in a postcolonial non-Western society. Nor does the reliance on the latest automated weaponry, drones, or a variety of technological innovations overcome the limited capacity of hard power superiority to achieve desired political outcomes, thus continuing to confound the realist calculus.

There is no doubt that in earlier periods of international history, hard power superiority was the principal agent of historical change and an efficient instrument of long-term conquest, domination, and exploitation. The puzzling feature of the present global context is why national leadership elites seem unable and unwilling to adapt to the changing nature of power, especially the decline of hard power in essentially exploitative international contexts. There is some ambiguous evidence that Europe, the birthplace of modern realist statecraft, has partially absorbed this understanding, at least with respect to relations *within* Europe, where a culture of peace has prevailed since 1945, although drawn into temporary question by the Balkan war late in the twentieth century and the more recent Ukraine War.

Elsewhere, especially in the United States, there exists an addictive relationship to militarism that reflects decades of wartime mobilization and the strength of the arms industry. The result has been a military-industrial-congressional-media complex that biases governmental policy toward an exaggerated correlation of security goals with military capabilities and away from a diplomacy of accommodation and reconciliation. What is depressingly evident on the part of American governing elites is a zero-learning curve hidden from public scrutiny by a compliant, uncritical media. The lessons of Vietnam were converted into "a Vietnam syndrome" that was treated as an advisory to the American military and political leadership that it needed to make some tactical adjustments: end the draft, rely on advanced technology to minimize American casualties, and generate fear of adverse security and economic consequences of defeat on the home front. What has remained unlearned is an adaptive reading of the historical record since World War II that shows the extent to which military superiority of a foreign intervener has been consistently overcome by the patience, motivation, and sense of entitlement of a militarily inferior national resistance fighting to control the destiny of its own homeland.

Post-9/11 Forms of Power

The 9/11, 2001, attacks on the United States and its militarist response further illustrate the hard power fallacy, this time in the guise of counterterrorism. In this instance, a small group of essentially unarmed, yet suicidal, political extremists were able to inflict unprecedented harm on the United States by commandeering four commercial airliners on behalf of their disruptive missions. Responding by principal reliance on American military reach and power signified once more, with heavy negative consequences, the inability to abandon inappropriate and heavy-handed hard power approaches.

The essence of the threat posed by transnational terrorist violence is neither based on hard power nor can it be nullified in most respects by hard power; it is essentially a soft power challenge in the form of a transnational underground network. Meeting such a challenge depends on law enforcement, global police/intelligence collaboration, and occasional small, sharply focused, hard power overseas operations undertaken in cooperation with national authorities. Fighting against such a hostile network more closely resembles controlling the Mafia than opposing a hostile sovereign state.

Despite several decades of disappointments with hard power reliance, the United States seems as preoccupied as it ever was with the pursuit of global hegemony with hard power. The obsessive character of American militarism is so great now that it is not even possible to have a responsible national debate as to whether the military budget is too large or the fact that reliance on hard power approaches toward national security have become dysfunctional in the twenty-first century. It is also not possible to seriously raise the relevance of the struggle over the symbols of legitimacy as a factor shaping the relation of political forces. In effect, there results a dangerous exaggeration of hard power relevance coupled with an exaggerated and inflated view of existing security threats. This dysfunction is reinforced by a corresponding lack of appreciation of both soft power ideas of entitlement and forms of coercion, especially when persuasively combined with ascending the high ground on matters of moral claims and legal rights.

What is also evident is that popular movements and civil society actors have a far greater appreciation of the legitimacy/soft power approach to security and conflict than do state actors and their entourage of advisors, bolstered in their misapprehensions by "groupthink" strategic elites and the manipulations of deep state operatives. Of course, this is partly a matter of movements and activists making a virtue of necessity, given their total lack of capacity to compete in hard power arenas of conflict. It is only by shifting the conflict away from military encounters that soft power forms of coercion (such as cultural, athletic, and academic boycotts; divestment initiatives; public opinion; and citizen protests) linked to legitimation and resurgent nationalism seem so formidable.

Consequences

This analysis has several consequences. First, it diverts global leadership as still situated in governmental and market elites from maximizing the problem-solving potential of cooperative and nonviolent approaches in conflict situations. Such inefficiencies are particularly serious at a time when ignoring global challenges will over time impact disastrously on the health and well-being of future generations. One result of this dysfunction is to undermine efforts to establish global governance in forms that could have a genuine prospect of producing a safe, equitable, and sustainable world order that could overcome poverty, reduce disparities in material conditions of livelihood, and mitigate the damage wrought by climate change and other global maladies.

Second, realist misunderstandings of power incline major states, and especially the global hegemon, to adopt unsuccessful responses to conflicts of all kinds, guided by the false supposition that military dominance could usually produce stability and recourse to subjugation followed by regime change where necessary. Such militarist postures tend to heighten resistance, escalating combat and strife, while nevertheless, more frequently producing costly defeat and public demoralization.

Third, it has proved to be almost impossible to learn the lessons associated with the global transformations of power because of the strong realist consensus that rejects evidence bearing on the severe limitations constraining the effective role of hard power in the twenty-first century. This rejection is partly an expression of the degree to which paradigms of thought are typically resistant to adaptive change, a condition that persists until the anachronistic system reaches a point of decline and becomes aware of the dangers of collapse. This resistance to adaptation is heightened in the case of sovereign states, which originally achieved internal legitimacy by their monopolization of hard power capabilities, providing their citizenry with internal order and a sense of civic identity, as well as with security against external threats. It is also maximized in relation to the United States, as hegemonic geopolitical actor, that has created a bureaucratic and informational set of domestic structures that are completely dependent on the suppression of this militarist fallacy. This can be shown by the absence of political debate on the size of the American military budget. Past empires have often fallen primarily by stretching their capabilities to sustain financial and strategic overextension.

Fourth, given the imperatives of cooperation to stabilize the world economy and address the menace of global warning as soon as possible, this continuing reliance on hard power modalities of security dangerously defer the need to construct a responsive system of global governance. For this system to work in the absence of world government, which is neither practical nor desirable as a goal at this stage of history, there must be a willingness to constrain hard power discretion within the limits set by international law. For these limits to be implemented, there needs to be greatly increased deference by both the leaders and the citizenry of dominant states to the United Nations system and to international law, including the prudent disposition to find peaceful solutions to international disputes.

Fifth, it is true that the form of hard power architecture in world politics has produced an antibody of non-state violence and disruptive events that subverts peace and tranquility. This is the challenge variously posed by 9/11, COVID-19, and ongoing warfare. It calls for responses that combine enhanced global law enforcement, robust transnational collaboration of police and intelligence capabilities, a willingness to settle justifiable grievances, and a readiness to work together when necessary.

Recourse to a global counterinsurgency/counterterrorist campaign has not facilitated the achievement of security for the United States, and the West generally. Reliance on the realist discourses of "war" and "terrorism" seem to discourage the guardians of national and global security from adopting new strategies, one of the costs of ignoring the insights of self-criticism. War tilts the West toward hard power solutions, while often portraying adversary violence as "terrorism," and so diminishing the roles of diplomacy, compromise, and negotiation, leaving only an open-ended military option with no clear terminal point.

Unfortunately, the realist consensus functions as an ideology that complements the structures of militarist behavior (weaponry, foreign bases, global navies, the greed of the arms industry). This type of dysfunctional global governance encounters specific pockets of resistance from a variety of social and national movements but, by and large, geopolitical actors resist all pleas for fundamental change, exhibiting their lack of imagination, fears, ideological closure, and abiding political ambition. Weaker states even accept a nuclear security blanket to protect their territory from potential foreign attack, thereby entrenching realist thinking and structures.

Conclusion

From these observations, an overall conclusion can be drawn: the realist understanding of power has lost its grip on reality, but it continues to control the outlook and policy moves of geopolitical actors, with the possible partial exception of China. As a result, a world order crisis of unprecedented magnitude has emerged. It features countervailing views of power and systemic resilience. Alternatives to outmoded realism are, at this stage, mainly associated with global social movements, which rest on the adoption of nonviolent political alternatives as the foundation of constructive change, which seeks changes in political behavior at all levels of social interaction. The current version of Westphalian realism remains closely tied to its experiences of war as the main arbiter of change and stability. As such, it displays almost no understanding of this revolt from below.

There are some hopeful signs. These signs include the culture of peace productively established in a widening circle of European countries and the relatively low investment in hard power capabilities by emergent statist poles of regional influence, including China, India, and Brazil. Whether these developments will be able, in time, to convince the United States and Russia to move toward a collaborative form of global governance, premised on a security system that is more reliant on nonviolent geopolitics and international law, constitutes a crucial unanswered question that confronts the peoples and governments of the world with extreme vulnerability to future catastrophes, whether arising from human activity or natural causes.

6

Constitutional Guidelines for Global Governance

Peace studies, including world order studies, has from its inception always felt the need to overcome skepticism as to its academic credibility, given the cultural endorsement of realism. Practitioners had to convince doubters that peace was as entitled to respect as the study of war, conflict norms, and modes of resolution. Peace studies has mostly pursued this goal of disciplinary credibility by relying on methodologies developed in such social science settings as political science, law, sociology, anthropology, and economics.

This methodological priority has inclined the dominant approach taken to peace and justice to be as grounded as much as possible in empirical, data-driven interpretations of global developments related to war/peace issues. This modernist epistemological orientation tends to over-generalize statistical or other forms of hard data that are available, even if following the data influences inquiry in misleading ways. The struggle for disciplinary respectability in the peace studies domain has been adopted at a high cost, given the nature of the subject matter being investigated and the implicit ethical premise. An insistence on social science and juridical methodologies has had the effect of devaluing and rendering irrelevant qualitative assessments of challenges to peace and peacefulness. The moral, political, historical, philosophical, literary, and spiritual imagination are ignored, or demeaned, as sources of insight, knowledge, and wisdom, which have much to contribute to any prescriptive inquiry into the foundations of peace in the context of global governance.

As mentioned earlier in a different context, books by Pinker (2011) and Goldstein (2012) offer high-profile examples of this academic tendency to constrain inquiry and distort findings and policy implications. Both authors are respected, influential scholars who have received exaggerated praise for their work from the scholarly and policy communities, at least partly because their encouraging claims about international trends are derived from data that supposedly demonstrate the decline of political violence and war, while not threatening the mainstream international relations (IR) realist paradigm, the arms trade, or military budgets.[1]

Another prominent example of gaining attention for inquiry via reliance on a technocratic methodology is illustrated by the extraordinary reception given to the *Limits to Growth* study in the early 1970s (Meadows et al. 1972). This heightened interest seemed mostly to reflect the fact that its rather startling conclusions about the allegedly approaching demise of industrial civilization resulted from computer-simulated studies that purported to be objective and claimed at least to have technocratic, if not scientific, credibility.

Although we appreciate the rationality of this search for acceptance within the academy, and in domains of public influence, it is misleading in a war/peace setting, especially in the nuclear age. The threat of use of weaponry to kill tens of millions of civilians and cause "a nuclear winter" that would bring famine to much of the world weakens the meaningfulness of data sets that confirm lower casualty rates in war and even a lower incidence of major wars. It is a manifestation of the reality that many peace-minded scholars were themselves socialized into the prevailing Enlightenment notions that advances in knowledge are valued to the extent that they are as science-based as possible, resting on instrumental reason, and give rise to measurable and testable hypotheses rather than being reflections of normative preferences of the author or derived from cultural traditions. Nevertheless, such a supposedly responsible epistemological path is a dead end if the purpose of inquiry is to understand and promote prospects for a more peaceful and sustainable human future, which is essentially and unavoidably a normative undertaking. It is our view that peace and justice studies, as an academic field of inquiry and discourse, will only begin to realize its full potential when it begins to self-identify as an avowedly *normative* branch of knowledge, situated in the DMZ (demilitarized zone) that provides a receptive interface between the social sciences and the humanities.[2] Such a normative epistemology views literature, cultural studies, religion, and philosophy as being of equivalent relevance to its preoccupations, combining hopes and fears, as the social sciences, and maybe more so.[3] In effect, it is time for peace studies to come out of its "normative closet."

There is more to this curtailing of the normative imagination than conforming to prevailing academic methodological fashions. There is also an ideological blowback effect from the outcome of the Cold War. The dismal failure of the Soviet socialist experiment to endure has been interpreted and manipulated by Western elites in a manner that discredits non-incremental advocacy, radical thought, and even socialist values. This is especially the case if a projected global future is perceived as a threat to private sector interests and anticipates major changes for the sake of greater justice and prudence in human affairs.

An ideological spin has been given to the Soviet collapse by presenting it as the inevitable effect of Moscow's collectivist effort to build a socialist state, posited as a dystopian undertaking allegedly bound to fail—and not only fail, but in its pursuit of inherently unattainable goals, inflict massive additional suffering on its adherents, as well as pose dangerous threats to its internal and external adversaries. In effect, utopian thinking is unfortunately interpreted by many Western ideologues and even serious thinkers as inherently dystopian and historically linked to the humanistic failures and military defeats of fascism and communism. Whenever it becomes operational in history, so goes the anti-utopian ideological litany, its praxis inevitably leads to the inversion of the emancipatory future it promises and vainly struggles to attain. Instead, in the process of questing after the unattainable, it actually produces a more oppressive and exploitative political order than the one it tries to supersede and discredit.

This fallacious reasoning, based on a selective interpretation of complex and contradictory historical developments, has been widely accepted within Western intellectual and elite circles, and for obvious ideological reasons. It completely devalues utopian thinking as dangerous mischief and devalues radical or transformative alternatives to the established order by attaching derogatory labels to "utopian," "socialist," and "collectivist," and indeed to whatever radical innovation is being advocated to achieve systemic transformations.

As a result, every projection of a better human future which is premised on structural changes or even drastic policy reforms tend to be derided and dismissed from consideration by both the informed public and governing elites at a historical time when such fundamental adjustments are needed if a catastrophic future is to be avoided. A benevolent human future depends like never before upon our capacity and willingness to think and act "outside the box" of conventional wisdom and vested interests that insist that responsible politics should limit itself to the politics of the possible. Such encoded language is innocently deferential to whatever elites deem attainable and nothing else. In Western practice this has meant resistance to world order innovations, confining *policy* adjustments to increments at the margins of established *structures*. If our speculative investigations are confined to horizons of feasibility associated with incremental reform as embodying non-utopian conceptions of politics, humanity will remain entrapped, mentally and behaviorally, in self-annihilating modes of belief and collective behavior that can neither address the most serious challenges currently threatening species well-being, nor take advantage of the opportunity to improve upon centuries of war, oppression, cruelty to marginalized minorities and to animals, and irresponsible disregard of ecological limits. These patterns deny humanity pedagogies that could teach us how to live together in better ways. To put this position more bluntly, we live in a historical setting in which only utopic possibilities have the necessary emancipatory potential to address such practical challenges to species well-being as climate change and nuclearism. And put more positively, by responding to these challenges through enhancing the life circumstances of humanity holistically conceived, almost all persons on the planet will benefit. Future generations will be born into far more benign historical circumstances than currently exist and be confident about moving ahead in benevolent directions that benefit not only individuals but collectives.

It is a contrarian view that the most daunting global challenges—for example, climate change and the abolition of nuclear weaponry—are global collective goods problems of great magnitude that will remain incapable of solution within the framework of state-centric global policy formation. This is because this framework continues to be dominated by calculations of short-term national interests, market-driven economics, and incremental adjustment that set realistic outer limits of feasible reform.[4] As matters now stand, any proposed reforms or transformative projects that cannot be justified by such calculations tend to get sidelined in the marketplace of ideas, being treated as outside the responsible scope of political discourse. The contrary position urged here is that only by encouraging engagement in promising "unrealistic" political spaces receptive to our imaginative faculties, including utopian thought and transformational assessments, that society can generate plausible escape routes from a condition of entrapped hopelessness and despair that are currently giving rise to escapism, denial, extremism, and dark apocalyptic expectations about the future.[5] Put differently, our most urgent and difficult policy dilemmas do not seem resolvable by recourse to normal politics that continues to be conceived within the self-limiting frame of "the art of the possible."

If anyone doubts this seemingly gloomy assessment, it is helpful to reflect carefully on the inability to achieve nuclear disarmament or to adopt policies responsive to the scientific consensus warning humanity of the menacing consequences of further atmospheric buildup of greenhouse gases. There are many contextual factors that help explain such systemic failures, but the most daunting explanation is undoubtedly the structural implications of state-centrism and market-driven capitalism as reinforced by the near universal adherence to a political ideology of nationalism, individualism, statist realism, and geopolitical managerial priorities, accentuated by a temporal view of short-termism that governs the behavior of political leaders and their publics. These factors dilute their motivations and capabilities to cooperatively solve the long-term challenges of planetary scope, which are characteristic of the rapidly unfolding Anthropocene age. Transnational private sector interests and influences also inhibit many commitments to produce global public goods undertaken for the sake of human and planetary well-being.[6]

There are some more hopeful ways to conceive of this dangerous set of conditions that confront humanity. For one thing, our political experience reassures us that the "impossible" happens, although not necessarily, nor in a timely and bloodless fashion. Positive outcomes seem to depend on the convergence of struggles from below by people-bonding movements that exert strong pressures for change, eventual recognition and supportive responses by awakened elites from above, and helpful unanticipated developments that extend the boundaries of feasibility beyond previous societal understanding (Hardt and Negri 2004, 2009). Extraordinary events, such as the Fukushima reactor meltdown in 2010 or Hurricane Sandy in 2012, produce a temporary atmosphere of heightened sub-systemic public concern and awareness that temporarily enlarges the political space available to leaders. There is never any assurance that a positive policy breakthrough will follow from these foretastes of impending catastrophe or be durable enough to withstand the pushback from vested interests despite public concerns about past traumas, losing their resonance, fading in relevance with the passage of time.[7]

Among examples of such patterns of induced diversion are the climate skeptic campaign heavily funded by the fossil fuel industry and the shift of attention in nuclear weapons states from the threat posed by the weaponry to a preoccupation about proliferation to additional states. Such inattention to nuclearism has been recently mitigated by Russian saber-rattling nuclear threats arising in the course of the Ukraine War. Diversions confuse citizens and leaders as to the real nature of the most pressing problems confronting humanity. This type of stultifying uncertainty has been underscored by the failure to treat the COVID-19 pandemic as a collective goods problem for the entire planet, rather than allowing it to become a postcolonial experience for the Global South that illuminated the class/race inequities that resulted in grossly favored access to life-saving vaccines, medical treatment, and hospital equipment for those living in the Global North. Our modern circumstances, heavily influenced by media manipulations especially responsive to corporate interests, help divert attention from underlying dangers. The result is an overall mood among elites and publics of collective denial, despair, and distraction. It is notable since the American presidential electoral campaign of 2008, there has been no significant reference to either climate change or the menace of nuclear weaponry by opposition presidential candidates. In effect, national political calculations led to complete acquiescence to such a politics of evasion. This surrender was undoubtedly reinforced by the priorities of most major funders of political parties and candidates, who seemed to care about little else than the short-term profitability of corporate and financial activities and, on some occasions, regressive social policies such as promoting prohibitions on abortion, gay marriage, and gender preferences.

Parallel to this plea for an epistemological enlargement of what we mean by peace studies is an insistence on the integration of the spiritual dimensions of human experience to our conception of "reality." Such openness to spirituality implies a distinctive pedagogic outlook toward the subject matter of peace and justice. Spirituality in this usage does not necessarily imply a religious consciousness, nor does it exclude it. The significance of spirituality for the normative concerns associated with the quest for peace, justice, and sustainability is to acknowledge the limits of reason as a basis for interpretation and behavior. This sense of limits is to be complemented by recognizing the importance of unfathomable complexity at all levels of apprehending reality, from the tiniest particle to the cosmic expanse of the universe.

In a prior generation, Paulo Freire inspired many of us with essentially secular ideas and practices set forth in his *Pedagogy of the Oppressed*, a book that deserves to be given a renewed spiritual resonance in the setting of present struggles of marginalized peoples everywhere (1970). And could we not all be considered marginalized in light of the failure of governance structures to uphold human security? We who declare ourselves dedicated to human betterment by way of minimizing war, global warming, and human suffering would benefit from forms of public reason that are not restricted to the ideas of instrumental rationality and empirical validation associated with the contextual Enlightenment emphases on repudiating supernaturalism and religiously induced metaphysical wishful thinking. The Confucian scholar Tu Weiming has reminded Western readers of the practical relevance of spiritual knowledge. He writes, "As we become acutely aware of our earth's vulnerability and increasingly wary of our own fate as an 'endangered species,' what are the critical spiritual questions we must ask?" (1996, 73).

Another aspect of normative pedagogy is sensitivity to what the Indian jurist Upendra Baxi has highlighted by asserting a moral injunction to scholarly endeavor to take "suffering seriously" (1985). Our main Enlightenment legacy does not encourage this kind of focused empathy in affairs of state, nor do prevailing capitalist ethics, by deeming such a call for public empathy as demoralizing—what Margaret Thatcher dismissed as "the nanny state" that allegedly replaced the capitalist work ethic of individualism and calculus of rewards and punishments with the corrupting state-administered bestowals of automatic "social protection." Virtues of sympathy and compassion are not easily encompassed by incremental problem-solving or market mentalities, and, according to prevailing tendencies in economic and political thought, are best confined to family, maximally extended to community neighborhoods, with an individualist society backstopped by voluntary charitable impulses to address severe national health and disaster-induced hardships.

To live ethically in a globalizing world entails the adoption and implementation of *a pedagogy and politics of empathy*. It is a matter of regarding the mass suffering of others not only as an occasion for the activation of charitable impulses to the less fortunate, but as sending a clear signal that our modern structures and procedures of governance at all levels of social interaction are normatively deficient and in need of reconstruction.

It is worth observing the cohesiveness of premodern family, community, and tribal patterns of interaction to gain perspective on the humanistic deficiencies of the more technologically sophisticated and elaborate modern patterns of social interaction, from the city to the world.

Another aspect of this proposed pedagogy is to conceive of global policy from the perspective of the human interest, an understanding prefigured decades ago in Robert Johansen's pathbreaking argument for the reconfiguring of American foreign policy (2006). Such an orientation directly challenges the realist paradigm that is premised on the predominant historical agency of statist hard power as used to calculate and promote *national* interests, epitomized by the stress on military capabilities, the outcomes of major wars, and twisted to serve powerful internal and foreign private sector interests.

What induces despair is this realization that a state-centric, market-driven world is structurally incapacitated from consistently apprehending and serving the global interests of humanity, which include adapting to the future as well as the present in situations where significant material sacrifices or substantial behavioral adjustments are required. In some circumstances the human interest, as measured by reference to global public goods, can be achieved. For instance, establishing through negotiations the public order of the oceans was an impressive display of intergovernmental cooperation on the basis of mutual interests and trade-offs to satisfy uneven and diverse interests; other examples include the suspension of sovereignty claims in Antarctica and the agreements reached to phase out the use of chlorofluorocarbons (CFCs) that were depleting the ozone layer that protected the earth's inhabitants from deadly forms of radiation.

In situations, however, where achieving human interests call for major economic cutbacks for which there are no compensatory alternatives, and which encroach on entrenched security commitments and military capabilities of important governments, cooperation in the pursuit of global public goods has achieved minimal results. Efforts to overcome antagonistic national interests are obstructed by the unevenness of perceptions and endowments that undermine cooperative responses, which are only rarely chosen, and even more rarely successful. These sources of systemic disappointment call attention to the inadequacy of global institutions that are *rhetorically* mandated to serve the human interest under current world conditions yet denied the capabilities to implement the mandate. The somewhat promising constitutional framework embodied in the UN Charter is illustrative of these tensions between rhetorical promise and existential performance. National political elites, when under pressure, give ground rhetorically, yet seldom performatively. And even rhetorical progress is slow. The UN took a giant step by its general prohibition of recourse to force in international relations, yet gave the most powerful countries a right of veto, which amounts to a right of exception when it comes to Charter prohibitions including Security Council decisions.

Old Realism Versus New Realism

The emphasis here on the need to develop a more cosmopolitan oriented epistemology and pedagogy for the study of global issues from a normative perspective is in line with Johansen's (2006) call for the displacement of an *old realism* based on national interest thinking by a *new realism* that acknowledges the relevance of the human and global interest. Such a reorientation does not resolve the challenge of praxis—that is, what needs to be done on the level of behavior to make this proposal more than a wish. A critique of the still prevailing realist paradigm has to be tempered by an appreciation that world order structures continue to be state-centric and geopolitically configured, which have not been seriously challenged by the establishment in the last century of centralized global institutions, first the League of Nations and then the United Nations, nor even by the more resource-endowed Bretton Woods institutions (Falk 2004). These institutions are essentially instruments of sovereign states, especially the dominant and more affluent states, but at best, operate as battlegrounds for clashing state interests, which is not to be confused with venues dedicated to global and human interests. Such institutions, established in postwar geopolitical climates, have become increasingly anachronistic, failing to adapt to the collapse of the Western colonial empires or to reflect the rise of non-Western political actors and the importance of regional developments (Ikenberry 2001; Paupp 2009). The use of a cosmopolitan rhetoric to affirm the existence of a phantom "world community" somewhat disguises persisting nationalist orientations and capital-friendly policymaking mechanisms, often compounding confusion.

In crucial respects, as already noted, the old realism was constitutionally embedded in the United Nations by way of conferring an unrestricted right of veto. This, in effect, elevated the logic and practice of geopolitics above any pretension that international law is the final authority even in global institutional arrangements pledged to pursue war prevention priorities. Double standards in applying Charter norms have further weakened the authority of the UN. It undermined the attempt to establish a common legal and political regime that would set a single set of ground rules applicable to all political actors. The legitimacy of the rule of law depends on treating equals equally. By labeling UN members as juridically equal while at the same time conferring this unrestricted right of exception on the most dangerous states or practicing double standards amounts to a somewhat veiled confession that the UN was always intended and expected to act as a creature of the old realism of power. Despite the preamble of the Charter the UN was not empowered to bring into being a new realism premised on peace, justice, and ecological sustainability.

In his book *Strategic Vision*, Zbigniew Brzezinski, a stalwart among political realists, revealingly shows his awareness of the new set of circumstances, yet proceeds with a traditional geopolitical perspective rooted in the national interests of the United States. His very first sentences set the tone: "The world is now interactive and interdependent. It is also for the first time a world in which the problems of human survival have begun to overshadow more traditional conflicts" (2012, 1). Of course, fundamental reorientations of worldview are rare, and it is thus not surprising that the argument of Brzezinski's book concentrates upon a reformulation of American grand strategy so that it might continue to perform as the global leader under these altered international conditions. In his words, "The world needs an America that is economically vital, socially appealing, responsibly powerful, strategically deliberate, internationally respected, and historically enlightened in its global engagement with the new East" (ibid.). He recognizes that the West is increasingly challenged by the rising Asia and the changing global context, by "serious longer-term risks to the survival of some endangered states, to the security of the global commons, and to global stability at large" (ibid.). But in the end, what Brzezinski proposes is nothing more than a reformulation of national interests of an American-led West under altered contextual conditions, with a nod of appreciation that a credible new realism must incorporate an ethical and spiritual vision responsive to *human* and *global* interests as manifest in the early twenty-first century.

What is missing in this reformulation is any recognition that economic globalization and climate change in different ways call for more geopolitically independent international institutions, systemic respect for international law and human rights, and a willingness to forgo American exceptionalism in the international realm, especially when it comes to uses of force to resolve international disputes or satisfy geopolitical ambitions. It is at least somewhat encouraging that someone who had spent his long career espousing hard power geopolitics has come to recognize the need to adapt to a new constellation of global influences in which effective governance can no longer be premised on the primacy of the West. Although welcome, such an adjustment is still far from enough as it takes the persistence of the obsolescent state-centric, geopolitical, market-driven structures as set in stone for all time.

What the new realism demands, above all, is a more effective set of procedures and institutions by which to address the most acute problems of global governance. These problems cannot be resolved by the methods available to a state-centric world order driven by nationalist, economistic, and geopolitical priorities and related short time horizons. Such a political realization briefly penetrated the public consciousness after the use of atomic weapons against Japanese cities at the end of World War II, occasioning a flurry of elite calls for the establishment of world government as the alternative to species disaster. For a short time, the sobering realization became prominent that any future major war would likely be fought with weaponry of annihilation that would result in massive, mutual devastation. Yet such a reactive embrace of new realism quickly disappeared from public consciousness in the wake of renewed geopolitical rivalry that became known as the Cold War, with hostility and security threats exaggerated by those private and bureaucratic interests benefiting from continuing over-investments in anachronistic militarized conceptions of global security. The main adjustment, which gave the world some borrowed time to transform its structure of institutions and prevailing ideas, involved the substitution of *threats* for the actuality of *warfare*, what became known as "deterrence," "mutual assured destruction" (or MAD), and "crisis management" in US–Soviet relations.

With respect to other categories of weaponry of mass destruction, there has been some success due to the establishment of regimes of prohibition for biological and chemical weaponry and some ambiguous managerial arrangements among nuclear adversaries known as "arms control," but coupled with a deceptive alleged geopolitical fix for nuclear weaponry in the guise of the Non-Proliferation Treaty (NPT), as given political potency by an American-led enforcement regime that is also delegitimized by operational double standards (Israel was given a secret pass, while Iran is threatened with military attack).

Revealingly, the treaty makes a rhetorical gesture toward balanced commitments by incorporating a denuclearizing provision in Article VI, obligating nuclear weapons states to undertake good faith negotiations to achieve nuclear disarmament. However, the practice over many decades is deeply disillusioning for those who believed that the treaty provided a reliable vehicle for reaching a world without nuclear weaponry. What the treaty process has revealed has been a consistent refusal by the nuclear weapons states, led by the United States, to consider seriously fulfilling its commitment to give up such apocalyptic weaponry.[8] The result has been to make seemingly permanent a hegemonic dimension of world order, which, if objectively viewed, constitutes a regime "nuclear apartheid," expressed both by the selective enforcement of the obligation to forgo the acquisition of nuclear weapons and by the hegemonic impacts of a few states retaining the weaponry while the others commit to forgoing the nuclear option.

Concerns about the carrying capacity of the earth that surfaced in the early 1970s were a second strong message that the consumptive patterns of the rich countries, combined with rising living standards throughout the world being achieved by a rapidly expanding population, were inviting a catastrophic future for the human species.[9]

Since the end of the last century, a third related and reinforcing warning about lifestyle has been delivered in the form of climate change, validated by the findings and recommendation of climate scientists and confirmed by a variety of indicators, including the increasing frequency of extreme weather events, melting polar and glacial ice, rising sea levels, intensifying floods, fires, and droughts. The COVID-19 pandemic temporarily awakened the world to the borderless nature of serious contagious disease, as well as to the dysfunctionality, from the standpoint of health and equity, of state-centric dominance and capitalist logic controlling relevant arrangements.

An extraterrestrial consultant hired to correct the ills of the planet would immediately notice this inability of state-centric problem-solving to overcome unconditional attachments to hard power assets, maximizing economic growth, and the unevenness of resource endowments. They would also take note of the fact that the smartest and most influential among policy-oriented political realists, Kissinger and Brzezinski, while acknowledging the new global context, fail to question the most fundamental of all dysfunctional world order patterns. As a result, nothing happens. Unresponsive thinking by governments continues to dominate policymaking, and unresolved problems of global scope are kicked down the road, time and again, to be solved on the next guy's watch. And public memories are regrettably short: the lessons of Hiroshima and COVID-19, that seemed to make a decisive impact, quickly lost their relevance as more abiding interests regrouped and recovered their control over the limits of policy adaptations.

Rethinking the Westphalian Structure of World Order

The state-centric world order that has been globalized in the aftermath of the collapse of colonialism started out as an essentially regional system in seventeenth-century Europe. It came to be conveniently associated with the Peace of Westphalia (1648). The basic structural innovation was to postulate an international society constituted by territorial sovereign states rather than as one with a variety of political actors, ranging from city-states to variously constituted multiethnic empires.

The League of Nations, a first attempt to institutionalize cooperative relations of states for the overriding purpose of war prevention, was premised exclusively on the formal postulate of sovereign equality (although bearing the colonial imprint of Western dominance). Its failure was partially interpreted as being due to the refusal to recognize the international role played by certain leading states in the period after World War I. The United Nations was constructed to overcome this failure of the League to appreciate statist inequality, giving an institutional expression to the realist views of Franklin Roosevelt, who held the belief that future international organization would be able to continue in peacetime the cooperative atmosphere among the Allies and, above all, between the United States and the Soviet Union. To ensure Soviet participation, and to take account of the geopolitical attributes of Westphalian and still West-centric world order, the

UN constitutional framework conferred upon the four main victors in the war permanent membership in the Security Council (plus China, accorded geopolitical status because of the size of its population, its victimization by Japan in World War II, and its West-leaning government at the time the UN was established).

There are now several additional challenges to the legitimacy and effectiveness of the UN. First, the privileged status of the victors in World War II no longer reflects the geopolitical landscape, denies a comparable role to such emergent major actors as India and Brazil, and remains overly weighted toward Western dominance. Second, established primarily to address war between states, the UN is constitutionally disabled from dealing directly with violent conflict within states, whereas the dominant conflict patterns of the twenty-first century are internal wars often intensified by proxy interventions of external actors, both states and non-state political movements. Third, the geopolitical leverage of permanent members of the Security Council, especially of the United States, China, and Russia, results in a delegitimizing pattern of strategically implemented double standards, perhaps most vividly evident in shielding Israel from adverse consequences of its multifaceted defiance of international law and UN authority. Fourth, the effort of global policy formation to meet challenges other than those of peace and security demonstrates the need for an international institution with *decisional* authority in relation to economic globalization, human rights, contagious disease, ecological resilience, and climate change. These disabling shortcomings of the UN, which remains, above all, an arena within which governments articulate and pursue *national* interests that may include major efforts to achieve and implement lawmaking norms binding on all states in the world, suggest the importance of establishing arenas where the institutional orientation is more responsive to human and global interests. To do this under present conditions seems unattainable by normal politics. The UN framework is frozen, and those states that benefit from these conditions lack incentives to give up their vested interests in structures and procedures no longer reflective of the global makeup of power or responsive to pressures to generate effective solutions.

Reform Proposals Within a Westphalian Framing: An Independently Funded UN Emergency Peace Force, Global Parliament, and Peoples' Tribunals

Several proposals have been put forward that would take steps to realize the normative potential of Westphalian structures to meet current world order/justice challenges. These include a UN Emergency Force that would be made available to address severe human rights abuses, humanitarian catastrophes, and natural disasters, and could be activated on the authority of the UN secretary general or General Assembly, thereby circumventing the veto and geopolitical manipulation (Johansen 2006). Such an approach would gain considerable credibility if tied to some kind of independent funding source. There has long been awareness of levying a Tobin Tax, or some variant, on financial transactions that weakened existing connections between the richest and most powerful states and responses to international situations of an emergency nature.

Another kind of proposal is to establish a global people's assembly or parliament that would give voice to the priorities of the peoples of the world rather than to restrict participation in international institutions to governmental representatives (Falk and Strauss 2011). The evolution of the European Parliament illustrates one model of popular representation that operates in a regional political space that is deliberately detached from both statist and hegemonic dimensions of Westphalian world order. From the perspective taken here, such an innovation weakens policy deference to statist and geopolitical dimensions of world order, and gives belated opportunities for participation to civil society actors as deserving of meaningful roles in the articulation of global policy.[10] It would also be a step in the direction of globalizing a more democratic form of governance.[11] As with any democratic institution, there is no guarantee that it would lend support to the pursuit of human and global interests. If the institutional space became influential, it would stimulate those with the greatest economic and political leverage to take action to protect their interests. As more recent elections for members of the European Parliament illustrated, the wave of reactionary populism that is sweeping across Europe resulted in the victory of many candidates who were deeply opposed to any weakening of European nation-states in deference to regional goals of an integrated political and social Europe. Since the economic troubles of recent years, there are increased societal demands to restore many of the features of a state-centric Europe. This has been accompanied by the recognition that strong nationalist antagonisms are resurfacing along with a weakening of the ethos of a uniting Europe. Whether the Ukraine War will tip the balance once again to the benefits of European unity are currently uncertain and seems to depend on how interplay between security concerns associated with Russia outweigh more nationalist preoccupations bearing on trade, immigration, money, and borders.

A further proposal is of a purely civil society character: the encouragement of people's tribunals that can be organized spontaneously, as was the case with the Russell Tribunal of 1966–67, or within an ongoing framework, as was the case with Permanent Peoples' Tribunal established in 1976 by the Basso Foundation in Rome. Such initiatives can challenge the impunity gap, at least symbolically, that allows dominant states to avoid accountability for violations of international law. They can also expose societal insensitivities on matters of race, gender, and environmental protection.[12]

Toward an International Rule of Law

Another path toward creating the kind of structure that is needed to meet current challenges would be to enhance the role of international law within international relations, generally, and with the UN system, in particular. A first step might be for permanent members of the Security Council to agree not to use their veto in situations of a humanitarian emergency, either caused by natural disaster, political strife, or contagious disease. A second initiative would be to make the Advisory Opinions of the International Court of Justice (ICJ), that are now downgraded by being treated as "advisory," binding. This could be achieved to some degree by dropping the word "advisory" from the jurisdictional authority accorded in the statute governing this eminent body's activities. A variety of ways could be undertaken to make it easier for governments and civil society organizations to implement authoritative judgments as to applicable international law from the ICJ. Similarly, the ICJ should be endowed with the power of judicial review in response to complaints by states, and possibly other entities, to the effect that the Security Council has overstepped its authority as set forth in the Charter.[13]

Another reform measure would be to make the International Criminal Court less tied to the hegemonic dimensions of world order via its manner of funding and appointments. In the first decade of its operation, the ICC seemed to reflect the double standards imposed by this hegemonic dimension. This has meant potential accountability for the non-Western governments, especially those in sub-Saharan Africa, and impunity for Western governments and large states, including China, India, and Russia. The non-hierarchical application of international law is an indispensable step in the direction of establishing a credible global rule of law, which in turn would move toward creating the sort of normative infrastructure required for the promotion of human and global interests.

Of course, if such reforms took place with the acquiescence of governments, which seems highly unlikely in the present atmosphere, the evolution of the Westphalian world order would demonstrate once again its extraordinary adaptive resilience and manifest a normative responsiveness to the emergence of human rights, international criminal accountability, and the importance of shaping global policy by reference to human and global interests as democratically interpreted. It is highly questionable whether conceiving of the normative potential of global reform as existing within Westphalian structures is a useful exercise, given the stubborn refusal by countries benefiting from the geopolitical overlay that qualifies the foundations of state-centric world order. Such an agenda of non-incremental reforms far exceeds reasonable expectations at present, and suggests that it may be more relevant to consider such reforms as essentially transformative, hopefully to be realized in the future within a post-Westphalian or non-Westphalian framework, if and when it emerges.[14]

It should be observed that the complexities of the present combined with uncertainties about the future suggest adopting a posture of humility. It is not possible to predict the actualization of ambitious reformist proposals in the absence of political will on the part of those governments that continue to believe that they benefit from this mix of power and order. It seems helpful to delimit changes that would serve in meeting the challenges that are not being currently met, but how to overcome patterns of resistance is a psycho-political matter that has yielded the most modest of results. In effect, we do not know what must happen to make governmental elites understand that they would benefit more from the existence of a global rule of law than from the present structures of impunity. Blueprinting a transition to the future we desire is deceptive and irrelevant, an instance of normative hubris. This observation applies to the proposals of the prior section as well as the discussion of enhancing the role of international law. We are destined to live with uncertainty and risk and manifest our beliefs by engaging in struggle and resistance.

Subverting Westphalia

Several developments have made continued reliance upon the Westphalian model of world order to be misleading.[15] At the same time, it is important not to lose sight of the persisting control of global policymaking mechanisms and international war-making capabilities by states, especially by leading states that constitute hierarchical/hegemonic and geopolitical dimensions of state-centric world order. This is more euphemistically known, especially in American international relations literature, as "global leadership," which in its more idealistic versions is often identified as "liberal internationalism."

Among the subversive developments one must note the advent of apocalyptic warfare that undermines the traditional role of war and military superiority as the main ordering principle in relations among sovereign states without achieving prudent adjustments by way of nuclear disarmament. This role is further undermined by the spread of nationalism and the success of nationalist wars of independence in the non-West that have greatly reduced the historical agency of nonnuclear military superiority, as evident in the outcome of recent American wars in Vietnam, Afghanistan, and Iraq; the Soviet Union has a similar confirming experience through years of costly failure in Afghanistan, repeated currently (and more dramatically) by Russia in Ukraine, which poses a geopolitical threat to the West, in addition to the dire societal threats to Ukraine. This trend is also evident in the rise of non-state actors that are capable of eroding the stability of world order in profound ways despite having only trivial resources at their disposal. This is illustrated most dramatically by the 9/11 attacks and the reactions of the Global War on Terrorism that it produced, as well as by the emergence of extremist movements in the Middle East (and elsewhere), capable of overwhelming traditional governing authorities.

Meanwhile, the rise of transnational and regional civil society and global actors, institutions, and procedures has rendered the Westphalian postulate of sovereign states as the only political actors entitled to full-fledged membership in world society increasingly anachronistic. This outmodedness of a sovereignty-oriented approach is also illustrated by the emergence of international standards of human rights, doctrines of humanitarian intervention, and the rise of the responsibility to protect norm (R2P). In addition, criminal accountability for international crimes attributed to leaders of states by overriding traditional doctrines of "sovereign immunity" and "acts of states" weakens notions of territorial sovereignty and dilutes basic Westphalian principles. Similarly, the overall impact of economic globalization in all of its aspects makes the contours of interdependence and interactive transactions far less focused on intergovernmental and international relationships, according more attention to transnational arrangements that institutionalize cooperation at regional and global levels.[16]

The cumulative weight of such developments is sufficient to justify the terminology *post-Westphalian*, but that does not necessarily imply a departure from the realist paradigm of analysis and prescription. The "normative potential" of the Westphalian frame will not be exhausted without replacing this paradigm and displacing it by the emergence of an epistemology and pedagogy of empathy—that is, sensitivity to the suffering of others, including treating "nature" as integral to the sphere of otherness that deserves ethical treatment. It would certainly benefit national societies, given the realities of interdependence, to move toward an orientation that was human and global as well as national, which viewed nature with ecological respect instead of as inertly present, there to be dominated, exploited, and managed for the sake of strictly short-term human gains: profits, power, and pleasure (Held 1995; Archibugi 2008).

What seems to be an original aspect of the historical present is the extent to which the problems confronting sovereign states are now best understood and approached as collective goods challenges. As such, they can only be solved by the give and take of regional and global cooperation, as well as by responsible statecraft on the part of political actors. There are multiple sources of resistance to such an adjustment that, if made, could over time produce a series of win/win outcomes. The most steadfast forms of resistance are habit, popular expectations, nationalist pride, as well as the unevenness of national circumstances and expectations. It will be up to the rich and powerful to make the first moves toward such reconfiguring of national identity in a manner responsive to the imperatives of the Anthropocene lifeworld.

Arguably, such moves have been taken in limited circumstances in the past, for instance, in the relatively benign global leadership exercised by the United States shortly after World War II, especially in the economic domain of transatlantic relations. In that period, with a special concern about the recurrence of a new global depression, Americans invested heavily in the restoration of European markets in countries devastated by the war, and created the kind of liberal international order that allowed many nations in the world to trade, invest and prosper in a relatively stable setting, including the creation of innovative institutional arrangements relating to money and credit, whose degree of effectiveness undoubtedly reflected the accommodation of international hierarchies by means of weighted voting.[17] A novel aspect of the contemporary setting is the inability to address the climate change challenge without a realization that human endeavors can only be sustained by altering the human/nature nexus from one of domination and exploitation to one of collaboration, resilience, and sustainability.[18] Despite the science-backed consensus on global warming and its existential confirmation in rising temperatures, sea levels, and the frequency of extreme weather events, it has proved almost impossible to put obligatory restraints on business as usual.

The post-Westphalian global setting has significantly weakened its state-to-state and pure sovereignty dimensions, especially by holding *most* states and their leaders accountable for behavior that violates international law and subjecting their sovereign territory to potential R2P claims.[19] This juridical sovereign equality deeply informs international law, indeed all law. It continues in many diplomatic contexts to show respect for the juridical equality of sovereign states and treats sovereign states as alone enjoying the benefits of full membership in international society. The UN General Assembly exemplifies this feature of world order by treating all states, regardless of size and stage of development, as formally equal. Lichtenstein and China each have a single vote, and no non-state actor, no matter the size of its budget or the extent of its influence, is admitted to full UN membership with voting rights. This statist framework, implied by such phrases as "the state system," is weakened by the role of international financial institutions and by a variety of disciplinary moves associated with neoliberal globalization that limit the freedom of national governments to determine their own economic policies.[20]

Such effects were magnified by the realization that the Great Power dimensions of world order, which enact on the level of policy, the political inequality that exists among states. Part of the confusion results from the Janus face of geopolitics that affirms sovereignty for its own purposes while compromising or ignoring altogether the sovereignty of weaker states. This meant virtually unlimited sovereignty at home for geopolitical actors and impunity and nonaccountability in relation to their interventions in the internal affairs of other nation-states or their wartime behavior unless, as was the case with Germany and Japan after 1945, such states were themselves on the losing side in a major war. This pattern particularly resulted from a violent struggle between geopolitical actors that produced a new scheme for the management of postwar power relations.

This development was coupled with imposing disciplinary constraints on the weaker states, most notably those located in sub-Saharan Africa, but also more or less spread throughout the world. In this respect, the seemingly reformist steps taken during the last several decades have the common features of exhibiting double standards in their application, perhaps most explicitly evident in relation to such varied issues as the selective and discriminatory implementation of the NPT, the use and non-use of R2P, and the pattern of indictments and non-indictments by the International Criminal Court recently dramatized by prosecutorial inhibition in relation to the United States and Israel as contrasted with its zeal in indicting Putin during the ongoing Ukraine War. In these instances, and many others, juridical equals are treated unequally, the weak being disciplined, the strong and geopolitically dominant exerting managerial authority and enjoying near total exemption from rules and procedures applied to the others. In aggregate, this pattern might be characterized as a regime of "geopolitical exceptionalism," which can be understood as an extension of American exceptionalism that is proudly proclaimed by US leaders who insist that their doings are "innocent" even though, if objectively evaluated, they would be considered "criminal." In various global venues, a hierarchy of influence among geopolitical actors is also present when it comes to issues of accountability in relation to UN or ICC authority.

To a slight extent, those parts of the UN not subject to the veto or the full disciplinary weight of geopolitics, such as the Human Rights Council or the General Assembly, have attempted to mitigate this inequality of accountability. For instance, the outreach of Pope Francis is a sign of the Catholic Church turning in such a morally responsible direction expressing inclusiveness and empathy with the poor and vulnerable, as well as a dedication to peace and justice. Such expressions by moral authority figures play a complementary role to that of the UN secretary general in shaping public opinion in the important symbolic domain of politics, which in certain settings can exert a benign behavioral influence, especially if it arouses global solidarity initiatives, as it did during the Vietnam War in the late 1960 or later in the anti-apartheid campaign directed against in South African racism in the last decades of the twentieth century.

The Spanish–Turkish leadership of a UN project to encourage an Alliance of Civilizations was premised on the reinforcing relevance of religion, culture, and spirituality while fostering a climate of opinion that is pluralist, inclusivist, and cosmopolitan in its essential claims. Other religious groups, while still perhaps in the minority, are also open to an orientation toward global issues that gives primacy to the human and global interests and are not aligned with selfish conceptions of national interests; it is appropriate to view these progressive religious bodies as espousing the new realism of a cosmopolitanism *to come.* An encouraging interpretation of such tendencies is to take note of a degree to which the public consciousness of modern society is being conditioned for a radical repositioning of its perceptions of spiritual self-awareness that could make the human and global interest more widely accepted by governments as the necessary foundation for global problem-solving.[21] At the same time, it would be a superficial reflection, and quite possibly a mistaken one, to overlook the degree to which many religious institutions and perspectives are also becoming more exclusivist and supportive of dogmatic positions that reject the kind permissive values that had been taking root, especially in liberal democracies and are internationally embodied in legally obligatory human rights standards. As these societies turn "illiberal," organized religion and religious activism often join in celebrating regressive moves, as has notably been the case for various evangelical churches in the western hemisphere or Buddhism in Sri Lanka and Myanmar.

As far as states that are not tied closely to geopolitical alliances, there exists an opportunity for important initiatives that can advance the case for humane and effective solutions to outstanding global public challenges by articulating the human and global interest at stake. Sweden until recently played such a role, as have several Latin American and Asian countries at various times on different issues.

A second role for such political actors that are less rooted in the Westphalian worldview is to form coalitions with civil society actors, as was done with impressive results in gaining support for the Anti-Personnel Landmines Treaty and the establishment of the International Criminal Court (ICC). The important Treaty on the Prohibition of Nuclear Weapons (TPNW) negotiated under UN auspices is perhaps the most illuminating example of the success of exemplary initiatives achieved despite the determined opposition and diplomatic efforts of the main geopolitical actors. Especially in relation to the ICC, it is true that the utopian perceptions of victory at the time of establishment of the ICC in 2001 has been partially undercut by the inability to fund properly the institution to enable it to operate more independently of back channel geopolitical manipulations that have damaged its legitimacy from the outset.

The world is catching up with Robert Johansen's plea a generation ago for adherence to the human interest, and his more recent, more comprehensive and contemporaneous development of the argument (Johansen 2021). There is at this time a greater sense of urgency and crisis than existed in the 1980s, including a reawakening to the acute dangers of nuclear war during the Ukraine War. Until about 2015, there was a period of relative geopolitical calm in the Westphalian sense of war dangers between leading states, as well as some gestures of acceptance of a more cosmopolitan worldview as to forming cooperative responses to global-scale challenges. Yet all along there were powerful forces of resistance associated with entrenched beliefs, interests, and habits, as well as fears associated with risking fundamental changes.

This can be observed in the drift toward renewed tensions with Russia since 2014, reaching a confrontational peak after the Russian attack on Ukraine in early 2022, which superseded for the present the prior drift toward heightened tensions and hostile competitive relations with an ascending China. This new phase of geopolitics is emerging without a credible cover of ideological antagonism and more closely resembles traditional rivalry among geopolitically ambitious states struggling to define a new post–Cold War geopolitical hierarchy and set of relationships with its agreed fault lines. Biden has vainly tried to inject an ideological element into this historical circumstance of geopolitical fluidity by dividing the world into democracies and autocracies or rule-governed and power-driven political actors, but the categorizations lack normative cohesiveness, especially among the countries grouped among the democracies, such as India, Israel, Poland, Saudi Arabia, and others.

More clearly than ever before there is present a widening public awareness that state-centric world order is dangerously anachronistic, and that only a globally constituted, inclusive, ecologically responsible, person-centered order can bring to the peoples of the world a promise of a brighter future. A haunting practical question is whether existing leaders and elites can be induced to embrace a cosmopolitan ethos, and implement a foreign policy sufficiently dedicated to the human and global interest in a timely manner. As with other issues of action associated with adhering to the global public interest, it is difficult for individual political and economic actors to take such a step until there is a more collective push from below in the form of militant popular movements. There were hopes a few years ago that climate change might provide the incentive structure and motivational basis for a transformative response, at least offering a further demonstration that a state-centric world order possessed the capability to engage in *global* problem-solving when so much is at stake. However, this hope now seems to have given way to disillusionment as a result of the pushback by strong private sector interests associated with fossil fuels, arms sales, agrobusiness, and by the American turn away from its earlier role of global leadership, distractions arising from the immediacy of COVID-19, the Ukraine War, food and energy price and supply issues, and by the repeated disappointments associated with annual COP (Conference of the Parties) climate change meetings of governments under UN auspices in which nationalist perspectives have so far held sway.

It is too soon to conclude that climate change will be ignored altogether as a global challenge, especially given the increasing frequency and the growing gravity of the harmful effects of global warming. Much energy was devoted to the high expectations associated with the Paris 2015 meeting of almost all governments, with its announced resolve to produce a binding treaty that would regulate carbon emissions sufficiently to avoid, or at least slow down, the buildup of greenhouse gasses to the point that further heat rises occur more gradually in coming decades. The results at Paris, while impressive if expectations were held at a low level, failed to seek action that would keep the earth's average temperature rise below 1.5 degrees Celsius. and settled for national *pledges* to reduce carbon emissions rather than impose legally specified obligations. In effect, better than nothing, but far from enough. A more negative assessment followed shortly when Trump sided with climate denialism and demonstrated his commitment by withdrawing the United States from the Paris Agreement in early 2018.

Disappointment about the responses to climate change will, perhaps, be widely interpreted as exhibiting the inability of intergovernmental diplomacy to uphold the human and global interest and, in this sense, failure to protect national interests. The postulate of the new realism is that national interests can under current conditions only be consistently upheld by a *selective* promotion of human and global interests. However, if this test of state-centric world order works out, it would not represent evidence of a structural shift but only the capacity of the existing mechanisms to act collectively to avoid catastrophic harm to the human species under emergency conditions. It is somewhat comparable in its impact to science fiction scenarios that envision political unity on earth in response to credible, if spurious, reports of an impending invasion from a hostile species inhabiting another planet. In effect, a unified response would be a wartime alliance against an enemy of the world rather than an alliance of one part of the world against another, the standard framework of international warfare. It is this view of the whole, as opposed to the outlook of the part, that will be needed to move the human agents of a changing world order from their fragmentary consciousness to a holistic sequel, whose identity is formed by the rise of species, planetary, and cosmic awareness that infuses public consciousness sufficiently to enable the kind of solidarity needed to make large-scale cooperation a reality.

The prospect of the sort of structural and ideological adjustment presupposed by new realism would likely be preceded by the formation of a strong transnational movement of people in many parts of the world demanding change for the sake of survival, sustainability, and global justice. There were some glimmerings of such a movement in the brief and disparate flourishes associated with the Occupy movement of 2011 that took hold in many urban centers in the West, itself inspired by the Arab Spring uprisings, especially in Egypt's Tahrir Square. There was present in these populist gatherings a strong critique of the legendary 1 percent who controlled the wealth and shaped global governance policies, but neither program, organization, leadership, nor mobilization were sufficiently present to produce, let alone sustain, a significant challenge, either ideologically or politically. Without the emergence of such a movement, there will be, at most, progress only in relation to solving one issue at a time, and only if the sense of urgency is sufficiently sustained to overcome the various obstacles. Yet this kind of issue-oriented populism will not lead to a transformed world order but, rather, demonstrate that one is not needed, that when the necessity is great enough, the state system can act on behalf of the global public good.

In this event, there will probably be renewed confidence in the resilience of state-centric world order, and one more evolutionary jump in what states can do collectively if severely stressed.[22] This kind of resilience, while welcome and offering a sign of a species will to survive, does not purport to involve an ideological and structural shift toward cosmopolitanism, and may even induce what might be described as "world order complacency." Such an attitude developed in relation to the menace of nuclear weaponry in the aftermath of the Cold War. The opportunity to replace a genocidal security system based on deterrence and subject to human error with a process of phased disarmament was not even seriously explored or widely advocated by political leaders. Instead, there was widely asserted the unverifiable claim that nuclear deterrence kept the peace despite international tensions in a more reliable fashion than could be expected in a disarming world vulnerable to cheating and covert nuclear rearmament.

We are arguing that the needed structural and ideological shift will not result from rational argument, even if persuasive in elite circles, although the apartheid-ending South African exception should not be forgotten. Similarly, there are few examples in history that give reason to hope that a sudden willingness by political leaders to embrace cosmopolitanism for functional reasons will arise to avert ecological or economic calamity. Such momentous changes in outlook and behavior usually have presupposed the formation of radical social movements around the world that capture the political imagination of the masses at unpredictable moments and mount a direct threat to the existing political order. Whether this will happen, and if so under what circumstances and with what effects, is impossible to foretell. There has never been a self-consciously global political movement, although certain religious movements and imperialisms, commanding communities of the faithful or obedient, are vivid examples of extensions of control and allegiance beyond enclosures of the normal sovereign states. The Holy Roman Empire and the Ottoman Caliphate are historical examples of this bonding of secular and religious, without regard to internal boundaries, and may be suggestive of what is to come. The United States, with its post–Cold War investment in limited governance of a unipolar world order, is the best modern example of a non-territorial global state, although seemingly vulnerable to decline, and even collapse, unless it diminishes it globalist ambitions.

It could be that a future catastrophic event, preceded by populist demands for transformation, could set the stage for a transition from statism to cosmopolitanism as the foundation of realist ideology. Such futures can only be contemplated by utopian imaginative projections with explicit normative agendas, not predicated on data-oriented, technocratically minded futurists. We should all have learned that history unfolds in mysterious ways that bring into reality ideas, practices, and realities that were previously dismissed as fantasy, or more moderately, as alluring dreamscapes (Taleb 2010). A haunting uncertainty is whether the early twenty-first-century travails are gestating the birth of new global arrangements of control, security, development, resilience, and sustainability, or will provide the occasion for patterns of collapse.

Notes

1   Both of these contain much valuable material but rely excessively on battlefield deaths and countable trends as the main basis for their overarching claim that war and political violence are declining. This misses many features of the changing pattern of conflict that convey a far less rosy picture of the future. For instance, drones kill fewer people than a ground attack, but spread violence further, terrorize targeted civilian communities, and erode prior limits on the scope of violence associated with respect for territorial sovereignty. Also, the spread of nuclear weaponry, and the risks associated with its possible use, need to be taken into account, as do nuclear energy facilities that are subject to natural disasters, human error, accidental or deliberate attack in the course of combat operations.

2   The World Order Models Project (WOMP), without being self-conscious about its methodology, was avowedly normative in the sense of creating a framework of inquiry based on *values* rather than on *data* or subservient to the postulates of political realism. The overall perspective, which makes its own claims to be non-utopian, is nevertheless dismissed as utopian by mainstream scholarship because it seems beyond the outer horizons of feasibility despite claims to be depicting "feasible utopias." See Mendlovitz (1975) and Falk (1975).

3   For an impressive book written from such a perspective, see Rees (2021).

4   The same problem would be posed nationally in the United States if there was no central government, and policy formation depended on achieving agreement among the fifty state governments each pursuing their separate

interests. It is not difficult to suppose that paralysis would exist on the level of action whenever large-scale collective goods issues arose that would impose heavy burdens on the diversely situated federal states.

5   For a powerful rendering of the inverted utopianism that derives from an outlook of hopelessness, see McCarthy (2006). On the positive contributions of even miserably failed utopias, see Žižek (2008).

6   A distinguished poet's rumination expresses this stultifying sense of historical entrapment: "Like many people I know, I often have a somewhat—no, a wholly frightening view of the future of humanity and of the earth. There are periods when I live in a state of acute anxiety, near panic, about what awaits our children and grandchildren" (Williams 2012). Such poetic voices are the canaries in the mineshafts of modern civilization, sensing the dangers but not able to pinpoint the cause or intuit a solution. Unlike the evasion and denial of politicians and most citizens, the poet's voice is one of solitary witnessing that we ignore at our peril.

7   That the leadership and citizenry of the world have not gained sufficient leverage to abolish nuclear weaponry is indicative of how a new normal can evolve even in the aftermath of the unprecedented Hiroshima/Nagasaki catastrophic events, which also served as a foretaste of future events.

8   The NPT obligation as set forth in Article VI of the Treaty was affirmed unanimously by the International Court Justice in July 1996.

9   My contribution to this literature also was to insist that the war system was producing a global crisis of such depth that only a transformative global politics could ensure a positive future for the peoples of the world (Falk 1972; Commoner 1972; Goldsmith 1972).

10 In Falk (1997), this kind of participation is depicted as "globalization-from-below," intending to create countervailing pressures to the convergence of governmental and private sector interests that are described as "globalization-from-above."

11 Held (1995) is a ground-breaking work on issues of international democratization; also important is Archibugi (2008).

12 Issues involving peoples' tribunals are more fully discussed in chapter 10 of this volume.

13 In the Lockerbie case, the ICJ set forth the view that the decisions of the Security Council were unreviewable, and that even contentions that the rights of states under international law were being violated was of no relevance. See decision in International Court of Justice Reports (1998).

14 A "post-Westphalian" framework is a construction of world order that suggests that the changes in structure, order, and conflict are so significant that they create a rupture with the state-centric system—depicted by many observers, perhaps most influentially by Bull (1977), Morgenthau (1960), and Jackson (2000); a "non-Westphalian" framework is one in which there is a shift away from realism in line with the acceptance of a normative (law, ethics, spirituality) epistemology and pedagogy as the interpretative foundation of world order, which includes a *critical* appreciation of the role of hard power diplomacy.

15   For earlier discussion of these structural issues, see Falk (1975).

16   See Bobbitt (2008) for a challenging depiction of this new configuration of conflict, intellectualized as "the long war" by the Pentagon.

17   For suggestive jurisprudential insights along these lines, although not with a world order focus, see Orford (2006).

18   See the Gaia writing of James Lovelock (2000, 2007). See also Hamilton (2010).

19   There is a certain irony present. In the very period during which the state system became universalized in the aftermath of the collapse of colonialism, a variety of developments eroded the unconditionality of sovereignty as a formal attribute of Westphalian world order, which certainly never existed in the pure form implied by its most influential doctrinal formulations (Krasner 1999).

20   This is a central argument of Cutler and Gill (2013).

21   For a comprehensive formulation along the lines being advocated in relation to human interest and cosmopolitan world order, see Tarnas (2006). The generalization at the outset conveys the perspective:

> Amidst the multitude of debates and controversies that fill the intellectual arena, our basic understanding of reality is in contention, the role of the human being in nature and the cosmos, the status of human knowledge, the basis of moral values, the dilemmas of pluralism, relationism, objectivity, the spiritual dimension of life, the direction and meaning—if any—of history and evolution. . . . Something is dying and something is being born. The stakes are high, for the future of humanity and the future of the Earth. (Preface)

See also Žižek (2010)

22   John Micklethwait and Adrian Woolridge (2014) explore whether the state can achieve a fourth revolution of adaptation. The first three were responses to various functional needs and populist demands: the formation of national states to overcome the dysfunctionality of medieval Europe with its small security units and religious wars; the reaction against royal absolutism in the form of representative government as flowing from the French Revolution; and the response by way of social democracy and the welfare state to the challenge of a rising labor movement and associated threats posed by revolutionary socialism. Their concept of the fourth revolution is the development of governance procedures and practices that can restore the confidence of the masses in the legitimacy of the state and overcome present patterns of disaffection. Note that their prescription of a revolution from within state-centric world order is essentially indifferent to the sorts of challenges that are high on the human interest/human security agenda.

References

Archibugi, Daniele. 2008. *The Global Commonwealth of Citizens: Toward Cosmopolitan Democracy*. Princeton, NJ: Princeton University Press.

Baxi, Upendra. 1985. "Taking Suffering Seriously: Social Action Litigation in the Supreme Court of India." *Third World Legal Studies* 4 (6): 107–32.

Bobbitt, Phillip. 2008. *Terror and Consent: The Wars for the Twenty-first Century.* New York: Knopf.

Brzezinski, Zbigniew. 2012. *Strategic Vision: America and the Crisis of Global Power.* New York: Basic Books.

Bull, Hedley. 1977. *The Anarchical Society: A Study of Order in World Politics.* New York: Macmillan.

Commoner, Barry. 1972. *The Closing Circle: Nature, Man, and Technology.* New York: Random House.

Cutler, Claire, and Stephen Gill, eds. 2013. *The New Constitutionalism.* Cambridge: Cambridge University Press.

Falk, Richard. 1972. *This Endangered Planet: Prospects and Proposals for Human Survival.* New York: Random House.

Falk, Richard. 1975. *A Study of Future Worlds.* New York: The Free Press.

Falk, Richard. 1997. "Resisting 'Globalization-from-Above' Through 'Globalization-from-Below.'" *New Political Economy* 2 (1): 46–56.

Falk, Richard. 2004. *The Declining World Order: America's Imperial Geopolitics,* 1st ed. Milton Park: Routledge.

Falk, Richard, and Andrew Strauss. 2011. *A Global Parliament: Essays and Articles.* Berlin: Committee for a Democratic UN.

Freire, Paulo. 1970. *Pedagogy of the Oppressed.* New York: Herder & Herder.

Goldsmith, Edward T. 1972. *The Blueprint for Survival.* London: Tom Stacey.

Goldstein, Joshua. 2012. *Winning the War on War: The Decline of Armed Conflict Worldwide.* New York: PLUME/Penguin.

Hamilton, Clive. 2010. *Requiem for a Species: Why We Resist the Truth About Climate Change.* Washington, DC: Earthscan, 2010.

Hardt, Michael, and Antonio Negri. 2004. *Multitude: War and Democracy in the Age of Empire.* New York: Penguin.

Hardt, Michael, and Antonio Negri. 2009. *Commonwealth.* Cambridge, MA: Harvard University Press.

Held, David. 1995. *Democracy and the Global Order: From the Modern State to Cosmopolitan Governance.* Stanford, CA: Stanford University Press.

Ikenberry, John G. 2001. *After Victory: Institutions, Strategic Restraint, and the Rebuilding of Order After Major Wars.* Princeton, NJ: Princeton University Press.

International Court of Justice Reports. 1996. *Advisory Opinion on Legality of Threat or Use of Nuclear Weapons,* July 8.

International Court of Justice Reports. 1998. *Questions of Interpretation of Montreal Convention Arising from the Aerial Incident at Lockerbie,* February 27.

Jackson, Robert. 2000. *The Global Covenant: Human Conduct in a World of States.* New York: Oxford University Press.

Johansen, Robert C. 2006. *A UN Emergency Peace Service to Prevent Genocide and Crimes Against Humanity.* World Federalist Movement.

Johansen, Robert C. 2021. *Where the Evidence Leads: A Realistic Strategy for Peace and Human Security.* Oxford: Oxford University Press.

Krasner, Stephen. 1999. *Sovereignty: Organized Hypocrisy*. Princeton, NJ: Princeton University Press.

Lovelock, James. 2000. *Gaia: A New Look at Life on Earth*. New York: Oxford University Press.

Lovelock, James. 2007. *The Revenge of Gaia: Earth's Climate Crisis and the Fate of Humanity*. New York: Basic Books.

McCarthy, Cormac. 2006. *The Road*. New York: Knopf.

Meadows, Donella H., Dennis L. Meadows, Jørgen Randers, and William Behrens III. 1972. *The Limits to Growth: A Report to the Club of Rome on the Predicament of Mankind*. New York: Universe.

Mendlovitz, Saul H., ed. 1975. *On the Creation of a Just World Order*. New York: Free Press.

Micklethwait, John, and Adrian Woolridge. 2014. *The Fourth Revolution: The Global Race to Reinvent the State*. New York: Penguin.

Morgenthau, Hans J. (1960/1948). *Politics Among Nations: The Struggle for Power and Peace*, 3rd ed. New York: Knopf.

Orford, Anne, ed. 2006. *International Law and Its Others*. Cambridge: Cambridge University Press.

Paupp, Terrence. 2009. *The Future of Global Relations: Crumbling Walls, Rising Regions*. New York: Palgrave.

Pinker, Steven. 2011. *The Better Angels of Our Nature*. New York: Penguin.

Rees, Stuart. 2021. *Cruelty or Humanity: Challenges, Opportunities and Responsibilities*. Bristol, UK: Bristol University Press.

Taleb, Nassim Nicholas. 2010. *The Black Swan: The Impact of the Highly Improbable Fragility*, 2nd ed. New York: Random House.

Tarnas, Richard. 2006. *Cosmos and Psyche: Intimation of a New World View*. New York: Penguin.

Wei-ming, Tu. 1996. "Beyond the Enlightenment Mentality: A Confucian Perspective on Ethics, Migration, and Global Stewardship." *International Migration Review* 30 (1): 58–78.

Williams, C. K. 2012. "Nature and Panic: Can Beauty Save Us?" *Poetry*, October. https://www.poetryfoundation.org/poetrymagazine/issue/71498/october-2012.

Žižek, Slavoj. 2008. *In Defense of Lost Causes*. London: Verso.

Žižek, Slavoj. 2010. x-xi. *Living in the End Times*. London: Verso.

PART TWO

Pillars of Order: Horizons of Aspiration

7

International Law:

Overcoming War and
Collective Violence

Effective international law has been a central goal of antiwar activists and pacifist-minded jurists in the Global West since the end of the nineteenth century, and even much earlier. Recalling the analysis of prior chapters, political realists who think war and militarism are an inherent in the human condition view claims and aspirations made on behalf of international law in the domain of peace and security as an awkward, marginal, and diversionary feature of foreign policy. Public advocacy of international law in war/peace contexts should be thought as belonging to the realms of adversary state propaganda. Otherwise, international legalism gives rise to moral hypocrisy, double standards, and one-sided diplomatic rationalizations of the behavior of sovereign states, especially in relations among the Great Powers. Political realism as the prevailing paradigm through which international relations is best understood and professionally practiced regards unlawful militarism and war making as indispensable, and somewhat counterintuitively, put it forward as the best available policy framework within which to maintain peace among antagonist sovereign states. This admittedly accords an enhanced role in war/peace contexts to the most powerful, wealthiest, and geopolitically ambitious states. An extreme affirmation of the realist ways of thinking lends a certain plausibility to the slogan of the US Strategic Air Command: "Peace is our Profession."

International public discourse is further confused by the tendency of national governments to mobilize support for militarist policies by alleging violations of international law by geopolitical adversaries. Thus, realist pronouncements among foreign policy elites become intermingled with state propaganda about unlawful international behavior by enemy states. Such legalistic partisanship is reflected in media treatments of international conflicts, which play a mobilizing role in depicting the enemy as evil and their own orientation based on nationality and alliances as good.

The contention of this chapter is that such a paradigm almost always throughout history served geopolitical ambitions, causing great suffering, waste, and destruction, as well as fracturing the unity of humanity. This dynamic was somewhat hidden from public view by the national glorifications of war and its fighters as the source of national security and societal pride, prestige, and material rewards. These positive outcomes are attributed to military success. Correspondingly, with harm coming to a country by failures in war and defensive credibility.

Beyond this, nation- and state-building generally involved relying on collective violence to achieve ethnic or religious coherence of the polity. Such coherence is typically a matter of inclusions and exclusions exhibiting various internal hierarchies, further fragmenting human identity into myriad we/them patterns. The dysfunctions of the political realist paradigm have become increasingly evident as the preceding century unfolded to the point of threatening the very survival of the human species, a postmodern imaginary gaining prevalence since the dawning the Anthropocene age, the onset of which is frequently associated with the harnessing the explosive energies of the atom in 1945 at the end of World War II. A world divided into territorially and ideologically bounded political units is headed for disaster if it cannot shift its behavioral priorities to take account more closely of this "new realism"—based on imperatives of unity, cooperation, nonviolence, and ecological sensitivity, and reinforced by a shared appreciation of human destiny as the common fate of the peoples of the earth. A destiny made tangible through transnational bonding, awareness of planetary codependence, and conservation of resilient natural habitats. This dual connectedness of every person with each other and with interdependent natural habitats seems replicated throughout the entire cosmos.

The cynicism of many political realists doesn't tell the whole story, which, from the point of war and collective violence, imparts an even darker tale. For centuries international law in the domain of strategic interests and global security functioned mainly to give cover to conquest and related geopolitical maneuvers of dominant states, while reinforcing unconditional claims of territorial sovereignty and white supremacy of behalf of the colonizing countries of Europe and their racialized settler colonial offspring. These policies and practices, including ethnic cleansing of resisting native or indigenous people, the adoption of genocidal policies as needed to complete settler colonial projects, and the exploitation and oppression of many less developed non-Western societies expose the roots of the contemporary war system. For centuries, peace treaties were a policy instrument that invoked legal mechanisms to validate and stabilize even the outcomes of outright wars of aggression. This conclusion follows from regarding war itself as a discretionary dimension of foreign policy to promote national security goals and to satisfy the strategic ambitions of political leaders to acquire control over territory, resources, investment opportunity, and trade routes.

In more recent times, international law in conflictual settings has generally served Great Powers, especially in the West, strategically as a propaganda tool for demonizing the behavior of geopolitical rivals and ideological enemies during the Cold War. Gaining the edge in legal debate and backing justice claims of moral superiority helped gain approval for positions taken in conflictual relations. The West and then "the free world" claimed to be the global disseminator of civilization, a guardian angel of manifest destiny, a trustworthy keeper of the peace, a steadfast opponent of barbarism, and the states responsible for bearing the weight of the "white man's burden." This was a self-justifying narrative, which contained bits of genuine belief and insight but, overall, exhibited the hubris of hegemonic modernity, an aspect of which was to undermine the potential role of international law as providing enforceable neutral standards shaped, not by expansionist and imperial dreams or paranoid delusions but by the needs of *human security* and the values of *peace, justice,* and *ecological sustainability.*

Fulfilling this normative potential of international law has become more *necessary* and *desirable* than ever before in world history, but the haunting question is whether such a role for international law can be achieved given the anachronistic worldviews of the political class managing the foreign policy of most sovereign states, including the most powerful ones. We distinguish four distinct historic roles played by international law with respect to the management of power and the pursuit of national, regional, and global security:

1. lending an aura of legal and moral validity to imperial expansion, especially European colonialism;

2. providing a self-justifying tool for actions undertaken and a policy tool of condemnation with which to attack adversaries;

3. projecting as an ideal a law-based order in which the norms of international law were widely respected, objectively interpreted, and effectively enforced against the strong as well as the weak; and

4. increasing the legitimation of law with the precepts and norms of justice.

Since the carnage of World War I, international law has continuously struggled to provide a normative framework that would inhibit and respond to recourse to aggressive war, as well as hold accountable those who were guilty of perpetuating international crimes. Despite notorious shortcomings, this existing framework should not be dismissed as a failure. It has enjoyed a measure of success in restraining the sustained military attacks across international borders, but not nearly enough to give any assurance of a peaceful future for world order, let alone address the suffering caused by civil strife and oppressive arrangements within states. Geopolitical ambitions remain robust despite being restrained by an awareness that international warfare has mostly become a problematic tool by which to advance national interests. Countervailing forces dedicated to nonviolent forms of peacemaking and human rights have mounted challenges to traditional manipulations of international law by the major players in international relations. These challenges to the precepts and practices of political realism are coming from the margins of intergovernmental interaction and from the transnational civic initiatives of a rising new, unacknowledged, and an emergent political class that remains still mostly powerless when it comes to the adoption and actualization of geopolitical policy. Members of such a rising political class are identified here as "patriots of humanity" or, more appropriately, considering the salience of ecological challenges, such persons might be also thought of as "patriots of the earth." The genocidal onslaught of Israel in Gaza in 2023–24 imparted a sense of urgency to overcoming the implementation or enforcement crisis that has so often rendered international law behaviorly helpless. In essence, it is not mainly the norms and procedures of the international legal order that are deficient, but their implementation and enforcement especially in the context of direct and indirect violations by geopolitical actors.

Some historical perspectives are helpful to illustrate the Western birthing process for international law, its gradual globalization, and partial de-Westernization as colonialism collapsed and world order accommodated the changes. This accommodation was profiled in the Charter of the United Nations and further developed by the practice of the organization over the course of decades following 1945. The UN was constituted above all to reflect the confusing dual character of world order: *formal juridical equality* based on territorial statehood and national sovereignty as offset by *political inequality* reflecting the differential size, population, resource endowments, military capabilities, diplomatic activism, and economic status of individual states. There were other markers of inequality that help us interpret the limits of international law as an imperfect functioning and flawed reality, none more vivid and consequential than the role of law in drawing dividing lines between nuclear and nonnuclear weapons states, or secondarily between the five winners in World War II alone vested with permanent membership in the UN Security Council and alone enjoying a right of veto.

International Law as It Emerged in Europe

The Westphalian System

As prefigured in earlier chapters, international law in the modern sense is associated with the emergence of sovereign states in Western Europe as a sequel to the prolonged religious warfare that afflicted European society for decades. The birth of this statist approach to world order is conveniently, but not entirely accurately, associated with the Peace of Westphalia (1648), given influential legal formulations by several European jurists, including Grotius, Vattel, and Pufendorf, and motivated by an effort to curtail several centuries of religious wars.

The basic characteristic of world order became one in which only fully sovereign independent states were entitled to participate as full-fledged members of international society. A central role of international jurists was to provide legal rationalizations for European expansion by way of colonial conquest, slave trade, appropriation of the natural resources of non-Western countries, and forcible debt collection. The Westphalian system was complicated, varying in application from region to region and through historical periods, but its defining characteristics were shaped over time to vindicate a set of rules and principles that validated and facilitated Western dominance as substantially extended beyond Europe by racially tinged settler colonialism as in North America, Australia, and New Zealand, as well as by regional imperialisms in Latin America and the Asia/Pacific. In this sense, international law professionals often functioned to provide ideological and nationalist justifications for the discretion in foreign policy that political leaders acted upon. On occasion, sometimes at the personal cost of marginalization or worse, individual jurists managed to maintain a more independent outlook that sought the minimization of violence and the maximization of respect for international law as objectively interpreted in international relations.

When it came to war and collective violence, international law and lawyers were largely silent or, at best, marginal until the onset of World War II. Up until 1945, war was treated effectively as a matter of national discretion that might be denounced for political reasons, while collective violence within states was of concern only to the territorial sovereign and its friends. Colonialism and imperial relations were treated by most jurists as generally compatible with international law. Political violence within national territory was generally viewed as *legally* subject exclusively to the sovereign authority of territorial governments. External states were legally entitled to help the *diplomatically* legitimate government, regardless of its inhumaneness, but forbidden to assist its insurgent challenger even if reacting to severe abuse. Internal warfare never became a proper object of dedicated international legal scrutiny until after 1945 when such conflicts engaged Cold War rivals on opposite sides. To some extent, the American Civil War was an exception to this generalization as it engaged foreign states on both sides of the conflict.

Just War Tradition

Antecedents to international law: Prior to Westphalia, and to some extent also subsequently, the main source of normative constraint with respect to war and collective violence was derived from prevailing religious treatment of war in canonical Christian commentary on how to reconcile war and morality through law. Catholic theologians, most notably St. Thomas Aquinas and St. Augustine, provided rationalizations for *recourse* to war and principles of constraint in the *conduct* of war based on Christian values, and with some ontological claims of a universalist outreach that was consistent with non-Christian traditions of belief and practice. These principles of constraint have infused the law of war, incorporated as binding norms under the heading of "principles of customary international law." Among such customary norms are the following: *proportionality* (restraints on magnitude of permissible force relative to military objective); *discrimination* (restraints on targeting based on prohibitions of civilian targets); *necessity* (restraints based on limiting use of force to the proportional pursuit of legitimate military objectives); and *humanity* (restraints in tactics and targeting based on the avoidance of cruelty, sadism, and unnecessary suffering).

Adherence to these principles in waging war, despite their vagueness, continues to the present to have some bearing on perceptions of legitimacy with respect to belligerent uses of force, which are particularly influential in shaping civil society perceptions of approval and disapproval. Most but not all governments during the last seventy-five years have made strenuous efforts to demonstrate their adherence to this customary law framework, especially with respect to minimizing damage to civilians and nonmilitary targets (hospitals, sites of worship, schools, civilian centers of habitation) while often complaining about the failure of their opponents to do the same.

A glaring weakness of this framework, particularly evident in situations of nondefensive uses of international force, is the vagueness of the criteria of restraint. These criteria lend themselves to manipulation by amoral political realists whose pronouncements go mostly unchallenged in domestic policymaking circles and the main media platforms in even democratically governed sovereign states. A further weakness, of course, is the absence in most circumstances of any pretense of objective interpretations of the facts and relevant legal norms, much less the capabilities for their nondiscriminatory enforcement. Wartime journalism is often indistinguishable from state propaganda in partisan situations.

Primacy of Geopolitics

It was always the intention of leaders of the more powerful countries to conceive of international law as a *tool* of foreign policy more than as a framework setting *limits* on the means and ends of their own foreign policy. Only with the rise of non-Western nationalism did international law begin to be envisioned in counter-hegemonic roles, including as a means to uphold the sovereign rights of the weaker states in the Global South, with the determination to hold the powerful as well as the weak to standards of legal accountability. Despite some important counter-hegemonic achievements of international law, principally in the economic sphere, the end results are disappointing. International law remains a mobilizing tool of the powerful, useful in justifying coercive means to bend the will of weaker states, and for mobilizing public support, and to sustain impunity for the strong and their friends. The punitive treatment of Cuba by prolonged sanctions is illustrative of such hegemonic behavior oblivious to international law rules and principles, to world public opinion, as well as the changed climate of the postcolonial world order.[1]

The opposite phenomenon was evident throughout the intensive military campaign undertaken by Israel in Gaza during 2023–24, when extreme encroachments on international humanitarian law were shielded from adverse commentary at the UN and elsewhere with help of the main states in the Global West giving unrestricted support to Israel despite the latter's reliance on its own halfhearted claims of self-defense.

The de facto impunity of the United States for the commission of international crimes in Vietnam, Afghanistan, Iraq, and elsewhere has also subverted the international authority of law. Its own practices during the "war against terror" following the 9/11 attacks expose shortcomings of international criminal law if, as is generally assumed, the morality, legitimacy, and coherence of the rule of law are dependent on treating equals equally.

Outlawing War

The heavy casualties and great destruction of World War I led to an upsurge of antiwar public opinion, given governmental credence by the antiwar passions of the American president, Woodrow Wilson. These feelings were reinforced by the widespread public sense that nothing beneficial was achieved by prevailing in such a costly and devastating war that had the further self-defeating effect of weakening respect by nationalist movements in the colonial structures under attack in the non-Western world.

This delegitimizing current of opinion was geopolitically reinforced by the anti-colonial outlook adopted by the leaders of the Russian Revolution. At the same time, wily statesmen in leading European countries refused to accept the view that colonialism was in its sunset phase and was now regarded by a consensus of governments as unworthy, a conclusion reached by many persons even in Europe. Instead, after 1918, European colonial ambitions mobilized their influence in the hopes of obtaining a division of the territorial spoils of the collapsing Ottoman Empire, especially in the Middle East. The result was a period of normative ambiguity for Europe with respect to hegemonic relations with many non-Western societies. The surfacing of these sentiments cast moral and practical doubts on war as an acceptable vehicle of change and order in the Westphalian dynamic of world order. These antiwar sentiments ran counter to US isolationist identities, struck hard boiled political realists as dangerously naive, and were a temporary postwar phenomenon soon displaced by a combination of resumed isolationism by the United States. and a return to Euro-centric realism by the colonial powers.

At the same time, there was present an antiwar momentum that shaped public attitudes in the West after 1918, possessing sufficient political traction to produce the Pact of Paris in 1928, which outlawed nondefensive war making and obtained the legal backing of all important governments in the Global West. Yet it seemed unlikely when such a mere normative declaration, even if formalized as a treaty with great fanfare, would alter deeply entrenched elite beliefs, interests, and patterns of behavior. It needs to be remembered that political realists continued to dominate the affairs of states with respect to matters of national security including war prevention, adhering in practice and belief to a militarizing consensus of "peace through strength." The United States remained an outlier to some extent because it still associated its national interests with non-involvement at the international level except in the Asia Pacific where it sought to establish its own imperial sphere of influence.

World War II sent new mixed messages to leaders and citizens alike, who both deepened antiwar sentiments, although again only temporarily, and simultaneously extended support to the realist belief that war, and particularly its preparation and credible threats, performed necessary functions in a state system of world order. The defeat of expansionist fascism in Europe and Asia was seen as a vindication of just war thinking and practice, as well as of political realism. The blood-drenched outcome of that war was widely accepted as justified by security and morality criteria, despite the enormity of the human and economic costs and menacing implications for the future. It reaffirmed standard realist thinking that liberal democracies needed to be permanently prepared and constantly ready to engage in wars to prevent the expansion of and encroachment by illiberal states such as Germany and Japan, and later the Soviet Union.

At the same time, the atomic bombings of Japanese cities in 1945 created great new fears of a future war that clouded the political and moral imagination of influential sections of the public as much as did the Holocaust, at least during the immediate aftermath of the war. A result of these contradictory biopolitical concerns was both a further effort to narrow the scope of "legal" warfare as, paradoxically, soon coupled with the greatest "peacetime" military buildup in human history. This reflected the realist view that "deterrence" of a nuclear catastrophe could only be achieved by relying on omnicidal retaliatory capabilities. The net result was a reassertion of the prevailing Westphalian idea that peace primarily depends not upon adhering to the normative framework of law and morality, but on maintaining a workable balance of power as continuously reassessed to ensure that rationality would discourage hostile uses of force by adversaries. In the Cold War phase of the nuclear age, this came to mean the vigilant management of Western deterrent capabilities so that any innovations in weaponry or doctrine would not undercut expectations that retaliatory options would continue to deter attacks, and if this effort should ever fail, a crippling retaliation would follow.

This post-1945 atmosphere definitely eroded the legitimacy of warfare as a discretionary instrument of state policy, especially for losers. This development was reinforced by the Nuremberg and Tokyo Judgments through delimiting and punishing "Crimes Against the Peace." Although these outcomes were criticized as "victors' justice," legal scrutiny relating to crimes committed by the victors never officially happened except in a scattered way by civil society jurists, especially in Japan. There were reassurances by the chief prosecutor at Nuremberg that the Nuremberg Principles, based on the standards applied to judge the German defendants, would be used in the future to assess the behavior of all countries, including those that had acted at Nuremberg on behalf of the victors. This Nuremberg promise has not been kept, nor was it even endorsed by the victorious governments. It's true that some effort with secondary countries has been made to assess criminality regardless of outcome by ad hoc tribunals set up by the UN to deal with former Yugoslavia and Rwanda. Yet, as previously mentioned, geopolitical actors continue to enjoy existential if not formal legal impunity, and this means that the universal phrasing of the Nuremberg Principles remain subject to what might be called "a geopolitical exception."[2] True, NATO countries called for action under international criminal law against Putin after the Russian attack on Ukraine in 2022, but nothing happened, and it was seen as more an expression of conflictual behavior by adversaries than a sign of respect for the antiwar norms of the UN Charter, which had on several earlier occasions been violated or circumvented by the United States and its allies, perhaps most flagrantly in the Vietnam War and the attack on Iraq in 2003.

The outlawry of aggressive war has enjoyed more impressive empirical support in the behavior of leading states. The UN Charter prohibits force except in conditions of self-defense, strictly defined. In several prominent instances, aggressive war across international boundaries have been effectively denied any lasting territorial effects by joint defensive responses:

the attack by North Korea on South Korea (1950–52); the Suez Operation (1956); and the attack, occupation, and attempted annexation of Kuwait (1991–92). Even geopolitical actors with territorial ambitions have tended to respect this norm of prohibition, seeking to reach expansionist goals by indirect means, through overt and covert forms of intervention, destabilization of governments perceived as hostile, and sanctions, as well as through trade and investment policies. As with so many developments bearing on global security, Israel has been an exception to the prohibition on forcible territorial expansion for decades without any meaningful pushback.

Civil society has taken the lead in challenging geopolitical impunity, including the accountability gap. Starting with the tribunal of conscience organized in 1966–67 by the British philosopher Bertrand Russell and brought into being by his principal assistant, Ralph Schoenman. There have been a series of civic initiatives to document the crimes of the powerful and pass judgment on their behavior. Several of these initiatives have achieved significant results, including some sessions of the Permanent Peoples' Tribunal, headquartered in Rome, and the Iraq War Tribunal of 2005, in Istanbul. The jurisprudential status of such undertakings remains problematic in most conventional international law circles, but it is an alternative to what has been perceptively called "crimes of silence," filling gaps of inaction by international institutions and national governments, and offering quicker results and less tainted documentation of war crimes than what would likely emanate from partisan formal tribunals.[3]

Paradigm Shift

Without a "new realism" there is little prospect of an escape from the Westphalian statist worldview, and its epistemic and geopolitical embrace of "political realism" as the paradigm governing peace, security, and the resolution of conflicts. Proposals for world government or "empirical realism" have achieved very little political traction even as the dysfunctions and catastrophic implications of the existing paradigm became more widely appreciated. There exists some possibility that the practical imperatives of fashioning survival in the face of climate change, biodiversity, and health challenges will give rise to both a revisioning of political realism and a greater reliance on international cooperative arrangements. For this to come about will almost certainly require a massive insurrectionary movement for a post-Westphalian world order that brought to the fore a new paradigm premised on human security, nonviolence, human rights, and augmented structures of ecologically sensitive global governance. Such an approach of new realism would likely foster centralized governance only where necessary (as with nuclear disarmament and global-scale ecological regulation) and rely on regional, national, and localized self-government (as with food sovereignty and ecological communal arrangements) wherever possible.

Reimagining Law and War

Reclaiming Realism

The first and primary challenge is to establish an epistemic community that understands the conditions for achieving peace and human security, given current and evolving historical circumstances. It is a two-step process: critique and renewal.

As expressed above, the frameworks of beliefs and behavioral patterns giving policy directives reflects the obsolescent worldview of "political realism" as developed within the Westphalian consensus. This outlook relied excessively on militarism—as exhibited by weaponry, foreign bases, deployments, technological innovations, and alliances to uphold security in an ever-evolving global setting. Such a security posture required credible potential and actual external adversaries or in pursuit of widely endorsed national ambitions. The advent of nuclear weapons and their spread beyond the West led to threats in the form of the doctrine of deterrence, largely displacing battlefield combat as the cornerstone of security in the developed world.

Warfare of a traditional character was mainly confined to struggles for the control of the governing process at the level of sovereign states, continuing in a variety of patterns of civil strife and geopolitical interventions throughout the Global South. Both patterns of warfare are costly, with ambiguous deterrent doctrines risking nuclear war—an apocalyptic catastrophe of potentially omnicidal and ecocidal proportions. The experience of conventional warfare under contemporary conditions is also alarming—long violent conflicts, massive human suffering and physical devastation, and political outcomes more reflective of the ethos of national self-determination than of the military balance, with the superior side on the battlefield generally failing to attain its political objectives, and thus effectively losing the war. This latter feature of post-1945 Global West/ Global South warfare contradicted Westphalian realism and ran up against the ideational and economistic embedded confidence in the continuing agency of military superiority.

The reclamation of reality presents a daunting challenge of substituting a normative framework more reflective of "reality" than what has long been believed and practiced by the political class in virtually all internationally active countries in the modern world, and especially those that enjoyed a meta-legal geopolitical status, with the partial exception of China. Resistance to such critiques of militarism result from a combination of entrenched habits of thought and policy, bureaucratic careerism, "groupthink," a variety of vested private and public interests, as well as the complacencies of habit in the form of the collective consciousness of society. It is hard to imagine a shift away from a militarist security mentality without strong national political movements in the United States, Russia, and even China that could be the revolutionary bearers of the connectedness of nonviolent or at least purely defensive conceptions of security and the reallocation of resources from military budgets to ecological and social protection. Even the wealthiest countries will not be able to, under present conditions, sustain political realism as it has functioned in the modern world and meet challenges of global scope that depend not only on profound changes in productive and energy systems, managing artificial intelligence (AI), and digitized networks. To construct adaptive patterns of behavior also requires reform of the UN and other international institutions. Reform is needed to facilitate both policy steerage at regional and global levels and unprecedented degrees of global solidarity to support cooperative problem-solving.

To wish fervently for an orderly transition to "new realism" in thought and action is understandable, but the evidence from the past is not encouraging. Deliberate adjustments in approaches to war, militarism, and security have come throughout the evolution of Westphalian world order only after major wars, and then predominantly at the level of political discourse without corresponding changes in modes of thought or regulation of capabilities believed to have relevance from the perspective of "military necessity." The normative shifts that have occurred since 1648, while not altogether cosmetic, have been of a character that has maintained the destructive dynamics of what Robert Jervis depicted as "the security dilemma," by which the pursuit of security by State A makes State B insecure, giving rise to cycles of insecurities of a character that fuels arms races among competitive states.

What is being proposed here is of an inter-paradigmatic nature, which depends on the revolutionary or insurrectional replacement of the present political class in key countries. It is possible that the rise of China presents the world with an example of a transition process to new realism that is less disruptive if it manages to split the political class in Western countries into an internal struggle between those that see China as a geopolitical, economistic, and ideological threat and those that appreciate China's overall ascent as the result of adopting a model of post-Westphalian world order than needs to be systemically emulated, further elaborated, and adapted to human security priorities and values, as well as ecological stability goals. An alternative discourse that has a similar transformative potential can be formulated as a post-Westphalian reset from a hard power approach to security and foreign policy to a soft power approach that prioritizes the pacific attributes of pluralist democratic practice and a cosmopolitan turn in nationalist and societal identity.

Envisioning Structural Reform

The logic of Westphalian world order flow from its major premise: only sovereign states with established international borders are formal and full participants in international relations and subjects of international law. Westphalian superstructures in international life consisting of networks of international institutions at the global and regional levels of international relations are funded and controlled by states, seen as more or less useful for the pursuit of national interests. The new realist framing of foreign policy and world order would endow such institutions with a higher degree of *autonomy*, greater *capabilities*, and more robust expectations that their decisions would ordinarily result in *compliance* with mechanisms of *implementation* available as needed.

This Westphalian state-centric model of world order was never truly either descriptive or prescriptive. It excluded states that were formerly called "Great Powers" and recently more often referred to as "geopolitical actors" that behaved as if their strategic interests took precedence over the obligations of international law. Such meta-legal status was by and large accepted by other sovereign entities either from choice, as allies, or from necessity, as lacking the capabilities needed to mount a challenge.

The initial focus of the structural dimensions of post-Westphalian patterns of global reform would be on the UN system, although it may turn out that regional institutional developments and ad hoc coalitions (e.g., the BRICs)[4] have a crucial role to play in making transformative moves that could influence the UN to make comparable adjustments or be faced with further declines in relevance when it comes to the management of global power and security. The European Union has shown some promise in this respect, cutting the level of its military investments, accepting a broad sphere of European regional law, and pledging to achieve net-zero carbon emissions by a year certain. To a discouraging degree, these European Union (EU) developments, temporarily at least, have been casualties of the Ukraine War. The EU as a regional system operates on the basis of the supremacy of the rule of law and sovereign equality, two areas of achievement that have so far eluded the UN, although its security arrangements continue to cling to the North Atlantic Treaty Organization (NATO) framework. The European Parliament has grown in stature through time, suggesting the appropriateness of such an institution at a global level, and illustrating the usefulness of global explorations of how new realism can be applied to improve the quality of human security.

The purpose of these reforms is to endow the UN with more political independence with respect to its membership, and especially to end the geopolitical right of exception and generalized impunity enjoyed by the five permanent members of the Security Council. As such, this would greatly weaken the rarely acknowledged central tenet of political realism in practice, the primacy of geopolitics in all policy arenas of principal states, including the venues of international institutions. This would by itself imply an upgrading of the role international law as a source of global security and a marginalizing of the war system in both its threat and war-fighting dimensions, greatly weakening the case for arms races and extravagant weapons innovations, although not entirely without a deeper de-Westernization of world order than occurred after the collapse of European colonialism.

Of course, such a vision of a strengthened UN seems utopian given the continuing grip of the obsolete political realist framework, which helps explain why the future of global security seems fragile and overly dependent on the continued workability of outmoded ideas about how international history is made. The emergence of this preferential pattern of international behavior likely will result, as previously indicated, more from movement politics than from rationality in the face of changed conditions. Put differently, when a paradigm shift is needed to overcome the weaknesses and vulnerabilities of present security systems, only revolutionary praxis is relevant, although even a partial breakdown of the old order may generate "a revolutionary situation." In effect, prospects for a transition of sufficient magnitude with respect to security depends more on civic activism than on elite rationality.

There are also bleaker scenarios that should be taken into account and are to some extent foreshadowed by the rise of autocratic, ultranationalist governments in this century, exhibiting extremist militarist political styles that are hostile to human rights at home and inimical to peace and global cooperation with respect to foreign policy. International law and the UN are further degraded, the regressive features of political realism are accentuated and no longer remain disguised behind a facade of normalcy. The Trump presidency (2017–21) gestured in these directions by its dysfunctional withdrawal from constructive international arrangements such as the Paris Climate Change Agreement and the Iran Nuclear Agreement (JCPOA). In this sense, the obsolescence of political realism does not ensure a benevolent sequel.

Post-Westphalian world order could assume various forms of what might be called "global anarchy" or, worse, "global barbarism" as enacted in the 2023–24 extreme violence in Gaza. It is not implausible to conjecture that the dominant political classes of many states will rely on oppressive governance within their own societies, coupled with contrived geopolitical encounters to foster illusions that the foreign evil "other" is intimidated or neutralized. In the process, such dysfunctional and opportunistic political leaders will devise techniques to shift as much ecological harm beyond national borders while some economic elites seek ecological sanctuaries for themselves by seeking living spaces in other planets, leaving the masses to endure the entropic effects of further ravaging the earth in this era of ultra-nationalism and a possible bonding of autocracies.

Avenues of Endeavor

The imaginary of new realism seems clear and convincing as does the persuasiveness of the critique of political realism. What we are left with is Lenin's famous question, "What is to be done?" As the transformative momentum must *not* come predominantly from the Global West, given its hegemonic and exploitative relationship with the rest of the world, it will likely take many forms in non-Western diverse civilizational settings. These will include a range of societal initiatives and coalitions that are intergovernmental, intrastate, regional, transnational, local, and traditional in their diverse and primary loci of energy, as well as event-driven and responsive to disasters of various kinds, especially those that expose the deficiencies of political realism.

The Archetypal Struggle Against Nuclearism

In 1945 the Trinity Test explosion in New Mexico revealed the terrifying power of the atom. It was followed shortly thereafter by the atomic bombings of Hiroshima and Nagasaki in the final phase of World War II. The subsequent struggle to rid the world of nuclear weapons has dramatized the radical opposition between the two dominant conceptions of "peace." On the one side, the political realists upholding the statist logic of Westphalia despite endangering multiple catastrophes of global scope and even the end of the world as we know it. On the other side, those disparate social forces that by their beliefs and actions uphold the promise of global community and practice a patriotism of humanity/earth, seeking collective and cooperative problem-solving that takes full account of equitable considerations in their search for agreements that are fair by the logic of statism and serve the global public good. This is of course a simplification. There exist many bewildered members of the political class caught in between, especially inhabitants of nonnuclear states, who are political realists without access to the weaponry, and many persons who believe antinuclearism is futile or are complacent about or ignorant of its dangers or place their trust in religiously ordained faith. And others still who remain strangely convinced that deterrence coupled with non-proliferation are the best way to keep world peace, and yet have the supposed benefits of hegemony.

Nothing more starkly reveals the contrast between political realists and new realists when it comes to peace and human security than these opposed approaches to nuclear weaponry. Einstein is often aptly quoted by referring to his saying that the atom bomb changed everything except "our modes of thinking," that is, the mentality of the political classes that upholds political realism. Such an insight, however, is incomplete without observing the economic, political, and cultural linkages between power and ideas. That is why, despite the evidence and the passion of antinuclear public opinion through the decades, and periodic elite gestures toward denuclearization, the deadly edifice of nuclearism has remained stable for more than seventy-five years. It is mostly a result of the resilience of the old mentality as Einstein insisted, but it is also more than a mental construct. The mental consensus is complemented by the material realities of vested interests of weapons developers and arms merchants, as well the benefits of hegemony.

On the level of rationality, the evidence is necessarily inconclusive because the future is unknowable, and the past could have generated different outcomes but for luck and other contingent factors. The risks tend to be compared by primary reference to worldview, experience, and social position. For political realists the optimal solution is *stability*, reflecting retention and continuous development of the weaponry, prudence (crisis management), robust deterrence (second strike invulnerability or defensive capabilities), and selectively implemented non-proliferation.

For new realists, the obvious solution is phased, monitored, and enforced nuclear abolition by way of a treaty administered by the United Nations system and tied in its final phases to nonnuclear demilitarization, culminating in general and complete disarmament and a UN International Peace Force. Of course, there are complexities arising from technological innovations of radical potentiality, including drones, robots, AI, and their linkage to the lethal potentialities of cyber and so-called cognitive warfare. The contrast can be clarified by the existence of two distinct treaty instruments, *operationally* expressive of clashing interpretations of reality despite seeming *normatively* compatible. Because the technology of weaponry is dynamic and potentially subversive of order and peace, constant vigilance will be required whatever policy path is chosen.

The Non-Proliferation Treaty (NPT) and Geopolitical Enforcement Regime

It is important to distinguish the widely ratified NPT (1970) based on a delusionary bargain: nonnuclear parties to the treaty agree to forgo nuclear weapons in exchange for legal pledges by the nuclear weapons parties to share peaceful use technology and to proceed in good faith to negotiate nuclear disarmament, and eventually, general and complete disarmament. In deference to Westphalian logic nonnuclear states retained the formal option to withdraw from the treaty after giving notice if their supreme national security interests so required. In effect, the NPT as a negotiated text seemed to pave the way toward nuclear abolition through a reciprocal exchange of rights and duties of nonnuclear and nuclear states that served the global public good. There are several reasons it didn't work out this way:

- Political realists in the nuclear weapons states never genuinely accepted the treaty path of denuclearization leading to abolition, continuing with development of new weaponry, retaining even first use options as integral to both deterrence and grand strategy.
- The primacy of geopolitics meant that the leading nuclear weapons states could ignore their legal commitments while insisting to the point of threatening war to enforce the commitments of *certain* nonnuclear states, implicitly claiming the authority to decide which states could be allowed to acquire the weaponry and which could not.
- Many leading nonnuclear states were complicit to the extent of basing their national security on alliance pledges of nuclear protection against future military aggression and others lacked the will or capability to challenge this prolonged failure to implement both sides of the NPT bargain.
- The resulting arrangement grounds "peace" in the nuclear age on a nuclear oligopoly or "nuclear apartheid" structure, which is a de facto modification of the Westphalia norm based on the mythic equality of sovereign states. This inequality pertaining to nuclear weaponry is analogous in systemic effects to the UN grant of a veto power to the permanent members of the Security Councils.

Treaty of Prohibition of Nuclear Weapons (TPNW): Abolition Aspirations

In 2017, 123 countries signed a treaty that finally came into force in 2021 after the deposit at the UN of the sixtieth instrument of ratification, committing parties to reject all aspects of nuclearism, including possession, development, deployment, and threat or use of the weaponry. The treaty was brought into being by collaboration between governments of non-geopolitical states and a global coalition of civil society nongovernmental organizations (NGOs). The TPNW was not endorsed, and actively opposed, by the leading nuclear weapons states, as explained in an official statement issued by the three NATO nuclear powers.

Explaining why the NPT upholds political realism while TPNW remains operationally meaningless:

- The governments and social forces behind TPNW lack geopolitical leverage.
- Without geopolitical implementation legal challenges to existing security arrangements have no prospect of altering the operational role of nuclear weaponry.

- Civil society mobilization that was vital to the TPNW undertaking is even more essential to achieve its inclusive implementation, yet lacks the capability and political will, and perhaps even the understanding, to do what is necessary to challenge geopolitics.
- At the same time, TPNW somewhat delegitimizes the NPT regime and is a step along a crucial avenue of endeavor, reflecting the growing challenge of new realism.
- New realism will remain in the geopolitical shadows until social forces within governing forces and transnational movements make an insurrectionary leap forward to challenge the nuclear divide between haves and have nots in a credible manner.

The main conclusion to be drawn is that although the two treaty instruments are textually compatible, the NPT as an operational reality is rooted in the old realism that continues to enjoy overwhelming support of geopolitical actors. In contrast, the TPNW lacks this support, and thus its new realism aspirations remain little more than a pious dream, at least until seriously acted upon by coalitions from the Global South and progressive civic activists.

No First Use (NFU) of Nuclear Weapons

Since the early period of the Cold War, denuclearizing advocates have emphasized NFU as a step that would at least manifest good faith with respect to the claim that nuclear weapons were exclusively deployed for defensive purposes, and to discourage recourse by adversaries to a nuclear attack and lessen the burdens of defensive prudence. Leaders of the leading nuclear weapons states have been often pressed by peace groups and arms control advocates to endorse NFU but have withdrawn support after encountering resistance from strategists and intelligence officials within their own governments. Strategic impulses to maintain ambiguity with respect to the use of nuclear weapons is a further indication that foreign policy managers of nuclear weapons states seek to retain strategic flexibility with respect to the threat or use of nuclear weapons and ill-disposed to take denuclearizing arms control steps as distinct from the embrace of arms control measures that add to the stability of the nuclear environment or cut costs and reduce risks of accidental or unintended usage.

Managing the Global Ecosystem

A signature focus of new realism must be placed upon the ecological dimensions of security, somewhat acknowledged even by military planners, and possibly the source of splits within the political class of geopolitical actors, which up until now continues to grossly overinvest in military capabilities. This is particularly descriptive of the United States with its global network of expensive military bases, separate naval commands for the oceans of the world, and expensively unstable development of space forces. This persisting militarization obscures a simultaneous acknowledgment of an ecological security agenda as well as the extensive social protection and human security agendas. There is some recent pressure evident for a partial demilitarization from within the political realist framing of security. If adopted, it is to be carried out in ways that do not undermine the Westphalian consensus that the security of states continues to depend on self-help either through military strength and preparedness or indirectly by way of alliances and collective security mechanisms.

Depending on the course of elite learning experiences and societal pressures, a transition to new realism could take place within a Westphalian framework. The irresponsible damage to the Brazilian rainforest that resulted from deliberate government policy of deforestation as a prelude to agricultural development in 2020 suggests that territorial sovereignty in relation to some critical circumstances is no longer compatible with human security on a planetary scale. The notion of a "global commons" that encompasses vital ecosystems, including those preserving biodiversity, natural habitats of animals and cultural habitats of indigenous peoples, underscores the obsolescence of political realism and state sovereignty as policy guides, and the need for a more comprehensive ecologically understanding of security, which either regards ecological security as part of human security, or may come to view human security as encompassed by ecological security.

Prioritizing the ecological agenda is likely over time to increase skepticism about the viability of the Westphalian framework, making way for thinking outside the militarist security frame and strict notions of statism, which has badly obstructed perceptions of the changing *realities* of international life, at least since the time of the first nuclear explosion. With the growing impact of climate change on the everyday life of increasing numbers of people, moral and political imagination is being revitalized to conceive of community in more universalist patterns. As mentioned earlier, this could lead to cruel and destructive intensifications of violence-based governance and security. More positively conceived, it could also lead to urgently needed emancipatory adaptations to changing conditions that both widen and deepen community procedures for collective problem-solving. Ecological sensitivity to multiple layers of connectedness is already a pillar of new realism.

Challenging Informal Censorship

The rational foundations of political realism have been undermined by a variety of studies that show the dysfunctional role and experience of relying on military approaches to diplomatic challenges. At the same time, an acceptance of international law as an authoritative source of policy in relation to international conflict has been shown to be more reliable and less costly as a basis for national, regional, and global security than a continuing reliance on threats and uses of force, including sanctions, called *unilateral coercive measures* (UCMs) in UN parlance. This essential good news has been kept from the public even in democratic societies by the corporativism and informal censoring filters of mainstream media and book publishing. Foreign policy debates on TV are totally dominated by think tank specialists or retired military and intelligence officers, with policy dissent rarely seriously voiced and considered. Almost never are legal proprieties of contested positions explored, or advocates of a law-based foreign policy given their day in the court of public opinion. Such closures distort reality, unreasonably limit debate to matters of cost and feasibility, and have led to a series of foreign policy failures, including loss of life, forever wars, and frozen conflicts, while avoiding objective reappraisals of what went wrong in past military engagements that resulted from outmoded hegemonic reasoning.

The US role in the Vietnam War was illustrative of this pattern, repeated in Iraq and Afghanistan, each ending in failure, but without facing the underlying misappraisals of reality bearing on conflict in the twenty-first century. Self-censorship insulates the anachronistic record of political realism from criticism and appraisal. It applies not only to the media but also to university education, which rarely indulges academic orientations and scholarship that deeply challenges prevailing modes of thinking and policymaking. Indeed, new realism perspectives tend to be dismissed as *normative* (that is, non-scientific) or *utopian* (that is, fanciful or pathways to dystopias) and, thus, unworthy of study. From this perspective the political and moral imaginative powers most in touch with the realities of contemporary insecurity are discredited and ignored, and past failures are continuously and mindlessly reproduced as thresholds of irreversibility are crossed, increasing already high risks of geopolitical confrontation and ecological disaster.

It is possible that social movements, the renewed activism evident in the Global South, and the pressures of ecological entropy will make media and public education at some future time more receptive to new realism, but this will involve a struggle with entrenched economic and political interests that continue to dominate mainstream media, political parties, and higher education. Such a benevolent transition will not happen without the friction of mounting pressures against the unipolar management of global security. Unipolarity has been equated with "global leadership" over the course of the last thirty years following the Soviet implosion. Such a pattern of geopolitical management of global security maybe is beginning to lose ground in the political imaginary of the Global West. NATO's inability to inflict a defeat upon Russia after its attack on Ukraine and as well as the BRICs search for an alternative to the dollar in the operation of the world economy are indicative signs of a deteriorating form of global governance.

Revisioning Citizenship

Civic education does not prepare young people to become participatory citizens much beyond exercising rights to vote in national elections. It is time to abandon old thinking when it comes to political participation in democratic societies. The widespread adoption of new thinking toward the responsibilities and opportunities of citizenship are crucial to the opening of the gates toward a better future for the peoples of the world. To have any realistic prospect of actualization, especially as to human security on levels of being-in-the-world, citizenship will have to manifest greater educational proficiency, ecological activism, anti-militarism, and increased empathy and hospitality to those foreign others entrapped in various ways, whether by poverty, oppression, or otherwise.

Making global framing humanly relevant is especially important under current historical circumstances. We now inappropriately speak of "global community" as globally shared values and identities, yet they remain the exception to the exclusivist promotion of nationalist and geopolitical priorities. There is an urgent need for the activism of those who claim to be "citizen pilgrims," who are ready to dedicate themselves to a journey through time and across space that is mindful of species identity and the urgent need to refashion human relations to enable resilient coexistence with national habitats. Citizen pilgrims are more evolved than "world citizens," who misleadingly believe and act as if a global community serving the public good of humanity and the natural surrounding already exists and only needs to be strengthened. The citizen pilgrim believes that time is as important as space, that the globalist behavior based on empathy, law, and respect for the carrying capacity and limits of ecosystems remains a post-Westphalian world order in the making.

The anachronisms of old thinking are also gestating highly regressive responses to the experience of modernity's growing dysfunction when it comes to security, which the citizen pilgrim must join in resisting while struggling to realize a brightly lit future. Instead of "liberal internationalism"—with its partial openings to cooperation, human rights, and international law—we are experiencing disturbing trends toward chauvinistic nationalism, geopolitical disregard of international law and the UN, and a preference for intergovernmental bilateral bargains as opposed to multilateral cooperative solutions. Instead of favoring extensions of the global commons by reference to the boundaries of ecosystems, the extreme forms of old thinking encourage national encroachments on existing global commons arrangements and

strong resistance to ecological challenges to sovereign rights with missions
of protecting major rainforests from irresponsible management. Projects of
epistemic renewal combine the best available knowledge of "reality" with
biopolitical interpretations that incorporates eco-humanistic ethics.

Two closing remarks acknowledge the limitation of a presentation that is
focused on the inadequacies of political realism for safeguarding the security
of people and their habitats:

- A concentration on behavioral patterns, which, while general, are
  exemplified by the behavior of the United States; there are many
  situational variations of Westphalian logic evident at the national
  level that need to be examined in a fuller treatment of this central
  theme, including the reliance on military alliances to oppose all
  postcolonial efforts to achieve de-Westernization of world order;
  persisting Westernization if symbolically expressed by three of the five
  permanent members of the Security Council being NATO members
  and no permanent representation for Muslim and Hindu majority
  countries, and from Latin America, Africa, and the Middle East.
- Violent conflict in the future is already drawing upon dramatic
  technological innovations ranging from drones, killer robots,
  cognitive manipulation and surveillance via hacking, the merger of
  government espionage and subversion with transnational crime,
  the protection of cybersecurity, and many other developments that
  make the future of warfare move its forms of combat away from
  conventional battlefields.

The basic contention being made in this chapter is that the political class
that runs the world is entrapped by obsolete patterns of thought, values,
feelings, and, hence, action, bearing on what is possible, necessary, and
desirable for the present and future security of humanity. The fundamental
flaw is a blend of fear and trust in the ways of violence to produce order
and guard national space against various types of unwanted intrusion. The
United States has been most responsible for shaping world order during
the last eighty years in this direction, but its views are mimicked by other
states, including its geopolitical rivals. At the same time, it is important
to recognize that the rise of China exhibits a different, more flexible, less
militarist model of the relations between state, society, and world, but it is
being threatened at present by its own mobilization of old thinking, which
seems to be leading it to embrace a dystopian conformism with Westphalian
statism. Whether China could survive geopolitical confrontations with the
Global West without such conformism raises an open, haunting question:
Are there existing alternatives to political realism that possess historical
plausibility?

There are many voices and initiatives that suggest a flourishing of new
thinking throughout the world, although so far they lack geopolitically

relevant leverage at governmental and intergovernmental levels. The planting of numerous seeds that challenge the postulates of "smart agriculture" by positing many alternatives that allow our food and water needs to be locally provided in accord with culture and tradition, the wisdom of "agro-ecology" pitted against the industrial mentality of agro-business. In this sense, food constituting the most indispensable link between human well-being and the well-being of nature serves as an illuminating metaphor for all forms of human security at this pivotal time.

Whether we think by way of paradigm transformation or a Great Transition or the onset of another axial age, this is a historical moment giving rise to a growing sense for those who reflect on the human condition that time is running out. Let us hope that imaginaries of "necessary utopias" and a surge of spiritual awareness lead to revolutionary revisioning of feelings, thought, imagining, and behavior that make their weight felt before it is too late.

Notes

1   An academic counter-hegemonic reconstruction of international law, known as TWAIL (Third World Approaches to International Law) has gained some political traction in recent years, but remains a dissident tradition of marginal influence in policymaking spheres in the Global West.

2   Commentaries on the seven principles appears in Principles of International Law Recognized in the Charter of the Nuremberg Tribunal and in the Judgment of the Tribunal. Text adopted by the International Law Commission at its second session in 1950 and submitted to the General Assembly as a part of the Commission's report covering the work of that session (International Law Commission 1957).

3   Israel's alleged genocide in Gaza is a partial exception as the ICJ and ICC have both been invoked by critics and given some encouragement in their efforts to instruct Israel to comply with international law.

4   An alliance originally consisting of Brazil, Russia, India, and China (now including several other major developing economies), created to challenge the West's dominance of existing international institutions such as the World Bank or the International Monetary Fund.

References

International Law Commission. 1957. "Principles of International Law Recognized in the Charter of the Nürnberg Tribunal and in the Judgment of the Tribunal." *Yearbook of International Law Commission 1950*, vol. 2, 374–78. New York: United Nations.

8

Appropriating Normative Geopolitics:

Civil Society, International Law, and the Future of the United Nations

Points of Departure

This chapter considers the extent to which international law and the United Nations (UN) serve as both obstacle and instrument in the pursuit of a vision of a just world order that is sensitive to the realization of human rights comprehensively conceived to include economic, social, and cultural rights as well as civil and political rights. This enumeration of human rights accepts the categorizations and boundaries set forth in the two covenants of human rights, the binding international treaties that were negotiated in 1966 as a sequel to the Universal Declaration of Human Rights. It may seem obvious to the more ethically minded commentators on world politics that the most worthwhile undertaking of international law and the UN is to restrain the wrongful exercise of power by states, and this task is deserving of the utmost and invariable respect of governments and citizens. But the realities of international life and experience are sufficiently complicated, contradictory, and confusing as to resist such formulaic enthusiasm.

In fact, moral imperatives and political opportunities may point in one direction, while law points in the opposite direction. For instance, when a government abuses its citizenry to the extent of committing crimes against humanity, an external attempt to protect such vulnerable people may run up against the legal prohibition on recourse to the threat or use of force by states except in circumstances of self-defense rather narrowly defined or under the authority of the UN Security Council. If the Security Council refuses to mandate the use of force, then the tension between respect for law and the humanitarian urge to protect an endangered civilian population is made manifest, which the Charter itself encodes in Article 2(7) in the domestic jurisdiction exception to its war prevention mandate.

Both international law and the UN, besides being intertwined, can be twisted in many directions by powerful political actors to advance regressive, as well as progressive, policy agendas. The rules and frameworks that constitute international law, as conventionally understood, continue to owe their authority largely to the advocacy and consent of the elites that control the governments of the most powerful sovereign states, and their non-Western allies, which manage the postcolonial Western hegemonic world order (see, for example, Henkin 1979; Sands 2005).

Such an acknowledgment of legal positivism, as description and prescription, needs to come to terms with the extent to which states, especially dominant or hegemonic states, tend to subordinate or manipulate legal obligations whenever these impinge upon geopolitical priorities that shape their strategic interests. It should also not be forgotten, and it often is, that international law was generated to serve the underlying strategic interests of Western-oriented global governance and, as such, was unresponsive to non-Western values and interests. Latin American countries were the first to perceive the counter-hegemonic potential of international law in the context of protecting national economic interests from US penetration and manipulation.

So conceived, international law from above is less useful as a source of behavioral restraint, and even less when it comes to justice. This is especially true in relation to non-Western uses of force contested by the West. International law can be systemically useful either as an instrument of mutually beneficial cooperation (for example, in relation to trade, investment, maritime safety, and a host of practical transnational concerns where the logic of reciprocity prevails) or as a universally understood language for interstate communication of claims and grievances (Manning 1975; Kennedy 2006). As well, international law since the beginning of the twentieth century increasingly included aspirational goals and humanistic rhetoric, a repository of hope for the future that departs from the realist consensus.

There has, in addition, emerged over the course of the last century a counter-tradition that might be characterized as *internationalism from below*, in which weaker states and populist forces have effectively used international law as a selective protective shield, and even occasionally a sword, to resist various forms of exploitative abuses of foreign sovereign rights. The orientation is highly critical of the European colonialist origins of international law, emphasizing its racialist coding of white supremacy that disregarded the rights of native peoples and Global South nations. The postcolonial Global South has been slow to develop a distinctive jurisprudential response as in many countries governing elites have induced to dilute the worth of political independence by accepting what we identify as "colonialism after colonialism."

More clarifying jurisprudential perspectives are being adopted as civil society projects, largely thanks to the critical of independent jurists and groups such as TWAIL (Third World Approaches to International Law), an active network of international law specialists, most of whom have Global South identities.[1]

Global North Critical Expositions of International Law

Martti Koskenniemi has provocatively critiqued international law very differently from the discourses of jurists of the Global South. We categorize these critiques as adopting a Global North perspective. In our judgment, he overstates his central illuminating insight that international law has habitually functioned either as a source of apology for the depredations of power (Kant in a similar spirit dismissed the celebrated international jurists of his time as "miserable consolers") or as a utopian bromide for sentimental idealists who fail to appreciate the historic role of military force in international relations (see, e.g., Koskenniemi 1999 and 2001). In essence, this critique contends that international law either rationalizes the machinations of power or blends in aspirational features that lack behavioral relevance. Either way, the preeminent role of the international lawyer, according to this skeptical assessment, is a matter of either deliberate or innocent obfuscation. It reduces the roles of international law to one of service to the state out of ambition and deference or to denigrate idealistic legal thinkers as too naive to appreciate the extent to which geopolitics based on strategic calculations trump law whenever the national interests of major states become engaged.

In this respect, Koskenniemi's outlook is insightful to the extent that it lifts the curtain drawn by apologetic invocations of international law. His purpose is unquestionably to unveil the realist drivers of Great Power diplomacy. It is also a matter of striking a policy posture that is simultaneously wary and even dismissive of fuzzy thinking by starry-eyed legalists. These legalists tend to believe that merely by positing legal rules, political traction automatically arises to enable implementation. On this basis, it becomes possible to formulate a new behavioral hierarchy of self-actualizing norms that by their very existence are assured of restraining oppressive or exploitative exercises of state-centric violence. The Kelsenite tradition, with its formal rigor and detachment of law from an interplay with religious, moral, and political authority, represented the most influential expression of this depoliticized legalism, especially in Europe between the two world wars (Kelsen 1951 and 1966). Totalitarian forms of legalism, both Nazi and Soviet, as well as apartheid South Africa, discredited legal positivism nationally, but not internationally. It should be observed that legalist approaches to international law continue to downplay the relevance of civil society to the formulation, adoption, and implementation of legal norms except in relation to adversaries where states act on their own.

The Question of Agency:
Military and Political Ascendancy

Nevertheless, the apology/utopia dualism is too simplistic in a number of respects, including overlooking the significance of law as a tactic in struggles to gain control over the often-crucial moral high ground in many conflict situations, especially in most "new wars," highlighting the role of social movements and non-state actors (Kaldor 1999). It is notable that ever since the end of World War II, the militarily dominant side in conflicts suppressing self-determination concerns have rarely been able to control the political outcome. Historically, this had not been the case. In the prior century or so, the militarily stronger side almost always achieved its political goals, often without great difficulty or sacrifice, with hard power properly credited with historical agency. So long as this sense of superior military capabilities, intelligently deployed, being invincible, the will by native or indigenous peoples to resist remained weak and chaotic. The establishment of the globe-girdling colonial empires provided territorial and economic confirmations of this generalization about the geopolitical efficiency of hard power, especially as deployed by the major states in Western Europe and several breakaway British colonies, up through World War II.

No single factor reversed this pattern, but an essential feature of the reshaping of conflict and dominion in the countries of the South was that the militarily weaker side increasingly understood and took advantage of the normative backing of law and morality (instruments of soft power) in carrying on its struggles. Other factors that supposedly contributed to this trend were the greater availability of small arms throughout the world after World War I and the weakening of political will in the Global West due to the debilitating effects of costly wars to uphold colonial claims that were widely experienced in the increasingly democratic West as producing an increasingly unsupportable loss of life and resources. This new sense of normative advantage was especially relevant to creating a potential mass willingness by a people held in bondage to endure heavy burdens over long periods of time due to this revitalized belief in the entitlement and capacity of oppressed or colonized peoples to win their freedom and independence.

After some expressions of ambivalence, the United Nations played an activist role in creating and reinforcing this normative consciousness and further stiffened the growing will to resist through its endorsement of the right of self-determination and the prohibition of intervention in the internal affairs of colonized states, as well as through the repudiation of colonialism and condemnation of apartheid as a distinct international crime.

The UN Fits In

The UN, at its start, was conceived and established as a purely Westphalian framework of world order, with governments constituted as the political actors representing sovereign states exclusively entitled to membership. States retained full legal authority over territories situated within sovereign boundaries. Yet from its inception, the UN was also an arena where issues of normative aspiration were prominently considered as relevant concerns of law and morality. That is, the shaping of the norms of international law within the UN was an expression of its soft power importance in a global setting that failed to possess compulsory supranational governmental authority to settle international disputes. Thus, despite the statist background of the UN (which with its Western orientation did not, in its early years, question the legitimacy of colonial arrangements) came over time to encourage the decolonization process, partly through its Trusteeship Council. This both reflected a changing climate of ideas and social forces, including the approval of norms that eventually legitimized and empowered armed struggles against established colonial and racist political arrangements, and disempowered and demoralized entrenched elites seeking to perpetuate older, once legitimate forms of political order (Falk 2004, 3–44 and 67–103). Of course, this dynamic of constructing such a people-friendly and emancipatory orientation for international law was itself the outcome of an ongoing political process complemented by the activism of nongovernmental organizations (NGOs) and popular movements, particularly those dedicated to the promotion of human rights, above all the right of self-determination.

Cold War populist geopolitics, such as détente from below, also made often unacknowledged contributions: what was empowering and disempowering in the decolonizing struggles was reproduced in relation to the demand for human rights in the Cold War settings of Europe (Keck and Sikkink 1999). It was here that the politics of civil society were shaped and tested by a variety of efforts to construct, validate, and then actualize a normative architecture embodying fundamental ideas of morality, fairness, and justice (Kaldor 2007). Although the historical trend validates the emphasis on gaining the moral high ground and reliance on soft power instruments, especially during the decades of anti-colonial struggle and throughout the last stages of the Cold War, there is no assurance about the outcome of a particular conflict. Where the historical trend seems strongest is in relation to the failures of foreign military intervention since 1945, despite hard power dominance, a pattern exemplified by the contours of the American defeat in Vietnam. The trend is less pronounced in state/society struggles in which the hard power state may prevail (as in relation to Tibet, Chechnya, or the Tamil region of Sri Lanka) or fail (as in the Shah's Iran or apartheid South Africa). Further, the outcome may produce a victory for a supposed liberation movement that itself turns oppressive almost as soon as it gains power, as in Iran after the victory of the Khomeini-led revolution or of the Taliban in the aftermath of the Afghanistan resistance to Soviet and, later, US large-scale intervention.

But while this portrayal of the continuity between the worldview of progressive activists, the United Nations, and the international legal process contains important insights, it is far from the whole truth about the role and character of the United Nations, international law, and civil society. It is also crucial to grasp the seemingly paradoxical significance of the constitutional provision that allows the five permanent members of the Security Council to veto decisions of the organization even when addressing international threats to peace and security. This reflected a deliberate and fundamental intention in theory and practice to acknowledge the geopolitical dimension of world order by conferring on the then most powerful states' permanent membership in the Security Council and an extraordinary exemption from any obligation or expectation that these five countries, the P5, would be bound by the norms or procedures of the UN Charter. This expressed a fundamental intention in theory and practice on the part of the drafters of the Charter to take account of the geopolitical dimension of world order.

The exemption has been treated as unrestricted and in practice has been extended to shield friends of the P5 from adverse Security Council decisions. What may be more troublesome in some respects is the other part of the state-centric bargain underlying the formation of the United Nations to the effect that every other member state would be legally obligated, whether large or small, to act within the bounds set by the UN Charter as interpreted by the Security Council, including being potentially subject to UN-sponsored enforcement actions.

There are at least two ways to view this dualistic legal structure built into the constitutional foundations of the United Nations. It can be seen as a Faustian Bargain that was needed to bring the organization into existence in the first place and to help ensure that it would not fall apart under the strain of political crises in the manner of its predecessor, the League of Nations. It should be recalled that the League could neither induce some important states to join in the first place, most notably the United States, nor retain the membership of several important states. In contrast, the UN has retained the membership of all major states despite severe strains at times, and entry into the organization has become a vital indicator of legitimate sovereign status, as the bitter struggle for and against admitting Palestine as a full UN member illustrates.

UN deference to the distribution and role of hard power capabilities is at the heart of the realist worldview, and the fact that the UN has achieved and sustained universality of membership would tend to vindicate this approach in many circles, but it also has had several negative debilitating consequences. Most obviously, throughout the Cold War, it meant gridlock in the Security Council, which translated into a discrediting ineffectuality whenever the superpower antagonists disagreed, which was virtually always whenever global security issues arose. The veto also explains a UN legitimacy deficit, embedding double standards into the constitutional sinews of the organization with respect to the implementation of international law and the accountability of violators. This has constrained UN effectiveness, as well as sending the disheartening message to those seeking a global rule of law that considerations of law and justice must generally give way to the vagaries of hard power and a subtle acquiescence to some degree to Western hegemony. Double standards, so subversive of a genuine rule of law, can be observed in other domains of world politics. This delegitimizing characteristic of UN practice was highlighted since 2022 by the contradictory responses of the Global West to the Russian attack on Ukraine and the Israeli attack on Gaza, including the dismaying dismissal of the relevance of international law in the latter case.

Why should this kind of veto have been conferred on those states whose adherence to international law is most important if the UN system was ever to become effective and legitimate? The same diplomats who were scorned as idealists for their dedication to the overall UN framework and vision were also attacked for giving a group of large countries realist reassurances by way of the veto as an enticement to become and remain members without jeopardizing their geopolitical maneuverability. After the Cold War, the assault on UN legitimacy was less about the veto than criticism of the newly exercised hegemonic authority of the United States as the sole surviving superpower.

When George W. Bush, in the lead up to the Iraq War in 2003, told the Security Council that the UN risked becoming irrelevant if it did not support the American-led attack on Iraq, he was openly articulating an hegemonic demand, insisting that the UN would lose credibility if it did not endorse an aggressive war by P5 member that transgressed the core norm of the Charter prohibiting recourse to force in an international conflict unless it could be justified as self-defense against a prior armed attack (Articles 2(4), 51). Fortunately, despite bullying tactics by Washington, the Security Council withheld endorsement of the US/UK recourse to aggressive force in Iraq, but from an international law point of view, this was not a sufficient or effective response with respect to a state wrongly threatened by and then subjected to an unprovoked massive military attack and occupation.

The UN failed to condemn the invasion of Iraq and undertake its supposedly pivotal mission of protecting countries subject to unlawful threats or uses of force, and after the American-led attack toppled the Iraq government, the UN established a presence supportive of the outcome of the aggression followed by belligerent occupation. Nowhere in the Charter or in international law is there a rule asserting that states lose their sovereign rights if governing abusively, although in UN practice, it is true that if the level of abuse reaches the level of imminent or ongoing genocide or ethnic cleansing, moral, legal, and political challenges to sovereignty have been made on behalf of the victimized population. If such challenges clash with geopolitical priorities (as in relation to the Israeli attack on Gaza in 2023), then the UN becomes neutralized even though the violations of minimum moral and legal standards have outraged global public conscience to a degree never before experienced by the UN.

With respect to Iraq, conditions warranting intervention were not present despite past internal abuses that might at the time have justified intervention from legal and moral perspective. In 2003, the reasons for intervention seemed overwhelmingly strategic, and moral arguments about liberating the Iraqi people from tyranny, while somewhat plausible, had little legal weight even in the realm of public relations, and the whole undertaking came to be widely regarded as a dangerous UN precedent. It needs to be remembered that the UN was formed with war prevention as its primary mission, conditioned by assurances of nonintervention in domestic life (Article 2(7)). Human rights emerged during the early life of the organization and did erode the UN commitment to unconditional respect for territorial sovereignty, but always problematically due to double standards and selective political will, overlooking some gross violations and reacting coercively to others of equal or sometimes lesser gravity.

After World War II, surviving Nazi and Japanese leaders were prosecuted for their abusive *international* behavior, yet the exemption of the victors from legal accountability gave rise to a new episode of cynicism associated with the apology/utopia dualism so influentially articulated by Koskenniemi and in different ways by other critics. It should be noted that twelve years before the Iraq War of 2003, the UN had gone along with an extremely punitive peace imposed on Iraq after the Gulf War of 1991, resulting in severe harm to the civilian population of the country resulting from years of sanctions (see Falk 2008; Gordon 2012). There is every reason to view the United Nations both as, at times, an instrument of geopolitics and, at other times, as a site of struggle for the establishment of norms and normative architecture that offer soft power encouragement to an array of struggles against oppression, abuse, and exploitation throughout the world. It would thus be wrong to regard the UN as either only a geopolitical instrument or as exclusively a bastion of law, justice, and peace. For better and worse, it is both. Sometimes, as during the anti-colonial period, when the General Assembly was more assertive in support of an emergent anti-colonial international law framework, making the UN seem for some years more aligned with a politics of liberation and justified resistance, and even global reform.

In recent decades, the UN became more overtly associated and identified with power-driven geopolitics and a unipolar world order that tended to reflect the priorities of American foreign policy. This was true whether the issue was regime change in Iraq or subsequently imposing sanctions and threats of a military attack against Iran. In both instances, the UN seems to be contradicting the foundational mandate of the Charter to save succeeding generations from the scourge of war.

Note on the UN and the Israel/Palestine Conflict

The relationship of the UN to international law in the context of the Israel/ Palestine conflict is also emblematic of a split organizational personality. With normative zeal, the idea of a "responsibility to protect" (R2P) was endorsed as a world community responsibility in the face of severe abuses by a state of human rights in the form of ethnic cleansing or genocide. The R2P ethos was a diplomatic effort to give "humanitarian intervention" a postcolonial orientation, but so far this linguistic trope has not overcome the well-founded suspicions that accompany such selective and geopolitically driven uses of force (Orford 2003). Since mid-2007, when Israel responded to the Hamas takeover of the governing process in Gaza by imposing a comprehensive blockade, restricting the entry of food, medicine, and fuel to the then 1.5 million inhabitants, more than half of whom were classified as children and 75 percent as refugees. The maintenance of the blockade, although controversial in international law circles, has been widely condemned as flagrant and deliberate collective punishment in direct violation of Article 33 of the Fourth Geneva Convention governing "belligerent occupation." Such a prolonged and abusive deprivation of basic rights in Gaza certainly appears to pose a dramatic challenge to the supposed R2P norm, but the geopolitical circumstances of Israel's posture of non-cooperation and defiance of law and international institutional authority combined with the US/EU willingness to support whatever Israel does makes any kind of meaningful UN response not even seriously discussable, much less form the basis for action needed to provide protection to an acutely vulnerable people that have endured continuing crimes against humanity for decades. These issues assumed a dramatic, and polarizing, climax after the Hamas attack of

October 7, 2023, leading Israeli to unleash a genocidal assault on the entire civilian population of Gaza, now 2.3 million, speciously claiming a right of self-defense, which is of dubious relevance in situations of belligerent occupation.

But this UN failure is not the whole story. If the conflict is looked at differently, it can be seen that the UN lends significant support to the Palestinian struggle for self-determination, especially in light of the more recent shift in emphasis within the Palestinian resistance movement to a soft power, non-territorial strategy that seeks to do two things: (1) exert coercive nonviolent pressures upon the Israeli government by recourse to such measures as boycott, divestment, and sanctions (the BDS campaign), as well as more recently, arms embargos and R2P initiatives, and (2) civil society militancy designed to break the Gaza blockade. This shift can be questioned as to its depth and breadth, especially after the October 7 Hamas attack, which although decidedly provoked did shatter the image of peaceful Palestinian resistance. Developments since October 2023 make it virtually certain that various Palestinian factions will, in the future, revert to sustained hard power tactics, quite likely having become firmly unified in renewed support for armed struggle and the shared goal of national self-determination.[2]

It can be questioned whether the totality of the Palestinian opposition was ever persuaded to adopt and practice a soft power approach to attain their goals, especially in light of Israel's undisguised expansionism that included a categorical denial of Palestinian statehood. The BDS (Boycott, Diversity, Sanction) Campaign definitely was strengthened by UN initiatives of the last several years, especially the Goldstone Report of 1999 on alleged war crimes associated with Israeli attacks on Gaza in the period between December 27, 2008, and January 18, 2009, as well as the Human Rights Council's formal inquiry into the lawfulness of the Israeli attack of the May 31, 2010, on the Mavi Marmara Freedom Flotilla carrying humanitarian assistance to Gaza. Ideally, these condemnations of Israel's behavior as being in serious and sustained violation of international criminal law would induce intergovernmental and UN sanctions, censure, and mechanisms to impose accountability on those Israeli leaders responsible for shaping and implementing the policies. In fact, a geopolitics of impunity continues to shield Israel and its leaders from any kind of negative effects despite these clear and authoritative UN findings. Whether such a pattern of impunity will follow the events of 2023 is unknowable at this point, but if past practice is any guide, it would seem a near certainty that no Israeli will be held accountable for this fundamental breach of international criminal law.

It is misleading to view this result as a reflection of something deeper and more general than geopolitical priorities (even if distorted from a realist perspective by the strength of the Israeli Lobby and strategic regional energy concerns) as is implied by the phrase often used of "a culture of impunity."

The unconditional support given to Israel by the United States has been sharply and persuasively criticized from a realist perspective, suggesting that it distorts US strategic priorities in the region, as well as discredits its claims to provide globally responsible and legitimate leadership (Mearsheimer and Walt 2002). Two qualifications need to be added: even if foolish from a realistic perspective, the use of American leverage in the UN is an instance of geopolitics; after the Israeli victory in the 1967 Six Day War, the Pentagon and Washington think tanks increasingly treated Israel as a valuable strategic asset in the region, a position further strengthened indirectly by the fall of the Shah as an outcome of the Iranian Revolution in 1979. When the geopolitical priorities fall on the accountability side of the balance sheet, vigorous efforts will then be made to impose responsibility as in the reverse setting was the effort at evasion. The criminal prosecutions of Slobodan Milosevic and Saddam Hussein illustrated this proactive selective approach to criminal accountability of leaders unshielded by geopolitical factors.

As Mary Kaldor has so persuasively argued over the years, a statist focus provides an inadequate understanding of contemporary conflict situations, as the relevance of civil society actors needs to be increasingly assessed. The Israel/Palestine conflict also illustrates the political importance of controlling the narrative about how to describe the conflict and attribute blame for its origins and persistence, which influences attitudes toward what would be a reasonable and acceptable outcome and under what conditions is resolution and reconciliation possible (Kaldor 1996; Beebe and Kaldor 2010). It also relates to what types of resistance are undertaken, and how the international public opinion reacts to the asymmetric relationships embedded colonial settler projects, to the plight of native populations, and the weaponization of anti-Semitism.

The conclusion in relation to Israel is that there is no requisite political will on the intergovernmental level of state-centric diplomacy, especially in the Global West, to hold Israeli officialdom accountable under international law, but at the same time there does exist sufficient political will within UN circles to carry out investigative inquiries as to *whether* Israel and Israelis are in violation of their legal obligations and should be held accountable. In other words, try as it might, the United States cannot completely insulate Israel from the adverse normative consequences of its policies that violate international law and affront the conscience of the world, but it can so far contain consequences within UN settings by blocking efforts to implement normative expectations throughout the UN or resulting from intergovernmental action.

Nullifying the behavioral impacts of rulings by the International Court of Justice, UN fact-finding commissions, and reports of Human Rights Council Special Rapporteurs as to remedies for noncompliance with international law can be achieved despite vigorous geopolitical interferences. This is far less so with respect to progressive elements of global civil society, which do take more literally views of law and morality derived from reliable sources. A midway, relatively underutilized, and controversial option to implement international criminal law is afforded by some national courts, especially in Western Europe, which allow complaints about violations of international criminal law to be made under the rubric of "universal jurisdiction" (Macedo 2004). There have been no dramatic results with respect to Israeli accountability achieved by way of universal jurisdiction, although on several occasions Israeli political leaders and military commanders have canceled travel plans to countries where courts possess this authority on their law books for fear of being detained to face criminal charges. Even this low level of informal accountability, a mildly intimidating concern about the possibility of prosecution, undoubtedly has some chastening effect on the comfort zone of Israeli leaders associated with policies widely viewed as involving serious violations of international criminal law. Israel has met these kinds of tactics, whether involving international criticism or the use of national courts to assess accountability, by relying on a politics of deflection, complaining about the alleged anti-Semitic bias of the messenger or the auspices rather than addressing the substance of the charges, as well as by mounting a major public relations campaign to discredit critics typically by charges of anti-Semitism (Winstanley 2023).

Looking at this experience in the ever-unfolding Israel/Palestine conflict through the Kaldor lens of "new wars" accord a much more important political role for these delegitimizing and legitimizing narratives, and related undertakings, that have proceeded under UN auspices than would be the case if a mainstream state-centric or geopolitical lens is relied upon as the main optic. Their high-profile character gives societal plausibility to the main accusations of criminality associated especially with the expansion of settlements in the West Bank and East Jerusalem, the blockade of Gaza, and contentions of Israeli apartheid, and, above all, of genocide. This in turn invigorates efforts to organize various civic forms of boycott and divestment activities, as well as develop a variety of civil disobedience initiatives to break the blockade of Gaza. In other words, the Goldstone Report and the Report of the Fact-Finding Mission on the Gaza Flotilla are important for mobilizing purposes, but their non-implementation at intergovernmental levels gives arguments that international law matters, despite patterns of noncompliance and non-implementation a rather hollow sound. Israel defies international law, enjoys impunity, and can only be effectively constrained by geopolitical actors or concerted action by the peoples of the world taking and sustaining punitive action on a global scale as was the case in the final years of South African apartheid. There is significant evidence that Israeli leaders view what they call "the delegitimation project" as now a more serious threat to Israeli security and ambitions than hard power (violent Palestinian resistance). The Israeli ordeal of enduring a wave of "suicide bombings" during the 1990s helped maintain the Holocaust imagery of

Jewish victimization, while weakening claims of Palestinian victimization, despite the systematic abuse of their fundamental rights in the course of occupying post-1967 Palestinian territories. Israel by its control over the international public discourse was enabled to retain most of the high moral ground in the media and governmental arenas of the Global West.

A further shift in the normative equilibrium of the conflict has taken place since 2006, starting with the Israeli tactics of bombarding civilian centers of population in the Lebanon War (Hovsepian 2008), accentuated by the brutality of the 2008–9 Gaza War involving the same tactics on a more intense scale directed at the entrapped and entirely vulnerable civilian population of Gaza, and culminating in the attacks of May 31, 2010, on the civilian freedom flotilla carrying needed humanitarian goods to Gaza. These developments have allowed the Palestinians to exert, for the time being at least, somewhat greater influence in the moral heights in relation to the conflict, putting Israel on the defensive with respect to the crucial struggle for symbolic soft power ascendancy. This new approach to the struggle for Palestinian self-determination by nonviolent reliance on a range of resistance initiatives has been identified as a "legitimacy war" strategy. Up until October 7, the Palestinians were winning most battles on this global symbolic battlefield. The ferocity and cruelty of the Israeli response again shifted the public discourse as to entitlement, producing widespread denunciation of Israeli tactics and generating widespread support for the Palestinian in the Global South and even causing diminished unity at societal levels in North America and the European Union. It is significant that this series of developments following the Hamas attack brought public scrutiny to the interplay of terrorism, counterterrorism, and political alignments.

Whether this exceptional recourse to violence followed by the capture of much of the high moral ground by the Palestinians will be sustained— and even if so, whether it will be enough to alter the balance of political forces in the conflict sufficiently to achieve a just and sustainable peace for the two peoples—remains, at this time, highly uncertain. Whatever the outcome, the legitimacy war track still seems to offer the Palestinians and other embattled peoples greater promise under most circumstances than either armed resistance or reliance on traditional state-centric diplomacy. It is important to draw distinctions among various Palestinian elements in waging legitimacy wars. It is also far from certain that a complete reliance on soft power can or should be maintained if there are no convincing signs of substantial progress toward the overriding goal of Palestinian self-determination in whatever form can be negotiated. Much will depend upon how Israel, the Palestinians leadership, regional forces in the Middle East, the Global West and Global South, and the UN shape the situation in Gaza after a ceasefire is finally established.

Up to now, the world of organized diplomacy, in contrast, has been offering the Palestinian people less than zero through its periodic convening of a "peace process" involving negotiations between governmental representatives of the two embattled parties as mediated by the highly partisan United States. These negotiations are the most cynical imaginable inversion of justice erecting temporary facades of pseudo-accommodation that forthrightly excludes any reference to the rights of the Palestinians under international law, while seeking validation of the main unlawful and deliberate features of Israel's encroachment on Palestinian territories during more than fifty-seven years of occupation, that is, legalization of the unlawful Israeli settlement blocs, separation wall, and total denial of Palestinian refugee rights, especially the right of return. As many observers have commented, there can be no just and sustainable peace, as distinct from a ceasefire disguised as "peace," until fundamental Palestinian rights and Palestinian security are accorded an equal respect and protection as has been accorded to Israel (Kattan 2009, xv–xx and 248–61). Recent frameworks of official negotiations have no hope of achieving, or even pretending to achieve, respect for rights, a process that alone would offer some prospect of justice. At present, negotiations are shoved forward without the long-abused people of Gaza even being represented in any formal or appropriate manner due to the disqualification of Hamas as an unfortunate result of its terrorist listing. What has been argued in relation to Israel/Palestine applies with equivalent force to the differing situations in Kashmir, in the Kurdish struggle for fundamental rights in Turkey, to the Western Saharan struggle for secession from Morocco, and in many other conflicts around the world, although in each setting the specifics of context are crucial. No one template fits all.

Generalizing these comments makes it evident that transnational civil society initiatives, whether the BDS (Boycott, Divestment, and Sanctions) Campaign or the Free Gaza Movement, are focused on two principal goals: (1) peace and reconciliation based on justice and rights for both peoples under international law and (2) urgent action to alleviate the daily suffering of the Palestinian people and avert this further unfolding of the worst humanitarian catastrophe since, at least, the Nagasaki bomb was dropped. In this respect, the United Nations can be viewed as a necessary component in the prosecution of a legitimacy war—not directly through its decisions or behavioral impacts but, rather, indirectly as the world's most influential source of moral and legal authority, a legitimizing and delegitimizing arena that provides guidelines and sets limits on and gives visibility to permissible civil society approaches to conflict resolution. Prospects for a just world order depend on this reliance on peace and justice from below, new forms of nonviolent and populist form of geopolitics that seeks to neutralize the violent and governmental modalities of traditional statecraft that continues to rely mainly on hard power calculations in the shaping of conflict resolution, which entails ignoring the rights at stake of the weaker side and disregarding the limits set by international law on territorial gains achieved by force. The experience of the Palestinians since 1948 is extreme in these respects, but the pattern of marginalizing the relevance of international law is paradigmatic of any conflict situation is which the imperatives of geopolitics are allowed to guide diplomatic initiatives.

Conclusion

This disappointing assessment is not confined to the peace and security agenda of world politics—it applies whenever international law and the authority of the UN are stressed by geopolitical pressures. The same sort of disillusionment with both state-centric diplomacy and the UN as problem-solver has resulted from the failure to achieve the kind of obligatory agreement urgently needed, according to a consensus of climate experts, to keep global warming from reaching even more dangerous and irreversible levels than at present.

International law contributes the markers of the impermissible at a time when the formal annals of state-centric politics are being simultaneously (mis)shaped by the hubris of hegemonic geopolitics and ambiguously resisted by people-centered politics from below. In the varied enactments of this bearing of witness, international law helps parties to put contested behavior within a historical and ethical context but leaves responsibility for implementing tactics mostly in the hands of the mobilized peoples of the world and their governmental representatives whenever the normative goals are at odds with the strategic priorities of geopolitical actors or strong, well-funded private sector interests. The obstructive influence of oil and gas energy producers in the climate change context has weakened efforts to curtail carbon emissions by the adoption of prudent restraints. In this respect, international law contributes to an ongoing vital discourse and should, whenever possible, be invoked and relied upon by those struggling to promote global justice, while at the same time remaining opposed to demystifying claims that international law vindicates this or that use of interventionary violence. This world order bromide of a necessary hegemon is likely to persist unless there is a global justice movement that safeguards and envisions the future from a people-centric viewpoint, or a revolt against the primacy of geopolitics, which up to now has taken the form of seeking to substitute to the post–Cold War realities of a unipolar world with a new multipolar world order, especially in relationship to the management of peace and security and the regulation of trade and investment (see, for example, Gilpin 1981).

What emerges from this analysis of a changing global setting, underscoring the illuminating and prophetic importance of engaged scholarship that creatively conceptualizes the state/society/planet interaction, are two momentous, not generally appreciated, conclusions: first, violent resistance for an embattled people is being displaced, although not everywhere or consistently, by reliance on soft power instruments of coercion, including the force of law and morality; and second, the traditional conflict resolving modalities associated either with hard power domination or state-centric diplomacy, whether under UN auspices or independently, are proving increasingly incapable of fashioning humane and effective problem-solving solutions (Falk 1999 and 2017). As a result, there exist expanding opportunities for civil society initiatives, especially as the symbolic battlefields in legitimacy wars are non-territorial and potentially global in scope. If these dynamics are activated, as occurred during the anti-apartheid campaign of the late 1980s and early 1990s, then the UN and states can play a crucial role in encouraging just and sustainable outcomes to conflict. In effect, the war system has become increasingly dysfunctional for both strong and weak actors, with a few exceptions, and the future of world order now heavily depends on the extent to which political elites around the world, especially the leaders of major states, absorb this indispensable understanding of altered geopolitical realities in the early twenty-first century.

Notes

1   Notably, Antony Anghie, Upendra Baxi, and B. S. Chimni; TWAIL publishes a journal and arranges conferences developing an anti-hegemonic jurisprudential discourse that is critical of Global West manipulations of international law as in the context of Israel/Palestine. For detailed account, see Erakat (2019).
2   As articulated in the Beijing Declaration on Palestinian unity.

References

Beebe, Shannon D., and Kaldor, Mary. 2010. *The Ultimate Weapon Is No Weapon: Human Security and the New Rules of War and Peace*. New York: Public Affairs Books.
Erakat, Noura. 2019. Justice for Some: Law *and* the Question of Palestine. Stanford, CA: Stanford University Press.
Falk, Richard. 1999. *Predatory Globalization: A Critique*. Cambridge, UK: Polity Press.
Falk, Richard. 2004. *The Declining World Order: America's Imperial Geopolitics*, 1st ed. Milton Park, UK: Routledge.
Falk, Richard. 2008. "The Power of Rights and the Rights of Power: What Future for Human Rights?" *Ethics and Global Politics* 1 (1–2): 81–96.
Falk, Richard. 2017. *Power Shift*. London: Zed.

Gilpin, Robert. 1981. *War and Change in World Politics*. Cambridge: Cambridge University Press.

Gordon, Joy. 2012. *Invisible War: The United States and the Iraq Sanctions*. Cambridge, MA: Harvard University Press.

Henkin, Louis. 1979. *The Rights of Man Today*. New York: Routledge.

Hovsepian, Nubar. 2008. *Palestinian State Formation: Education and the Construction of National Identity*. Newcastle, UK: Cambridge Scholars Publishing.

Kaldor, Mary. 1996. "A Cosmopolitan Response to New Wars." *Peace Review* 8 (4): 505–14.

Kaldor, Mary. 1999. *New and Old Wars: Organized Violence in a Global Era*. Cambridge, UK: Polity Press.

Kaldor, Mary. 2007. *Human Security: Reflections on Globalization and Intervention*. Cambridge, UK: Polity Press.

Kattan, Victor. 2009. *From Coexistence to Conquest: International Law and the Origins of the Arab—Israeli Conflict, 1891–1949*. New York: Pluto.

Keck, Margaret, and Kathryn Sikkink. 1999. "Transnational Advocacy Networks in International and Regional Politics." *International Social Science Journal* 51 (159): 89–101.

Kelsen, Hans. 1951. *The Law of the United Nations: A Critical Analysis of Its Fundamental Problems*. New York: Praeger.

Kelsen, Hans. 1966. *Principles of International Law*, 2nd ed. Revised and edited by Robert W. Tucker. New York: Holt, Rinehart and Winston.

Kennedy, David. 2006. *Of War and Law*. Princeton, NJ: Princeton University Press.

Koskenniemi, Martti. 1999. "'The Lady Doth Protest Too Much': Kosovo, and the Turn to Ethics in International Law." *The Modern Law Review* 65 (2): 159–75.

Koskenniemi, Martti. 2001. *The Gentle Civilizer of Nations: The Rise and Fall of International Law 1870–1960*. Cambridge: Cambridge University Press.

Macedo, Stephen, ed. 2004. *Universal Jurisdiction: National Courts and the Prosecution of Serious Crimes Under International Law*. Philadelphia: University of Pennsylvania Press.

Manning, Charles. A. W. 1975. *The Nature of International Society*. London: Macmillan.

Mearsheimer, John J., and Stephen Walt, 2002. "'Realists' Are Not Alone in Opposing War with Iraq." *Chronicle of Higher Education*, November 15.

Orford, Anne. 2003. *Reading Humanitarian Intervention: Human Rights and the Use of Force in International Law*. Cambridge: Cambridge University Press.

Sands, Philippe. 2005. *Lawless World: America and the Making and Breaking of Global Rules*. London: Penguin.

Winstanley, Asa. 2023. *Weaponizing Anti-Semitism: How the Israel Lobby Brought Down Jeremy Corbyn*. New York: OR Books.

9

Global Inequality and Human Rights:

An Odd Couple

Ever since the emphasis on economic globalization in the 1990s, there was a technical awareness among economists that growth patterns were accentuating income inequality in the United States and in most other affluent and rapidly developing countries in the world, but this trend did not cause any significant political backlash so long as the national and global economies were experiencing satisfactory rates of overall growth. This changed when national economies in the North, and especially the United States, hit a series of bumps in the road with respect to growth, culminating in the Great Recession of 2008. It was in this period, roughly correlated with the years since the turn of the century, that inequality achieved political salience in the United States, being blamed in contradictory ways for socioeconomic distortions, regressive allocations of public revenues, and class inequities.

Such realities surfaced in the Occupy movement of 2011 with its influential division of the country into the superrich 1 percent and the other 99 percent, which became the centerpiece of the anti–Wall Street populist rhetoric of Bernie Sanders's presidential campaign of 2016, and whose resonance lingers. Donald Trump mounted a similar argument from the extreme right, blaming the distress of those being economically victimized on the ineptitude of a government catering to special interests and faulty international applications of contemporary capitalist ideology and practice. He pointed with particularly venomous language to disadvantageous international trade arrangements that deindustrialized the United States and displaced its workers while making China rich and economically ultra-dynamic in the process. During the 2016 electoral campaign, Sanders and Trump agreed from opposite ends of the political spectrum on the toxic impacts of intensifying inequality on the quality of life in the United States, and by implication, elsewhere. After a year of Trump's presidency, it was evident that although Trump's campaign rhetoric was populist, his performance as president intensified income and wealth inequalities and political elitism dramatically, particularly by way of new IRS (Internal Revenue Service) tax legislation that funneled more than 80 percent of the reduced taxes to corporations and the richest individuals (Tax Policy Center 2017).

In this chapter, the main goal is to analyze the phenomenon of "toxic inequality"—that is, the extent and patterns of inequality that are generally perceived as a fundamental political failure that harms and undermines the core commitment of democratic forms of governance to what the French philosopher Montesquieu called "the spirit of equality" (1748). Part of the policy debate unleashed by this development relates to the responsibility and role of the state under such circumstances, and whether the state over-regulates or under-regulates the private sector, which in turn has to do with deciding whether some limits on inequality are a core feature of true democracy. Alexis de Tocqueville was among the first acclaimed observers of American political life to associate democracy with the gradual, inevitable, and continuous increase in social and economic equality, which he mistakenly projected as an inevitable consequence of the repudiation of preexisting hierarchical governing arrangements, with monarchy and empire principally in mind.[1] Conversely, the dramatic recent rise of inequality, especially if seen as toxic, would seem to explain, in part, the de-democratization of society, although other factors, including a priority accorded to homeland security and to the technology of surveillance of the citizenry after the 9/11 attacks, are widely accepted as being among the most important proximate causes of the decline of democracy. This toxic sense is politically disruptive if it leads to lifestyle declines for other segments of the social spectrum and can become inflammatory, especially if it pushes substantial numbers from lower-middle-class living standards to those of varying degrees of impoverishment or exclusionary immigration policies.

The attempt is also made in the sections that follow to explore the complex relationships between the protection of human rights and the emergence of inequality as a high-profile societal concern (Milanovic 2016; Therbon 2017). The individualism of liberal Western traditions that underpinned the rise of human rights within the framework of international law, as distinct from its earlier embodiments in moral and religious thought and practice, helps explain why inequality does not figure prominently in the legal architecture of human rights as it was developed after World War II. It is noteworthy that capitalist logic is challenged by extreme poverty, but not by inequality as such, except as it pertains to radical critiques of class relations that link revolutionary potential to classist views on the perceptions of inequality. In later sections of this chapter, it is proposed that steps be taken to link human rights directly to inequality, with the objective being not the elimination of inequality but the avoidance of toxic forms of inequality. "Toxic" refers to forms of inequality that provoke controversy fueled by widespread perceptions of income/wealth distribution patterns, which are almost always accompanied by widespread, often political, embitterment and alienation. Such inequalities usually result in declining standards of living for the poor and middle classes, and if severe, is reflected in higher suicide rates, reduced average longevity, and the rise of diversionary, disruptive political finger-pointing, such as at migrants or marginalized minorities.

Inequality Discourse in the United States and the Global South

Barack Obama made a stir in 2013 when he identified "inequality as the defining challenge of our time."[2] His comments were a response to trends toward greater inequality in the United States, but there is growing evidence that rising inequality is a global issue, at least in relation to the rich and highly developed Organization for Economic Development and Cooperation (OECD) countries. Obama declared that this "dangerous and growing inequality" is imperiling the American dream, as well as undercutting the "middle-class America's basic bargain—that if you work hard, you have a chance to get ahead." Obama's basic objection is not about inequality, per se, but directed at the overall social impact of economic inequality given the particular stage of development reached by richer, fully industrialized countries and, in particular, the United States. Although not often explicitly stressed, the focus on inequality in the United States is on extreme levels, especially the disproportionate increases in the wealth of the wealthiest, with the most questionable concentrations of wealth allocated to the top 1 percent of the population. This would seem to be true even if the aggravating features of a detrimental impact on aggregate purchasing power and middle-class stagnancy were not perceived as caused by increasing inequality. Also, as in the Arab world, if economic growth has not lifted from poverty notable numbers of the most disadvantaged parts of society, the political relevance of inequality may be expressed at either extreme of repression or revolution, as well as by scapegoating styles of governance designed to distract potentially explosive discontent from its real explanation.

Inequality in America and some other developed countries is having strong negative impacts. It contributes to the stagnancy in the middle classes, undermining opportunity, exerting a downward impact on public revenues available for social goods, increasing youth unemployment, shifting power to the ultra-wealthy, and causing alienation and despair among workers. The most devastating overall or structural implication of this severe inequality, according to its critics, is the transformation of America into a plutocracy, defying the will of the public by mobilizing lobbyists and special interest pressure groups.

Global inequality presents a related but different kind of challenge than the national inequality that Obama found so disturbing. While the negative impacts of inequality on richer, more developed countries are widely acknowledged, the positive impacts of growth in developing countries have so far mostly outweighed the perceived negative effects of inequality, although this balance varies when national and regional contexts are taken into account. Rampant corruption and billionaire elites in the Middle East, Africa, Eastern Europe, and parts of Asia often appear linked to repressive governance patterns, attacks on resistance movements, and a delegitimizing dependence on security protection from a foreign state. Although these conditions are not normally explained by reference to inequality, the presence of severe and increasing inequality would appear to have a definite causal relevance to adverse political behavior.

Critiques of global inequality from the perspectives of the South, historically, did not contend that moves to promote greater global equality should be understood as a human rights issue but rather as a rich/poor issue or, at most, an issue of the "right to development" and associated critiques of the Bretton Woods institutions (the World Bank and the International Monetary Fund), the World Trade Organization (WTO), and international trade agreements (Rachman 2017). In a central respect this seems strange, as it neglects the effects of inequality on individual well-being, giving attention only to collective considerations associated with asymmetric trade, intellectual property, and investment structures. If inequality—as it deepens—imperils lives and diminishes the quality of life, it erodes the societal foundations needed to support the realization of human rights, especially those of an economic and social character, and less directly, those of a political nature.

In other words, if inequality crosses certain thresholds, it becomes toxic, manifesting itself in various political forms that discredit the established order. By way of illustration, it is quite plausible to interpret the election of Donald Trump as a type of sublimation on the part of a plutocratic political order, even if unwitting, disguised and rationalized by a reliance on the mobilization of a populist, anti-immigrant, ultranationalist, and antiestablishment base.[3] Trump's message was to keep jobs at home and to encourage more investment in American development via renegotiation of major trade agreements, while at the same time reforming health and tax policies in ways that would actually aggravate existing inequality ratios, yet satisfy his conservative political base by shrinking the so-called administrative state, which is in part a move against statist forms of social protection. Of course, a part of the Trump message was and continues to be the adoption of a radically anti-immigrant set of policies that especially undermines the human rights of vulnerable undocumented immigrants and subjects Muslims to special scrutiny. Such moves are ways of diverting the attention of those most victimized from grossly unequal distributions of wealth and income without correcting unfair levels and patterns of inequality.

Against this background, the next section will further explore why the evolution of international human rights standards were not more explicitly devoted to identifying limits on inequality that would better insulate society and its citizens from toxic forms of inequality and its adverse social and political repercussions, including tendencies to fragment identities within and across international borders. These tendencies work against the construction of the normative foundations of the unity of humanity, and the kind of postmodern patriotism we are advocating.

Explaining the Disconnect

At first glance, the connections between international legal standards upholding human rights and the realities of global inequality, however interpreted, are vague and ambivalent, implicit at best, and, until recently, rarely thought about. There are several reasons for this. Perhaps the most obvious explanation is the degree to which the canonical human rights instruments[4] overwhelmingly reflect the values of the West and the ideology of liberal individualism (Wolin 2004). The normative rationale of human rights clearly emphasizes endowing the *individual* with the material foundations of well-being and with protection against abuse by the state. Whether there is some sort of upper acceptable limit on the Gini Coefficient[5] that prevails within or among sovereign states is rarely raised as a matter of public debate, and never with respect to human rights, partly because it is a matter of collective conditions, while human rights is concerned only with individual conditions.[6] Twenty years ago, efforts under the auspices of United Nations Educational, Scientific, and Cultural Organization (UNESCO) to balance respect for "human rights" with a code of "human responsibilities," stressing collective perspectives on proper behavior, turned out to have zero political traction.[7]

A second explanation for this disregard is associated with the ethos of capitalism, which emphasizes—to varying degrees at different historical periods—that persons are entitled to the fruits of their labor as determined by the dynamics of the market. In this regard, inequality is presented as an inevitable side effect of meritocracy, even if conditioned along the lines advocated so influentially by Amartya Sen of working toward the establishment of equality of opportunity. This line of reasoning used to be reinforced by reference to the normative failures of socialism as practiced in the Soviet Union and Eastern Europe, or by comparing the standards of living prevailing in North and South Korea. The recent experience of some Asian countries, especially China, renders questionable, if not irrelevant, the ideological claim so prominent during the Cold War that capitalism is, under all social conditions, the best possible economic system, stimulating creativity and risk-taking, and rewarding success.[8]

A third line of explanation is linked also to the nature of neoliberal globalization, with its emphasis on the rule-based efficiencies of transnational capital and financial flows, which has been understood by national economic policymakers as support for minimizing interference with market dynamics, thereby maximizing growth. Until recently, virtually the sole criterion of economic performance has been the rate of net global economic growth, with no public attention accorded to the relationships between growth and income distribution except by a few dissident economists here and there.[9] It was claimed by most policymakers and politicians that there would be collective benefits from maximizing growth associated with the image of "lifting all boats," and so there was no need to worry about inequality if the concern was overcoming material deprivation and poverty. In the recent phase of neoliberal globalization, there has been a growing backlash of anger and alienation that is expressed by the rise of right-wing populism in response to the privileging of lower global costs while diminishing the national economic well-being of some sectors of society (UNESCO 2002). The most salient argument in this respect has been the outsourcing of manufacturing and some low-grade servicing jobs (for example, customer complaints and online sales) to low-wage, minimally regulated societies with harmful effects resulting from low safety and environmental protection standards.

A Reframing of Human Rights and Inequality

When considering issues of economic policy from a global standpoint, the distinction between relations of growth to existing class structures and to particular stages of development is crucial. Moreover, these relationships help explain the barriers to the formation of a global consensus as to how to fix the world economy. As a result, it is difficult, yet far from impossible, to find a constituency with an authoritative mandate to draft and present for adoption a UN Declaration on Human Rights and the Limits of Economic Inequality, however relevant such a text might be to the various global forms of economic growth in richer countries increasingly perceived to be proceeding in ways that give rise to economic malaise. If social and economic rights are given proper respect by such mainstream human rights nongovernmental organizations (NGOs) as Human Rights Watch and Amnesty International, the political opportunities to address income and wealth inequality within a transnational activist framework of international human rights law would immediately increase, at least among OECD countries.

A second conceptual concern is the overall relevance of internal class structure to assess the varying impacts of global inequality on the existential circumstances bearing on human dignity, as well as the interconnections between global growth trends, income distribution, and the mix of beneficial and detrimental consequences that can be attributed to different levels of internal inequality, including the effects of reductions and increases of poverty levels. As will be later discussed, it may be desirable to prepare a declaration or manifesto that explains, and insists upon, the relevance of inequality to the realization of human rights, issuing an urgent call for the reduction of disparities to measurable targets.[10]

So far, there has been an overall failure of those challenging inequality to express their grievances by reference to human rights, although more general complaints about injustice are frequently made (e.g., Sen 1992; Nussbaum and Sen 1993, 30–53). Despite this failure, there exist good reasons to suppose that a human rights approach to the struggle against toxic forms of inequality may be tactically useful to those seeking to address social injustices and tensions derived from inequality. To ground grievances in established traditions of legality may remove the debate somewhat from a partisan ideological standoff about the ills and benefits of capitalism to the peoples of the world and related controversies about the optimal levels of market regulation.

To some degree, the inequality discourse is already embedded, although indirectly, within the international law architecture of human rights. This is particularly true of the seminal Universal Declaration of Human Rights (UDHR), as well as the language contained in the preambles of the two human rights covenants. The widespread acknowledgment of the equality of the person as a central pillar of human rights calls attention to some potential and actual tensions in both capitalist and noncapitalist societies between formal legal and substantive material equality. Inheritance and unrestricted property accumulation have clear implications for the capabilities of many societies to fulfill minimum requirements of human rights concerning the material necessities of life and could exert downward pressures on political and civil rights due to the perceived need to control citizen discontent related to impoverishment, unemployment, and the lack of opportunities for upward mobility.[11] This seems to be especially the case in the Middle East and North Africa, which helps to explain recent interactions between revolutionary upheavals, counterrevolutionary backlashes, and massive restiveness and discontent.[12]

As earlier suggested, when assessing "global inequality," it is essential to distinguish between inequality within societies (which is rising in every part of the world) and aggregate inequality between sovereign states (which has decreased temporarily, though this trend was explained primarily by the economic rise of India and China). In general, in the international law of human rights, the conditions of individuals within states are alone regarded as a proper legal object of concern. The preamble of the UDHR does imply a connection between realizing human rights within countries and the overall conditions prevailing in international society by this assertion: the "recognition of the inherent dignity and of the equal and inalienable rights of all members of the human family is the foundation of freedom, justice and peace in the world" (UNGA 1948, Preamble). Also of relevance is Article 28 of the Universal Declaration that sets forth a very embracing pledge that could be interpreted as requiring limits on inequality: "Everyone is entitled to a social and international order in which the rights and freedoms set forth in this Declaration can be fully realized" (UNGA 1948). Presumably, to the extent that global inequality is considered to infringe upon the capacity of states to realize these rights, its relevance is at least acknowledged. Such a provision has so far been of interest only to critics of the moral order of international relations, for the political will to implement this potentially radical approach has so far been absent on the part of governments and even among mainstream civil society organizations.

The preamble also affirms the relevance of human rights to the maintenance of "friendly relations" among states and also to overall peace and stability by removing the occasions for "rebellion against tyranny and oppression." Although far from setting forth binding norms, a preamble represents a diligent and carefully scrutinized effort by negotiators and drafters to capture the spirit of an international law text, offering a formulation of an ethos to guide subsequent interpretations of substantive provisions in accord with reasonable expectations.[13]

There are also provisions in the UDHR that can be considered, at least, plausible candidates for acknowledgment and potential implementation as norms of customary international law, for example Article 25(1): "Everyone has the right to a standard of living adequate for the health and well-being of himself and his family, including food, clothing, housing and medical care and necessary social services" (UNGA 1948).

The various forms of social democracy, especially as developed in Europe, and more recently extended to rapidly developing Asian countries, reconcile creating conditions for a good life, including public systems of education and health, through an indirect assault on extreme inequality by way of the tax system. Upper-class Scandinavians complain about high taxes, the loss of incentives, and the deadening impact of social leveling on cultural vitality, implicitly arguing that significant degrees of inequality are necessary ingredients of societal vitality, including a dynamic economy.

Depending on the overall social structure within a country, the ability of governance structures to realize this aspiration is undoubtedly affected by different levels of inequality resulting from both national and global policies. It might be difficult to overcome by impartial analysis divergent explanations for persisting poverty and challenges to subsistence, but it is certainly plausible in some settings to contend that inequality of income and wealth within a society bears centrally on whether a given number of people are denied fundamental economic and social rights. At the very least, such a proposition deserves empirical investigation.

Similarly, it can be maintained, although, again, difficult to demonstrate, that civil and political rights are less frequently upheld if high levels of inequality are present, and especially if there appears to be trends toward even greater concentrations of wealth and income among the dominant elites of a society. If such a pattern is validated by neoliberal rationalizations of market forces that incorporate a Social Darwinian ethos, it may occasion a societal backlash. The relevance of context is of great importance. Efficient successful economies, such as Germany, fulfill economic and social rights in the natural course of political life, able to combine market-led operations with a generous social contract in ways that make degrees of inequality of minor societal concern. In contrast, deep pockets of distress affecting many millions in the United States combine with extreme disparities between the very rich and the rest to make inequality a prime target of left populist reform. The growing realization that it is not just the poor but also the middle classes in America that have been victimized by stagnant wages, poor social services, and rising health and education costs gives added political weight to critiques of inequality that stress the injustice of the polemical, but suggestive, 1-to-99-percent ratio. As observed in recent decades, by recalling the America of the 1920s before "the crash," economic inequalities were seen as organically linked to social injustice, and not just to poverty. These underlying conditions also give rise to status-quo-oriented extremisms that situate the blame for social distress on immigrants and unfair international trade while inducing fear in the population by manipulating and exaggerating security threats, as recently in relation to China and Russia.

In effect, there are degrees of inequality that have varying connections with human rights and democracy in different social circumstances and cannot be generalized. It may be that future research could help establish that Gini Coefficients beyond a certain range would make the satisfaction of the standard of living aspirations of Article 25(1) effectively unattainable for parts of the population, and therefore arguably making a Gini Coefficient above a specific level by itself a violation of the human rights standard.[14] Of course, it could be argued that 25(1) is only aspirational or conjectural. It is often argued by conservatives that a higher minimum wage or reduced inequality would not necessarily lead to a greater proportion of a given society enjoying an adequate standard of living because it would inhibit investment and overall growth. Here is an area where social science research confirming causal links could contribute to sensitizing the human rights discourse and community sentiments, and maybe even judicial interpretations, to the relevance of high levels of inequality, as affected by specified levels as present in particular countries, regions, and the world.

The link between inequality (both among and within states) and human rights is more pronounced in Article 28 of the UDHR, although this article has implications so radical as to make it seem utopian: "Everyone is entitled to a social and international order in which the rights and freedoms set forth in this Declaration can be fully realized" (UNGA 1948).

This provision, as suggested, is likely to be dismissed as utopian or, at best, wildly aspirational and conjectural. It can also be read, in light of the preamble, as an encouragement to governments to establish conditions sensitive to human well-being, and the concrete appreciation of the equal worth of each person, both of which are central ingredients of any human rights culture. At least within some societies current levels of inequality are creating conditions that are widely regarded as inimical to material and spiritual well-being of many persons as well as undermining the vitality and credibility of political democracy. This line of moral reasoning is the thrust of the critiques of inequality associated with Barack Obama's 2013 speech and the Sanders presidential campaign in 2016. Even Trump's attack on the connection between the displacement of American workers and the global trade framework could be understood as an indirect call for a greater effort to comply with Article 28, although on the basis of experience, be more appropriately dismissed as a diversionary polemic without any serious attempt to show a causal relationship to the overall international order or to act in a manner that takes the analysis seriously. Trump then racialized the employment and income challenges by the inflammatory tendency to place blame on undocumented immigrants for stealing jobs and depreciating wages of American workers. As the economists Paul Krugman and Robert Reich, among others, have shown, job displacements are being principally caused by automation, robots, and artificial intelligence, and not by immigrant low-wage workers and outsourcing.

The Trump presidential victory in 2016 shifted attention away from inequality for two main reasons: Trump's own emphasis on economic nationalism as the key way to "make America great again," as well as the preoccupation by liberal constituencies with the broad spectrum of threats associated with the worldwide rise of right-wing populism, anti-immigration politics, and thinly disguised Islamophobia.[15] Such a loss of focus, however, does not really refute the critiques of inequality that commanded such attention a few years ago and that political figures such as Bernie Sanders and Elizabeth Warren articulated so effectively in the political arena. Arguably, the current situation may obscure the centrality of inequality while at the same time reflecting its overall influence.[16] Although such a counterfactual cannot be proved, it is nonetheless plausible to suppose that a more equitable distribution of income over the last twenty years would have avoided the stagnancy of the middle classes and the anger of workers and overall polarization, especially if coupled with more forthcoming public policy relating to education, health care, and job training. A legacy of the Cold War was the persisting rejection of any approach to social and economic policy that could be discredited as "socialist," however relevant it was to creating a humane economic order based on capitalism. Such an ideological flexibility would also involve shifting policy emphases from a blind devotion to gross national product (GNP) growth as the prime indicator of economic performance to more nuanced assessments that include social satisfaction and the relations between inequality and growth at various stages of economic development.

Toward a "Universal Declaration on Human Rights and Inequalities of Income and Wealth"

The preceding discussion could be understood as arguing that overcoming excessive inequalities was *impossible* because of the capitalist ethos of unregulated capital accumulation and a cult of individualism that accords priority to the efficiency of capital, bolstered by the false sense that human well-being is best upheld by not tampering with market forces. There is also the misleading belief that interference with the market is *superfluous* as the normative framework of human rights is already sensitive to the challenges posed by existing levels of inequality. Even if this is in some sense true, the benefits of consciousness raising and encouragement of direct action with respect to the harms attributable to inequality make a campaign against inequality valuable at this time.

Along these lines, it would seem beneficial to encourage the formulation of an authoritative document linking severe forms of inequality to a range of economic and political disturbances in state/society relations. The advantage of adopting a human rights framework is that it provides the only universally accepted normative language within which to express rights and aspirations, as well as to acknowledge wrongs and deprivations.[17] Such a declaration, ideally adopted by a resolution of the UN General Assembly, would not attempt to formulate obligatory standards but, rather, would set forth a series of concerns that recognize that inequality in many national, regional, and global settings has reached levels that demonstrably interfere with the implementation of many existing human rights standards. In effect, reducing inequality would make it more feasible to satisfy the expectations set forth in Articles 25(1) and 28 of the UDHR, although inequality in certain societal contexts is far more detrimental than in others. It is also arguable that the removal of incentives to compete by a maximum leveling of outcomes in society also could have certain negative effects on the cumulative achievement of human rights, although this seems rather remote given the extent and detrimental effects of certain forms of inequality.

Rather than attempt to draft the text of the proposed declaration on global inequality and human rights, the goals and some factors that should be taken into account are set forth. The complexity of the challenge is partly due to the undesirability of condemning inequality as an unqualified global wrong, a designation that seems more appropriate for certain types of conduct, such as torture and extrajudicial executions. Inequality needs to be appraised according to its effects within given contexts. In this respect, a proposed declaration is, to some extent, in the nature of sensitizing peoples to the relevance of curtailing certain forms of inequality so as to be better able to uphold human rights. Even those who might regard Obama's contention that inequality was "the defining issue of our time" as hyperbolic would nevertheless agree that certain trends and benchmarks bearing on inequality weaken existing patterns of compliance with human rights standards and impair prospects for progress toward more humane types of governance on all levels of social interaction.

There are many ways to anchor a declaration on global inequality and human rights. Our recommendation is to tie the declaration directly to the unfulfilled normative potential of Article 25(1) and 28 of the UDHR. The obvious reason to proceed in this way is that the declaration would flow from an existing widely respected human rights text, conveying a sense of normative continuity. There is also an important disadvantage of this approach. It is significant that 25(1) and 28 were not carried forward in the two human rights covenants, which are the treaty sequels to the UDHR. As the covenants were conceived as obligatory treaty instruments, it was taken for granted that the more aspirational features of the UDHR would not be incorporated. Even if such provisions were advocated for inclusion, at least in the Covenant on Economic, Social, and Cultural Rights, it would have been virtually impossible to obtain a consensus for their inclusion among the negotiating governments, especially given the ideological cleavages of the then-prevailing Cold War atmosphere. As a result, a project to propose and draft a declaration on the relevance of inequality could on similar grounds be dismissed as yet another utopian elaboration of goals unattainable in a state-centric system of world order underpinned by a neoliberal version of capitalism.

There are several lines of response. First, such a text would not aspire, at first, to be obligatory but only declaratory and aspirational with respect to legal authority. Second, there is a growing recognition of a crisis of capitalism, accentuated by the global rise of right-wing populism, which has given political traction to concerns about levels of global inequality that did not exist earlier.

Although mindful of the difficulties and the controversial nature of such a proposed declaration, the undertaking seems to be a politically and ethically responsible initiative. This is especially the case in light of recent developments. Among these developments is the ideologically motivated effort by those at the top of the socioeconomic pyramid to shift the conversation away from inequality on the grounds that it foments class warfare, limits freedom, and is inherently anti-capitalist, negating the alleged benefits of a neoliberal approach to trade, investment, and growth (Wodak 2015; Judis 2016). Support for a declaration would have the important beneficial effect of grounding human rights on ideas of social justice, as well as on the regulation of abuses of people by the exercise of state power directed at suppressing popular discontent.

With these considerations in mind, the Declaration of Human Rights and Inequality should be drafted with the following goals in mind:

- a summary of trends and profiles of inequality within and among states and regions;
- an analysis of the relationship between economic growth and inequality trends as differently affecting developing and developed economies, with particular attention to alleviation of poverty in developing countries and impacts on wage stagnancy, unemployment, and social mobility in developed countries;
- a recognition of the correlation between heightened inequality and the spread of illiberal forms of governance that highlight deteriorating respect for fundamental human rights;
- an inquiry into whether respect for human rights can be protected and promoted in the face of increasing inequality, and whether there is a need for a protocol to the human rights covenants that affirms collective rights of societies to set boundaries on the acceptable degree of inequality at national, regional, and global levels; and
- a framework of principles and guidelines that would be more responsive to the contextual complexities of inequality than would a code of conduct to guide governments and shape public discourse.[18]

Conclusion

Given the rise of autocratic leadership in important countries, including the United States, Russia, India, Turkey, Egypt, Philippines, Hungary, and Poland, it is highly unlikely that inequality can be immediately addressed head on in the manner advocated above. Nevertheless, an insistence on doing so might highlight and expose tensions between rising inequalities and falling human rights. The undertaking itself would serve pedagogic and political purposes even if in the end not formally adopted.[19]

Plan B would be to discuss and draft a declaration along the lines proposed above as a transnational undertaking of civil society, sponsored by human rights NGOs in various parts of the world.[20] It is notable that the World Economic Forum before Brexit and the rise of Trump downplayed concerns about the challenge associated with prominent critiques of inequality.[21] It might be that the World Social Forum, if still sufficiently ambitious, could be induced to produce such a declaration in the spirit of promoting social justice and encouraging a civil society campaign.

If the goal is a better understanding of why certain levels of inequality do such social damage to the pursuit of human rights in some contexts, it might make more sense to put a critique and prescriptions in the form of a manifesto rather than a declaration. Such a choice of format would depend on auspices, and whether goals were educational rather than political.[22] What is most needed and desirable would be both educational and political efforts in governmental and civil society arenas to explore the interactions between inequality and human rights. The purpose would be to gain insight and agreement on acceptable limits and guidelines for constructive planning. Currently, regulation has a toxic political character because it is accompanied by wage stagnancy, declining middle-class standards of life and future expectations, and a large number of persons enduring extreme poverty and homelessness (Falk 2009, especially chapter "Toward a Necessary Utopia," 13–24). These features of the socioeconomic landscape of the wealthiest countries in the world is what makes the allocation of public expenditures and the regulation of private income and wealth often not only regressive but, for those with eyes to see and a democratic consciousness, a moral scandal that casts shadows of illegitimacy over the state and its approaches to achieving economic equity while promoting aggregate economic growth.

Even in the "success stories" of Asia—India, China, and the Asian Tigers—there are signs that toxic levels of inequality are producing storm clouds on the horizons given the recent trends toward both stagnancy and rising inequality. This assessment mainly rests on a recognition that economic growth lifted hundreds of millions out from the grip of extreme poverty in a stunningly short period of time, which is an extraordinary social and political achievement, even if during this same time a small elite in these societies, whether "market socialist" or "crony capitalist," has gained disproportionately in wealth and income. Such disparities not only tend to make the rich much richer but also nurture a culture of corruption. In this regard, the normative focus, even among those who bring needed attention to the excesses of inequality, is on its contextual effects on the poor and middle-income segments of society. From the dominant human rights perspective, the existence of inequality is not in itself treated as an assault on human dignity that would by itself require remedial action.[23] This may reflect a deficient grasp of societal coherence as there may be disruptive weakening of the social fabric if inequality is allowed to remain or exceed present levels.

This inquiry into the harmful consequences of toxic forms of inequality is linked to the underlying argument in other chapters of this book: that is, that a shift in the center of patriotic gravity from the state or nation to the species is an indispensable precondition for achieving a future world order premised on the *unity of humanity*. So long as patriotism is primarily attached to fragmentary embodiments of political and personal identity, humanity as an organizing category will not seriously challenge the Westphalian framework of world order and its hybrid twenty-first-century evolution combining state-centric and hegemonic geopolitical structures of practice and belief.

A second aspect of this inquiry into humanity as an organizing category is a deeper consideration of whether modifications of or alternatives to neoliberal capitalism might offer paths toward frameworks anchored in humanity as an organizing category for problem-solving, which might include a consideration of whether China offers a partial model, with greater adaptive potential to the imperatives of twenty-first-century humanity than do the models being generated in the Global West. Part of such an assessment would be the response of different ways of handling technological innovations with major structural impacts within a historical setting of mounting global challenges.

Notes

1   Fred Dallmayr comments on de Tocqueville (1945) in *Democracy to Come: Politics as Relational Praxis* as follows: "Focusing on the egalitarian character of democracy, as contrasted with the structural hierarchy of earlier regimes" (2017, 1).

2   In his speech (White House 2013), Obama gave some telling statistics to underscore his quite dramatic and oft-quoted assertion: "The top 10 percent no longer takes in one-third of our income—it now takes half. Whereas in the past, the average CEO made about 20 to 30 times the income of the average worker, today's CEO now makes 273 times more. And meanwhile, a family in the top 1 percent has a net worth 288 times higher than the typical family, which is a record for this country." For a more detailed global statistical profile, see Roser and Ortiz-Ospina (2016).

3   The dominant human rights perspective is compatible with neoliberal versions of economic policy that validate unequal income and wealth outcomes to varying degrees, mitigated by progressive tax policies. There are other social and political ideas that link the quality of democracy to the development of a more egalitarian society in all of its dimensions (see, e.g., Dallmayr 2017, which positively correlate progress in human rights with policies designed to produce reductions in all dimensions of inequality).

4   The instruments referred to as "canonical" are the Universal Declaration
     of Human Rights and the two human rights covenants. For representative
     writing emphasizing the Western bias of the human rights mainstream, see
     Falk (2000, 87–96); Mantua (2002); de Bary (1998).

5   The Gini Coefficient is the best-known measure for a nation's income
     inequality. It is worth noting, however, that it isn't the best measure to reflect
     today's trends. The Chilean economist Gabriel Palma (2011) observed that
     the middle of the income distribution is relatively stable across countries and
     across time, meaning that the real changes and differences between countries
     occur on the tails—that is, in levels of extreme poverty and in income
     concentration within the top 10 percent of the distribution. The Palma ratio
     (national income shares of the top 10 percent of households over the bottom
     40 percent) suggests that global inequality is significantly more problematic
     than we initially thought when using only the Gini measurement.

6   The closest analogy to the recent focus on inequality and global reform were
     the efforts in the early 1970s at the UN General Assembly to establish what
     was being called a "new international economic order" that was intended to
     level the North/South playing field with respect to trade and investment. This
     third world project was not explicitly justified by reference to human rights.

7   This connection between plutocratic leadership and policies associated with
     extending inequality is evident in both the tax reform and health plans being
     proposed by the Trump presidency, as well as by the plutocratic orientation of
     appointments. For a deeper assessment of the connection between inequality
     and related distortions of public policy in defiance of citizen preferences in
     such areas as gun control and legalization of marijuana, see Mounk (2018).

8   The countries that became known as the "Asian Tigers"—Hong Kong,
     Singapore, South Korea, and Taiwan—are known for their rapid
     industrialization in the 1960s to 1990s. What is less known about them is
     that they did so while pursuing policies that directly contradicted the Western
     free-market consensus of our time. Their governments rejected foreign loans
     and free trade agreements to protect their infant industries, heavily subsidized
     manufacturers, and invested into universal healthcare and education. China
     has followed similar market-shaping policies, with similar economic success.

9   Such a concern with inequality is certainly at the core of Marxist analyses,
     and their normative aspirations to establish a classless society. Indeed, the
     Marxist critique of capitalist societies has always accentuated the distorting
     human effects of inequality of material conditions as between entrepreneurs
     and workers. Leninist projections of class analysis with regard to international
     capitalism also focuses on the global inequalities that result from power
     structures. Marxism-Leninism does not invest its hopes in overcoming these
     deficiencies in socioeconomic relations through the promotion of human
     rights, but rather as a result of revolutionary seizures of state power. At
     least until very recently those who championed the liberal international
     economic order as established after World War II under American leadership
     were unconcerned with inequality. See, for example, the failure to consider
     inequality trends and effects in Ikenberry (2011).

10   Goal 10 of the UN Sustainable Development Goals calls for reducing within- and between-country inequality through more equitable resource distribution, investment, and social programs, as well as through special attention to regularizing migration and remittances. While supporting migrants and facilitating remittances would likely have positive impacts on reducing poverty, the UN text remains vague on how, for example, "resource distribution" is to be achieved and by whom, as well as to what degree inequality should be reduced.

11   The growing demands for reparations in the United States are based on the understanding that today's severe wealth inequality significantly reflects the extraction enabled by slavery and that the institutions that facilitated such wealth accumulation persist (e.g., protection of inheritance from meaningful taxation). A parallel, though at the time of this writing, less vibrant movement is happening in Europe with regards to reparations for colonialization.

12   A notable exception is Morocco, which between 1975 and 1984 experienced a dramatic decrease in inequality (a 27.3-point drop, as measured by the Gini Coefficient). In an unpublished master's dissertation (2016), Sasha Milonova shows that this was due to a conscious effort by the monarchy to reduce poverty and create a middle class to shield itself from political unrest following two attempted coups against the king. This episode also gave rise to some harsh policing of dissent, but through redistribution policies such as food subsidies, land reform, expansion of state employment, and nationalization of foreign assets, the government managed to reduce inequality to a level tolerable to the population, though it's hard to know how long this brokered peace will last, given that Morocco's inequality is once again on the rise.

13   Of course, the publication of Thomas Piketty's *Capital* (2014) had a huge impact on public awareness and influenced the language of politicians. See also Milanovic (2016) and Piketty (2015).

14   Empirical evidence already suggests that inequality impedes long-term economic growth, particularly in low- and middle-income countries (e.g., Benerjee and Duflo 2003).

15   Rather than aim their attacks on the underregulated world economy or on job losses associated with automation, politicians scapegoat immigrants and outsourcing.

16   For an important exception that carefully links human rights with inequality, see Alston (2015).

17   For insight into the complexities of interpretation, see McDougal et al. (1967).

18   There are other interesting ideas in this vein. Economist Richard Parker argues that the existing way of reporting economic activity using GDP growth obscures the fact that most of that growth is captured by the wealthiest 1 percent. He suggests the creation of a gross domestic distribution index, which, if reported alongside GDP, would direct the policy debate toward addressing the growing inequality within and between countries (for his GDD proposal, see Parker 2023).

19   We are aware that such a project requires, besides a legal reframing, changes to the dominant economic paradigm of the day. If it is the responsibility of states to guarantee human rights, it would then become their responsibility to intervene in activities that exacerbate inequality, which could mean, for example, regulating private sector actors or withdrawing from trade agreements. The concept of a government directing an economy toward social outcomes challenges the neoliberal idea that freer markets and smaller governments are best for maximizing welfare.

20   The highly regarded and widely praised NGO, Oxfam, has conducted notable research and campaigning along these lines: their reports focus not on a utopian goal of absolute equality, but rather on problematizing an economic system that enables nine billionaires to hoard the combined wealth of the poorest 3.5 billion people (Hardoon 2017). It is a level of inequality so deep that it renders precarious or altogether impossible the livelihoods of 50% of the world's population. Oxfam regularly publishes inequality reports - see for example "Takers not Makers" (Taneja et al., 2025).

21   For representative views linking inequality to the electoral success of Trump, see Anderson et al. (2016) and Dennin (2017).

22   The other alternative universal normative language is associated with the overlapping core values of world religions. This approach is complementary to human rights although it lacks the backing of intergovernmental diplomacy and legal status (see Küng 1997); a similar argument can be made on the basis of overlapping ethical values as between the different ethical orientations of major world civilizations, but the emphasis of various writers on the distinctiveness of Asian values contests claims of a universal normative language based on shared ethics.

23   The World Economic Forum highlighted economic inequality (and suggested it was behind Trump and Brexit)—see Elliot (2017).

References

Alston, Philip. 2015. "Report of the Special Rapporteur on Extreme Poverty and Human Rights." UN Human Rights Council, A/HRC/29/31, May 27.

Anderson, Sarah, Chuck Collins, Josh Hoxie, and Sam Pizzigati. 2016. "Inequality Gave Rise to Donald Trump's Presidency." *Nation*, November 9. https://www.thenation.com/article/inequality-gave-rise-to-donald-trumps-presidency/ (accessed April 11, 2018).

Ballard, Charles. 2017. "Many of Trump's Policies will Further Intensify Income Inequality." *Hill*, February 10. http://thehill.com/blogs/pundits-blog/economy-budget/318941-many-of-trumps-policies-will-further-intensify-income (accessed April 11, 2018).

Banerjee, Abhijit V., and Esther Duflo. 2003. "Inequality and Growth: What Can the Data Say?" *Journal of Economic Growth* 8: 267–99.

Boaz, David, and Edward H. Crane, eds. 1993. *Market Liberalism: A Paradigm for the Twenty-First Century*. Washington, DC: Cato Institute.

Dallmayr, Fred. 2017. *Democracy to Come: Politics as Relational Praxis*. New York: Oxford University Press.

de Bary, William Theodore. 1998. *Asian Values and Human Rights: A Confucian Communitarian Perspective*. Cambridge, MA: Harvard University Press.

Dennin, James. 2017. "Inequality Helped Elect Donald Trump—and would Grow Wider under his Policies." *Mic*, December 7. https://mic.com/articles/161422/income-inequality-helped-elect-donald-trump-and-would-grow-wider-under-his-policies#.znBazvovg (accessed April 11, 2018).

de Tocqueville, Alexis. 1945. *Democracy in America*. Edited by Phillips Bradley, vol. 1. New York: Vintage Books.

Elliot, Larry. 2017. "Rising Inequality Threatens World Economy, says WEF." *Guardian*, January 11. https://www.theguardian.com/business/2017/jan/11/inequality-world-economy-wef-brexit-donald-trump-world-economic-forum-risk-report (accessed April 11, 2018).

Falk, Richard. 2000. *Human Rights Horizons: The Pursuit of Justice in a Globalizing World*. New York: Routledge.

Falk, Richard. 2009. *Achieving Human Rights*. New York: Routledge.

Forbes, Steve. 2012. *Freedom Manifesto: Why Free Markets are Moral and Big Government Isn't*. New York: Crown Business.

Hardoon, Deborah. 2017, "An Economy for the 99%: It's Time to Build a Human Economy that Benefits Everyone." Briefing Paper, Oxfam. https://policy-practice.oxfam.org.uk/publications/an-economy-for-the-99-its-time-to-build-a-human-economy-that-benefits-everyone-620170

Ikenberry, John G. 2011. *Liberal Leviathan: The Origins, Crisis, and Transformation of the American World Order*. Princeton, NJ: Princeton University Press.

Judis, John B. 2016. *The Populist Explosion: How the Great Recession Transformed American and European Politics*. New York: Columbia Global Reports.

Küng, Hans. 1997. *A Global Ethic for Global Politics and Economics*. Oxford: Oxford University Press.

Mantua, Makau, 2002. *Human Rights: A Political and Cultural Critique*. Philadelphia: University of Pennsylvania Press.

McDougal, Myres S., Harold D. Lasswell, and James C. Miller. 1967. *The Interpretation of Agreements and World Public Order*. New Haven, CT: Yale University Press.

Milonova, Sasha. 2016. "Political Economy of Income Redistribution in Postcolonial Africa: Cases of Morocco, Mali, and Malawi." Unpublished master's dissertation, London School of Economics.

Milanovic, Branko. 2016. *Global Inequality: A New Approach for the Age of Globalization*. Cambridge, MA: Harvard University Press.

Montesquieu, Charles-Louis de Secondant. (1748/2001). *Spirit of Laws*, Book VIII. Translated by Thomas Nugent (1752). Ontario, Canada: Batoche Books.

Mounk, Yascha. 2018. "America Is Not a Democracy." *Atlantic*, March, 80–87.

Nussbaum, Martha, and Amartya Sen, eds. 1993. *The Quality of Life*. Oxford: Oxford University Press.

Palma, Gabriel. 2011. "Homogeneous Middles vs. Heterogeneous Tails, and the End of the 'Inverted-U': The Share of the Rich is What It's All About." *Development and Change* 42 (1): 87–153.

Parker, Richard. 2023. "What We Don't Measure—but Should." *The American Prospect*, December 6. https://prospect.org/economy/2023-12-06-what-we-dont-measure-but-should (accessed September 15, 2024).

Piketty, Thomas. 2014. *Capital in the Twenty-First Century*. Translated by Arthur Goldhammer. Cambridge, MA: Harvard University Press.

Piketty, Thomas. 2015. *Economics of Inequality*. Translated by Arthur Goldhammer. Cambridge, MA: Harvard University Press.

Rachman, Gideon. 2017. *Easternization: Asia's Rise and America's Decline from Obama to Trump*. New York: Other Press.

Roser, Max, and Esteban Ortiz-Ospina. 2016. "Income Inequality." *Our World in Data*, October. https://ourworldindata.org/income-inequality (accessed April 11, 2018).

Sen, Amartya. 1992. *Inequality Reexamined*. New York: Russell Sage.

Taneja, Anjela, Anthony Kamande, Chandreyi Guharay Gomez, Dana Abed, Max Lawson and Neelanjana Mukhia. 2025. "Takers not Makers: The Unjust Poverty and Unearned Wealth of Colonialism." Oxfam. https://africa.oxfam.org/latest/publications/takers-not-makers.

Tax Policy Center. 2017. "Distributional Analysis of the Conference Agreement for the Tax Cuts and Jobs Act." Urban Institute and Brookings Institution, December 18. https://taxpolicycenter.org/sites/default/files/publication/150816/2001641_distributional_analysis_of_the_conference_agreement_for_the_tax_cuts_and_jobs_act_0.pdf.

Therbon, Göran. 2017. "Dynamics of Inequality." *New Left Review* 108 (January/February): 1–19.

United Nations Educational, Scientific, and Cultural Organization (UNESCO). 2002. "Declaration of Human Duties and Responsibilities." Fundación Valencia Tercer Milenio.

United Nations General Assembly (UNGA). 1948. *Universal Declaration of Human Rights*. GA Res. 217A. December 10, Paris.

Wodak, Ruth. 2015. *The Politics of Fear: What Right-Wing Politics Discourses Mean*. London: Sage.

White House. 2013. "Remarks by President Obama on Economic Mobility." Office of the Press Secretary, Town Hall Education Arts Recreation Campus, Washington, DC, December 4.

Wolin, Sheldon. 2004. *Democracy Incorporated: Managed Democracy and the Specter of Inverted Totalitarianism*. Princeton, NJ: Princeton University Press.

10

International Law and Transformative Innovations:

The Case of Criminal Accountability

Point of Departure

Global governance has aspired to achieve a framework of law that sets limits on national sovereignty and geopolitical primacy in the context of peace and security. The results have been mixed with some observers affirming the glass half full and others in despair reflecting a focus on the glass half empty. The crux of this diversity of assessment arises from the uneven record of implementation, which is blamed for the erosion of the basis logic of law that equals be treated equally. Realists tend to accept the structural constraints of a state-centric world order while some global reformers derive satisfaction from partial implementation and incremental progress. The issue can be approached from various angles, including recourse to international force, individual accountability for violation of international law and human rights norms, compliance with the Non-Proliferation Treaty (NPT), and indicators of respect for the authority of the United Nations (UN).

There is no doubt that the future of global governance will reflect the degree of success in overcoming the present "implementation and accountability crises" that weaken the roles of international law in sphere of collective behavior and, often, enforcement where it is most needed.

A Conceptual Prologue

For almost a century, there has been a concerted and cumulative international effort to place limits on the discretion of sovereign states and their political and military leaders to embark upon wars of aggression or to commit atrocities that inflict severe and deliberate harm on individuals or targeted groups.[1] Norms, procedures, and institutions have been established to carry out these ambitious goals, which have, to varying degrees, been both abetted and obstructed by the flow of political developments. Above all, the destructiveness of modern warfare became evident in the enormous losses of life that were sustained in World Wars I and II, as well as the widespread devastation of urban habitats, giving rise to calls for and support of global reforms.[2]

The emergence of nuclear weaponry made even the most hardened politicians schooled in political realism recognize the catastrophic prospects of a third world war, although this recognition quickly faded from relevance with the passage of time and the challenges of post-fascist geopolitics, although periodically revived in response to international crises throughout the Cold War, and now somewhat again with concerns growing about a confrontation with China that might yet produce a new, very different kind of cold war, but at least as dangerous.[3]

Complementary to the concerns surrounding war prevention is the emergence of the human rights architecture given impetus by the Cold War rivalry and by civil society activism. Respected human rights organizations, including Amnesty International and Human Rights Watch, have consistently supported post-Nuremberg efforts to establish norms, procedures, and institutional venues with mandates to uphold legal protections of individuals in times of peace as well as wartime by holding perpetrators of abuse criminally accountable. Such civil society pressures have not worried too much about shortcomings of coverage but focused their energies on holding leaders and others responsible for major criminal violations of human rights standards or for crimes against humanity.

In effect, there were ideological turns against war as a discretionary instrument of national policy with legal entitlements to the fruits of aggression and against the absolute claims of territorial sovereignty that were formally endorsed by leading governments (Stone 1954). Such proposed normative innovations represented a potentially radical challenge to the Westphalian system of world order that had unfolded in Europe since the middle of the seventeenth century, becoming globalized after the two twentieth-century "world wars." Yet the behavioral impacts of these rhetorical challenges were seriously undermined by failures to seek credible political implementation in the peace diplomacy that followed the Allied victory in World War I. Instead, the Westphalian fusion of state sovereignty and "Great Power" geopolitics was restored, and the League of Nations turned out to be an empty shell when it came to establishing a durable peace (Coffman 1998; Bull 1968), although it made valuable contribution to the quality of human life in other domains, including labor rights and standards, as well as preparing the world for transitions from colonial rule to political independence. Yet the League was regarded as weak when it came to war prevention and West-centric with respect to overall outlook and policy agenda.

What became evident after World War I was the unwillingness of leading Western states to implement such an aspirational view of war and sovereignty in a manner that created any confidence that these internationally mandated normative shifts in behavior and entitlement would be reflected in altered political behavior. It was immediately evident that the political will to erode sovereign rights or establish credible enforcement mechanisms did not exist, nor could ad hoc mechanisms be brought into existence except in very selective circumstances, and even then, such initiatives were more reflective of geopolitical priorities and preoccupations than normative imperatives.[4] States were unwilling to transfer authority or meaningful capabilities to policy arenas in which they gave up control. Political elites managing national governance structures continued to believe that security policy bearing on issues of war and peace, and to a lesser degree human rights, could not be addressed by normative fiat at a global level. These elites were unwilling to delegate national authority to an international institution, nor could territorial sovereignty be operationally diluted to protect fundamentals of human dignity against internal instances of abusive state behavior. The operationalization of normative innovations in these policy spheres continued to depend on national self-enforcement and pragmatic self-restraint.[5]

The Westphalian form of world order, as previously noted, was influentially depicted by Hedley Bull as a form of anarchy that depended, for humane results, on the moderation, prudence, and wisdom of "Great Power" diplomacy to advance the common good, extend standards of reciprocal benefit, and achieve functional measures of societal cohesion (1977). In effect, international law could be effective when it was mutually beneficial as with the facilitating lawmaking treaties on matters of shared and reciprocal concern such as maritime safety, diplomatic immunity, and contexts where power differentials were almost irrelevant.

Bull cautioned against more ambitious normative initiatives, especially with respect to personal accountability for alleged state crimes, suggesting that the war/peace and territorial sovereignty agendas were firmly entrenched in the realms of power and diplomacy and could not constructively be rendered subservient to law or ethics (1968). This was an uncompromising realist response to the legalist hopes of the innovators who seemed to believe that morality, law, and reason, if activated properly, were sufficient to establish new canons of behavior. Such beliefs were widespread among ordinary citizens but scorned by foreign policy experts.

And yet, the normative assault on the permissiveness of the earlier Westphalian ethos did not disappear, nor totally disappoint. As the case for international normative modifications of world order increased due to the further development of weaponry of destruction and greater interaction among nations, attention to human rights and global interdependencies, civil society engagement, digital administrative capabilities, and global-scale challenges posed by climate change, pandemics, artificial intelligence (AI), and nuclear weaponry, the gap widened between political realists, critical realists, and new realists.[6] The status quo realists believed that maintenance of peace and security depended on stability, which in turn depended on balance of power geopolitics backed up by military preparedness and adequate weaponry, and attuned to changing circumstances. Normative markers of statist world order, such as borders or refraining from forcible interferences in domestic affairs, were the grammar of international relations, identifying red lines, which, if crossed, would more than likely provoke retaliatory actions.[7]

This chapter is devoted to the legal struggle for international criminal accountability, which falls into a hybrid category of its own, reflecting evolving normative aspirations, and exhibiting the impacts of "geopolitical nullification." This is expressed in international relations by double standards that treat equals unequally. The hybrid character of the quest for criminal accountability can be depicted by three interrelated generalizations:

1. double standards that result in imposing accountability on the weak, while granting impunity to the strong;

2. an overall growing commitment embodied in international criminal law to achieve maximal accountability, challenging, and eroding to some extent, the selective acceptance of impunity; and

3. frequent abandonment or dilution of accountability procedures in contexts of transition from criminality to the rule of law; the adoption of pragmatic adjustments to achieve domestic social peace in the aftermath of a voluntary transfer of power involving the replacement political leaders who perpetrated state crimes during their period of governance. For instance, Obama did not pursue allegations of torture against his predecessor, George W. Bush.

Each of these generalizations can be illustrated and elaborated to expose the contradictory pulls and dilemmas that explain the confused and complex reality of international criminal accountability. The underlying tension is between the claims of sovereignty as beyond the reach of international law and of international law as taking precedence over national law in the event of conflict. A secondary tension is between the primacy of geopolitics and the authority of international law.

For and Against Normative Determinism

Contrary to the hybridity model of world order put forward in the preceding section, Oona Hathaway and Scott Shapiro offer a Hegelian interpretation of international political order that gives decisive weight to normative innovation relative to a unitary structure of world order. In their words, "[a] key theme of this book is that *ideas* matter, and people with ideas matter" (2018, 249). The central argument of their book is clearly conveyed by its title—*The Internationalists: How a Radical Plan to Outlaw War Changed the World*. Its central thesis is that when certain ideas are given a sufficiently prominent endorsement by relevant authority figures in a political order, they have an impact on political behavior, maybe not immediately or in a linear fashion but cumulatively, in keeping with the ebb and flow of historical processes of change. These authors believe that the formal renunciation of international war as a legitimate instrument of national policy has, over time, transformed international relations in fundamental respects, and in their view, for the better. And further, that the initial advocates of normative innovations, in this instance influential professors of law, give ideas a political, moral, and legal weight that can lead to their actualization if the historical circumstances are receptive and reinforcing. We regard the evidence as mixed, especially in the contexts of war prevention and implementation/accountability challenges.

They believe that central stages in the evolution of world order relative to the legal status of war can be associated with influential jurists: Hugo Grotius in the seventeenth century for his learned endorsement of war and its limits as a partial corrective for wrongdoing by sovereign states, and then Hersch Lauterpacht in the twentieth century for his repudiation of the legitimacy of war as an instrument of national policy. These jurists are singled out in intriguing fashion, but somewhat arbitrarily, for preparing the groundwork for the rupturing of the structure of world order between the old and new.

Hathaway and Shapiro draw a sharp distinction between what they call the old world order (OWO) and the new world order (NWO) with respect to the subject matter of discretionary war making, which they convincingly put forth as the defining issue of international political life. In essence, these authors regard the Westphalian Treaties ending the Thirty Years' War, as preceded and prefigured by the indispensable juridical contributions of Grotius to mark the beginning of the historical era that they label as the "old world order" (OWO). This OWO had as its dominant feature the justifiability of war for purposes of overcoming perceived injustices, posited as a necessity given the absence of internationally available and effective institutional procedures for the peaceful settlement of disputes between states.[8] In effect, war is assigned a quasi-legislative and institutionally primitive character of the highly decentralized structure of state-centric world order.

The NWO is connected with the analysis and advocacy of the twentieth-century jurist Hersh Lauterpacht, who developed his ideas about war in reaction to the terrible human losses associated with World War I. These ideas were translated into a legally relevant format only in 1928 when most of the leading countries became parties to the Pact of Paris, which outlawed aggressive war and formally renounced war as an instrument of national policy. Even Germany, surprisingly, became a party to the treaty in 1934, a year after Hitler's ascent to power. The main thesis argued by Hathaway and Shapiro is that this dramatic change in the legal status of war between sovereign states was of such a character in intention and eventual behavioral effect as to create a before and after, constituting a systemic rupture in the character of world order.[9] The experience of World War II was treated, despite its magnitude, as an anomaly from the contrary antiwar normative momentum resulting from the Pact of Paris. A derivative feature of the NWO for Hathaway and Shapiro, explored below, involves prohibiting the use of aggressive force in international relations making it a logical juridical sequel to attribute individual criminal responsibility to its human perpetrators, and thus helps explain the major push toward international criminal accountability at the Nuremberg and Tokyo Tribunals held after World War II.[10]

While setting forth their stimulating thesis, the authors make the rather far-reaching claim that the NWO deserves credit for producing an unprecedented period of relative peace and international warlessness in international relations, a great achievement only partly diminished, in their view, by increases in the numbers of failed states and intrastate wars.[11] It seems reasonable to question this conclusion by regarding the peace achieved as not measurable in terms of the frequency and magnitude of international wars, nor can many intranational wars in recent years be so sharply distinguished from international wars, especially in cases where external actors intervene and the autonomy of internal actors is subordinated.[12] Although Hathaway and Shapiro acknowledge the relevance of developments other than normative advocacy and innovation, their claim is one of "normative determinism," that is, that changing the norm on the legal status of war provides a decisive explanation of why it becomes appropriate to refer to post-1928 experience as the origins of the NOW.[13] Fears of wars fought with nuclear weapons seem like a crucial new factor that encourages geopolitical prudence and conditions the pursuit of strategic ambitions in many, but certainly not all, contexts.

As already suggested, the concern with the criminal accountability of leaders for wrongdoing was presented by Hathaway and Shapiro as derivative from the underlying influence of the anti-aggression norm. In that regard, the punishment of German and Japanese transgressions of this new grand norm demonstrated to the world its reality, and helps account for the decline of war in international relations during the last eighty years.[14] What is certainly true is that the Nuremberg Judgment did give a leading emphasis to its designation of "crimes against peace" as the international crime that embraced the other two categories of criminality involving crimes of war and crimes against humanity, and this is definitely supportive of the contention that the Pact of Paris initiated a decisive ideational turn against aggressive war.[15] But it could also be argued that the motivations for the Nuremberg/ Tokyo trials were more associated with the interest of the victorious power in demonstrating the just cause and outcome of the conflict, and less with the vindication of the anti-aggression norm. Indeed, the public justification for the trials related more closely to Nazi and Japanese atrocities than to being appalled by their recourse to war as instruments of national policy.

Subsequent international behavior shows a weakening of the norm during and after the Cold War.[16] Although the refusal of the Security Council to authorize the attack on Iraq in 2003 is notable, the rationalization of aggressive war relied upon by the United States was more in accord with the OWO attributed to Grotius than to the NWO. It is also notable that the inability to agree on a definition of aggressive war finally overcome by its deferred inclusion as a distinct crime in the Rome Statute governing the operations of the International Criminal Court, whereas other categories of criminality were included without causing intergovernmental disagreements.

In summary, while the Hathaway and Shapiro thesis is interesting jurisprudentially and historically, it does not hold up from the perspective of explanatory power for several reasons. Properly appraised, it seems unconvincing to contend that we are living in a more peaceful world than existed before 1928, even if we accept the fact that much violent political conflict has shifted to intranational struggles. In other words, the anti-aggression norm has not had the impact attributed to it, even accepting the acknowledgment that their data-driven assessment (number of international combat and territorial conquest per year) is somewhat reflective of the inhibiting impacts of nuclear weapons on the behavior of states, a growing awareness post-1945 that international trade was more efficient and effective than conquest to enhance state power, and on the temporary spread of democracy as elevating sentiments discouraging war as an instrument of policy. With the passage of time, an assessment of the present global setting as culminating in the Ukraine War, political violence in Gaza, and the worldwide rise of autocratic forms of national governance signals the end of the post–Cold War moderate phase of international relations and a new test of diverse conceptions of preferred world order perspectives.

Our view is that there is hardly any reason to attribute any aspect of the decline in the incidence of wars and territorial conquests to the Pact of Paris, and even to its subsequent development. There has been, in fact, a de facto juridical retreat to just war thinking, that is, to a revival of OWO or

Grotian perspectives on recourse to war, even if the rhetorical pattern of contemporary justifications for recourse to international force has somewhat shifted in response to technological, tactical, and normative innovations.[17]

There are at least three reasons for rejecting the normative determinism of *The Internationalists*. By far the most important is the persistence of *geopolitical primacy* with respect to the war/peace agenda overriding and marginalizing more legalistic readings of international legal norms. Expressing this in the conceptual language of Hathaway and Shapiro, we are still living in a framework delimited by Grotian OWO, although the reasons for undertaking war as an instrument of national policy have shifted, and become more constrained in some respects, while the overall risks of unwanted escalation have risen dramatically (Schell 1982). This OWO primacy was even evident in the "victors' justice" aspect of the World War II trials that avoided accountability for the victor despite Hiroshima; it was not law, but politics and morality, that encouraged a legal framing of personal accountability, which contrasted with the less hypocritical preferences of Stalin and Churchill for summary execution of captured Nazi senior officers and high officials.[18] Although hypocritical, the Nuremberg approach could be justified in other ways, including for exposing to a broader public, especially in Germany, the evil nature of Nazi policies and practices, and creating a precedent that had archival, pedagogical, developmental, and, possibly, deterrent effects.

The continuity of geopolitics reflects the fact that the political elites responsible for foreign policy of the major governments remain skeptical or strategically opposed about subjecting their own foreign policy to law as a guide to political behavior.[19] Their "political realist" worldviews suggest that recourse to war remains a rational calculation conditioned by prudence in settings where escalation above nuclear thresholds is relevant, but historical research yields a different, more complex understanding of when wars start and when they are avoided.[20] It is conceptually plausible that the factors mentioned by Hathaway and Shapiro as explaining the decline of war-making and territorial conquest could have been integrated into a NWO altered "political realism" in which adherence to the Charter framework served national interests. Such interests pertain to avoiding the potential catastrophic effects of a nuclear war, as well as the interference with economic benefits of a peacetime neoliberal world economy and the diminished glorification of war in most national societies, but this did not happen. Why such revised rationality was never seriously considered by the leadership of P5 countries (i.e., the five members of the UN that were accorded permanent membership in the Security Council as well as an unrestricted right of veto), and some others, is itself worth pondering, and seems to reflect private sector pressures to keep military budgets high and arms industries profitable in peacetime in response. Such factors explain the tendency to exaggerate security threats as a key uncontested aspect of post-1945 capitalism that also marginalized the advocacy of disarmament and the funding and political support of strong global institutions, including the UN.[21]

We argue that the most significant pressures that discouraged major wars after 1945 were perceptions that preparing for international wars was *prudent*, but engaging in such war was highly *imprudent* and to be avoided as a matter of supreme national interest. There was no existentially significant political shift in behavior that can be convincingly attributed to the post-1928 reformulations of international law norms bearing on the use of international force.[22] In other words, pursuing geopolitical ambitions shifted away from winning international wars, but not away from global militarism, and without deepening respect for more restrictive normative constraints adopted in several important peace and security contexts: the UN Charter was put forward to the public as a virtual constitution for a state-centric world order. This kind of strategic reasoning takes account of the need to have the kind of military capabilities that would discourage future adversaries from attacks and provocations even if not seeking to engage in actual combat. Geopolitical prudence and self-restraint, not deference to normative innovation, is what became the most relevant explanation of the modification of war making. Also relevant was the changing nature of global capitalism, as further affected by the normative and political turn against colonialism and imperial modes of trade and investment that have made territorial conquest and traditional forms of imperial exploitation less viable, more indigenously contested, and less profitable.[23]

The third deficiency in the Hathaway/Shapiro major premise is its insistence on drawing a sharp distinction between intergovernmental and intranational wars. The prudential incentives to keep war within limits explains why international wars have been so often fought within the boundaries of sovereign states, a pattern identified in the literature and practice of international relations as "proxy wars."

The United States government in the Vietnam War justified the expense and human costs by the contention that, by assisting the Saigon government of South Vietnam, it was actually waging a war of containment against communist China, as well as discouraging the spread of communism in the region (the "falling dominos" metaphor). Saudi Arabia makes the same kind of claim with respect to Iran in justifying its involvement in violent struggles taking place in Syria and Yemen.[24] The principal rationale for confining the theater of warfare reflects pragmatic efforts to avoid the occurrence of major wars rather than a show of greater respect for normative prohibitions formulated to restrict recourse to international uses of force.

Also suggestive of the failure of the Pact of Paris approach is the previously mentioned degree to which the ICC had great difficulty even adding the crime of aggression to its jurisdiction, although heralded at Nuremberg as "supreme" among the crimes being prosecuted and inserted in the UN

Charter as its most basic normative claim. Ever since the Russell Tribunal was convened in 1966–67, the effort to bring law to bear on the geopolitics of war has been much more an undertaking of civil society initiatives rather than reflecting intergovernmental ambitions at the UN or elsewhere.[25] In this respect, civil society tribunals have taken more seriously the Pact of Paris approach to major instances of aggressive war making, although relying mainly on the UN Charter norms, and according no particular attention to the diplomatic consensus expressed by the 1928 treaty. The most comprehensive legal narratives documenting the failure to adhere to the Pact of Paris renunciation of war are to be found in the commentaries about and the proceedings of these citizen initiatives (Duffett 1968; Sokmen 2008).

In this regard, the struggle for individual criminal accountability has proceeded without any overt causal linkages to the NWO hypothesis, or to the alleged dividing line of 1928 between the OWO and the NWO with respect to war as a discretionary instrument of national policy. The inconsistent record of implementation reflects geopolitical calculations and material capabilities much more than the rhetorical claims of imposing individual accountability for violations of international criminal law. The overriding motivations for imposing such accountability when it occurs has to do with strengthening just war reasoning, that is OWO thinking, maintaining Western civilizational hegemony in a postcolonial world. Similarly, the motivations for impunity with respect to accountability have to do with maintaining geopolitical maneuverability and keeping the leadership of Western countries and their allies free from all forms of international accountability.[26] The "clash of civilizations" hypothesis of Samuel Huntington has enjoyed a second coming in the opposed alignments of the Gaza struggle, featuring the West on one side and Islam on the other.

The conclusion reached is that normative determinism is a conceptually intriguing way of interpreting the evolution of world order over the past century, but it is fundamentally flawed for multiple reasons. Most fundamentally, this stress on norms as ideas mistakenly attributes significant *political* traction to *rhetorical* changes in the status of recourse to war in nondefensive circumstances. These rhetorical changes are not trivial, playing important roles in the domain of "symbolic politics" within which longer-term lawmaking is often situated, and more potently in recent "legitimacy wars" involving struggles for the high legal and moral grounds by antagonists in political conflicts.

There is little doubt that without the normative development dramatized by the Pact of Paris, the inclusion of the crime against peace in the London Charter would have seemed legalistically more problematic for reasons of retroactivity, which explains the failure to include "genocide" either as a distinct crime or under the category of crimes against humanity. The Nuremberg Judgment relied heavily on the Pact of Paris in building their case for the propriety of including the novel indictment for crimes against peace against these defendants, surviving Nazi leaders, climaxing with this dramatic yet misleading language: "to initiate a war of aggression, therefore, is not only an international crime, it is the supreme crime, different only from the other war crimes in that it contains within itself the accumulated evil of the whole."[27]

What emerges from viewing this wider century-long struggle to criminalize war as practice is a dominant sense of *geopolitical continuity* and *normative discontinuity*. This gap has created various tensions over the decades, which has more generally eroded respect for law-governed behavior in war/peace contexts and added confusion as to the content of international obligations pertaining to it.[28] The unfortunate result is regression with regard to the relevance of international law to this defining area of international life, while international law plays an increasingly important role in other domains, ranging from climate change to the world economy.[29] Despite the rejection of their normative determinism, the Hathaway/Shapiro approach is important because of its systemic contention that the manner by which international law deals with "war" as constitutive of the nature of world order in post-Westphalian international relations. The Hathaway and Shapiro line of argument seems more convincing, at least as measured by media and public opinion, than the main alternative explanation of the structure of world order by uncritical references to state-centrism and territorial sovereignty.

Hathaway and Shapiro view the evolution of this crucial sector of international law from a top-down perspective—that is, reflecting the formal commitments of governments as exemplified by the significance attributed to the Pact of Paris and the Nuremberg Judgment. In our view, they do not accord sufficient attention to the meta-legal impact of geopolitics that greatly constrains international criminal law in war/peace contexts, sometimes by way of impunity and at other times by way of discriminatory policies as in "victor's justice." What is even more absent from their study of how law alters the behavior of sovereign states is their disregard of the relevance of symbolic politics and a bottom-up "implementation" role in the application of international law by various forms of transnational civil society activism. In analyzing political resistance to aggression or oppressive governance, the successful waging of "legitimacy wars" to capture the high moral and legal ground has been most effective over the course of the last seventy-five years in curtailing the role of geopolitics in perpetuating international criminality. This has been especially evident in the major anti-colonial and regime-changing wars that have mostly been "won" at the level of normatively shaped symbolic politics despite military inferiority and combat defeats.[30] The Vietnam War is paradigmatic: the United States exercised military dominance in almost every dimension of combat, yet lost the war due to the perseverance and tactical ingenuity of national resistance, and the eventual unpopularity and expense of the war to the militarily superior side.[31]

The situation with respect to international accountability is related, but it is affected by somewhat different influences. The most relevant difference is that the legal evolution of accountability norms is consistent with the geopolitical continuity with respect to war as an instrument of national policy. This becomes clear by examining the Nuremberg experience in two parts: the Nuremberg Judgment and the Nuremberg Principles (as well as the ad hoc tribunals for former Yugoslavia and Rwanda established by the General Assembly).[32]

The Nuremberg Judgment[33]

In a typically paradoxical manner, among geopolitical actors in the course of the last century, the United States is both the principal proponent of a law-oriented and institutionally networked world order and the least willing to renounce its own sovereign prerogatives. In effect, law-governed behavior is good for others, especially adversaries, while conditioned on a cost/benefit calculus when it comes to itself or those enjoying "special relationships." In a sense this peculiar stance can be viewed as one of the negative sides of "American exceptionalism."[34] Such a paradoxical posture can be traced back to the leadership role played by the United States in the formation of the League of Nations, followed by its unwillingness to become a member.[35] To moderate this double movement at the end of World War II, the decision was made to locate the headquarters of the UN in the United States (preliminary meetings were also held in the United States—San Francisco, Turtle Bay, and Bretton Woods). This geographic Americanization of institutional internationalism has worked, as the United States has been a P5 member from the time of establishment of the UN and the largest funder of the organization. Yet the geopolitical, ecological, and militarist footprints of the United States have also been larger than of any country. It has used its leverage openly and via back channels to shape UN policy and to exert control over the behavior of its institutional leader, the secretary general, as well as to express displeasure, especially over the frequent clashes within the UN system arising from Israel's denials of Palestinian rights and reliance on excessive force.

The Nuremberg experience can be interpreted as exemplifying this paradoxical pattern. There is little doubt that a law-oriented approach to accountability for surviving Nazi political officials and military commanders would not have happened without US insistence. Churchill and Stalin would have proceeded by way of summary executions without the pretense, delay, expense, and hypocrisy of war crimes trials. Reflecting on the idea of normative determinism discussed in the prior section, neither Churchill nor Stalin seemed convinced that the rhetorical shift embodied in the Pact of Paris had any impact on the discretionary nature of war as the chief mechanism of dispute and conflict resolution in international political life, as well as believing that the gravity of German atrocities was so evident as to make trials a waste of time. The United States, in contrast, as epitomized by its wartime leader, Franklin D. Roosevelt, wanted to deliver both a just war message to the world and its own citizenry by showing that the political identity of the victorious powers was based on an ethos of fairness even to a defeated enemy accused of evil acts and at the same time build an antiwar and accountability narrative that would influence the future. There were other considerations at stake, including the recognition that the punitive manner of dealing with Germany after World War I created an atmosphere of humiliation that helped explain German receptivity to Hitler's demagogic message of depravity and revenge, and it was thus widely believed desirable to avoid postwar arrangements that seemed punitive to the German nation as a whole.

The reach of criminal accountability extended well beyond the prosecution of the twenty-one most prominent Germans who were perceived as playing leadership roles in the Nazi governance and military processes. The secondary Nuremberg trials reached many more Germans involved in the Nazi war-inducing and atrocity-generating operations, with separate trials of corporate managers, doctors, and other categories of defendants.

At the same time, the United States no less than its partners at Nuremberg had no difficulty exempting its own criminal acts from legal scrutiny. What Philippe Sands (2005) refers to in passing as a "strong whiff of 'victor's justice'" should not be allowed to distract commentators from the achievement of the Nuremberg approach, arguing that "there was no doubt that the case was catalytic, opening the possibility that the leaders of a country could be put on trial before an international court, something that had never happened before." And unlike the Pact of Paris, there seemed to be some greater resolve to integrate the Nuremberg experience into the evolving character of Westphalian world order, especially with respect to the second and third categories of Nuremberg crimes as prescribed by the London Charter, namely war crimes and crimes against humanity. It is notable that the first category of Nuremberg crimes, crimes against peace, have not been accompanied by any serious efforts in the course of eighties years to hold leading perpetrators of war crimes by sovereign state individually accountable, with the instructive example of the very dubious spectacle of the trial of Saddam Hussein in the aftermath of the Iraq War of 2003 in circumstances where it was particularly ironic as the "victor" was, from an international law perspective, also the aggressor in the war. The prosecutions of former Yugoslav and Rwandan leaders are also illustrative of non-geopolitical approaches in the setting of conflicts between or within second-tier sovereign states.

All the noteworthy post-Nuremberg governmental and international tribunals were concerned with war crimes or crimes against humanity, including the controversy over the extradition and prosecution of the Chilean dictator, Augusto Pinochet, the prosecutions of the Ad Hoc Tribunal for Former Yugoslavia and Rwanda, the attempted ICC prosecutions of Omar al Bashar of Sudan and Charles Taylor of Liberia.[36] In one respect it could be argued that this string of events, including institutional initiatives, was evidence of a serious intention to carry forward the Nuremberg experience, at least as bearing on the responsibility of individual leaders in the former colonial world to adhere to international legal standards of their behavior in combat situations, including within their sovereign territory. In another respect, these post-Nuremberg events reinforced the impression of geopolitical primacy, impunity for major countries, and double standards when it comes to imposing international legal accountability on individuals for their criminal wrongdoing.[37]

What has become evident over the years since the Nuremberg Judgment is a continuing struggle to uphold the ideas of criminal accountability for individuals, yet an undertaking subject to major geopolitical limitations and manipulations. The idea of exempting the crimes of the victor from legal scrutiny was obvious in the contexts of World War II and more recently with regard to the Iraq War.[38] Geopolitical interference with the application of international criminal law is also apparent in contexts of lost wars. The American defeat in the Vietnam War is widely acknowledged, yet there was no Vietnamese attempt, even symbolically, to do to the American aggressors anything comparable that was done to the Germans or the Japanese. True, the circumstances were dramatically different. There was no occupation of US territory, and Vietnam was devastated and preoccupied with the immense challenges of economic and societal recovery. As well, there were no practical means to gain personal jurisdiction over those alleged to be perpetrators of the main war policies. In addition, there was an utter unwillingness by the defeated country, the United States, to apply international criminal law to its leadership, or even to consider doing so. Vietnam could, in theory, have held a trial prosecuting such defendants as Robert McNamara, Henry Kissinger, and Richard Nixon in absentia, and compiling a just war narrative vindicating their victory.[39] It should be remembered that the main rationale for Nuremberg was not the punishment of these defendants but the pedagogical objective of controlling the narrative of the war without the Versailles mistake of imposing responsibility on the entire nation. Vietnam possessed the evidence to mount such a legal proceeding, and could have produced powerful testimony, including from antiwar American veterans. In fact, such a retributive undertaking collided with Vietnamese cultural predispositions to reconcile with former enemies once foreign troops departed. Vietnam seemed far more interested in achieving diplomatic and economic normalization with the United States after its historic success in upholding its central claim to exercise its right of self-determination. Legal vindication seemed irrelevant and unnecessary, and Vietnam very soon turned its attention to the brewing conflict with its former ally, China,[40] although it is true that, a half century after the Vietnam War, the country remains haunted by the environmental effects of Agent Orange, which continues to cause genetic disabilities among Vietnamese children exposed to stockpiles of the toxic chemical in the soil and underground water left behind by departing American forces.

That is, without a surrender by the alleged criminal government and the occupation of its homeland, implementation of even victor's justice is difficult, and restricted to such special circumstances that existed in Iraq after 2003, when the country was occupied and its offending leader, Saddam Hussein, was captured and put on trial by an Iraqi counter-elite put in charge of the country by its US/UK conquerors, but subject to the guidance and supervision of these intervening powers. A similar dynamic was present regarding the indictment of Slobodan Milosevic after the Kosovo War of 1999. In both settings, the governments responsible for what was declared at Nuremberg as "the supreme crime" escaped any formal legal scrutiny.[41]

Another source of limitation arises from prudential considerations of two main kinds. First of all, there is insufficient political will in many instances of conflict management to impose geopolitical enforcement by way of achieving a political victory followed by occupation and trials. For instance, the so-called First Gulf War deliberately refrained from pursuing regime-change, limiting its goals to restoring Kuwaiti sovereignty and teaching Iraq a lesson. Similarly, regarding reactions to crimes against humanity, even approaching genocide, there is present in many contexts the assessment that the effort to enforce international criminal law is too costly, unduly provocative, or inconsistent with geopolitical alignments—among many examples, interference with China's abusive treatment of the Uighur minority, Russia's oppressive treatment of Chechens and other minority peoples, and Israel's treatment of Palestinians. Such practical considerations discourage implementation even in the face of massive crimes against humanity, as was the case with India's criminal abuses of Kashmiris or Myanmar's genocidal assaults upon the Rohingya.[42]

Second are the limitations that arise internally from according "domestic peace" a priority over "implementing international criminal law." In the United States, President Barack Obama made clear shortly after he became president in 2008 that there would be no attempt to hold George W. Bush accountable for authorizing the torture of terrorist suspects in the aftermath of the 9/11 terrorist attacks in 2001. Obama explained his implicit grant of impunity to his predecessor by declaring that he was looking forward not backward in seeking to prohibit torture. Similarly, in Chile after the defeat of Pinochet in national elections, there was an ambiguous attitude of seeking accountability for past crimes as conditioned by worries about disturbing the transition to restored constitutional order in the state, especially given the continuing strength of the former governmental supporters, particularly in the armed forces and the police.[43]

In reaction to these limitations, which extend to the geopolitical constraints relative to UN operations, the main efforts to keep the struggle for criminal accountability alive have been waged by civil society activism, often borrowing the tribunal framing established at Nuremberg. This path was first pursued as a result of leadership provided by the British philosopher Bertrand Russell and highlighted through the establishment of the Russell Tribunal that investigated the allegations of criminality directed at the United States for its role in Vietnam, involving the participation of some legal experts but relying more heavily on moral authority figures with cultural and religious credentials (Duffett 1968; also continuation via Russell Foundation in Brussels). The impact of such tribunals can be partly evaluated by reference to compiling an accurate and useful legal narrative on accountability issues and for its impact on public opinion.[44] By now extensive experience has developed, perhaps most prominently evolved under the auspices of the Basso Foundation in Rome, and within a framework set by the Declaration of the Rights of Peoples. An important continuation of this kind of struggle of accountability was organized by a group of women in Istanbul in 2005 with a jury of conscience presided over by Arundhati Roy and a panel of experts (Sokmen 2008).

Beyond Nuremberg

Even though the Nuremberg Judgment was presented to the world as an appropriate, indeed admirable, example of forward-looking international jurisprudence because it accorded the accused defendants a fair trial—including due process, transparency, and competent defense counsel—there was a gnawing feeling that all was not right from the perspective of international criminal law. This was famously acknowledged even by Justice Robert Jackson, the chief prosecutor at Nuremberg, when he reminded the panel of judges assessing the guilt of these defendants that the quality of their legal conclusions would be tested by whether the law would be applied in the future to their own countries if the circumstances warranted such a process. In this liberal internationalist spirit, Nuremberg was seen as part of an accountability-strengthening *process* rather than an *event* to be interpreted as limited to its time/space zone of occurrence.[45]

In contrast, there were prominent Western skeptical voices that viewed Nuremberg as little other than a stage-managed show trial. There were several pointed dismissals of the Nuremberg experience by prominent legal figures in the United States, including the chief justice of the American Supreme Court, Harlan Fiske Stone, who called the trials "a sanctimonious fraud" or left-oriented Associate Justice William O. Douglas, who made the cogent point that Nuremberg was guilty of "substituting power for principle."[46] In effect, the skeptics in the West perceived Nuremberg not as a building block of accountability but as a flawed self-congratulatory event that exhibited the continuity and moral cynicism of geopolitics rather than a significant turn toward a law-governed world order. In contrast, the skeptics in Asia, most notably represented by Justice Pal's elaborate anti-imperial dissent in the Tokyo War Crimes Judgment, sharply challenged the use of law hypocritically as a platform for glamorizing the hegemony of the victors in the war.

Such perceptions, rather common among non-Western jurists, get the political animus wrong as it pertains to the attitudes toward the country to which the defendants belonged. In the aftermath of World War II, as distinct from World War I, the overriding motivation was to strengthen, not weaken, Germany (and Japan). One reason for supporting Nuremberg was to impose accountability on individuals while not acting punitively toward the German nation, and to thus end the war enmities, enabling the former enemies to be quickly treated as friends facing a new common adversary. After 1945, there were pressing reasons for this shift. There was a strong interest in restoring the devastated German economy, in part to address fears of a resumption of the Great Depression of the 1930 and in part to look ahead to the emergent geopolitical and ideological rivalry with the Soviet Union, where Germany was viewed by the West as a crucial potential ally.[47]

The UN General Assembly affirmed the principles of international law as contained in the London Charter and the Nuremberg Judgment in Resolution 95(I) that was unanimously passed, although there were several abstentions. A further step in incorporating the Nuremberg experience into authoritative international law was taken by requesting (in GA Res. 177(II)) an authoritative formulation of the Nuremberg Principles by the International Law Commission (an expert body charged with the codification and development of international law, and part of the UN system). In 1950, the text of the Nuremberg Principles was provided to the General Assembly, which sent the text to member states for comment. No further action was taken, but later formal action involving accountability proceeded on the basis of this Nuremberg framework, including the Ad Hoc Tribunal for Former Yugoslavia and the Ad Hoc Tribunal for Rwanda, as well as the Rome Statute framing the legal authority of the ICC.[48]

The Nuremberg Principles, and their operational relevance to later developments, is a major step forward, at least in the realm of *symbolic politics*, in the process of developing legal accountability for individuals under international criminal law. The first observation is to take note of the jurisprudential difference between the wartime context within which the London Charter was drafted and then applied by the Nuremberg Tribunal and the peacetime setting within which the Nuremberg Principles evolved. The London Charter was basically assimilated into the anti-European Axis alliance dynamics, adopted on August 8, 1945, apparently oblivious to the incredibly awkward timing, the date being situated between the two atomic bombs dropped on Japan, actions taken without even the benefit of a legal justification based on "military necessity." There seems little doubt that had the Japanese or Germans developed the atomic bomb before the United States and had used it against Allied cities after their governments already decided to accept defeat, the relevant defendants would have been prosecuted for the crime—the most memorable breach of law and morality in World War II other than the German death camps—if not by the international tribunal, then according to Article 4 of the Four Power Agreement, establishing the International Military Tribunal, which affirmed the commitment to "the return of war criminals to the countries where they committed their crimes."[49] It is hard to conceive of a more geographically specific potential crime than that of the atomic bombings, underscored by the purely symbolic judicial assessment made in response to the complaints brought by Japanese survivors.[50]

The public release of the London Charter is not only historically insensitive but the idea of framing a criminal trial by one side in a war would virtually guarantee conviction and remove discretion, even though the judges and prosecutors were chosen exclusively from the victorious powers.[51] For instance, the London Charter, rather than the Nuremberg judicial process, imposed the following guiding principles: that the defendants could not avoid legal responsibility because their alleged criminal acts were legal under *national* law or were done in response to *superior orders* of an official nature, nor could a defendant leader or government official claim *sovereign immunity*. These seem like reasonable doctrinal constraints, but the appearance of a more genuinely fair judicial process would have left these issues to the tribunal where there could have produced controversy if any of the appointed judges turned out to be legal skeptics in the face of such an orchestrated self-serving legal event.[52]

Perhaps more significantly, the Nuremberg Principles were submitted for endorsement to the General Assembly representing the entire membership of the UN, contrasting with the wartime alliance that drafted the London Charter, and were in turn entrusted for authoritative formulation to the apolitical body of legal experts within the UN system, the International Law Commission. But the legalization of the Nuremberg framework should not be exaggerated as overcoming the tendency toward the geopolitical manipulation of individual accountability for international crimes. As a matter of the development of law, the Nuremberg Principles were widely supported at the time, mainly to give added legitimacy after the events to what had transpired at Nuremberg through the initiative by four of the five permanent members of the Security Council. Such an endorsement of the legal framework at Nuremberg seemed an uncontroversial move, since, by and large, the anti-fascist, anti-Japanese imperialism war was viewed positively throughout the world. Properly considered, the Nuremberg Principles looked backward in legitimizing the post–World War II war crimes trials but also forward to set up a general framework based on the legal ideas that shaped the Nuremberg experience, but without the selectivity built into the process by aiming at only Axis survivors rather than all persons for whom evidence existed to support criminal prosecution. Needless to say, the retrospective validation of the Nuremberg Judgment was much less problematic than the prospective application promised by adopting the Nuremberg Principles and considering them as even deserving of a jus cogens status of irreversibility (Schwelb 2008).

Jurisprudentially, the Nuremberg Principles in scope, language, and prospective application were formulated without regard to geopolitical relevance, much less primacy, and have been widely regarded in liberal circles, and so interpreted, as a major innovation in international political life. The Nuremberg Principles as written threaten even the heads of the most powerful states: those who carry out state policies that were international crimes are subject to criminal accountability and denied the legal right to claim immunity from prosecution. As we have learned over the years, this generalization of the Nuremberg approach has been difficult, if not impossible, to implement on an international level.[53] Although there is no explicit or de jure veto as in the Security Council, ensuing practice has shown an equally effective de facto geopolitical veto.

Paradoxically, this Nuremberg framework has had more impact on *national transition politics* than on international politics, although here too there have been obstacles and pragmatic compromises. The most interesting compromise is to forgo the pursuit of criminal accountability for the sake of negotiating a peaceful transition and settling for some kind of peace and reconciliation commission that documents past wrongdoing, even identifying wrongdoers, but coupled with an understanding that amnesty will be accorded and criminal prosecutions not undertaken if perpetrators take part in whatever reconciliation mechanism is agreed upon. One kind of obstacle is to forgo accountability of those who committed international crimes in the past but have voluntarily given up political power in the present. The United States underwent a testing process to determine whether it would hold Donald Trump and his closest associates accountable *within* the American legal system. Given severe polarization in the United States, and the persisting strength of the Trumpist support base, attempts at prosecution would undoubtedly have given rise to unrest and quite likely insurrectionary violence. Yet given the flagrant character of criminality during the Trump presidency of 2017–21, the failure to take action struck a severe blow to rule of law claims that the American constitutional republic is ultimately governed by law, not men (and women). Now that the country and the world face a second term under Trump's leadership, the spirit of legality seems weaker than at any time since the founding of the Republic. The Biden presidency laid the groundwork for this by undercutting respect for international law by way of active complicity with the Gaza genocide and his refusal to engage in diplomacy to end the Ukraine War.

Without renouncing the prerogatives of "victor's justice" the geopolitical actors rely on a tacit grant of "impunity," reinforced by national legislative action, which is an offensive manner of resisting threats of international accountability.[54] As mentioned earlier, both the Kosovo War and the Iraq War gave rise to criminal prosecutions, although the wars were initiated in violation of the UN Charter's core principle—the leaders and officials of the attacked country faced war crimes tribunals. The treatment of Iraq in the First Gulf War of 1991 reproduced the discredited punitive peace diplomacy of Versailles by imposing harsh sanctions on those allegedly responsible for hundreds of thousands of deaths of innocent Iraqi civilians (von Sponeck 2005). The Trump presidency carried the logic of impunity to a political extreme by imposing sanctions targeting the ICC prosecutor for daring to investigate well-evidenced charges of US war crimes in Afghanistan.

The liberal view of this struggle for international accountability is to regard the process as gradual, uneven, but overall, going forward with momentum. The emphasis is placed on the various international tribunals that have been set up, with UN approval, after the occurrence of atrocities in warfare (as following the breakup of Yugoslavia) or genocidal internal struggle (as in Rwanda). Beyond this is the assertion that those charged are guilty of massive violations of international criminal law and yet receive a fair trial, including rights to offer a full defense, cross-examine witnesses, and make a statement in court. This liberal approach to international accountability, characteristically adopted by leading human rights NGOs, is to view as encouraging the developments of the last eighty years. As elsewhere, liberalism backs off in silence when structural contradictions arise. The liberal mentality accepts as a given that Western geopolitical actors and their allies enjoy impunity from criminal accountability regardless of their behavior, while military autocrats in sub-Saharan Africa are approvingly prosecuted. An extreme example was the appearance of Netanyahu as an honored speaker before a joint session of Congress despite being the chief perpetrator of an ongoing genocide in Gaza.

There is no question that there has been an accelerating, if uneven, momentum to strengthen international accountability procedures, but as the experience of warfare and the ICC has demonstrated, the geopolitical resistance to accountability is as strong as ever. This resistance is not even limited to impunity from prosecution. It extends to making selective use of accountability mechanisms to deal with adversaries (e.g., Milosevic in Serbia, Saddam Hussein in Iraq) as helpful for purposes of justifying foreign wars and "humanitarian interventions" (Chomsky 1999). There are two issues: first, is there any reason to be optimistic that the accountability momentum will gradually overcome this dynamic of geopolitical manipulation? There are no present signs of such a challenge being mounted to curtail geopolitical leverage, much less succeeding. Indeed, the trend toward autocratic leadership of national governing processes, accompanied by an ideological turn away from globalist undertakings and toward chauvinistic nationalism, is evidence of a turn away from all types of internationalism. Such a trend is openly dismissive of the struggle to achieve international criminal accountability and would seem even to be critical of the Nuremberg approach as hypocrisy, double standards, and power politics, contending, in effect, that straightforward revenge tactics would be more truthful. Our belief is that accountability gaps act as stimulants of civic activism and give rise to normative pedagogy that is grounded in the hope that strong governments as well as weaker ones need to be held to the same standards if international law is to be respected.

The second issue is suggested by this question: Does elemental justice not require that equals be treated equally in a legal regime that is premised on international accountability? The comparison here is between impunity for geopolitical actors and accountability for the rest. Such a jurisprudential postulate rejects the liberal view that, as long as those convicted and punished are guilty as charged and receive a fair trial, the legal process is doing the best that can be expected.

Having pointed to the persistence of geopolitical primacy as a significant shortcoming of the struggle to extend the Nuremberg Principles to the most serious international criminal activities, should we pronounce the quest for accountability a failure and abandon all legal efforts to challenge the international crimes of geopolitical actors? On this issue, we definitely affirm the ethos of the Nuremberg Principles as expressed by reliance on universalist language. We also affirm the various efforts of civil society activism to extend the coverage of accountability procedures. The unfinished drama associated with efforts of the ICC to investigate Israeli and US crimes in Occupied Palestine and Afghanistan is an important challenge to impunity. The heightened threat posed to impunity is illuminated by the fury of the pushback in Jerusalem and Washington. Even without any prospect of obtaining jurisdiction over Israeli or US defendants, much less enforcement, an ICC challenge has political impacts taking the form of the delegitimizing effects of even a preliminary investigation.[55] A similar indication of extreme sensitivity to allegations of Israeli crimes was exhibited by the

Israeli reaction to the Goldstone Report in 2009, a fact-finding report that presented extensive evidence of Israeli war crimes during its Operation Cast Lead attack on Gaza in 2008–9. Israel reacted similarly to the 2017 ESCWA (Economic and Social Commission on West Asia) report on whether to consider Israeli practices and policies a violation of the prohibition against apartheid (Falk and Tilley 2017).

In this regard, the struggle for legal accountability creates opportunities and responsibilities to make the Nuremberg Principles live up to their explicit positivist mandate with respect to the impunity exclusions on the one side and the inappropriate geopolitical manipulations on the other. There is a new form of global movement politics that joins in coalition transnational civil society activism and those governments that favor a law-governed world order on issues of international peace, security, and justice.

Returning a final time to the Hathaway/Shapiro argument that the Pact of Paris started a process of remaking the world: in our contrary view, a benevolent process of remaking the world would entail minimizing geopolitical leverage and enhancing the forms of global governance responsive to the public good of humanity.[56] We would be somewhat more sympathetic with an argument that anchored the remaking the world hypothesis in 1950, the time that the Nuremberg Principles were authoritatively endorsed, although this, too, might be persuasively dismissed as a wild exaggeration, given international experience over the course of the last seventy-plus years. Perhaps a more promising focus for such a radical idea is the UN Treaty on the Prohibition of Nuclear Weapons (TPNW) that came into force in early 2021 after receiving fifty formal ratifications (in the face of strenuous objections from the United States, the United Kingdom, and France). The implementation of this treaty would be a major victory over the geopolitical right of exception with regard to nuclear weapons and posit disarmament as a demilitarizing alternative to the present nuclear apartheid regime that is as explicit as the UN veto in vesting authority to opt out of international legal obligations.[57] In the end, it is our unhappy conclusion that ideas capable of remaking the world exist but, so far, none have achieved sufficient political traction to give rise to rational transformative expectations.[58] And yet, given the fragilities of the human condition, the struggle for accountability should continue to be pursued. The complexities of an ecologically unstable world living perilously with nuclear weapons arsenals requires global governance that includes universally applicable accountability procedures and institutions, and not only as part of the normative architecture. Without consistent implementation of accountability, norms in relation to the most powerful states would still leave most people of the world vulnerable to the primacy of geopolitics and the excesses of state-centrism. The paths leading to implementation involve self-restraint and the emergence of widely shared beliefs in the reciprocal benefits of a global governance structure that is enforceable against all political actors.

Notes

1   In the United States, walking the tightrope that connects being both a leading liberal democracy and a dominant geopolitical actor is rhetorically handled in domestic policy debates by speaking of "wars of aggression" as "wars of choice."

2   But see Klein on disaster capitalism (2008): the devastation and human disaster of war being converted into an opportunity for reconstruction, investment, and renewal of production.

3   See Graham (2018) and Sherwin (2020); a cold war with China would likely be a very different experience than with USSR due to weapons innovations, the backgrounding of ideological differences, and the more directly competitive approaches to investment and trade, especially in the Global South.

4   See Chomsky (1999) for a recent critique of hiding geopolitical motivations behind a fog of justification. It is not only claims of humanitarian intervention and Responsibility to Protect (R2P) but the failure to act consistently, as when abuses are not addressed at the global level.

5   It is illuminating to appreciate the general reliability of international law in bringing stability and predictability to routine transactions across borders in which reciprocity exists, as in diplomatic protocol, international maritime and air safety regulations, communications networks, and others policy domains where a regulatory framework is mutually beneficial regardless of differences in relative power. And the frustration of most efforts to extend international law to achieve similar results is in asymmetric situations where relative power differentials and antagonistic strategic interests are salient.

6   The *critical realists* include system theorists in the Wallerstein tradition, Marxists, and anti-imperialists; the *new realists* are preoccupied with fashioning responses to the bio-ethical-eco crisis of our time, and reconceptualize world order by reference to three levels of overlap and interaction: state-to-state, hegemonic states-to-law-and-order, and transnational civil society; also, rebalancing and reconceptualizing the relations of whole and part.

7   Allegations of the use of chemical weapons by the Syrian government was a red line, the crossing of which justified a retaliatory strike that did not reflect international legal prerogatives. It reflected geopolitical managerial directives; the debate about the Douma chemical weapons attack in April 2018 was not about legal prerogatives, but about the validity of the accusations by the evidence by the UN agency.

8   Hathaway and Shapiro do not want to connect the origins of OWO with Westphalia, which they interpret as mainly concerned with curtailing the bases for the struggles between Catholic and Protestant polities in the period of the Holy Roman Empire and not concerned with the legal status of war as an instrument of national policy. See Kegley and Raymond (2001).

9   See Davutoglu (2020) for a more convincing analysis of systemic change at the global level.

10   See their earlier treatment of the effort to prosecute the German leader Wilhelm Kaiser after WWI, as mandated by the Versailles Treaty (Hathaway and Shapiro 2018, 249–98).

11   This is covered in Pinker (2011), but as discussed in chapter 6, data-driven views of "peace" tend to be deceptive and existentially unconvincing.

12   Such a rosy portrayal of the decline of war overlooks the catastrophic risks associated with the existence of nuclear weapons and the moral and opportunity costs of preparing for a war that deliberately targets tens of millions of innocent civilians. See discussion in chapter 6 and Thompson (1982).

13   Compare George H. W. Bush on Soviet collapse as enabling the implementation of the anti-aggression norm at the UN but also note the rapid abandonment of the language and practice of this version of "new world order" after Kuwaiti sovereignty was restored. Washington made it clear that the Bush advocacy was a one-time commitment designed to mobilize support and legitimate the use of international force. There was no political will present to seize upon the collective security response to Iraqi aggression, and attempted territorial conquest, as offering an opportunity to fulfill the UN Charter expectation of establishing a collective security system set up to protect future victims of aggression. As the uncontested geopolitical leader after the Soviet collapse, it became clear that the United States did not want its geopolitical hands tied when future security issues arose.

14   But see Judge Pal's (1948) dissenting opinion that does not question the validity of the norm but its applicability to Japanese recourse to war.

15   For Hathaway and Shapiro, reliance on Pact of Paris is decisive; for relevant discussion, see Taylor (1992); Sands (2005).

16   See literature on Charter prohibition in Henkin (1968); Reisman (1984); McDougal and Feliciano (1961).

17   For example, the *Goldstone Report* on the Israeli attack on Gaza in 2008–9 did not even consider whether the initial Israeli attack was legal or not but just concentrated on the relevance of norms to the weaponry and tactics used by the two sides.

18   Although addressing the flaws of the Tokyo Tribunal, Richard Minear's *Victor's Justice* (1971) is equally relevant to Nuremberg.

19   Kissinger, Morgenthau, and Kennan are typical exponents of realism in foreign policy (referred to throughout this book as "political realists," and in previous articles as "old realists.")

20   See also Sherwin (2020), which shows that normative inhibitions played almost no role in avoiding nuclear war, and rational calculations have a relevance, but less than psycho-political factors, as in poker.

21   See Sorensen (2020). Additional factors are also present—including ideological rivalry, leadership, and nationalism—that exert varying degrees of influence with respect to war-proneness.

22   Perhaps the most authoritative confirmation of the prohibition of aggressive recourse to war was formulated in the majority opinion of the ICJ decision in the *Nicaragua v. United States* case (ICJ 1986).

23 The failures of militarism in colonial wars and regime-changing interventions to achieve positive results at acceptable costs had less of a war-reducing impact than might have been expected. It exposed the internal factors that led to exaggerated external threat perceptions and private sector high stakes in global militarism (see chapter 5).

24 Syria also had similar proxy features; parallel arguments with respect to regime-changing interventions generating endless wars and failed states as in Libya, Afghanistan, Iraq; see Franklin (2018).

25 At the UN and ICJ, greater emphasis has been placed on the prohibition and proliferation of nuclear weapons than on the antiwar norm. See, for instance, the UN Treaty on the Prohibition on Nuclear Weapons (UNGA 2017), also highlighting the tensions between nuclear weapons states and the rest of the world community.

26 For an argument against seeking legal accountability for crimes of state committed within a geopolitical actor, see Posner (2020).

27 Note Sands (2016) on the differing views of the two most influential jurists behind the scenes, Lauterpacht emphasizing the aggressive war dimension whereas Lemkin emphasized the genocide, human rights dimension as the "supreme crime"; for Lemkin became for him the "Nuremberg nightmare" as the exclusion of any mention of genocide in the Nuremberg Judgment became "the bleakest day" in his life. It is important to understand that the jurisprudential background of Nuremberg was shaped by European international law scholarship that was overwhelmingly shaped by the legal positivist school (in reaction to the religious, moral, and imperial background of the "just war doctrine.") In this regard, the American embrace of "legal realism" or a more sociological approach to international law had almost no influence.

28 The allusion to "law-governed foreign policy" should not be confused with Antony Blinken's advocacy of an undefined "rules-governed world," which treated "rules" as a way of distinguishing the behavior of democracies from that of autocratic adversaries, or, more bluntly, US state propaganda.

29 With the rise of ultranationalist leaders around the world, there is a definite decline in attention to the rule of law either internationally or internally, and hence, to efforts seeking to impose accountability for crimes of state. Whether this pattern is a temporary phenomenon or expressive of a continuing trend is difficult to discern at this time.

30 For exposition of the legitimacy war argument, see Falk (2014), with emphasis on the Palestinian national struggle. Some political outcomes do reflect military balances despite legitimacy war outcomes, for example, Tibet.

31 This assessment explored in Andersson (2017).

32 See the UN ad hoc criminal tribunals to deal with serious crimes in former Yugoslavia and Rwanda, formally known as International Criminal Tribunal for Rwanda and the International Criminal Tribunal for the Former Yugoslavia.

33 The Tokyo Judgment is also worthy of scrutiny, but the interest here is on the larger ramifications of the accountability efforts, and these seemed to

be dominated by the Nuremberg undertaking, perhaps in part reflecting Western preoccupations with European victimization by Hitler's wars and the emergence of fascism; this is not to say that the Japanese experience is not relevant to the themes under consideration. Because of the economic strangulation of Japan, the victors' justice argument was more clearly articulated. See Pal (1948); Minear (1971). In the Nuremberg context, the composition of the Court and the binding guidelines of the London Charter indicated a clear intention to control the legal narrative in a manner vindicating the West's just war justifications, which meant excluding the causative relevance of punitive peace diplomacy after World War I.

34   For exploration of American exceptionalism, see Ignatieff (2005).

35   The same pattern of engagement and withdrawal by the US government is evident in many different settings, including the Law of the Sea Treaty and the Genocide Convention, and of course, in relation to the League of Nations.

36   Also, the International Criminal Tribunal for Rwanda, a UN mechanism addressing serious crimes associated with the 1994 genocide.

37   Not only relating to war and peace, but human rights, humanitarian intervention, and accountability.

38   Although over time, the victory became questionable; in modern settings, the battlefield outcomes may not tell who eventually wins the war.

39   See the backlash unleashed by the MyLai massacre that was kept secret as long as possible in Hersh (1970).

40   An interesting question is whether this concern with outlawing war and imposing accountability was a largely Western project with little resonance in non-Western societies, which viewed history through the lens of harmony and chaos rather than legal and moral right and wrong. On the continuing significance of the Vietnam War, see Andersson (2017).

41   In the Kosovo context, an International Commission was established to examine legal allegations and report to the UN secretary general—it made a judgment; Canada Commission on State Sovereignty and Intervention evaded the accountability issues and came up with the R2P approach.

42   Although the Gambian recourse to the ICJ on charges of genocide is an instance of seeking an outcome that imposes a kind of accountability in the realm of symbolic politics.

43   See the Pinochet case in Woodhouse (2000).

44   Also as movement networking and transnational antiwar politics that is people-oriented rather than governmentally driven; see Cubukcu (2018).

45   In effect, the law was directed only at these German defendants, with the acts of the victors immune from scrutiny, but would the countries that convened the Nuremberg Tribunal live within the legal standards it had set forth, and if so, offer a retroactive validation of Nuremberg? (Jaspers 1953).

46   As quoted by Pathak, an article that can only be read as an anti-Nuremberg screed, with an opening sentence that expresses its outlook: "The Nuremberg Tribunal had virtually been victor's justice with sanctimonious scam and

lynching body rather than a free, and fair body. The war winner USA and its allied victors established threatocracy and crowdocracy against the poor victim and defeated war loser nation to further discourage and further weaken them" (2020, 2).

47 After WWI, the contrasting idea of the peace diplomacy was to weaken Germany as a future military threat and to punish it by way of reparations burdens. Note also the neglect of any attention in WWII peace diplomacy to the supposed transformative impact of the Hathaway/Shapiro argument about the Pact of Paris initiating a world-changing dynamic of which Nuremberg was a major confirming development, although the norm prohibiting aggressive war became the core idea of the UN Charter as drafted and anchored in the featured finding of crimes against peace at Nuremberg.

48 See the Moscow Declaration of 1943 (United Nations Information Organization 1943). See Darton (2020), for comprehensive coverage of documentary material associated with the Nuremberg tradition.

49 The complainants in Shimoda were seeking token damages to make clear that the concern was the legal status of the atomic attacks, not compensation for injury and suffering. See Falk (1965).

50 The Japanese Tribunal was less orchestrated, and the results revealed the difference, with a touch of irony: the Nuremberg Judgment has received the bulk of commentary despite the somewhat more neutral framing of the Tokyo Judgment.

51 See London Charter, Articles 7 and 8; Article 12 authorizes prosecution of an absent defendant if the situation warrants (United Kingdom et al. 1945).

52 Along the lines of criticisms referred to above by Pathak (2020).

53 From the outset, as Article 107 of the UN Charter made clear, the defeated countries were still considered threats to the postwar order established by the victors.

54 For example, the congressional Act known as The Hague Invasion Act which protects US servicemen from criminal prosecution by an international tribunal.

55 Past experience has shown that even without formal legal decisions, persons accused of war crimes in the public domain are reluctant to travel to countries with domestic legislation giving courts universal jurisdiction over enumerated international crimes.

56 This outlook can be given more conceptual and institutional content by referring to "global mechanisms" charged with promoting and protecting "the human interest" as distinct from the national interest and involved the autonomy and enlarged the budgets of the institutional venues making up the UN system and related transnational and other actors so oriented.

57 See critique of the NPT regime as both hegemonic and selectively implemented in chapter 7.

58 The emergence of an ecologically oriented civilizational structure is one such approach.

References

Allison, Graham. 2018. *Destined for War: Can America and China Escape the Thucydides's Trap?* Boston: Houghton Mifflin Harcourt.

Andersson, Stefan, ed. 2017. *Revisiting the Vietnam War and International Law: Views and Interpretations of Richard Falk.* Cambridge: Cambridge University Press.

Bull, Hedley. 1968. "The Grotian Conception of International Society." In *Diplomatic Investigations: Essays in the Theory of International Politics*, edited by H. Butterfield and Martin Wight, 51–73. Cambridge, MA: Harvard University Press.

Bull, Hedley. 1977. *The Anarchic Society: A Study of Order in World Politics.* London: Palgrave.

Chilcot, John. 2016. *Report of the Iraq Inquiry.* UK House of Commons, July 6.

Chomsky, Noam. 1999. *The New Military Humanism: Lessons from Kosovo.* Chicago: Pluto Press.

Coffman, Edward M. 1998. *The War to End All Wars.* Lexington: University Press of Kentucky.

Cubukcu, Ayca. 2018. *For the Love of Humanity: The World Tribunal on Iraq.* Philadelphia: University of Pennsylvania Press.

Darnton, Geoffrey, ed. 2020. *Nuclear Weapons and International Law*, 3rd ed. Dorset, UK: Durotriges Press.

Davutoglu, Ahmet. 2020. *Systemic Earthquake and the Struggle for World Order.* Cambridge: Cambridge University Press.

Duffett, John, ed. 1968. *Against the Crime of Silence: Proceedings of the Russell International War Crimes Tribunal.* New York: Simon & Schuster.

Falk, Richard. 1965. "The Shimoda Case: A Legal Appraisal of the Atomic Attacks upon Hiroshima and Nagasaki." *American Journal of International Law* 59: 759–93.

Falk, Richard. 2014. *Palestine: The Legitimacy of Hope.* Washington, DC: Just World Books.

Falk, Richard. 2017. "What the Chilcot Report Teaches Us." *International Journal of Contemporary Iraqi Studies* 11: 13–22.

Falk, Richard, and Virginia Tilley. 2017. *Israeli Practices Regarding the Palestinian People and the Question of Apartheid.* UN Economic and Social Commission on West Asia (ESCWA), Beirut. https://aardi.org/wp-content/uploads/2020/04/ESCWA-2017-Richard-Falk-Apartheid.pdf.

Franklin, Bruce. 2018. *Crash Course: From the Good War to Forever Wars.* New Brunswick, NJ: Rutgers University Press.

Hathaway, Oona A., and Scott J. Shapiro. 2018. *The Internationalist: How a Radical Plan to Outlaw War Remade the World.* New York: Simon & Schuster.

Heller, Kevin Jon. 2012. *The Nuremberg Military Tribunals and the Origins of International Criminal Law.* Oxford: Oxford University Press.

Henkin, Louis. 1968. *How Nations Behave.* New York: Colombia University Press.

Hersh, Seymour. 1970. *MyLai 4: A Report on the Massacre and Its Aftermath.* New York: Random House, Inc.

Ignatieff, Michael. ed. 2005. *American Exceptionalism and Human Rights.* Princeton, NJ: Princeton University Press.

Ikenberry, John G. 2020. *Prospects for a World Safe for Democracy: Liberalism and the Crisis of Democracy.* New Haven, CT: Yale University Press.

International Court of Justice (ICJ). 1986. *Nicaragua v. United States of America, Military and Paramilitary Activities.* Judgment of June 27, 1986. http://www.icj-cij.org.

Jaspers, Karl. 1953. *Origin and Goal of History.* London: Routledge.

Kegley, Charles W., and Gregory A. Raymond. 2001. *Exorcising the Ghost of Westphalia: Building World Order in the New Millennium.* London: Pearson.

Klein, Naomi. 2008. *The Shock Doctrine: The Rise of Disaster Capitalism.* London: Picador.

McDougal, Myres S., and Florentino P. Feliciano. 1961. *Law and Minimum World Order.* New Haven, CT: Yale University Press.

Minear, Richard. 1971. *Victor's Justice: The War Crimes Trial.* Princeton, NJ: Princeton University Press.

Pal, Radhabinod. 1948. "Judgement." In B. V. A. Roling and C. F. Riter, *Tokyo Judgment: The International Military Tribunal for the Far East, April 29 to November 12, 1946.* Amsterdam: APA-University Press.

Pathak, Bishnu. 2020. *Nuremberg Tribunal: A Precedent for Victor's Justice.* Transnational Media Service, September 21.

Pinker, Steven. 2011. *The Better Angels of Our Nature: Why Violence Has Declined.* London: Penguin.

Posner, Eric. 2020. "Why Prosecuting Trump Is a Very Bad Idea." *New York Times,* December 4.

Reisman, W. M. 1984. "Article 2(4): The Use of Force in Contemporary International Law." *Proceedings of the Annual Meeting (American Society of International Law)* 78: 74–87. http://www.jstor.org/stable/25658214 (accessed September 15, 2024).

Sands, Philippe. 2005. *Lawless World: America and the Making and Breaking of Global Rules.* London: Penguin.

Sands, Philippe. 2016. *East West Street: On the Origins of "Genocide" and Crimes Against Humanity.* New York: Vintage.

Schell, Jonathan. 1982. *The Fate of the Earth.* New York: Knopf.

Schwelb, Egon. 2008. "Crimes Against Humanity." In *Perspectives on the Nuremberg Trial,* edited by Guénaël Mettraux, 120–65. Oxford: Oxford University Press.

Sherwin, Martin. 2020. *Gambling with Armageddon: Nuclear Roulette from Hiroshima to the Cuban Missile Crisis.* New York: Knopf.

Sokmen, Muge Gersoy. 2008. *War Tribunal on Iraq: Making the Case Against War.* New York: Olive Branch Press.

Sorensen, Christian. 2020. *Understanding the War Industry.* Atlanta, GA: Clarity Press.

Stone, Julius. 1954. *Legal Controls of International Conflict.* New York: Rinehart & Co.

Taylor, Telford. 1992. *The Anatomy of the Nuremberg Trials.* New York: Skyhorse.

Thompson, E. P. 1982. "Notes on Extremism, the Last Stage of Civilization." In *Beyond the Cold War,* by E. P. Thompson, 6–13. Nova Iorque: Pantheon Books.

United Kingdom of Great Britain and Northern Ireland, United States of America, France and Union of Soviet Socialist Republics. 1945. *Charter of the International Military Tribunal—Annex to the Agreement for the Prosecution and Punishment of the Major War Criminals of the European Axis (London Charter)*. United Nations, August 8. https://www.refworld.org/legal/constinstr/un/1945/en/21123 (accessed June 14, 2024).

United Nations General Assembly (UNGA). 2017. *Treaty on the Prohibition of Nuclear Weapons*. Res. 71/258. March/July, New York. https://documents.un.org/doc/undoc/gen/n16/466/69/pdf/n1646669.pdf.

United Nations Information Organization. 1943. *Moscow Declaration on Atrocities*. London: United Nations, November 1.

von Sponeck, H. C. 2005. *A Different Kind of War: The Sanctions Regime in Iraq*. New York: Berghahn Books.

Walt, Stephen, and John J. Mearsheimer. 2006. "The Israel Lobby and US Foreign Policy." *KSG Faculty Research Working Paper Series* RWP06-011, March.

Woodhouse, Diane, ed. 2000. *The Pinochet Case: A Legal and Constitutional Analysis*. London: Hart Publishing.

11

Peoples' Tribunals and the Peace Movement's Quest for Justice

The Judicial Dimension of Global Governance

As with the implementation of international law, in general, the role of courts in providing dispute settlement and accountability for perpetrators of violations of international law has, in form and practice, displayed the consequences of state-centricism, sovereign rights, and geopolitical primacy. As indicated in earlier chapters, the implementation of international law by way of the decisions of international tribunals is often denied implementation. This more often occurs if the legal proceeding has rested upon the "advisory opinion" jurisdiction of the ICJ as delimited in the Statute of the International Court of Justice. Nullification also occurs frequently if the rulings are geopolitically controversial as subject to the exercise of the right of veto if implementation by the United Nations (UN) is needed.

The work of the International Criminal Court (ICC) has been subject to different lines of appraisal. In the past the ICC has been blamed for focusing far too much on alleged criminality of Global South leaders while failing to investigate and seek the prosecution of Global North perpetrators of international crimes, for example, in Afghanistan or Occupied Palestine. It is reasonable to conclude that international courts, despite their institutional affiliations, are not able to implement international law where it is most needed. There are exceptions in those rare instances where geopolitical actors are in agreement or not involved. This negative assessment should not be interpreted to mean that international judicial action is useless in relation to challenges of implementation and accountability but rather that it must be informally produce enforcement initiatives by stimulating creative civic action.

As suggested, such internationalist approaches are subject to the constraints on UN effectiveness with respect to achieving *behavioral* compliance. Yet even intergovernmentally such tribunals remain useful in the *symbolic* domains of global politics, exerting an influence on media treatments and civil society activism by its determinations of the competing legal claims of political antagonists.

It is against this background that the formation of peoples' tribunals occurred and, over time, attained significance in the context of global governance. This was especially true in settings of conflicts engaging geopolitical actors or substantive issues that national courts were generally unable or reluctant to address. The first important such undertaking involved the Russell Tribunal established during the Vietnam War and, while summarily dismissed by Western media and Western governments as without "legal" or political relevance, managed to persuade a distinguished cast of known international personalities to become members of its jury of conscience dedicated to upholding international law on the basis of abundant incriminating evidence. The outcome was transcribed and disseminated in various formats, offering the public a comprehensive, persuasive, and credible documented record of war crimes committed by the United States in Vietnam.

After the Russell experience, civil society tribunal mechanisms have been developed as a valuable tool of populist opposition to controversial wars, human rights abuses, and ecological wrongdoing. In this respect, these society generated judicial mechanisms have gained relevance to issues of implementation, accountability, and citizen engagement in relation to global governance, and to a certain extent have mounted challenges to media complacency, state propaganda, and normative repression that is present when geopolitics and international law are in tension.

After the World War II, a legal and moral threshold was crossed. Leaders of Germany and Japan were held individually responsible for their contributions to state crimes committed by individuals on behalf of their governments during the war at special tribunals established for this single high-profile set of criminal indictments and prosecutions. It was flawed to the extent that it exempted even notorious crimes of the winners from legal scrutiny, making the formal tribunals into *political* actors, which used law as a medium for the one-sided endorsement of the norms of international criminal law. The official tribunals were at least constructed in ways that satisfied due process expectations and, therefore, proceeded without a vindictive edge, although several German defendants chose suicide rather than endure the indignity of trial and punishment.

These trials at Nuremberg and Tokyo were heralded at the time as the start of a new era for the rule of law, which meant that political and military leaders would no longer be able to benefit from sovereign immunity to avoid legal accountability for their alleged criminality by rationalizations based on following "superior orders." Up until then, acts of states were effective in placing the behavior of political leaders and military commanders beyond formal legal scrutiny and either left unpunished or victimized by revenge scenarios of the battlefield victor. It was naively supposed that there would be in the future individual responsibility for political leaders and military commanders based on international criminal law, which was to be given precedence over any claims based on national sovereignty, the exclusive authority of domestic law, and the primacy of geopolitics. In other words, the post–World War II experience of holding Germans and Japanese responsible was approvingly conceptualized by liberal public opinion and reflected in the treatment of these issues by the most influential media platforms as a stepping stone to accountability for winners as well as losers. It is our view that this desirable development did not occur, and will not, until the primacy of geopolitics is effectively curbed, or the nature of geopolitics is transformed into a source of global law governance.

It was obvious at the time to more sensitive observers that "victors' justice" could not satisfy the requirements of a "regime of law," much less fulfill requirements of "justice" and prudence. The American chief prosecutor at Nuremberg, Justice Robert H. Jackson, acknowledged in his closing statement such an anomaly with this widely quoted language: "If certain acts in violation of treaties are crimes, they are crimes, whether the United States does them or whether Germany does them. We are not prepared to lay down a rule of criminal conduct against others that we would not be willing to have invoked against us" (Avalon Project 1945). Contrary to Justice Jackson's high-minded expectations, the United States and its allies would insist to live in the future with impunity for themselves and accountability for their adversaries.

In recent years, such adversary leaders, including Slobodan Milosevic and Saddam Hussein, were indicted for war crimes, while such Western stalwarts as George W. Bush and Tony Blair have not even been *investigated* for possible charges in relation to the initiation of an aggressive war against Iraq in 2003 that had punishing effects on a large segment of Iraqi civilian society (Ismael et al. 2024). There are signs of a more detached approach of national courts faced with allegations of criminality by the territorial government. In 2023, the Center for Constitutional Rights (CCC), a respected US nongovernmental organization (NGO), initiated a legal action in American Court charging Biden, Blinken, and Austin with complicity in carrying out the crime of genocide alleged being committed in Gaza by Israel (CCR 2023).

Civil Society Justice

Beyond this historical context created by the Vietnam War, the Russell experience did accomplish its purpose of speaking truth to power, establishing through the adaptation of a tribunal format the viability and worth of such a symbolic undertaking. An influential and progressive Italian jurist and legislator, Lelio Basso, inspired by this civil society experiment in his role as a member of the Russell Tribunal process, moved to establish what at first was called "Russell II," but later developed its own framework and adopted the name of Permanent Peoples' Tribunal (PPT), headquartered in Rome, which is still operative.

It developed a textual framework to guide its operations in the form of a Declaration of the Rights and Liberation of Peoples, and therefore positioned its various inquiries as people-oriented, as distinct from the state-centrism of the United Nations and other international institutions (PPT 1976). Over the course of years since its founding in the 1970s, the PPT has organized some fifty sessions of its tribunal, addressing such neglected international issues as military interventions in third world countries, the rights of indigenous peoples in Brazil and ecological devastation in Amazonia, the Marcos dictatorship in the Philippines, the predatory behavior of corporate capitalism under conditions of economic globalization, and the 1915 Armenian genocide. Many of the sessions resulted in published volumes of testimony and commentary that provided readers with a comprehensive and well-documented account of important issues that had been otherwise neglected or manipulated by governments and the UN.

This model was also imitated and adapted to the particular outlook of the main organizers in a number of national settings unaffiliated with the PPT. In 2000, a moving and quite influential peoples' tribunal was set up in Tokyo to inquire into the use of "comfort women" by imperial Japan. Perhaps the most extensive and spontaneous of these civil society initiatives arose in response to the American-led invasion and occupation of Iraq in 2003. In different parts of the world, including in the United States, twenty preliminary sessions examined various allegations of criminality connected with the Iraq War, culminating in the 2005 Iraq War Tribunal in Istanbul at which fifty-four experts and witnesses testified. A distinguished jury assessed the charges and wrote a strong condemnation of the role played by the United States and the United Kingdom, as well as by corporations and private contractors. The results of this initiative are explicated and appraised in Sokmen (2008) and Cubukcu (2018).

Investigating State Criminality

The Russell initiative of the 1960s has endured through the work of the Russell Foundation, now located in Brussels, that organizes civil society inquiries into state criminality in various controversial situations. In recent years, it has given primary attention to the Israel–Palestine conflict, organizing four sessions in different cities to explore the dimensions of war crimes charges arising from Israel's behavior in the Palestinian territories occupied since 1967. Its investigative activities include examinations of the complicity of global corporations and criminal charges of apartheid associated with Israel's repressive occupation of Palestine, featuring constant collective punishment, discriminatory laws, policies and practices, and persistent violations of international humanitarian law that support the view that Israel intends the occupation since 1967 to become permanent and irreversible.

In September 2014, in response to the Israeli attack on Gaza, given the code name Operation Protective Edge, the Russell Foundation convened an event in Brussels in which a jury of conscience listened to evidence relevant to the allegations of Israeli criminality and particularly considered charges of "genocide" put forward by critics of the attack. This kind of proceeding, because of the personalities involved, made some impact on the media and had a beneficial effect on public awareness, but it had no discernible influence over Israel's behavior on the ground.

As with the Russell initiatives in response to the Vietnam War, these civil society pronouncements have consistently encountered dismissive criticisms, and the Brussels initiative was no exception. It was criticized as lacking in legal authority and failing to appreciate the security situation facing Israel as a result of hundreds of Hamas rockets launched against its population. To put this argument in perspective, it is helpful to note that the UN has never acted to protect the people of Gaza or to challenge Israel's legal entitlement to carry out massive and unlawfully disproportionate attacks against an occupied people who lacked any means of defense and for their security were forced to rely on Israel's legal duty of, as the occupying power, to protect the civilian population under its supposedly temporary control.

It should also be observed that the Brussels Tribunal failed to uphold the most serious charge leveled against Israel in relation to Protective Edge: that the massive assault carried out against the defenseless civilian population of Gaza constituted genocide. On the basis of the evidence presented, the jury in Brussels did agree that Israel was guilty of the lesser crime of "incitement to genocide" as set forth in Article 3(c) of the Genocide Convention. It also agreed that the additional treaty duty to prevent genocide had definitely been violated by Israeli behavior and its enablers during Protective Edge. Unlike the original Russell Tribunal in relation to the Vietnam War, the initiative to expose Israeli criminality was more a response to "indifference" and "complicity" than to "silence" and "active engagement," although in both instances the effort was made in the shadows cast by the failures of organized international society to adopt effective measures to uphold the rule of law in a wartime situation.

Such tribunals are created almost always in exceptional circumstances of defiance of the most elemental constraints of international law and morality. Despite their limitations, peoples' tribunals have the potential to make crucial contributions to public awareness in situations where geopolitical realities preclude any reliance on established institutional procedures. Such initiatives exemplify and foreshadow the spirit of "a patriotism to humanity," which is not yet strong enough to challenge traditional modern patriotism with its passionate attachment to the nation, tending to withhold judgment on what its government undertakes in the name of foreign policy. The reactions of the Global South and of the younger generation of adults in the Global North to the Israeli genocide in Gaza is a glimmer of hope that "humanity," rather than "nationality," is becoming a significant signifier of political identity, at least in extreme situations.[1]

When strong interests of the West are at stake, as in the Ukraine, Kosovo, and Qaddafi's Libya, there is usually less need to activate unofficial international law initiatives through the agency of civil society. However, in circumstances such as resulted from the United States' and Western Europe's unconditional support for Israel, the need for a public accounting is particularly urgent, even if the prospects for achieving institutional accountability are virtually nil. The long-suffering people of Gaza and the West Bank have endured four major criminal assaults by Israel since 2008, while the governments of the world looked on without lifting a finger, a posture of dehumanizing detachment culminating in the 2023 spectacle of genocide where, to the extent that Western involvement took place, it was supportive of Israeli criminality. Under such circumstances, it is only civil society initiatives that retain some ability to respond meaningfully to the widely felt moral outrage and possess the capacity to provide reasoned views as to why such extreme defiance of international criminal law, and accompanying morality, is intolerable. Even such a check on state power, precisely because of its rootedness in witnessing, truth-telling, and shared values, threatens the established order in ways that produce repressive reactions even in countries that claim to be the guardians of freedoms and global security.

The Russell Tribunals, the PPT, and the various ad hoc civil society initiatives thus act to challenge the normative vacuum that currently afflicts the world. Such undertakings do not pretend to be substitutes for courts of law. In fact, the Brussels jury conclusions included a call on the Palestinian Authority to make use of the International Criminal Court and present its grievances to the formal authorities in The Hague for their investigation and possible indictments. Even then, the political realities of the world are such that prosecution would not be possible, as Israel is not a party to the treaty establishing the ICC and refuses to honor any arrest warrants issued by The Hague, even if the process is legally impeccable. And although the ICC has jurisdiction over all international crimes committed on the territory of parties to the Rome Statute, a trial could not proceed without the physical presence of those accused, which would be impossible to obtain.

As with the Nuremberg Judgment, flawed by victors' justice, the various civil society initiatives of recent years can be criticized as being one-sided on behalf of the defeated and vulnerable in world society. Even admitting that such a criticism has a certain validity, these carefully analyzed assessments of geopolitically controversial wars and policies will be greatly valued in the future as contributions to the long struggle to make the rule of law applicable to the strong as well as the weak. In the interim, such initiatives should be seen as feeble challenges to state-centric, geopolitically driven mechanisms of state propaganda, which encompass the most influential media platforms even in the liberal societies of the Global West.

Note

1   These issues are well covered in Cubukcu (2018).

References

Avalon Project. 1945. "Report of Robert H. Jackson, United States Representative to the International Conference on Military Trials." Department of State Publication 3880, London.

Center for Constitutional Rights (CCR). 2023. *Defense for Children International v Biden, Blinken, Austin*. United States District Court for the Northern District, Case No. 3:23-cv-5829. November 13.

Cubukcu, Ayca. 2018. *For the Love of Humanity: The World Tribunal on Iraq*. Philadelphia: University of Pennsylvania Press.

Ismael, Jaqueline S., Tareq Y. Ismael, and Leslie T. MacDonald. 2024. *Pax Americana: America's Unending War on Iraq*. London: Palgrave Macmillan.

Permanent Peoples Tribunal (PPT). 1976. "Algiers Charter: Universal Declaration of the Rights of Peoples." Fondazione Lelio e Lisli Basso. July 4, Algiers.

Sokmen, Muge Gersoy. 2008. *War Tribunal on Iraq: Making the Case Against War*. New York: Olive Branch Press.

12

Reparations, International Law, and Global (In)Justice:

Extensions of Reparations to Global Governance

If properly used, and not as a punitive measure adopted against an enemy in the aftermath of armed conflict (like in the imposed "peace" arrangements following World War I and the First Gulf War of 1992), reparations may serve to redress past wrongs. This pattern was evident in recent years during which reparations within the United States were mainly thought about as rectifying past wrongdoing, often associated with the abuse of a distinct minority, as with native or indigenous peoples, slavery, discrimination against racial and religious minorities, and harsh forms of political repression.

Reparations may mitigate grievances and make indirect contributions to future war prevention by way of the Charter Article 2(3) "to settle their international disputes by peaceful means." In this respect, reparations are a policy instrument that governments, civil society movements, and even individuals, can use to obtain justice for claims without recourse to force. Although the Charter discusses the "peaceful settlement of international disputes," the same logic of violence avoidance applies to the resolution of similar disputes internal to sovereign states. These dimensions of the reparations experience are relevant and present in relation to temporally or spatially remote severe wrongs associated with international and internal forms of slavery, and also to the exploitative economic arrangements imposed by the European colonial powers during the transition to political independence in sub-Saharan Africa, or in the course of the ecocidal destruction of tropical rain forests as in Brazil.

A New Frontier

This chapter assesses recent trends in international law regarding the availability and character of rectification for past wrongs. The most serious recent reparations issues have arisen particularly in domestic societies searching for transitional justice in the aftermath of abusive forms authoritarian rule or foreign occupation. These issues are shaped by national legal systems but are also influenced by international practice. In these transitional settings, the search for justice is affected by political preoccupations such as the persistent influence of displaced persons during a prior period of authoritarian rule, as well as by real and alleged limitations on the financial capabilities of transitional states.

No general approach is currently available to address the interplay between national and international law in relation to past injustices. Reliance needs to be placed on a case-by-case approach, considering matters of context, such as the degree of suffering and disability inflicted on particular categories of claimants, and the balance of claims versus societal demands for capabilities to provide resources to fund sustainable and equitable development. Remoteness in time bears on the credibility of the claimants as present victims tend to be given priority over victims in the distant past when assessing relative merits. Scale and selectivity suggest that if the total claims overwhelm the administrative and material capabilities of the state, a strong tendency will form to substitute apology and symbolic gestures for material ones, and if reparations are awarded at all, they will be based on specific individual needs associated with earlier instances of deprivation. International law informs the conceptual background of moral and political thinking about reparations, but practical considerations of capability and prudence are decisive in most instances, making the influence of international law indirect and sometimes marginal to debates on the merits of reparations claims, conceived broadly as forms of rectification for past wrongdoing.

Points of Departure

It is only in the last decade or so that international law has moved significantly in the direction of providing the means to pursue global justice, that is, in global arenas or by reference to global standards and procedures, on behalf of the individual and collective victims of severe injustices of the sort associated with oppressive governing regimes.[1] Prior to that time, this class of issues pertaining to global justice were treated as marginal at best to the principal endeavors of international law, although overseas economic interests of individuals from the North received periodic protection if encroached upon by governments in the South. But in the 1990s, the combination of the end of the Cold War, the rise to prominence of international human rights, trends away from authoritarianism and toward constitutional democracy, and the partial eclipse of sovereignty in a globalizing world gave unexpected attention to the many facets of global justice, hitherto mainly neglected, including steps designed to rectify the harm endured by individuals or persecuted groups at the hands of dictatorial and abusive governments.

At the forefront of these moves was the reinvigoration of efforts to impose accountability on individuals associated with the perpetration of crimes of state, highlighted by such high-profile cases as those associated with the transnational pursuit of Augusto Pinochet and of Slobodan Milosevic (Falk 2004b). This emphasis on accountability of leaders was reinforced by institutional and procedural innovations enabling indictment and prosecution.

Of almost equal prominence was the temporarily increased acceptance of an international responsibility on the part of the organized international community to protect vulnerable populations facing catastrophic challenges, whether from an abusive government or from an inability to provide governing authority, giving rise to a series of humanitarian interventions as responses to chaos, oppression, and natural disasters. This historical climate of moral/legal concern, mixed in with strategic interests of the North Atlantic Treaty Organization (NATO) alliance, reached a climax with the Kosovo War under NATO auspices in 1999 and has subsequently markedly declined as a protective, as distinct from a geopolitical, force. In Kosovo, the duty to protect an oppressed and endangered Albanian majority in the province of Kosovo was assumed by a regional security alliance to validate military action against a sovereign state, in this instance Serbia, even without the benefit of a legitimating mandate to use force from the United Nations Security Council. Such a use of force, even if credibly undertaken for protective purposes, was always controversial from the perspective of international law—it depended upon the presence of political factors that were selectively present in the 1990s to a greater degree than at any other historical moment, which have subsequently almost disappeared. The inability to mobilize support for humanitarian intervention in the setting of ongoing, massive ethnic cleansing and genocidal tactics in western Sudan during mid-2004, in Myanmar in 2021, or more markedly in Gaza in 2023–24, is indicative of how restricted to context was the surge of humanitarian diplomacy in the 1990s. And even then, without the presence of more strategic objectives of the sort present in Kosovo but absent in Rwanda during the genocide of 1994, the prospects for genuine humanitarian intervention by either the UN or a coalition of the willing remain minimal. The advent of the Responsibility to Protect (R2P) is indicative of some earlier impulses, but as with humanitarian intervention, its credibility as a policy tool has been undermined by its selectivity of application and geopolitical manipulations, most pronouncedly by NATO in relation to an R2P undertaking in Libya in 2011.[3]

As part of this climate of global opinion that seemed, in the 1990s, more sensitive to injustice than ever before, a new disposition to consider historic injustices endured by individuals and groups was evident in international relations. As Elazar Barkan (2000), a perceptive analyst of this welcome, yet brief, mutation in international attitudes notes, there was "the sudden appearance of restitution cases all over the world," leading him to postulate the possible beginnings of "a potentially new international morality." It is within this normative setting of redressing historic grievances that issues of reparations make their reappearance, especially in the setting of transitional justice arrangements. Part of this incipient normative revolution of the 1990s was a concern with rectifying harm previously done to individuals and groups, as well as punishing perpetrators and repudiating their documented wrongdoing in an authoritative forum. What accounted for this focus on this redress agenda at such a historical moment is uncertain, but it undoubtedly reflected a loss of a guiding geopolitical purpose after the end of the Cold War, combined with the growing prominence of human rights and an impulse in leadership circles to overcome the chorus of criticisms directed at the amorality of neoliberal globalization.

Barkan and others, for persuasive reasons, approached these issues of restitution and reparations as primarily matters of morality and politics rather than law, that is, treating these humanitarian initiatives as reflecting the impact of moral and political pressures rather than exhibiting adherence to previously established or newly emerging legal standards and procedures.[4] The changes in the 1990s reflected almost exclusively a combination of special circumstances generating political pressures and a mysteriously supportive moral "window of opportunity" in a global setting. But to the extent that morality and politics created new, widely shared expectations about appropriate behavior by governments, international law was being generated, even if it did not assume in most instances the positivist formality of treaty arrangements or the specificity of a meaningful legal obligation that included measures designed to ensure consistent implementation. Throughout the history of international society, the evolution of international law has been closely related to prevailing political and economic currents, evolving moral standards, and dominant trends in religious thought.

Such a linkage has been particularly evident in the war/peace context, international law essentially embodying the just war tradition as evolved by theologians, but it is also true with respect to the recent prominence of a global justice agenda, in which redress and restitution play such a large part. In one sense, the role of international law has been generally one of codifying behavioral trends in state practice and shifting political attitudes on the part of governments with the intention of stabilizing and clarifying expectations about the future.

It seems essential to distinguish three sets of circumstances: the first, the main preoccupation of international law and lawyers, involves disputes between states, and increasingly other actors, in which the complaining party seeks relief from alleged wrongs attributed to the defending party; the second involves war/peace settings in which the victorious side imposes obligations on the losing side, "victors'" justice, which may or may not correspond with justice as perceived from a more detached outlook; the third, achieving attention recently, involves transitions to democracy settings in which the prior governing authority is held accountable for alleged wrongs and, again, reflect political outcomes of sustained struggle but not international war. These three contexts should be kept distinct for both analytical and prescriptive purposes. In the first and second, there exists a more obvious role for international norms, procedures, and institutions than in the third, which is treated for most purposes as a matter of domestic discretion, although influenced by wider trends of national practice in comparable instances and by wider global trends toward individual accountability for crimes against humanity.

To what extent these mainly encouraging developments involving the rendering of global justice have been stymied by the September 11 attacks in 2001 and the American-led belligerent response are matters of uncertainty and conjecture at present. The complicity of liberal democracies, especially the United States, in Israel's genocide in Gaza undermines their reputation for global leadership in relation to the normative agenda of world order, shifting this role partially to China. The refocusing of governmental and public attention on global security issues has remarginalized the pursuit of the global justice agenda, including the drive for reparations and compensatory actions associated with various forms of historic redress other than those associated with transitional issues in a given country relating to the recent past.[5] As developments in 2003 within Argentina or the United States in 2009 suggest, a change of governmental leadership at the national level can affect in contradictory ways the approach taken to justice claims in a transition process. In Argentina a renewed resolve to invoke individual criminal accountability and compensation for past abuse arose, while in the United States a presidential transition included a resolve to suppress any action prompted by allegations of aiding and abetting torture during the war of terror after 9/11 against the prior leader. Against this double background of an inchoate normative revolution in the 1990s and the altered historical setting of the early twenty-first century, this chapter considers the relevance of international law to reparations and especially whether and to what extent reparations have acquired an international obligatory character of any practical significance.[6]

Such significance is difficult to assess, especially as its most tangible impact may be to encourage the provision by national legal systems of remedies for various categories of losses sustained due to prior abuses of human rights.

To the extent that international law is relevant at all, it is to provide legal arguments or jurisprudential background useful for representatives and advocates of victims' rights in domestic political arenas to the effect that victims are legally entitled to reparations, and that the domestic system is obliged to make this right tangible by providing meaningful procedures. As stressed throughout this book, the pedagogical role of international law should not be underestimated as potentially helpful for the long struggle for a just world order rooted in the public good universally considered.

International Law: Authority and Instruments

The fundamental norms of international law bearing on reparations and redress of past wrongs are contained in customary international law and reflect widely accepted ideas about the nature of law, its relation to legal wrongs, and the duty to provide recompense. The Permanent Court of Justice, set up after World War I, gave the most authoritative renderings of this foundation for the legal obligation to provide reparations. This most general international law imperative was set forth most authoritatively, although without any equally wide-range prospect of implementation, in the Chorzow Factory (Jurisdiction) Case: "It is a principle of international law that the breach of an engagement involves an obligation to make reparation in an adequate form."[7] The Advisory Opinion by the International Court of Justice involving the Israeli security wall reaffirmed this cardinal principle in ruling that Israel was under an obligation to provide reparations to the Palestinians for damages sustained resulting from the illegal wall built on their territory (ICJ Reports 2004, para. 152).

A second, equally important idea embodied in customary international law had to do with the nationality of claims associated with wrongs done to individuals. In essence, this norm expressed the prevailing understanding that only states were subjects within the international legal order, and that wrongs done to foreign individuals were, from a legal perspective, inflicted upon their state of nationality. Accordingly, if the individual was stateless, a national of the wrongdoing state, or a national of a state unwilling to support the claim for reparations, there was no basis on which to proceed. This limiting notion was expressed succinctly by the Permanent Court of International Justice in the Mavrommatis Palestine Concessions Case: "[b]y taking up the case of one of its subjects and by resorting to diplomatic action or international judicial proceedings on his behalf, a state is in reality asserting its own rights—its right to ensure, in the person of its subjects, respect for the rules of international law."[8] It is important to appreciate that these formulations were made before there existed any framework of internationally protected human rights.

A third important idea that has persisted in customary international law forbids a state from invoking national law as a legal defense in an international dispute involving allegations of wrongdoing by the injured state. Such a principle pertains to the settling of international disputes, which is where the main precedents and doctrines of international law relative to reparations are fashioned. The International Law Commission (ILC) Articles on state responsibility clarified to some extent this earlier teaching, refining and codifying it conceptually more than changing it substantively.[9] The ILC approach to remedial or corrective justice was based on distinguishing between restitution, compensation, and satisfaction. Restitution is defined in Article 35 as the effort "to re-establish the situation which existed before the wrongful act was committed." Such a remedy is rather exceptional. It is usually illustrated by reference to the temple case before the International Court of Justice (ICJ) in which Thailand was ordered to return religious relics taken from a Buddhist temple located in Cambodia (ICJ 1962). This primary reliance on restitution where practicable has been recently reaffirmed by the ICJ in its ruling on Israel's security wall, an important restatement of international law, although contained in an Advisory Opinion, attaining legal authoritativeness because it was endorsed by fourteen of the fifteen judges. The language of the Advisory Opinion expresses this viewpoint with clarity in paragraph 153:

> Israel is accordingly under an obligation to return the land, orchards, olive groves and other immovable property seized from any natural or legal person for purposes of construction of the wall in the Occupied Palestinian Territory. In the event that such restitution should prove to be materially impossible, Israel has an obligation to compensate the persons in question for the damage suffered. The Court considers that Israel also has an obligation to compensate, in accordance with the applicable rules of international law, all natural or legal persons having suffered any form of material damage as a result of the wall's construction.
>
> (ICJ 2004, para. 153)

Article 35(a) and (b) of the ILC Draft Articles indicates that restitution is not the appropriate form of reparations in circumstances where it is "materially impossible" or would "involve a burden out of all proportion to the benefit deriving from restitution instead of compensation" (ILC 2001, 98). Compensation, resting on the fungibility of money, is more widely used to overcome the adverse consequences caused by illegal acts. In the Chorzow case, it was declared that where restitution cannot be provided to the wronged state, then the wrongdoer should be required to compensate up to the level of the value attributed to whatever was lost, including loss of profits. Articles 36 and 37 go along with this approach of full reimbursement, without qualifications based on capacity to pay.

Satisfaction is the third, and lesser known, manner of providing reparations. The ILC Articles make it a residual category in relation to restitution and compensation. As explained by du Plessis, "[s]atisfaction provides reparation in particular for moral damage such as emotional injury, mental suffering, injury to reputation and similar damage suffered by nationals of the injured state" (du Plessis 2003, 631).

Customary international law, as well as the ILC Draft Articles of State Responsibility, impose an undifferentiated burden, as stated in Article 37, on the wrongdoing state "to make full reparation for the injury caused by the internationally wrongful act" (ILC 2001). As such, it gives very little guidance in specific situations where a variety of considerations may make the grant of full reparation undesirable for various reasons, although commentary by the ILC on each article does go well beyond the statement of the abstract rule.

International treaty law does no more than to restate these very general legal ideas in a variety of instruments, and without the benefit of commentary attached to the ILC Articles. Because property rights are of paramount concern, the language of reparation is not used, and the more common formulations emphasize compensation for the wrongs suffered. The basic direction of these treaty norms also derives from international customary law, especially legal doctrine associated with the confiscation of foreign-owned property. The legal formula for overcoming the legal wrong accepted in international law involved "prompt, adequate, and effective compensation." Discussion of "restitution" and "satisfaction" is abandoned as the wrongdoing states are acknowledged by the United Nations to possess "permanent sovereignty" over natural resources.[10]

The Universal Declaration of Human Rights shifts the locus of relief to national arenas and away from international disputes between sovereign states. Individuals are endowed with competence, and the notion of wrongdoing is generalized to encompass the entirety of human rights. Article 8 reads: "Everyone has the right to an effective remedy by the competent national tribunals for acts violating the fundamental human rights granted him by the constitution or by the law." Of course, such a right tends to be unavailable where it is needed most, that is, against an offending government, although the existence of the right does provide a legal foundation for reparations in future circumstances when political conditions have changed.

Article 10 of the Inter-American Convention on Human Rights particularizes a "right of compensation" in a limited and overly specific manner: "Every person has the right to be compensated in accordance with the law in the event that he has been sentenced by a final judgment through a miscarriage of justice" (OAS 1969). It seems to refer exclusively to improper behavior of the state associated with criminal prosecution and punishment within the judicial system. It is available only on the basis of an individual initiative.

Article 14 of the Convention Against Torture and Other Cruel Inhuman and Other Degrading Treatment or Punishment (UNGA 1984) imposes on parties the obligation to "ensure in its legal system that the victim of an act of torture obtains redress and has an enforceable right to fair and adequate compensation, including the means for as full rehabilitation as possible." Again, the emphasis is on the legal duty of the state to provide individuals who are victims with a remedy within the domestic system of laws. That is, victims are not dependent on governments of their nationality pursuing claims on their behalf, nor are nationals barred from relief by the obstacle of sovereign immunity. Article 9 of the Inter-American Convention to Prevent and Punish Torture similarly obligates parties to "undertake to incorporate into their national laws regulations guaranteeing suitable compensation for victims of torture."[11] In the absence of case law, it is difficult to know what this standard might mean in practice and whether it is purely aspirational or represents a genuine effort to acknowledge the full spectrum of injury that often results from torture and severe abuse. Beyond this duty of the state, Article 8 allows persons alleging torture to internationalize their claims for relief "[a]fter all the domestic legal procedures of the respective State . . . have been exhausted" by submitting their case "to the international fora whose competence has been recognized by that State" (OAS 1985).

Within the European regional system there is a right of an individual in Article 50 of the European Convention for the Protection of Human Rights and Fundamental Freedoms to seek "just satisfaction" if national law provides "partial reparation" due to injury sustained as a result of a violation of the Convention (Council of Europe 1950). A proceeding of this nature would fall within the authority of the European Court of Human Rights. Here, too, the idea is to provide individuals with a remedy at the regional level beyond what is available within the national legal system.

These international law developments over the last half century have several important consequences for the wider interest in reparations as provided to a victimized group, especially in the context of transition from authoritarian regimes:

- first, there is the shift in the emphasis of international law from the protection of the rights abroad, and especially property and investment interests, to the protection of individuals who experience abuses of human rights within their states of residence;
- second, there is a legal recognition that the state responsible for the abuse should legally empower those who claim to have been victimized to pursue relief by way of compensation through recourse to the national judicial system;

   –   third, the national identity of the victim and the sovereign immunity
       of the state should not affect the availability of legal relief in the
       event of abuse; and
   –   fourth, in the event of frustration at the national level, then some
       further mechanism for providing relief is becoming available at
       either regional or global levels, or both.

In summary, the importance of these international law developments is
probably indirect, but the shift from a concern with dispute settlement
to human rights does involve a major reorientation. The obligations
embodied in legal instruments are vague and abstract, and are difficult and
cumbersome to implement, but they do contribute to what might be called
the formation of "a reparations ethos" to the effect that individuals who
have been wronged by reference to applicable international human rights
standards, especially in the setting of torture and kindred maltreatment,
should be compensated as fully as possible. This ethos is a challenge to
notions of sovereignty associated with earlier ideas that a state can do no
wrong that is legally actionable, and that the wrong done to an individual
is legally relevant only if understood as a wrong done to the state of which
he or she is a national.
    At the same time, the most important circumstances of reparations,
leaving aside postwar arrangements, are not really addressed directly by
contemporary international law. In authoritarian political settings, by
definition, there is an absence of judicial independence, and there is no
prospect of relief even in extreme situations. In post-authoritarian political
settings, where there is an impulse to achieve redress, the magnitude of the
challenge requires some categorization of the victims as well as a recognition
of severe limits on the capacity of the new government to provide anything
approaching "adequate compensation." The actual dynamics of reparations
and redress arrangements reflect a variety of specific circumstances that
exist in particular states. These arrangements have an ad hoc character that
makes it impossible to draw any firm conclusions about legal expectations,
much less frame this practice as legal doctrine. For this reason, among others,
it is appropriate to view reparations as primarily expressions of prevailing
political and moral convictions reflecting relevant contextual variables.

Shadows of Misunderstanding

Any broad consideration of the relevance of international law to the subject
matter of reparations needs to be sensitive to several background factors
that could invite misunderstanding if not addressed. Such factors illuminate
the tensions that have historically existed between considerations of global

justice and political relationships shaped by hierarchical relations between the strong and the weak.

For most people (other than specialists in international law concerned with international disputes about wrongdoing), the idea of "international reparations" recalls the burdens imposed on Germany at the end of World War I that were embodied in the Versailles Treaty.[12] These burdens were widely interpreted as accentuating the postwar hardships faced by German society in the 1920 and 1930s, and were viewed in retrospect as a damaging example of a "punitive peace" that contributed to a surge of German ultranationalism, producing a political climate conducive to extremism of the sort represented by the Nazi movement. From an international law perspective, the reparations imposed were perfectly legal, indeed specified in a peace treaty formally accepted by Germany, but from a political perspective such reparations were viewed as imprudent, if not disastrous. And from a moral perspective, they were widely viewed as ill-deserved, mainly exhibiting the vengeful appetite of the victors in the preceding war in which neither side could convincingly claim the moral high ground. This "lesson of Versailles" was heeded after World War II, Germany being assisted in economic recovery and political normalization despite the existence of a far stronger case for collective punishment of German society than existed in 1918, given the multiple legacy of crime and tragedy generated by Hitler's regime.[13] And the results are generally viewed as vindicating the soft approach, reinforcing the repudiation of Versailles, although the experience needs to be contextualized in relation to the perception in the West of a common front between the defeated Axis powers and the victorious alliance in which the primary security, strategic, and ideological concerns shifted from fascism to communism and the main adversary shifted from Germany to the Soviet Union.

And yet, perhaps surprisingly, the "peace" imposed on Iraq after the First Gulf War in 1992 seems to have adopted the previously discredited Versailles model of punitive peace, although the terminology of reparations was largely displaced in this instance by the language of sanctions and claims, perhaps to avoid evoking bad memories. At the same time, extensive assets and oil revenues were made available, along with a procedure within the UN to provide compensation to Kuwaiti victims of Iraqi harm arising out of its invasion of Kuwait in 1990, and so there was a justice dimension so far as individual victims of Iraqi wrongdoing were concerned.[14] Thus, overall, an important ambiguity emerges: the Iraqi people were punished collectively and severely despite being entrapped in a brutal dictatorship, while the various categories of victims arising from the international crimes of Iraq as committed in Kuwait were the recipient of substantial reparative efforts to compensate for losses sustained. In this respect, the positive side of reparations was present. This whole framework of "sanctions," combining the punitive with the compensatory, was given legal stature in the form of unanimous UN Security Resolution 687, the harsh terms of which were accepted by a defeated and devastated Iraq in the 1991 ceasefire that ratified the results of the First Gulf War, inflicting severe harm in subsequent years on the innocent Iraqi civilian population.[15]

There are two observations to be made. First, in the sphere of interstate reparations, there is a confusing association of "reparations" in language and policy, both with a largely discredited process of imposing postwar collective punishments upon a defeated state and its civilian population, and as seeking to give the victims of illegal and criminal conduct on behalf of a state a meaningful remedy for harm sustained in the form of substantial monetary compensation. Second, there is a flexible capacity for international law to provide a legal imprimatur, either by treaty or Security Council decision that ratifies a mechanism for the award of "reparations" and give legal expression to the geopolitical relationship that exists at the end of a war, without regard to whether the motivations for reparations are punitive or compensatory, or a mixture of the two. If the outcome of the war is "just" and the victors are "prudent," then the reparations imposed may contribute to global justice, but if not, not. International law provides at this point no substantive guidelines as to these assessments, and its main role is to provide victorious powers with a flexible instrument by which to shape a peace process in accord with their strategic goals and give their values an authoritative status.

The analogous dynamics of establishing reparations in the context of transitional societies also reflects power variables, although there is often not a clear dividing line between victory and defeat but, rather, a political process that produces a negotiated compromise that inhibits to varying degrees the redress of past injustices by the newly emerging constitutional leadership. The arrangement is formalized exclusively through a reliance on mechanisms provided by the governing authorities enlisting the national legal system and establishing special administrative procedures. There is no direct role for international law, except to the extent of taking account of past wrongdoing as instances of "crimes against humanity" or indirectly as responsive to international pressures associated with imposing national means to determine accountability and rectifying past wrongs to the extent possible, given the political and economic realities. In the context of the Holocaust, and to some extent in relation to authoritarian antecedents to constitutional government, the goal of reparations is also a deterrent message to future leaders and a pledge of sorts by present leaders to repudiate the past and build a just constitutional order.

Certainly, in the background of the sort of moral and political pressures effectively brought to bear on Swiss banks by Holocaust survivors and their representatives during the 1990s was the strong sense that these individuals, or in this case, sometimes their descendants, had truly been victims of internationally criminal conduct and deserved some sort of redress, even if belatedly.[16]

Decades had passed since the occasions of wrongdoing, and it was only a change in global setting that abruptly lent political credibility to claims that always had been actionable from legal or moral perspectives. It was this credibility that overcame the impulse to disregard old claims as stale and allegedly avoid opening old wounds. Such belated redress went against the traditional disposition of law to reach finality with respect to claims, both for the sake of stability and because evidence becomes less reliable and often unavailable with the passage of time.

An additional source of misunderstanding pertaining to international law relates to its state-centric orientation and traditions, which have been increasingly challenged in a variety of ways in the last few decades. The modern structure of international law was based on the idea that states were the only formal members of international society, and that the legal interests of individuals associated with the actions of foreign governments were protected, if at all, by one's country of nationality on a discretionary basis.[17] International wrongs of aliens were thus treated as generating potential legal claims by a government on behalf of their aggrieved nationals, but purely as a matter of political and moral discretion, and under international law the wrong was done to the state, not to the individual who was harmed. The practice by states of reacting to such wrongs was described as "the diplomatic protection" of nationals or aliens abroad and was usually associated with the protection of foreign property rights. The individual beneficiary of such claims had no legal entitlement, and a government could ignore or waive the claims of its nationals. This statist pattern was further reinforced by ideas of nonaccountability with respect to wrongs inflicted on nations, both internationally and domestically. The doctrine of sovereign immunity meant that an individual suffering injury could not initiate any legal action in the courts of either the country where the harm took place or the country of his or her nationality. Claims of allegedly injured aliens in third world settings were sometimes addressed by claims commissions assessing the merits of particular claims or by a lump sum settlement, the funds of which were then allocated on some basis to the claimants. This background of international law is highly relevant to the circumstance of societies in the midst of transitions to democracy and, overall, indicative of a turn toward nonviolent geopolitics and the implementation of an ethos of peaceful settlement of disputes, increasing prospects for governance structures and procedures responsive to the goals of a patriotism for humanity and the whole earth.

There are three further observations that are relevant to this inquiry. First, the political reality of such dynamics reflected the geopolitical and hierarchical structures of the colonial era. These claims made by governments in the North involved only losses sustained by Western individuals and corporations in Global South settings. There was no reciprocity or equality given the manner with which investment and property rights were dealt with in international law. A bit later these claims for compensation involved opposition to socialist approaches to both private investment and economic development, and resisted the legal effects, as far as possible, of the rise of economic nationalism in the decades following World War II. The protection of nationals abroad was not at all in the spirit of "reparations" (conceived as corrective justice) and reflected an opposite policy, generally associated with protecting foreign investors who had characteristically been beneficiaries of "unjust enrichment" in a variety of exploitative center–periphery relations. Ideas of state responsibility were also formulated with an eye toward fashioning an international law instrument designed for the protection of transnational private property interests of investors from the Global North, especially in the face of allegedly confiscatory forms of nationalization. Even the most recent formulation of the law of state responsibility by the International Law Commission treats the state as the sole subject of wrongs whose victims are its nationals and fails to address the existence of rights under international law of the victims if they are conceived of as individuals or groups. With moves toward neoliberal globalization since 1990, there has emerged a widespread intergovernmental consensus supportive of private sector autonomy, which has ended the widespread emphasis on balancing territorial rights against those of foreign investors in third world countries. In this regard, the capitalist ethos has prevailed, at least for the foreseeable future, yet has come under a renewed challenge by resurgent nationalism in various forms.

Second, the kind of concerns that have been associated with transitions to democracy were completely absent from these earlier concerns of international law with harm sustained by individuals. For one thing, victims within society were left completely vulnerable to abuse by their own governments due to ideas of territorial supremacy of sovereign states, and thus the abuses of oppressive government toward their own citizenries remained outside the legal loop of potential responsibility. International law was completely silent as to state–society abuses so long as the victims were nationals (Booth 1993). The emergence of international human rights, by way of the Universal Declaration of Human Rights in 1948 and the 1966 covenants, were at first only politically feasible because there were minimal expectations of legal implementation, much less remedies for victims seeking reparations. The majority of governments were authoritarian, fully dedicated to traditional notions of sovereign rights, and would have opposed a legal structure that had explicit ambitions associated with implementation of individual rights. It is here where the emergence of transnational civil society actors challenged the traditional political equation weighted in favor of state interests, creating pressures to promote degrees of implementation for human rights that went far beyond what had been anticipated at intergovernmental levels.[18]

Third, since international law failed to protect the human rights of individuals as a matter of law until after World War II, there was little pressure on national legal procedures to do so. But in more than a half century since the adoption of the Universal Declaration of Human Rights there has been an extraordinary set of regional and global developments enhancing the position of the individual as the formal holder or subject of rights.[19] What is important here is less the exceptional international initiative on behalf of the victims of human rights abuse, than the influence on the erosion of sovereign exemptions from accountability in domestic legal arenas (Donnelly 2003). Here the indirect impact of the human rights movement has been strongly felt. It includes the empowerment of civil society actors, creating intense perceptions of injustices endured by individuals, expectations of some sort of remedial process, and the importance of taking official steps toward corrective justice by a government in the struggle to renew an atmosphere of political legitimacy. This is the case with respect to its own citizens by means of a signal of the repudiation in the past and to aid efforts to acquire or reacquire legitimacy within international society.[20] In effect, some of the traditional veils of sovereignty are lifted to facilitate transition, but this is overwhelmingly and directly disguised by the adoption of a self- interested national political and moral discourse. But what seems national, even nationalistic, is undoubtedly influenced by varying degrees by what has been going on internationally, transnationally, and in other kindred states. What is most evident, particularly in Latin America, which provided the main experimental frontier, was the degree to which justice for victims was complementary to what often appeared from the outside to be a more strident insistence, effectively promoted by civil society actors, on combating what came to be described as "the culture of impunity" toward past wrongdoing by leaders. More properly considered, this effort to impose accountability on leaders was integral to restoring the dignity of victims, constituting a direct repudiation of the past, and was thus an aspect of rendering justice to the victims, however retrospectively.[21]

There is also evidence of a mimetic element in which national dialogues listen to one another, while adapting to their own particularities, building a trend that establishes a new pattern of expectations about justice in transitional circumstances. Such a drive for corrective justice was tempered by resource constraints and by the search for normalcy or social peace, tending to produce compromise approaches, especially encouraging an approach to feasible levels of "satisfaction" for victims by reliance on truth and reconciliation processes adapted to the particularities of a given country. The result is an acknowledgment of the past, but without great efforts either to punish perpetrators or to compensate victims. Symbolic forms of redress prevail, with both corrective and deterrent goals.

Such a historical process of innovative practice is somewhat puzzling from an interpretative perspective. Whether we call such patterns "law" or "international law" is a matter of the jurisprudential outlook, either positivist or constructivist. It is also a question of what might be called the politics and epistemology of law. A positivist approach would not regard the existing rules of international law as sufficiently clarifying as to permissible behavior to qualify fully as law. A constructivist jurisprudence attributes to the interpreters of law, both judges and scholars, a dynamic role in imparting authoritative meaning, and proceeds from the belief that legal standards cannot be objectified by language and strict canons of interpretation. We favor such an acknowledgment of the uncertainty of law on the books as a means to encourage those with discretion to interpret, apply, and enforce the law to act responsibly, which we regard as meaning that ambiguities be resolved by opting for morally guided outcomes to decision-making. Of course, discretion is not unlimited but confined by rules of reason that identify the boundaries of interpretative reasonableness and thus accord with the idea that those interpreting the law are not free to give expression to private ideas of morality and political prudence. Legality as a clarifying condition is left in abeyance until patterns of expectations are shaped by interpretative trends and practice.[22] Such a prism of evaluation would seek to relate law to widely endorsed expectations about behavior that exist in society but would not "legalize" moral sentiments that lacked such backing, however appealing, by pretending that these sentiments qualified as "law." From such a perspective, then, there is a greater relevance for international legal obligations in relation to reparations practice, and wider issues of corrective or remedial justice, than would seem to derive from a strictly positivist jurisprudence. The normative revolution that seemed to get underway in the 1990s had a lawmaking potential if expectations of legality are created by influential institutional and societal actors. Such expectations would acknowledge as valid specific claims and demands for justice and thereby set precedents that shape perceptions as to the evolving character of "the law." If victims' rights become established legally, expectations of participants alter in circumstances of future victimization.

Some Limiting Conditions

Reparations, if conceived as central to corrective justice, pose difficulties from the perspective of international law, but these are encountered in analogous form in transitional justice settings. Even more than efforts to impose individual accountability, a reliance on reparations, especially as a means of addressing the various dimensions of harm endured by victims, is inevitably context driven.[23] And because context is so decisive, the guidance functions of international law tend to be minimal beyond affirming the existence of an underlying obligation as a generality. As the 2004 ICJ Advisory Opinion on the legal status of the Israeli security wall clearly reaffirmed, there does exist in international law a well-established entitlement for the victim of legal wrongs to appropriate reparations. But between the affirmation of the legal right/duty and its satisfaction, there exists a huge contextual gap. In this instance, Israel, backed by the US government, immediately repudiated the World Court decision, and nullified the preexisting minuscule prospects of compliance. The international legal standard is authoritative and context free, but its implementation is context dependent.

Several dimensions of this unavoidable contextuality can be identified, but such a reality also pertains at least as much to reparations within national settings, where a wide measure of prosecutorial discretion reinforced by pragmatic polical calculations has been an attribute of efforts to bring justice to perpetrators and victims in transitional situations. What is set forth as applicable in international contexts is also relevant with some adjustments to national contexts.

Unevenness of Material Circumstances

To the extent that reparations attempt to compensate victims for losses endured, some assessment of an ability to pay needs to be made. This assessment should take account, as well, of the extent of victimization and whether certain forms of victimization should be excluded from a reparations program. The question of fiscal capabilities at the disposal of the perpetrators, or their successors, is crucial. Of course, this is also true of prosecutorial efforts to impose accountability on perpetrators, which reflects the unevenness of national capacities to sustain the "shock" of prosecutions.

Iraq, after the Gulf War, with extensive oil revenues, and South Africa, with a generally impoverished population, are at opposite ends of the fiscal spectrum in two respects: Iraq was an instance of reparations doubling as sanctions, whereas in South Africa, any attempt to provide monetary reparations would necessitate a massive diversion from the priorities of the new leadership to promote economic growth and address the challenge of massive extreme poverty.

The case of South Africa is significant for this inquiry.[24] The new political order had repudiated its criminal precursors mainly by way of a truth and reconciliation process. It was deeply committed to the improvement of the material circumstances of an extremely poor, majority black African population. Of course, the new leadership could have taken greater account of the high degree of victimization, as well as the unjust enrichment of the white minority, by combining constitutionalism with a program for the redistribution of wealth based on past injustice. To have done so, however, would likely have doomed the political miracle of a bloodless transition from apartheid and might have led to prolonged civil strife. The role of reparations in transitions to democracy is especially complicated, taking into consideration the entrenched interests of those associated to varying degrees with the old order, seeking to avoid overtaxing available capabilities to ensure the success of the newly emerging order, and yet providing some needs-based relief to those who suffered incapacitating harms due to earlier wrongdoing.

Similarly, in the setting of many African countries that are extremely poor, it seems unrealistic to impose corrective burdens of a monetary character because of resource constraints.[25] This is especially so for national settings where prolonged civil strife has victimized many, if not all, living in the society; many severely, if massive atrocities were committed on a large scale, as was the case in South Africa. Normally, symbolic measures of acknowledgment (via truth and reconciliation) would be more appropriate and less disruptive, along with a needs-based conception of reparations that tries, at least, to enable those who have been disabled, or find themselves in acutely vulnerable circumstances, to be given the means to restore a modicum of dignity to their lives.[26]

Remoteness in Time

Because some claims for redress of grievances arise from events that seem in the remote past and their redress is of a magnitude that would be disruptive to present social and economic arrangements, there is a vigorous resistance to material forms of compensation.[27] It is partly a matter of responsibility: the unwillingness of most members of a present generation to believe that they owe obligations to the descendants of victims of even severe past wrongs. It is partly a matter of changed mores: a sense that injustice needs to be measured within the historical setting of the contested behavior. It is also a matter of scale and impact: the realization that restoring the rights of victims would be enormously expensive, subversive of currently vested property interests, and diversionary from contemporary social protection priorities. As well, it reflects societal refusals to treat those in the present as genuinely victimized by occurrences that took place long ago. The reality is complicated, as old wounds often have not completely healed despite the passage of many generations as the persistence of racial tensions in the United States illustrates.

At the same time, remoteness has not altogether stymied efforts to obtain redress in the form of reparations under certain conditions. The exemplary case is the pursuit of Swiss bank deposits by Holocaust survivors and their heirs, as well as claims on behalf of those who were compelled to do forced labor in Nazi times. Swiss banks agreed to pay survivors $1.25 billion, and the German government agreed to pay compensation for slave labor (Bazyler 2003). Related efforts produced agreements with France to compensate for stolen assets during the Vichy period: "truth" commissions have been set up in twenty-three countries that are continuing to assess claims relating to looted works of art and unpaid insurance proceeds owed to relatives of Holocaust victims.

At the same time, beneficiaries are often disappointed by the level of compensation received, and more than this, distressed by the monetization of their suffering that can never be materially or otherwise compensated. When one survivor of Auschwitz, Roman Kent, was asked whether he was happy about the results, his reply was typical: "Why did it take the German nation 60 years to engage the morals of the most brutal form of death, death through work?" (quoted in Authers 2006) The pursuit of these claims on behalf of Holocaust victims has produced mixed assessments from observers, but the main relevant point is that the process has been primarily driven by moral and political pressures, with law playing a facilitative role. Lawyers have assumed a rather controversial role by siphoning off a considerable proportion of negotiated settlements as legal fees.[28] In a technical sense, the recovery of wrongfully taken property is an instance of reparations, but in its more unusual mode of restitution rather than as a means of providing compensation for injuries sustained.

In some respects, the relative success of Holocaust claimants has stimulated other categories of remote victims to be more assertive about seeking redress, although not necessarily in the form of reparations. To begin with, Asian victims of imperial Japan mounted pressures on behalf of survivors and their descendants in relation to forced labor, as did representatives of "comfort women." Asian claimants were able to take advantage of national laws in the United States that had been drafted in response to pressures associated with the Holocaust, although in the end were unable to proceed as potential claims had been waived in the peace treaty with Japan that included an exemption from responsibility that the US State Department continues to insist upon in litigation brought before American courts. Note here that the obligations to compensate written into American law does not purport to be the enactment of international legal obligations but are presented as instances of discretionary national legislation that results from moral appeals and political leverage.

Yet remoteness has not inhibited certain categories of claims for reparative justice in the United States, especially those associated with indigenous peoples and the institutions of slavery and slave trading. These claims, building credibility in the wake of efforts on behalf of Holocaust survivors, gained unprecedented visibility in the atmosphere of the 1990s.[29] To the extent that symbolic reparations were pursued, there were positive results in the form of acknowledgments, apologies, and increased media attention was given to past injustices.

Remoteness limited the capacity of such claimants to implement the very broad legal imperative to give victims remedies for harms endured, but it did not formally preclude relief. There was no statute of limitations applicable to bar claims. Those with limited claims and a small constituency, most notably Japanese Americans who had suffered enforced detention in World War II, were recipients of nominal compensation payments.[30] These payments were important to the victims as much, if not more so, as formal acknowledgments of past injustice, that is, as symbolic reparations in the sense of acknowledgment and apology, even though a nominal payment was involved. In contrast, descendants of slaves, although receiving some satisfaction, including a legal affirmation in authoritative global settings that slavery constituted a crime against humanity, have not been able to gain satisfaction in the form of compensation.[31] Unlike the case of Japanese Americans for whom compensation was not a huge financial tax on the present and unlike Holocaust survivors who had the benefit of supportive American pressures (which appeared to push the Swiss banks and others into accommodating gestures), indigenous peoples and descendants of slaves found themselves without political leverage, despite generating significant moral pressures arising from the documentation of horrendous past atrocities. Beyond this, redress in these latter instances would have been economically and politically disruptive, imposing a major and politically unacceptable burden on present public revenue flows and probably giving rise to an ugly racist backlash as experienced by "affirmative action" designed to offer redress for past discrimination based on gender and race.

Absence of Individuation

The magnitude of the harm done, especially when directed at a large class of victims, makes it impractical to evaluate individual claims on a case-by-case basis in most instances and, therefore, is not consistent with the international law approach based on the individual that is embedded in human rights. It has been historically possible under certain circumstances to create claims commissions to deal with efforts to achieve restitution of property and compensation arrangements, as was done in relation to the Iranian Revolution and the First Gulf War. In both instances, there were large pools of resources available that belonged to the accused governments, as well as antagonistic international attitudes toward the government that was being charged with improper taking of private property rights. Redress for claimants did not impose any burdens on the states that established the reparations mechanism, which distinguishes the situation from those where payment of reparations would be imposed from within. That is, the geopolitical climate was supportive of efforts to implement reparations on an individuated basis in Iran and Iraq. But these instances are the exception rather than the rule. No such redress occurs when the accused government is victorious or beyond the reach of the international community, as has been the case in relation to the United States, considering the wrongs associated with its conduct of wars in Vietnam, Panama, Afghanistan, and Iraq in the course of the last forty years, as well as in relation to both world wars of the twentieth century. There are many other instances of open wounds from past wrongdoing, especially in parts of Asia, sub-Saharan Africa, and Latin America.

More common are those many circumstances in a wide range of countries where an oppressive past has been finally repudiated by new political leadership, but not necessarily in a conclusive fashion. Beyond this, there are neither the administrative nor financial capabilities to process claims on an individual basis, particularly if the abuses do not involve property rights that can be established by the claimants. In such circumstances, the dynamic of redress has tended to emphasize accountability for the main perpetrators of atrocities and a collective truth-telling procedure for the community of victims, especially reliance on truth and reconciliation commissions.[32] Reparations are certainly not excluded, but they have not been consistently part of the process and rarely reach the majority of victims, except in pitifully small amounts. In Latin America, several countries have implemented significant reparations programs, including Argentina, Chile, and Brazil; others have made efforts that have been made are little more than token. Reparations have received less attention than efforts at criminalizing the perpetrators of gross wrongs but have been at least as significant an aspect of attempts at overall rectification.

Generality of Obligation

Any attempt to evolve a law-centered approach to reparations must accept the frequent inability to specify the level of responsibility with the kind of precision that makes it more likely that equal circumstances will be treated equally. Of course, this difficulty with reparations should not be exaggerated, and it should be appreciated that the more demanding rules of evidence and standards of persuasion that apply to criminal prosecution make problems of ascertaining responsibility and entitlement with respect to reparations somewhat manageable. The provision of reparations, however constructed, usually must depend in the end on a rule of reason, which accords those who administer the program, whether judicially or administratively, wide discretionary authority. Only where the idea of full compensation for losses is sustained, as in Kuwait after the Gulf War, is there operational guidance for those making decisions. Or where uniform payments are decreed, which overlook the unevenness of harm sustained, as with compensation accorded to Japanese Americans detained during World War II, is specificity attained.

In other settings, the legal mandate to award reparations operates in a manner similar to other areas of the law where the specific and the general are only loosely connected, as when such standards as "due process" or "the reasonable person" are used to judge legal responsibility in particular circumstances. Where the number of claimants is very large, there is a greater disposition to rely on administrative procedures that compensate victims by category of harm, and usually with no pretension that the level of reparations corresponds to the level of harm. Again, the human rights approach based on individual rights challenges this flexibility.

Extreme Selectivity

To the extent that reparation claims are given support in national legal systems, there are present critical geopolitical factors that inhibit any kind of standardization of treatment. It is one thing to initiate litigation to give some remedial relief to Holocaust victims, but it would be inconceivable that comparable relief, even of a symbolic character, were to be accorded to Indochinese victims of the Vietnam War or to Palestinian victims of Israeli abuses of international human rights and international humanitarian law during the period of extended occupation of the West Bank and Gaza. The victims require political leverage, and the target of remedial abuse must be discredited or defeated for such remedies to exist. Whenever geopolitical factors become relevant to the application of legal standards, the issue of legitimacy casts a shadow over discussions of legality, especially because selective implementation means that equals cannot be and are not treated as equals. Should such a realization be allowed to taint those applications of law that can be explained by reference to geopolitical patterns of influence?[33]

What International Law Can Do

So far, the emphasis has been placed on the limitations of international law in relation to the imposition of obligations to provide reparations to victims of past injustices and deprivations of rights, especially in the setting of transitions to democracy. But international law also has contributed to a generalized atmosphere of support, a reparations ethos, for compensating victims as part of its overall dedication to global justice and the enforcement of claims and, thus, lends support to the domestic willingness to provide reparations when contextual factors are favorable. Beyond this, international law is part of the normative context, giving a higher level of credence to victims and their supporters who insist on reparations as part of a new political regime of "fairness." Such a change in the climate of credibility with respect to claims of reparations for past wrongs is perhaps most evident in the greater seriousness accorded to the grievances associated with the descendants of slaves and the representatives of indigenous peoples. These claims had previously been hardly ever mentioned in influential political settings in the United States, being treated as too frivolous to warrant governmental attention, much less action.

International law also helps by clarifying those forms of governmental abuse that constitute international crimes and, therefore, cannot be shielded from legal accountability (Robertson 1999). The establishment of the International Criminal Court (ICC) is a step in the direction of accountability for perpetrators, there is an agreed-upon framework that might in time to exert an indirect influence upon those transitions to democracy that occur against an established background of gross abuse and international criminality. That is, by linking accountability for perpetrators to compensation for victims, there is encoded in international law a conception of fairness and rectification of past harm that includes victims.[34] This is a major conceptual step forward, with policy consequences, although disappointments also arise to the extent that compensatory steps are either trivial in relation to the quantum of harm endured or are never implemented beyond nominal awards.[35] Perhaps the most important impact of this level of generalized obligation is to influence the approach of national legal systems, which in any event have the most opportunity to actualize international standards, including those associated with human rights, in relation to the persons who endured the wrongs or their representatives. To the extent that national programs of reparations are enacted, there are expectations generated that a transition to democracy is incomplete if it does not include efforts to address to the extent practical, considering contextual constraints, the harms endured by victims of a prior oppressive regime. At the same time, there exists a margin of appreciation that allows a given national government a wide range of discretion in determining what is a reasonable appropriation for the satisfaction of past claimants.

To the extent corrective justice is considered, then the pressure to overcome the culture of impunity relating to transitions to democracy is of at least symbolic benefit to the victims, as well as to their families and friends. The difficulties of providing material compensation are partially offset by publicly and officially acknowledging past abuses, documenting the record of wrongdoing associated with a prior regime, discrediting perpetrators while expressing solidarity with a community of victims, issuing apologies, and challenging self-serving grants of amnesty. In this process, not only is the harm to those most victimized repudiated as a legal wrong but the public is educated about the limits on permissible government behavior.

Given the degree to which transitions to democracy are carried out within national legal frameworks, where the contours of arrangements are determined exclusively by reference to domestic law, the role of international law is inherently limited. Of course, if international human rights and criminal law are somewhat internalized, the norms influence national approaches, in circumstances of transitional justice, in the direction of providing "just compensation" for victims as determined contextually. Beyond this, international remedial procedures could impose legal obligations on states and other actors to provide financial capabilities via the ICC, and elsewhere, to enable those countries with limited resources and very widespread claims of victimization to receive special credits and loans for the purpose of satisfying certain categories of victimization.

Whether such an undertaking could fit within the writ of existing international financial institutions such as the World Bank or International Monetary Fund (IMF) is doubtful, but a special commission could be created within the UN system to receive voluntary contributions earmarked for such purposes. The record to date is not encouraging if the UN Voluntary Fund for Victims of Torture established by General Assembly Resolution 36/151 on December 16, 1981, is taken as indicative. The Fund receives contributions from governments, nongovernmental organizations, and individuals, but has managed to raise only $54 million during its entire course since coming into existence in 1983.

Another possibility, undoubtedly remote, would be to affix a "Tobin Tax" on international currency transactions or on activities that pollute the commons, such as commercial jet travel, thereby providing a pool of funds to be used to bolster the capabilities to realize the goals of corrective justice in transitional societies and other circumstances where international victimization has occurred. This kind of mechanism could also be used to address categories of claimants on a group basis, thereby circumventing the extraordinary bureaucratic burdens associated with judicial and administrative approaches that are based on assessing the merits of individualized claims.

This chapter has explored the general status of reparations as representing a trend within the last several decades to align international law more closely with the realization of justice for individuals and wronged or abused groups. It is on this basis that reparations enter the domain of global reform relative to governance and the universalization of patriotism as seen through dual lens of humanity, the global public good, and resilient ecological behavioral norms.

Notes

1   For review of this dynamic see Falk (2002a).

2   The conclusion of the Independent International Commission on Kosovo was that the action was "legitimate" (as it prevented an imminent instance of

ethnic cleansing) but "illegal" (as it lacked a required UNSC mandate). See the report of the commission (Independent International Commission on Kosovo 2000); along similar lines, but with a more comprehensive approach, see the report of the International Commission on Intervention and State Sovereignty (2001).

3   The most robust instances of humanitarian intervention during and after the colonial era were on behalf of Western interests as arising in states situated in the Global South.

4   De Greiff (2006) defends a nuanced position with respect to the relationship between reparations and international law: the main point is that what international law has to say about this issue is still mostly geared to the case-by-case resolution of claims, and that both this and the (related) adoption of *restitutio ad integrum* as the criterion of justice in reparations, make the guidance provided by international law less than clear when the task is to create a massive program.

5   Even in the aftermath of the Afghanistan War and the Iraq War, there does not seem to be a disposition to set up a procedure to provide reparations for the numerous victims of these brutal regimes. Unlike after World War II or the Gulf War, the main goals of the occupying powers, aside from selective criminal prosecution of the leaders of the former regime, seem to involve the establishment of stability and a sense of normalcy.

6   Of course, there are a series of affirmations of a legal obligation to compensate victims of abuses that can be found in such influential documents as Article 8 of the Universal Declaration of Human Rights, Articles 2(3), 9(5), Article 14 of the International Covenant on Civil and Political Rights, Article 14 of the UN Convention Against Torture, and Article 6 of the International Convention on the Elimination of All Forms of Racial Discrimination, as well as the elaborate consideration of victims' rights in the Statute of the International Criminal Court (see van Boven 2000). It is to be noted that most of the assertions of this right to compensation situate the remedy within national legal systems. With the exception of the ICC approach, there is no attempt at an international remedial option made available to a victim even if there is no meaningful national remedy. The Basic Principles document, in Principle 12, affirms the victim's right to pursue a remedy in all legal arenas "under existing domestic laws as well as under international law," but without any clarification as to how such rights can be upheld in concrete circumstances. States are obliged to "[m]ake available all appropriate diplomatic and legal means to ensure that victims exercise their rights to a remedy and reparation for violations of international human rights or humanitarian law" (UNGA 2005).

7   In explaining the bearing of international law, we have adapted the framework clearly set forth by Max du Plessis (2003).

8   Mavrommatis Palestine Concessions Case (1924, at 12); for fuller account, see (1982).

9   For the definitive account of the ILC treatment of reparations see Crawford (2002); for a useful assessment, see Shelton (2002). Professor Shelton asserts that these Draft Articles, that is, not yet in the form of an international

convention, combine persuasively the descriptive function of "codification" with the prescriptive function of "progressive development" in accord with the mission of the International Law Commission. She also confirms the influence of this statement of the law despite its lack of a formally obligatory character, including extensive reliance by the International Court of Justice in its decisions, and by parties in their submissions.

10   See especially GA Res. 1803 (UNGA 1973); also Declaration on the Right to Development (UNGA 1986).

11   OAS (1985); For a careful study of reparations in the Inter-American Human Rights System, see Carrillo (2006).

12   For a sense of the professional viewpoint on reparations associated with international law practice see Shelton (2002). A typical view of the Versailles approach, primarily because the reparations features were regarded as symbolically humiliating and substantively burdensome for Germany and Germans, and thereby leading to a backlash, is the following: "The Treaty of Versailles . . . represented a peace without justice. The desire of the First World War victors to seek revenge against the vanquished is widely believed to have contributed to conditions which led to the Second World War" (Rees 2003). Of course, it would be simplistic to explain the rise of Hitler by reference only to an extremist reaction to Versailles—see Arendt (1952). For a recent inquiry into the origins of "radical evil" as a political reality, see Katznelson (2003).

13   The issue of punishment and responsibility was individualized after World War II, as exemplified by the Nuremberg trials. See the instructive account in Bass (2000, esp. 14–205). For the international law foundations of the Nuremberg approach, see Falk et al. (1971, 73–176). The lesson of Versailles was reinforced by geopolitical considerations that regarded the reconstruction of Germany (and Japan) as an essential element in the containment of the Soviet Union as the Cold War unfolded and came to dominate the political imagination of those shaping the policies of leading Western states in the 1940s and 1950s.

14   See the study of the UNCC by van Houtte et al. (2006) and Bederman (1998).

15   For a range of critical assessments of sanctions imposed on Iraq, see Arnove (2000); a broader perspective is to be found in Cortright and Lopez (2000, esp. 37–61). Also, Falk (2004a).

16   Bazyler (2000). For a general study, see Richman (1999).

17   See Lillich (1962) on the nationality of claims, and their discretionary prosecution, as well as international practice.

18   This argument is set forth in greater detail in Falk (2002b); for scholarly treatment that fails to address this hypothesis of non-implementation, see Morsink (1999).

19   For various aspects of this evolution, see Andreopoulos (2002) and Falk (2000); for theoretical inquiry into the expanding status of individual rights, see Donnelly (2003); the most comprehensive assessment of this trend can be found in Steiner and Alston (2000).

20   For a pioneering study of legitimacy, see Franck (1990); further elaborated and explored in impressive detail in Franck (1995). Despite the sweep of

coverage in this latter study, Franck gives no attention whatsoever to issues of corrective justice and limits his relevant coverage to issues of "fairness" associated with alien property claims (453–73).

21 Of course, from another perspective, Germany after 1945 could be described in a similar manner, but Germany was taking steps in the aftermath of a devastating military and political defeat, and in the midst of a foreign occupation, to restore its standing as a legitimate state. It seems like an antecedent case to that of victim-oriented reparations as conferred by Latin American legal initiatives. See the studies on German reparations by Colonomos and Armstrong (2006) and Authers (2006).

22 Although not so formulated, this jurisprudence derives from the work of the New Haven School, especially Myres McDougal, Harold Lasswell, and Michael Reisman. For the most comprehensive overview, see Lasswell and McDougal (1992). A constructivist account of political and conceptual reality is most explicitly set forth by Wendt (1999).

23 Reparations can also be conceived, in part, as punitive, or at least directed toward burdening perpetrators with obligations. For insightful discussion of some of these issues, see Minow (1998).

24 See the study of South African reparations by Colvin (2006).

25 For one such example, see the study of reparations in Malawi by Cammack (2006).

26 A harm-based conception is more in accord with ideas of corrective justice, treating the victim as an autonomous subject entitled to compensation, at least to the extent feasible.

27 The issue of intertemporality is carefully considered by du Plessis (2003), in relation to efforts to obtain reparations on behalf of descendants of slaves. Interesting issues are posed as to the nature of victimization, and whether the grant of reparations, even in symbolic amounts, would not heal the inherited wounds of slavery and past forms of racial persecution and discrimination.

28 Among the treatments of this process, see Eizenstat (2003) and Bazyler (2003); for a skeptical account, see Finkelstein (2000).

29 These claims categories are included in Barkan (2000) and du Plessis (2003); see also Falk (2002a).

30 See study on reparations for Japanese Americans by Yamamoto and Ebesugawa (2006).

31 For instance, in the declaration adopted at the 2001 Durban UN Conference on Racism and Development (UNGA 2001). It is notable that the US government withdrew its delegation from the conference, partly to protest criticism of Israel and partly because of reparation claims advanced in relation to the condemnation of slavery. See du Plessis (2003) for extensive treatment.

32 For an admirable overview, see Hayner (2001).

33 It should be noted that this same selectivity applies in many crucial areas of international law, including that of humanitarian intervention, regulation of non-proliferation of weaponry of mass destruction, and enforcement of UN Security Council resolutions. It is an aspect of the balancing act that conjoins

law and power within any social order, but its influence is more salient and pronounced in relation to global policy concerns.

34   For an analysis of reparations and the ICC, see de Greiff and Wierda (2005).

35   Such nominal forms of satisfaction can be worse than nothing if the claimant continues to feel the anguish associated with harm while the impression is spread that reparative justice has been rendered, setting the stage for reconciliation.

References

Andreopoulos, George J., ed. 2002. *Concepts and Strategies in International Human Rights*. New York: Peter Lang.

Arendt, Hannah. 1952. *The Origins of Totalitarianism*. London: Allen and Unwin.

Arnove, Anthony, ed. 2000. *Iraq Under Siege: The Deadly Impact of Sanctions and War*. Cambridge, MA: South End Press.

Authers, John. 2006. "Making Good Again: German Compensation for Forced and Slave Laborers." In *The Handbook of Reparations*, edited by Pablo de Greif, 420–48. Oxford: Oxford Academic Press.

Barkan, Elazar. 2000. *The Guilt of Nations: Restitution and Negotiating Historical Injustices*. New York: Norton.

Bass, Gary J. 2000. *Stay the Hand of Vengeance: The Politics of War Crimes Tribunals*. Princeton, NJ: Princeton University Press.

Bazyler, Michael J. 2000. "Nuremberg in America: Litigating the Holocaust in United States Courts." *University of Richmond Law Review* 34 (1). https://ssrn.com/abstract=1508046.

Bazyler, Michael. 2003. *Holocaust Justice: The Battle for Restitution in America's Courts*. New York: New York University Press.

Bederman, David. 1998. "The UN Compensation Commission and the Tradition of International Claims Assessment." *NYU Journal of International Law and Politics* 27 (1): n.p.

Booth, Ken. 1993. "Human Wrongs and International Relations." *International Affairs* 71 (1): 103–26.

Brownlie, Ian. 1982. *Principles of Public International Law*, 3rd ed. New York: Oxford University Press.

Cammack, Diana. 2006. "Reparations in Malawi." In *The Handbook of Reparations*, edited by Pablo de Greif, 215–56. Oxford: Oxford Academic.

Carrillo, Arturo J. 2006. "Justice in Context: The Relevance of Inter-American Human Rights Law and Practice to Repairing the Past." In *The Handbook of Reparations*, edited by Pablo de Greif, 504–12. Oxford: Oxford Academic.

Colonomos, Ariel, and Andrea Armstrong. 2006. "German Reparations to the Jews after World War II: A Turning Point in the History of Reparations." In *The Handbook of Reparations*, edited by Pablo de Greif, 390–419. Oxford: Oxford Academic.

Colvin, Christopher J. 2006. "Overview of the Reparations Program in South Africa." In *The Handbook of Reparations*, edited by Pablo de Greif, 176–214. Oxford: Oxford Academic.

Cortright, David, and George A. Lopez, eds. 2000. *The Sanctions Decade: Assessing UN Strategies in the 1990s*. Boulder, CO: Lynne Rienner.

Council of Europe. 1950. "Convention for the Protection of Human Rights and Fundamental Freedoms." Council of Europe Treaty Series 005.

Crawford, James. 2002. *The International Law Commission's Articles on State Responsibility: Introduction, Text and Commentaries*. Cambridge: Cambridge University Press.

de Greiff, Pablo. 2004. "Universal Jurisdiction and Transitions to Democracy." In *Universal Jurisdiction: National Courts and the Prosecution of Serious Crimes Under International Law*, edited by Stephen Macedo, 240–59. Philadelphia: University of Pennsylvania Press.

de Greiff, Pablo, ed. 2006. "Justice and Reparations." In *The Handbook of Reparations*, edited by Pablo de Greif, 451–77. Oxford: Oxford Academic.

de Greiff, Pablo, and Marieke Wierda. 2005. "The Trust Fund for Victims of the International Criminal Court: Between Possibilities and Constraints." In *Out of the Ashes: Reparation for Victims of Gross and Systematic Human Rights Violations*, edited by Marc Bossuyt, Paul Lemmens, Koen de Feyter, and Stephan Parmentier, 225–43. Antwerp: Intersentia.

du Plessis, Max. 2003. "Historical Injustice and International Law: An Exploratory Discussion of Reparation for Slavery." *Human Rights Quarterly* 25: 624–59.

Donnelly, Jack. 2003. *Universal Human Rights: In Theory and Practice*. Ithaca, NY: Cornell University Press.

Eizenstat, Stuart. 2003. *Imperfect Justice*. New York: Public Affairs Press.

Factory at Chorzow (Germany v. Poland). 1927. P.C.I.J. (ser. A) No. 9, July 26.

Falk, Richard. 2000. *Human Rights Horizons: The Prospect of Justice in a Globalizing World*. New York: Routledge.

Falk, Richard. 2002a. "Reviving the 1990s Trend toward Transnational Justice: Innovations and Institutions." *Journal of Human Development* 3(2): 169–97.

Falk, Richard. 2002b. "The Challenges of Humane Governance." In *Concepts and Strategies in International Human Rights*, edited by George J. Andreopoulos, 21–50. New York: Peter Lang.

Falk, Richard. 2004a. "Iraq, the United States, and International Law: Beyond the Sanctions." In *Iraq: The Human Cost of History*, edited by Tareq Ismail and William W. Haddad, 111–34. London: Pluto Press.

Falk, Richard. 2004b. "Assessing the Pinochet Legislation: Whither Universal Jurisdiction?" In *Universal Jurisdiction: National Courts and the Prosecution of Serious Crimes Under International Law* 97, edited by Stephen Macedo, 189–211. Philadelphia: University of Pennsylvania Press.

Falk, Richard, Gabriel Kolko, and Robert Jay Lifton, eds. 1971. *Crimes of War*. New York: Random House.

Finkelstein, Norman. 2000. *The Holocaust Industry*. London: Verso.

Franck, Thomas M. 1990. *The Power of Legitimacy Among Nations*. New York: Oxford University Press.

Franck, Thomas M. 1995. *Fairness in International Law and Institutions*. New York: Oxford University Press.

Hayner, Priscilla B. 2001. *Unspeakable Truths: Confronting State Terror and Atrocity*. New York: Routledge.

ICJ Reports. 2004. "On the Legal Consequences of the Construction of a Wall in the Occupied Palestinian Territories." July 9.

Independent International Commission on Kosovo. 2000. *The Kosovo Report: Conflict, International Response, Lessons Learned*. Oxford: Oxford University Press.

International Commission on Intervention and State Sovereignty (ICISS). 2001. *The Responsibility to Protect: The Report of the Commission on Intervention and State Sovereignty*. International Development Research Center, December.

International Court of Justice (ICJ). 1962. Temple of Preah Vihear (Cambodia v Thailand), June 15.

International Law Commission (ILC). 2001. "Draft articles on Responsibility of States for Internationally Wrongful Acts, with commentaries." United Nations. https://legal.un.org/ilc/texts/instruments/english/commentaries/9_6_2001.pdf (accessed September 25, 2024).

Jaspers, Karl. 1947. *The Question of German Guilt*. Fordham University Press.

Katznelson, Ira. 2003. *Desolation and Enlightenment: Political Knowledge After Total War, Totalitarianism, and The Holocaust*. New York: Columbia University Press.

Lasswell, Harold D., and Myres S. McDougal. 1992. *Jurisprudence for a Free Society: Studies in Law, Science and Policy*. New Haven, CT: Yale University Press.

Lillich, Richard B. 1962. *International Claims: Their Adjudication by National Commissions*. Syracuse, NY: Syracuse University Press.

Mavrommatis Palestine Concessions Case (Greece v. UK). 1924. P.C.I.J. Reports (Ser. A) No. 2, August 30.

Minow, Martha. 1998. *Between Vengeance and Forgiveness: Facing History After Genocide and Mass Violence*. Boston: Beacon.

Morsink, Johannes. 1999. *The Universal Declaration of Human Rights: Origins, Drafting, Intent*. Philadelphia: University of Pennsylvania Press.

Organization of American States (OAS). 1969. *American Convention on Human Rights*. Inter-American Specialized Conference on Human Rights, San José, Costa Rica, November 22.

Organization of American States (OAS). 1985. Inter-American Convention to Prevent and Punish Torture. Cartagena de Indias, Colombia, December 9.

Rees, Stuart. 2003. *Passion for Peace*. Sydney, Australia: New South Wales University Press.

Richman, Gregg J. 1999. *Swiss Banks and Jewish Souls*. New Brunswick, Canada: Transaction.

Robertson, Geoffrey. 1999. *Crimes Against Humanity: The Struggle for Global Justice*. New York: Norton.

Shelton, Dinah. 2002. "Righting Wrongs: Reparations in the Articles on State Responsibilities." *American Journal of International Law* 96 (4): 833–56.

Steiner, Henry J., and Philip Alston, eds. 2000. *International Human Rights in Context*, 2nd ed. New York: Oxford University Press.

United Nations General Assembly (UNGA). 1973. "Permanent Sovereignty over Natural Resources." A/RES/3171, December 17.

UNGA. 1984. "Convention Against Torture and Other Cruel, Inhuman or Degrading Treatment or Punishment." GA Res 39/46, December 10.

UNGA. 1986. "Declaration on the Right to Development." GA Res 41/128, December 4.

UNGA. 2001. "Report of the World Conference against Racism, Racial Discrimination, Xenophobia and Related Intolerance." A/CONF.189/12. Durban, August 31—September 8. https://www.refworld.org/reference/themreport/unga/2002/en/68534 (accessed June 18, 2024).

UNGA. 2005. "Basic Principles and Guidelines on the Right to a Remedy and Reparation for Victims of Gross Violations of International Human Rights Law and Serious Violations of International Humanitarian Law." GA Res 60/147, December 15.

van Boven, Theo. 2000. "Basic Principles and Guidelines." E/CN. 4/2000/62, January 18.

van Houtte, Hans, Hans Das, and Bart Delmartino. 2006. "The United Nations Compensation Commission." In *The Handbook of Reparations*, edited by Pablo de Greif, Oxford: Oxford Academic, 321–389.

Wendt, Alexander. 1999. *Social Theory of International Politics*. Cambridge: Cambridge University Press.

Yamamoto, Eric K., and Liann Ebesugawa. 2006. "Report on Redress: The Japanese American Internment." In *The Handbook of Reparations*, edited by Pablo de Greif, 257–83. Oxford: Oxford Academic.

13

Transformational Justice in a Neoliberal and Statist World Order

Transitional and Transformational Justice: Conceptual Points of Departure

There is no obstacle to a transformative imaginary in relation to patriotism overcoming the fragmented identities of a state-centric world. Resistance to globalizing identities derives from imperial, nationalist, and even subnationalist ideological and essentially tribalist loyalties that reject more inclusive identity politics. Such fragmentations also preclude many forms of deference to the requirements of ecological sustainability and the development of high standards of ecological responsibility. Such an ethos depends on a greater privileging of species unity by conferring epistemological and existential status on "humanity" as an encompassing category, and the time/space attributes of eco-systemic durability as entirely complementary. In this sense, the quest for transformational justice starts with weakening the destructive bonds of nationalism and reorienting of geopolitical roles, especially in the context of war/peace agendas and the geopolitical management of global power relations.

If we imagine an interval of political transition of sovereign states from an antidemocratic governance structure to a democratic sequel, we can at least inquire as to "what kind of justice is capable of realization?" The intellectual focus on transition until the most recent decade has been prompted by encouraging trends toward democratization in the Global South, and specifically the challenges associated with a shift from an authoritarian repressive governing process to one that is constitutionally constrained and respectful of basic human rights within specific national contexts, in which the old governing establishment has not been criminalized or its influence altogether eliminated.

In this respect, the transitional challenges are dramatically different from the situation that exists if the old order has been defeated, discredited, and altogether excluded from the governing process, especially if the country is occupied in a postwar setting and a new political order is imposed by collaborative action of an occupier and domestic social and economic elites, as happened in West Germany and Japan after World War II, enabling a more drastic form of democratic restructuring, but one that still struggles internally and internationally with the threatening remnants of antidemocratic governance.

There is a further element of focus. The transitions under consideration are not a consequence of a *revolutionary* process but involve varying forms of partial accommodation between governing and oppositional forces that leave governmental bureaucracies intact and do not normally directly or deeply challenge the privileged status of *economic* and *social* elites. The varying contexts of transition are influenced, for better and worse, by the perceived need of an emerging leadership to strike a top-down compromise with former adversaries. This dynamic has seemed just as pronounced in the reverse transitions underway during the last fifteen years of somewhat democratic to somewhat autocratic.

Typically, a form of governance loses legitimacy at the point that either forces from above or below put forward sustained and intense demands for changes of leadership and public policy that go beyond marginal policy adjustments and generally represent a rising opposition to severe abuses associated with the personality, practices, and policies of a reigning autocrat or an ineffectual democrat at times of societal crisis. It is normally the case that the opposition seeking fundamental changes in governance will also insist on some accompanying form of transitional justice that takes account of and documents severe past injustices and strong personal grievances. Such a process often concentrates on agreeing to establish mechanisms for truth-telling and documentation of the past in relation to alleged grievances, including criminality. The process of such a reconstruction of the past is generally softened by arrangements providing amnesty with respect to former wrongdoing, which helps explain why the transition interval is seen as a time of compromise between formerly antagonist societal segments—a means to bring closure rather than achieving a satisfying sense of rendering justice or overcoming the deeper inequalities and inequities that afflict the social order, which would presuppose a transformative mandate. The reverse transition from democracy to autocracy is far more likely to signal change by vengeful action against the earlier leadership.

The national context in which transitional policy is formed plays a decisive role in the choice of instruments, mechanisms, policies, and goals. The weaker the transitional mandate, the more limited will be efforts to extend justice to those with pre-transition grievances. Contrariwise, if the transition is supported by highly mobilized societal forces that give rise to what amounts to a political surrender and a renunciation of the old governing process, then the discontinuity between past and future is likely to be symbolized by a much more ambitious approach to transitional justice, and such a process is better described and understood as "transformational."

Paul and Simon Robins make a creative contribution to the literature on transition by emphasizing "transformation" as a radical alternative in thought and action that is preoccupied with a societal agenda addressing the grievances of the previously marginalized, and less focused on adapting the apparatus of the state to new political circumstances (Gready and Robins 2014.) In this regard, transformative justice seeks radical changes in the economic and social order so that the mass of society formerly victimized by oppressive leadership and underlying socioeconomic structures are benefited by more equitable arrangements that benefit the whole of the population, and especially those that suffered from past marginality, deprivations, and exclusions. The transformational orientation plays a crucial role by emphasizing the need to redress societal grievances and the underlying conditions that gave rise to them, as well as to reorder the behavior of governing elites (ibid.).

What remains to be clarified is whether the articulation of such a transformational agenda can become relevant in political contexts other than those that reflect the success of a revolutionary social movement or arise in the aftermath of political surrender due to wartime occupation and defeat. In this regard, it is helpful to contrast transformation-from-within with transformation-from-without. It is our reluctant hypothesis that, absent such a revolutionary process or external occupation, the best that can be hoped for is an inter-elite bargaining process that yields compromises that can be endorsed from the perspective of "transitional justice" and are rhetorically sensitive to past atrocities, somewhat buffering the society against their repetition. In other words, there are preconditions for the realization of transformational justice that have been rarely present in antiauthoritarian movements of recent decades, which have turned out to be mainly demands for changes in the style of governance and its leadership (leader and entourage), and not the result of mass mobilization around an agenda of drastic social and economic reform, or even implementation of violated national and international criminal law provisions. In effect, these transitions have sacrificed legality for the sake of inducing voluntary transfers of power and a greater prospect of social peace. In reverse, legality is also suspended in the transition interval by vengeful acts of violence for which impunity is accorded by complicit government approval.

The Transformational Option
After World War II

Our understanding of the transformational approach as an alternative to the transitional framework can be clarified by reference to the situation that existed in Germany and Japan after 1945, when both became partially occupied countries after formally surrendering and acknowledging defeat. One of the circumstances that are amenable to transformation is where the political conditions accompanying the end of the old order do not presuppose compromise and negotiation or, more accurately, provide a setting where deeper changes can be made in an atmosphere of pervasive inequality. In the historical instance of 1945 that inequality was between the democratizing Allies and the defeated Axis powers. The Russian Revolution of 1917 illustrated another type of situation where the new order claims a mandate to reconstruct the social, economic, and political order in accord with radically different normative orientations.

Germany and Japan were occupied and devastated countries initially placed under military rule by the victorious powers, which included the resolve to destroy fascist/imperial structures of governance and ruling style and reconstruct the shattered economies along capitalist lines. The American occupier, after hesitating, did agree to allow Japan to retain "the emperor system," which was a strategic compromise made to encourage societal acceptance of the broader program of reconstruction that was being imposed on the country.

In the West this transformational mandate was partly validated and rendered politically acceptable by holding some of those previously governing and in command of military operations accountable for their allegedly criminal behavior in war crimes trials. The one-sidedness of the accountability procedures was reinforced by disallowing any formal process to assess claims that the victors also committed crimes during the war as, for instance, in strategic bombing campaigns directed at Japanese and German cities and by the atomic bombs dropped on Hiroshima and Nagasaki. The spirit of compromise and mutuality was completely absent in the assessment of criminal accountability, and the occupied population was split between those welcoming liberation from their prior political circumstances and those who resented being re-victimized by the self-justifying and coercive procedures rendering victors' justice (Minear 1971).

By and large, at least in Western liberal circles, this dramatic form of transitional justice was viewed as an advance for the rule of law, but it was sharply challenged in the dissenting opinion of the Indian judge, Judge Pal, at the Tokyo War Crimes trial and by several independent authors.[1] The parallel Nuremberg claim of legitimacy was made conditional by Karl Jaspers, dependent on whether in the future the victorious powers sitting in judgment would apply the same principles of accountability to their own behavior as had been used to judge surviving German and Japanese leaders.[2]

In effect, a governmental form of transformational justice was achieved during the transition period—the imposition of constitutional governance, sustained by periodic free elections, political parties, and rule of law did firmly ground a new type of governance that attained widespread international and provisional national legitimacy. By and large, such dynamics of transformation did not attempt to alter socioeconomic structures of wealth and privilege, and so should be considered as partial. However, if compared to the punitive peace imposed on Germany after World War I that generated an extremist backlash against democracy, the approach taken after 1945 took hold in the political soil of the occupied countries and brought an era of sustained prosperity and stability. This more enlightened approach to postwar reconstruction was undoubtedly also encouraged by the American realization of a need for quickly restored European markets to avoid a feared recurrence of economic depression, as well as by the lessons learned from the failure of the Versailles diplomacy.

There were also pragmatic considerations present, especially the early recognition in the West that the defeated enemies in Europe and Asia would be indispensable allies in the emergent rivalry with the Soviet Union. The process of postwar economic recovery and state-building in Europe was greatly facilitated by a large-scale international assistance program developed by the United States, known as the Marshall Plan. The American-led occupation policy was decidedly oriented toward instituting some version of capitalism as the basis of economic reconstruction and future strategic cooperation, although which version was left up to the domestic politics of the occupied country, so long as it clearly repudiated communist and fascist alternatives.[3] By contrast, the Soviet occupation did exhibit a mixture of vengeance with an insistence on political/ideological domination. It imposed its will on governing elites and peoples of Eastern Europe, which fell under its heavy hand, as compared with Western Europe, where the occupiers were successful in their promotion of compliant political elites that came to view the Soviet threat in a similar manner to that of their "liberators" and enjoyed the satisfaction of a rapid economic recovery that raised living standards.

In other words, the nature and sustainability of transitional justice was context driven. Part of this context was to observe that the ideological orientation of transformational politics reflected the values, policies, and skills of the occupier. Thus, the countries occupied by the Soviet Union in East Europe were dogmatically "socialist" in spirit and substance, governed by anti-liberal and state socialist states that the West would not acknowledge as "just," "legitimate," or "democratic." Moscow labeled these states as "socialist democracies" while deriding West Germany and Japan as retaining reactionary remnants of the old order. Whether these regimes in East Europe were transformational in a normative sense is widely doubted, but if such factors associated with what it means to be a legitimate sovereign state are not given precedence, then the implanting of these nominally socialist arrangements did result in major discontinuities when compared with their fascist past on all levels of the social and economic order.

A transformational outcome of a transition process, if imposed from without, is inherently one-sided, often lacking in legitimacy with the subordinated population, and makes selective use of the old order through co-option and collaboration rather than compromise. In such situations, the impact on social and economic relations depends on the orientation and agenda of the intervener or occupier, and whether the newly designated elites are competent and committed to meeting the challenges of implementation. There were notable reasons to compare and contrast these post-1945 transformational occupations with the transformations promoted by European colonialism throughout the Global South.

World Order Constraints on Transitional and Transformational Justice

As previously noted, Hedley Bull (1966) influentially argued against the Nuremberg and Tokyo ideas of accountability as forms of transitional justice on the grounds of incompatibility with what he described as "the anarchical society" that constituted the structure of world order. Bull's essential argument was that given the state-centric structures of international society, it was little other than an arbitrary and inappropriate display of power to posit a meta-law to judge the wrongs of individuals acting on behalf of sovereign states.[4] Although rejected de jure, Bull's skepticism seems validated from a de facto perspective. Neither the extension of the Nuremberg approach has been achieved to encompass the whole of international society, nor have the main geopolitical actors been prepared to limit their sovereignty by accepting the authority of international law or the United Nations.[5] Bull's opposition to intervention in the internal affairs of sovereign states, with its attendant affirmation of international pluralism, would also presumably make him critical of transformational ambitions if imposed from without, rather than coming about from within as a result of the inner dynamics of self-determination.

In effect, the prevalence of states, the weakness of international institutions upholding the *global* interest, means that the forms that "justice" assumes during transition are determined by national factors, matters that the elites in sovereign states retain control over overt or covert intervention and wars. In this respect, the normative architecture of international law, including human rights, is not usually given much explicit weight in addressing fundamental structural issues affecting the distribution of social and economic benefits and burdens. What seems most influential in the context of political displacement is the experience of other states when viewed as positive or negative models with respect to managing the replacement of an autocratic governing process by reformed governance structures committed to democratic procedures, reflecting the values of a liberal secular state. Again, the reverse transition is not symmetrical, as the autocratic reformers are less interested in peace, rule of law, and social justice and are preoccupied by the challenge of establishing effective control, managing power relations by inducing fear and intimidation rather than earning the respect and affection of their citizens and world public opinion due to the benevolence of their governance procedures.

Transformational outcomes associated with economic and social conditions are also deeply affected by the degree to which the challenges directed against the old order give emphasis to the mitigation of inequities and corruption. The ideological hegemony and the strong structures of neoliberal globalization make it very difficult to sustain such a domestic challenge, especially given the extent to which the provision by international financial institutions of economic credit and investment assistance seems to depend on an essential acceptance at the national level of the international economic status quo. It is true that several Latin American states in the period of transition repudiated both autocracy and the extreme application of neoliberal economic policies, as operative in such countries as Chile, Argentina, and Brazil, pushed by "the Chicago boys" of Milton Friedman and other endorsements of market fundamentalism.

In these countries, there was a revived adherence to moderate versions of social democracy, but without challenging the hegemony of national economic elites or breaking the links with the world capitalist economy. The weight of what was labeled "the Washington Consensus" is what Fernando Henrique Cardoso, while president of Brazil, brought to global attention when he declared that neoliberal globalization was "the only game in town" (an adaptation of Margaret Thatcher's "there is no alternative," or TINA.) The World Social Forum refused such economic determinism, adopting as its counter-slogan the phrase "there are alternatives!" and insisting that latent transformational options existed if the appropriate political will exists and massive social mobilization occurs. The Cardoso view seemed far more descriptive of the constraints on economic policymaking at the level of the sovereign state and for a time reinforced the assessment of the neoliberal world order as resilient, flexible, and able to retain its totalizing dominance.[6] With the dramatic economic success of China and some noncapitalist approaches, especially in Asia and South America, it does seem that there are indeed alternatives, but these are so far sustained by autocratic politics, or some hybrid of democratic and autocratic.

The Failures of Transition in the Arab Spring

Nearly fifteen years after the Arab Spring, it seems appropriate to assess what went wrong, at least temporarily. As the uprisings of 2011 unfolded, there was a widespread perception that the autocracies that had governed for so long were being effectively challenged by mass movements seeking a democratic constitutional order that would also address issues of joblessness, poverty, corruption, and unfair distribution of the gross domestic product (GDP). Leaders were overthrown in Tunisia, Egypt, Yemen, and Libya and were challenged elsewhere to various degrees by protests and street demonstrations. Egypt as the lynch pin of the Arab World seemed, at the start, to be engaged in a promising and important break with the past that augured well for the Middle East, generally. Egypt adopted an approach to transition that featured a series of parliamentary elections, followed by a presidential election that included the promise of a new constitution. These developments went as smoothly as could be expected given the long Egyptian background of autocratic governance and the sharp secular/religious split evident in the citizenry. The electoral outcomes exhibited the greater organizational and mobilizing skills of the Muslim Brotherhood, which performed far better than secular forces expected, challenging the long-standing secular control over the economy, as well as in relation to the post-Mubarak social and cultural order. This development quickly led secular liberals to be ambivalent and even antagonistic toward democratization reforms. Many liberal secular participants in the anti-Mubarak uprising changed sides when they came to appreciate that their material interest and societal hegemony would be undermined by the unexpected potency of political Islam. In effect, when Egyptians faced a choice between secular authoritarian rule and an Islamic-oriented constitutional leadership, many opted for the old order, and this move was extended to the Egyptian masses when the new political leadership of the Muslim Brotherhood failed to revive the economy or stimulate trade, investment, and tourism. There were also anxieties among the traditional secular elites that once the Muslim Brotherhood took over the government, the practices of parliamentary democracy would be abandoned and a theocratic government put in control of Egypt's political future.

From its outset, the Egyptian uprising left intact the bureaucracy and armed forces that had operated for thirty years under the authoritarian aegis of the Mubarak regime and, due to its strong stake in the private sector, placed a premium on ensuring the persistence of the social and economic order that had evolved under the prior regime. In that kind of atmosphere, a second movement from below emerged shortly after the 2012 close electoral victory of Mohamed Morsi, the Muslim Brotherhood candidate. This secular movement successfully created a crisis of legitimacy that gave rise to an initially overwhelming populist backing for a military coup and even supported the criminalization of the leadership elected by the Egyptian people only a year earlier. The slogan chanted in the anti-Morsi demonstrations was "the people and the army are one hand," which in certain respects is extraordinary given the abusive economic and political order that brought such widespread suffering to the Egyptian people in a governance structure presided over by the Egyptian armed forces, with their own direct stake in the exploitative economy that had dug deep roots of profitability and privilege during the Mubarak era.

What these Arab uprisings, each following a distinctive national pattern and each in its own way illustrated, is the impossibility of even transitional democratizing justice if the central aspects of the former governing process are kept in place and allowed to exert a decisive influence on contemplated reforms. In effect, in the Arab world, as elsewhere, you cannot make an omelet without breaking eggs. In Egypt this was dramatized by the reversal of the judicial conviction of the former dictator, Mubarak, leading to his impunity and the absence of transitional justice. Such action freed the long-time dictator and his associates from any accountability despite thirty years of abusive and deeply corrupt rule. Elsewhere, as in Yemen and Libya, the old order has been destroyed, but no transition to a new order took place. Instead, these states are experiencing devastating forms of chaos and strife, weakening of the state, and creating a political vacuum that is being filled by the rise of ethnic and tribal militias. Syria has experienced the worst outcome of a failed challenge to an authoritarian political order, enduring widespread devastation, acute human suffering, political fragmentation, sectarian strife, and multiple interventions by regional and global political actors. Out of this Syrian cauldron of fire, further aggravated by developments in neighboring Iraq, emerged ISIS and other non-state expressions of Islamic political extremism.

In Tunisia, a nominal, yet unstable, transition has taken place, as the dictator was removed from the scene and genuine elections followed, yet the newly elected leader was closely associated with the old Ben Ali regime and relative stability was achieved for some years by maintaining economic and social continuity with a corrupt past that reduced Tunisian masses to a collective experience of poverty, joblessness, and seeming political impotence. Yes, the hated leader and his immediate entourage had been forced off the political stage, but the old structures of privilege and oppression remain, and this has given rise to terrorist opposition challenges and to calls for renewed authoritarian governance, which has now happened with the accession to power of a new dictatorial figure, Kais Saied.

The Arab Spring gave rise to two different sets of developments. In Egypt and elsewhere, it became obvious that the desired transition could not go forward unless the movement that challenged authoritarianism also insisted on a democratizing state-building reform process. In effect, "transformational justice" would involve an equal emphasis on achieving economic and social justice, that is, jobs and equity, as had been presupposed by the promised transition to a democratic electoral process. In other words, transition would be impossible unless credibly coupled with and sustained by transformational ambitions and capabilities, and this depended not just on an appropriate form of domestic mobilization for change but also on a regional and international receptivity to such developments. The evidence suggests that from the moment that opposition succeeded in inducing Mubarak to give up his role as leader, the most significant national, regional, and international actors were intent on containing the Egyptian process of change and restoring the old structures, regardless of what the Egyptian people desired. Somewhat surprisingly, this transformational conservatism included the Muslim Brotherhood. The point here being that transformational justice, and even transitional justice, cannot be understood only as national phenomena but also as increasingly embedded in a globalizing economic and political order that sets and often enforces limits on what can be done. The contrast of the Egyptian relapse with the Iranian Revolution of 1978–79 is instructive. Both ended up with autocratic governments after democratically motivated movements were victorious over prior secular autocracies, but in the Iranian case the revolution safeguarded its victory by relying on autocratic governance with a theocratic structure. In the Egyptian case, it was a matter of restoring the former secular autocracy and renovating its policies of control.

This Middle Eastern experience contrasts with Latin America, where there was enough of a societal base sustaining the antiauthoritarian consensus that it could achieve and sustain moderate forms of transition without being reinforced by a transformational mandate. This relatively positive atmosphere in Latin America was also helped by the perceived economic failures of the military regimes that had been incompetently implementing extreme versions of market-driven styles of development. Furthermore, the transitional situation in Latin America was not nearly as complicated by some version of the secular/religious split or by the rise of anti-state tribalist subnational militias that doomed the Arab Spring in several countries. At the same time, the stagnant social and economic development in Arab countries in the aftermath of transition has contributed to counterrevolution in Egypt, chaos in Syria, Yemen, and Libya, and a temporary continuity in Tunisia that was later reversed. What seems to be the case in the Arab world is that, despite widespread popular discontent in every country, there is lacking the cohesion and consensus required to achieve even top-down transitional justice, much less bottom-up transformational justice. This resilience of the status quo is strengthened in the region by the antidemocratic and wealthy Gulf monarchies, led by Saudi Arabia, that are deeply threatened by even moderate democratizing processes and rely on co-option and suppressive tactics at home to deter challenges from below or above, as well as on overt and covert interventions throughout the Middle East to blunt if not defeat such movements wherever they arise. These tendencies are also reinforced by the antidemocratic regional priorities and strategic energy interests of Israel and the United States.

The Iranian/Islamic Revolution: A Sustained Transition and a Successful Transformation

To clarify these assessments, it seems helpful to further develop the contrast between the failed Egyptian transition following the Tahrir Square uprising in 2011 with the sustained Iranian transition/transformation in the period after the overthrow of the Shah's dynastic regime in early 1979. What seems clear are two elements of what happened in Iran during the anti-Shah mobilization: first, a popular movement from below that drew on suppressed Islamic cultural values and identities; and second, a revolutionary vision and leadership that understood that, to make a transformed structure of governance sustainable, transitions must include state reconstruction. This is an imperative if transformational ambitions are to be realized. It seems some circumstances require the replacement of the old with the new at all levels of the social order.

I had the benefit of a sustained meeting with Ayatollah Khomeini in late January 1979 that exhibited his thinking at the time about how to conceive of the future of Iran. He stressed the view that it was not "an Iranian revolution" but "an Islamic revolution," manifesting an important, often overlooked, transformational perspective, that is, a rejection of Westphalian notions of revolutionary change as territorially delimited.[7] In retrospect, more than forty-five years later, it seems accurate to conclude that the revolutionary process in Iran turned out in its unfolding to be mainly statist *and* Islamic in its effects, although not totally so.

It led to the restructuring of the Iranian state along theocratic lines outlined in earlier writing by Khomeini, achieving a form of "Islamic constitutionalism" that claimed democratic legitimacy. This theocratic regime has been sharply contested from human rights perspectives and by internal and external critics (Saikal 2016). In this respect, the Iranian "transformation" did succeed in bridging the gap between popular mobilization to challenge the old order and a drastic process of institutional reform to construct the new order. The latter relied on a strictly top-down basis, with the political dimension shaped by the uncontested authority of the hallowed religious leader. It was repressive toward those who advocated departures from Sharia law or who participated in public protests against the tactics or policies of the government.

In fairness, from the outset of its existence, the anti-Shah revolution in Iran was threatened by regional and global enemies, especially Israel, Saudi Arabia, and the United States. US regional interests were under attack, especially in relation to Israel and energy politics in the Gulf countries. The Iranian Revolution, despite preceding the end of the Cold War, was the first major indication that political Islam would not accept any persistence of Western imperial presence, and vice versa. This contrasted with the later, milder embrace of Islam in Erdoğan's Turkey that seemed able to allow a postcolonial margin of appreciation at the national level. Also, so-called moderate Islam was seen in the West as an alternative to be preferred over radical nationalism and political elites in Arab countries were more threatened by indigenous challenges than by Western or US encroachments on regional autonomy and national sovereignty. More concretely, conservative religious regimes like in Saudi Arabia were more fearful of the Islamic Revolution in Iran than of the alien values and interests of Israel and the United States.

What happened in Iran also spread the influence of political Islam throughout the region, with contradictory *ideological* reverberations that persist until now. Khomeini challenged the legitimacy of Saudi Arabia, not on sectarian grounds that Sunni Islam was heretical, but because of the alleged decadence and oppressiveness of dynastic monarchical governance. He insisted that the dynasty in Saudi Arabia was illegitimate in ways similar to his bitter indictment of the Pahlavi dynasty in Iran, a position that has received increasing support in light of Saudi behavior, including its interventions in Yemen and Syria, beheadings and other atrocities at home, and the backing given to the bloody regime of General Sisi in Egypt (Falk 2015a).

What ensued in the Arab world is not transformational movements of the sort that Iran experienced, and not even movements seeking a reformist reckoning with the past in the spirit of the Latin American and African countries, but uprisings unable to follow through, giving rise to prolonged strife and chaos or to counterrevolutionary restoration of the challenged old order, often (as in Egypt or Tunisia) in harsher form.

The Egyptian uprising failed to achieve any positive transition after its first democratic initiatives became so controversial that they provided the occasion for a counterrevolutionary backlash (Lynch 2012; Ayoob 2014). Unlike the situation in Iran after the Shah abdicated and his regime collapsed, in Egypt much of the entourage surrounding the Mubarak leadership remained in place. The embedded Egyptian judiciary and media reacted with hostility to the rise of the Muslim Brotherhood in an impressive series of electoral victories. The unreconstructed armed forces of the Mubarak period were relied upon, accorded trust and authority by the secular liberals that mobilized the effective 2011 challenge. Restorative politics along these lines were strongly, if covertly, encouraged by both Saudi Arabia and the United States.

The assigned overt mission of the Egyptian military was to ensure an orderly transition to a new era of constitutionalism and to oversee some reckoning with the past. This made the transition process susceptible to regression in light of the failure of the Morsi Brotherhood leadership to produce an economic recovery or to retain the political confidence even among the majority of those secular activists who were initially the backbone of the anti-Mubarak movement. In these respects, a growing deference to the pre-uprising governmental status quo made the transition to democratic constitutionalism extremely fragile, and subject to challenge and reversal. Arguably it was a combination of moderation and incompetence on the part of the Morsi governing process that allowed the crisis of legitimacy generated by a determined opposition to deepen and become the basis of a new, vigorous, and populist challenge with counterrevolutionary goals to succeed. The refusal of the United States, Saudi Arabia, and Israel to view Egyptian democratization favorably, given its nationalist agenda, undoubtedly contributed to the vulnerability of the transitional process to resistance and reversal.

In this respect, what happened in Egypt can be seen as negatively transformational, not only restoring the old authoritarian order, but liquidating those who had gained power through the democratic procedures instituted during what purported to be a transitional phase having as its goal nothing more ambitious than the establishment of a stable constitutional democracy.[8] The progressive transformational agenda associated with economic policy and emancipatory politics was never pushed in practice by either the original uprising in 2011 or by the Muslim Brotherhood, and certainly not in the course of the counterrevolutionary sequel.

The contrasting Iranian transition can be understood in two phases: first, the period of several months in 1979, when the government was under the control of a Westernized Iranian technocratic leadership adhering to the modernizing outlook of moderate Islam; this was followed by a second period of theocratic or radicalized Islam guided by the assertion of direct religious control over the governing process by Ayatollah Khomeini and the Shi'a religious establishment. There exists an unresolved ambiguity that concerns this shift from the moderate phase to the radical theocratic phase that institutionally implemented the vision that Ayatollah Khomeini had developed while living for seventeen years as an exile from the Shah's regime, mainly in Najaf, Iraq. During my meeting with this charismatic leader, he was then seemingly sincere about his intention to resume his religious life upon returning to Iran. He expressed the view that the movement he led embraced political action only to rid Iran of dynastic rule (that he ardently believed was responsible for "creating a river of blood between the ruler and the people"), and this being done, the revolution could go forward under the aegis of politicians and technocrats. But what this extraordinary historical personage seemed to believe in Paris did not accurately prefigure his activities and role upon returning to Iran.

When Ayatollah Khomeini returned from Paris in January 1979, in line with his earlier intentions, he took up residence in a madrassa in the holy city of Qom that is relatively remote from the political nerve center of the country in Tehran. The explanation of his resumed domination of the political scene some months later remains an unresolved mystery. Was it always part of a master plan? Did it arise due to his contentions that the post-Shah Iranian leadership in Tehran was weak, putting the revolution at risk by failing to carry out the promised transformational program? Was it the case that Ayatollah Khomeini only came to appreciate his extraordinary influence and stature in the country after his return to Iran at the start of 1979 or was he pushed to be more politically engaged by other religious leaders who believed that the opportunity to reshape the future of the country was of short duration and depended on Khomeini's personal engagement? As these questions have yet to receive convincing answers, it is impossible to determine the degree to which the enduring changes brought about in Iran were the result of a top-down process or somehow combined leadership by the new theocratic elite with the power of an aroused mass movement dominated by religious believers.

Overall, Iran is illustrative of a transformational process that altered the state and its governing process in fundamental ways, but did not have either the ambition nor the means to alter the social and economic experience of most Iranians to nearly the same degree. The impact of perceived enemies from without and within also seemed to be part of this aborted Iranian transition narrative, seeking to destabilize the Islamic government through diplomatic isolation, ideological rejection, and coercive diplomacy. Although the post-Shah regime safeguarded its security in ways that Egypt failed to do, it was forced act defensively, adopting an economically austere policy agenda that made life difficult for ordinary Iranians. Tehran's direct attacks on the legitimacy of Israel and its regional encroachment and beachhead for the reassertion of European and US influence contributed to a variety of failed regional efforts to reverse the revolutionary process.

What can be confidently concluded is that despite opposition and aggression by Iraq, mounted with encouragement and support from the United States, the governing process in Iran brought about by the overthrow of the Shah withstood these difficult external challenges in the 1980s. It also withstood challenges that came later, which were focused on Iran's alleged pursuit of nuclear weapons and its supposed role as a promoter of terrorism and proxy warfare in the region. In other words, unlike Egypt, the ongoing and recurrent crises of legitimacy never effectively challenged regime stability despite an array of domestic, regional, and global forces arrayed against the Islamic Republic of Iran.[9] Iran managed the transition to a form of theocratic governance which, although flawed, harsh, and repressive, operated within a constitutional frame that managed somewhat free and periodic elections. Iran's leadership administered this novel governing process by successfully transforming the Iranian state and its armed forces to serve loyally the new political order. Oddly enough, the Iranian experience of revolutionary transformation has parallels with the Leninist understanding that a revolutionary challenge from below can only be sustained if the state and armed forces are totally reconstituted and reoriented, and this can only happen if the process is guided by strong, perhaps ruthless, leadership that is itself committed to coherent programmatic ends rooted in an ideology that promises deliverance and emancipation from oppression. In practice, these kinds of political movements do not necessarily perform as initially promised, thereby betraying and sometimes punishing their earlier supporters. In effect, once the people were no longer needed in Iran, the top-down processes were reestablished, although the new leaders were primarily drawn from the previously excluded religious elites of the country. Under very different conditions, several Asian countries achieved high levels of political independence and economic progress by adopting highly centralized and autocratic state/society relations, most notably China, that proved impervious to the postcolonial interventions of the imperial West.

Applying the Lessons of Transition and Transformation to the Palestine/Israel Struggle

The Palestine/Israel struggle is a variation on the normal consideration of transitions from authoritarianism. Here the idea of establishing peace and democracy involves transforming oppressive structures of occupation, dispossession, and exile in the direction of shared sovereignty, equality, and mutual respect for rights. Such a transition requires in this instance territorial and governmentality compromises, repatriation of refugees, and some Israeli reckoning with past wrongs done to the Palestinians. It does not necessarily entail the dismantling of Israel that has long exerted dominance over the Palestinian people and was responsible for the first two major dispossessions of indigenous Palestinians in 1948 and 1967, but it does require that the Palestinian right of self-determination be achieved in a manner that produces a sustainable peace, which in turn must be perceived as just, or at least fair, by the great majority of Palestinians. Whether this is done by top-down intergovernmental diplomatic interaction, through the pressures exerted by bottom-up civil society activism, or by some combination that includes pressures from without, will likely influence whether the new political order for Israel and Palestine is to some degree transformative.

Such speculative commentary is certain to reflect the impact of the 2023–24 prolonged genocide against the Palestinian people living in Gaza, as well as the violent, government-sanctioned violence of West Bank settlers intent on provoking a third major dispossession of ethnic Palestinians by means of an international forced evacuation.

If the essence of this struggle is tension relating to overlapping and antagonistic territorial claims and opposed nationalist movements, then the challenges of peaceful transition and transformation can be achieved by a negotiated compromise, political surrender, or armed victory that imposes a solution. It has been long assumed since the British gave the responsibilities of their Palestine mandate to the UN after World War II that a diplomatically generated solution would enable transition to a peaceful and democratic future for both peoples, taking the form of some kind of partition of historic Palestine within its mandate borders.

First, the UN attempted to propose a compromise by way of General Assembly Resolution 181 that was based on the partition of Palestine, which led to a series of wars, and has since 1967 involved the Israeli occupation of territories set aside for Palestinian governance, a coercive status quo that blocks transition to an internationally preferred outcome of coexistence. After partition failed, the second major effort was to create a framework that allowed direct negotiations between the Israeli government and the legitimate representatives of the Palestinian people, with the United States acting as the convening intermediary in this self-proclaimed peace process that was initiated in 1993 by the adoption of the Oslo Framework of Principles. The implicit assumption was that a top-down transition by way of intergovernmental diplomacy could be achieved, leading to the establishment of an independent Palestinian state existing alongside the Israeli Jewish supremacy state, with transformative one-state solutions being treated as irrelevant (Falk 2015b, 1–12).

With the issue of Palestinian representation in doubt due to the fragmentation of administrative control between the Palestinian Authority and Hamas, it increasingly appears to be the case that alternate forms of representation linked to civil society activism have attained gradually increased legitimacy among the Palestinian people. It is not currently possible to assess whether this resituating of Palestinian representational legitimacy can be formalized in some relevant political form, but should this happen, the transformative dimensions of any genuine peace process are almost certain to gain credibility as it will be a people-driven political process. Of course, the mobilization phase will highlight incentives for social justice that may then disappear at a subsequent institutionalization phase, when social and economic elites will be poised to capture the political process.

This kind of accommodation to societal structures has often made the outcome of progressive movements that seemed built on populist enthusiasm—as was the case with many of the anti-colonialist struggles, and the anti-apartheid campaign challenging racist South Africa—seem disappointing in the end, as elites give ground with respect to political control while retaining benefits conferred by the basic socioeconomic hierarchies of the old order to facilitate transition, which in the Israel case never came, and increasingly took the form of apartheid subjugation while the challenge of ethnic cleansing of Palestinians from their own homeland was being overcome. Developments since the Hamas attack of October 7, 2023 have given this process a genocidal edge, shocking and alienating peoples the world over while Israel's North American and European supporters remain silent or commit crimes of complicity. China has sponsored a process by which the Palestinian Authority and twelve Palestinian resistance groups agreed to overcome their differences and work cooperatively to achieve self-determination for Palestine (2024 Beijing Declaration on Ending Division and Strengthening Palestinian National Unity).

The Liberal Bias Toward Transition Without Transformation

Hannah Arendt developed an influential argument in *On Revolutions* that insists that revolutionary dynamics achieve positive humane outcomes only when they do *not* attempt to promote radical changes in economic and social structure—that is, revolutionary success depends on removing transformational goals from the political agenda (Arendt 1963; Brinton 1962). The relatively benign transition managed by American elites from British colonial rule in the United States to political independence serves as the primary positive example of her position. The French and Russian Revolutions provide the main negative cases in which lofty transformational ambitions were abandoned and at the same time incremental progress toward an improved human future was rarely achieved. The logic behind this differentiation seems clear. When class divisions are unchallenged, elites can at certain points accept, or even favor, the outcome of challenges to the established *political* order, but will resist, violently, if necessary, any deeper challenge to their positions of economic privilege and social status. To the extent that this conservative analysis of historical experience is accepted, it poses a dilemma for those seeking change at the grassroots level, possibly discouraging movements from demanding transformative change at the level of state and society, and shifting attention in two alternative directions, the local and the global, and the hybridity associated with their interplay.

Such a framework of assessment can be further illustrated by reference to the cases discussed in earlier sections. Overcoming apartheid in South Africa and militarism in the Southern Cone countries of Latin America was sustained in the transition period and subsequently, but there were no challenges mounted in these instances to the underlying racially delimited class inequalities associated with great disparities of wealth and income. Similarly in Latin American and Asian instances, except in China, oligarchical distributions of economic and social power were not significantly altered by strong challenges mounted against the political status quo.

In contrast, the movements that overthrew the old order in Egypt and Iran did attempt to displace the traditional governing and privileged elites, provoking a counterrevolution in the Egyptian case and a coercive theocratic regime in the Iranian case. In Egypt, democratic aspirations were completely thwarted by the counterrevolution, while in Iran, a partial, tightly controlled and limited theocratic form of democracy was institutionalized, with some ups and many downs during its more than forty-five years of governmental authority. In neither the Egyptian nor Iranian cases was any effort made to achieve "peace and reconciliation" in the transition period but, on the contrary, a repudiation of the past leading to an intensive polarization as to the desired character of a new political future. For Egypt, the transformative ambition was repudiated by the coup in mid-2013, and even modest transitional hopes were abandoned and reversed. In Iran, the original revolutionary claims have been rhetorically maintained but managed on the basis of a theocratic structure that incorporated nationalist values in such ways as to block transformational gains based on bottom-up demands for participatory rights, secular freedoms, and socioeconomic equity.

From this experience we can draw some tentative lessons. In post-authoritarian situations, prospects for sustainable constitutional democracy depend on limiting goals to a self-consciously liberal political agenda focused on such concerns as leadership, rule of law, due process, the prohibition of torture and overt racism, and by avoiding questioning inflammatory structural issues such as property rights and distributional equity. These limits imply a circumspection with respect to the advocacy of change, being satisfied by modest *policy* reforms designed to reduce corruption and abusive state power, promote employment and investment, and increase tax revenues. These reforms steer clear of issues that would depend on *structural* changes requiring the alteration of domestic alignments of social and economic class forces operative within the country. Both the sustained compromises negotiated by Nelson Mandela and F. W. de Klerk in South Africa and the fragile democracy that emerged in Tunisia for some years are illustrative of reliance on a minimalist transitional approach to overcome a prior condition of autocracy. Such a practical foreshortening of goals leaves the most embedded economic and social inequities in place and essentially unchallenged. Transformational goals are quietly abandoned by the new elites and structural continuity achieved, which embodies the essence of what is understood by transitional justice in theory, and even more so in practice. Of course, radical critics are unhappy with this course of events, and are either marginalized or directly repressed, as in Iran.

Another way of understanding these outcomes is to regard liberal style transition as inevitably a Faustian Bargain in which peace and order are given priority at the expense of social and economic justice. It is also a recognition that most political challenges to authoritarian or oppressive established orders are not revolutionary in ideology, program, and leadership, with most oppositional movements seemingly content to achieve the removal of oppressive leadership, entrusting the future to a new elite committed to establishing and managing a constitutional democracy. This is a political process that may currently be reaching a historical dead end, signaled by mass migrations from impoverished and war-torn societies, with stability threatened by the havoc wrought by climate change, and by the inability of governing forces to deal with unemployment and poverty. Such developments help us grasp the logic of reversals that move toward or restore autocratic styles of governance.

This was certainly the case in Egypt and Tunisia, with the difference in the immediate aftermath of the upheavals in the two countries, reflecting the results of the Egyptian moves to institutionalize democracy that unexpectedly brought the Muslim Brotherhood into a brief period of wielding governmental control, inducing a powerful counterrevolutionary coup. In effect, the liberal reliance on elections posed a perceived threat of structural change both at the top (by substituting Islamic for secular elites) and at the bottom (by empowering an Islamic collective consciousness). After the Tahrir Square success in causing the downfall of the Mubarak regime, there was a temporary societal consensus in Egypt among secular elites that free parliamentary elections would not result in more than 25 percent of the legislative body being controlled by Islamically oriented political parties. The established civilian order and armed forces believed that an Islamic presence on such a scale was manageable within existing structures. This prospect was initially reinforced by a voluntary Muslim Brotherhood pledge not to compete for either legislative seats in large parts of Egypt or to seek the presidency. When it turned out that Brotherhood support was double what had been expected in a series of parliamentary elections in 2011 and early 2012, the organization adopted more ambitious goals, withdrawing its earlier pledge, competing everywhere for seats in the legislature and fielding their own presidential candidate. When this move by the Muslim Brotherhood was followed by a close victory for their candidate, Mohammed Morsi, in the 2012 runoff presidential elections, a backlash ensued that was able to reverse the transition arrangements so enthusiastically endorsed only a year and a half earlier.

The Ennahda Movement, an Islamic political organization in Tunisia, was more cautious about its approach to political participation. Some extremists in Tunisia resorted to violence to promote a transformational outcome, but the liberal transitional scenario unfolded in a manner that gave rise to a constitutional democratic sequel to the Ben Ali autocracy.

The situation in both countries was fluid, in part because of the stressed economic situation of joblessness, stagnant growth, and mass poverty on one side and an affluent, privileged small elite linked to the neoliberal world economy on the other. Despite the appearance of a successful transition to democracy in Tunisia, the old order was restored to power after some years, and now resembles Egypt, constituting a reverse transition from glimmers of democracy to the restoration of autocracy.

This mix of results produces an unstable future. In some national settings, for instance in Latin America, transitions based on liberal goals have proved sustainable for several decades. In the more turbulent setting of the Middle East, even minimal scenarios of transitional justice have been challenged in most instances, although internal circumstances can be described as continuing to exhibit *unsustainable* conditions of economic and societal injustice. Posed in this manner, only transformational movements can seek to overcome these national conditions, but without much encouragement from historical experience, which seems disillusioning. If the transformational mandate should be backed by a populist victory in electoral democracy, as for instance in Venezuela after the victory of Hugo Chávez, then a counterrevolutionary effort will be made, with varying degrees of external backing, to discredit, defeat, and reverse the democratic results. This poses the underlying question whether it is realistic to consider transformational options, given the strength of the internal status quo as backed by the international ideological consensus and geopolitical support systems, including military intervention, associated with the neoliberal world economy and the strategic and ideological priorities of geopolitical actors, especially the United States and China.

Conclusion

What emerges from the assessments made is that transformation-from-below is certainly desirable, and probably necessary, but its attainment and maintenance within a democratic framework is exceedingly difficult given the intersecting realities of domestic socioeconomic structure and neoliberal globalization. Both Cuba and China are examples of countries that achieved degrees of transformation in the aftermath of successfully overthrowing deeply rooted authoritarian political orders by reliance on armed struggle. Their revolutionary mandates called for drastic societal restructuring that reached many impressive results despite formidable internal and external obstacles, but in each country a process is being pursued that calls into question whether the transformational dimensions of their governing process will be retained or superseded by new socioeconomic hierarchies of privilege and gross disparity.

In China, the slogan of "market socialism" masks, to a degree, the transformational concessions being made, as well as new forms of elitism and subjugation that have now given rise to a new authoritarianism in the country. In Cuba, a similar process seems to be underway in which an announced receptivity to global market forces seems in the process of being allowed to encroach upon the socialist achievements of the country. The Cuban orientation toward development is embraced to promote economic growth, investment, and trade, as well as to achieve political normalization with the United States and the West, but without attaining these reasonable ends even though the Cold War ended more than thirty years ago. A similar repudiation of Maduro populism in Venezuela reinforces this impression of continuing hemispheric intolerance in Washington. These are shocking instances of official US postwar refusals to respect the dynamics of self-determination in Latin America.

In effect, a state-centric world order in the age of neoliberal globalization makes liberally constituted transition mark the outer limits of political feasibility, and even this kind of humane adaptation presupposes the right mix of conditions that seem absent in the Middle East, most of Asia, sub-Saharan Africa, and even parts of Latin America. One implication of this assessment is to make transformative visions unrealizable, and dangerously susceptible to outcomes that are either an intensified version of the old authoritarian system or an open invitation to counterrevolution and foreign military intervention.

A further implication of this analysis is to seek greater regulation of political behavior on behalf of the human interest in a variety of global venues that legitimizes the pursuit of transformative goals. This understanding is complemented by a recognition that the best prospects of grassroots movements may be in local struggles for transformed social and economic conditions, including through the agency of independent labor activism. As the prior discussion has confirmed, the particularities of national, regional, and global context are responsible for a series of limitations and opportunities at all levels of political action, empowering liberal programs of transition in some national settings and shattering transformational hopes in most others. What remains clear is that the workings of neoliberal capitalism are widening income and wealth disparities within most national settings in ways that might give rise to a new cycle of extremist politics and of transformational protest movements. If this happens, it will be important to avoid having such radical energies captured by liberal transitional frameworks and security practices that function to put constraints on all efforts to transform underlying socioeconomic relationships. Such developments prompt the emergence of movements for radical restructuring and responses, either by way of marginal concessions or reactionary retreats that end up producing autocratic forms of governance.

Although this discussion has been dominated by the internal dramas surrounding movements dedicated to liberal or radical reform, the implications for global governance are profound, producing political outcomes that reinforce rather than transcend statist forms of patriotism. Perhaps a series of developments in the third decade of the twenty-first century foreshadow a different future, including de-dollarization campaigns, the rising dominance of the BRICS economies, the decline of the Global West, and the vision of geopolitical balance being espoused by China (an implicit alternative to the "rules-governed world" touted by Antony Blinken, in which the rules are a facade for hegemonic governance administered by Washington). In effect, the tensions between state-centrism and eco/species centrism will become increasingly salient with the passage of time.

Notes

1   For authoritative positive account see Taylor (1992); compare Minear (1971) and particularly the dissenting judgment of Judge Radhabinod Pal (1948). For a different type of liberal justification for reliance on judicial criminal proceedings in the special transitional context that existed after World War II, see Bass (2000).

2   For an influential interpretation, see Jaspers (1961); see also the opening statement of the American prosecutor at Nuremberg, Justice Robert H. Jackson, reprinted in Falk et al. (1971).

3   There was less pressure placed on Japan to renounce its imperial antecedents except with respect to its militaristic dimensions. In this regard, and expressive of an antiwar mood in Japan, the new Japanese Constitution committed the country to limit military capabilities to self-defense and military expenditures to 1 percent of the national budget. Gradually, these constraints have weakened, and the present government of Japan is seeking "normalcy" by claiming the discretion to act internationally as any other sovereign state.

4   Henry Kissinger made a similar, although more self-serving, argument in opposing universal jurisdiction (2001); see in response, Roth (2001); and for an argument that prosecution of Kissinger would be justified, see Hitchens (2001).

5   Compare Goldsmith and Posner (2005) with Ohlin (2015).

6   This neoliberal world order is given a coherent rationale in Ikenberry (2011).

7   For comments on subsequent radical challenges to the core Westphalian conception of world order, see Falk (2004, 3–44).

8   Egypt gave rise to this peculiarity of a "counterrevolution" even though the 2011 uprising had never been "revolutionary" in organization, ideology, and program, which instructively distinguishes it from the political process in Iran. The original idea was to proceed with elections and a new constitution

without any formal effort to assess past wrongdoing, a minimal transitional scenario that proved to be overly ambition considering the deep polarization of Egyptian political culture.

9   Even the Green Revolution of 2009 was transitional, not transformative, seeking reform not regime change, and was easily suppressed by the government. See Hashemi and Postel (2013).

References

Arendt, Hannah. 1963. *On Revolution*. New York: Viking.

Ayoob, Mohammed. 2014. *Will the Middle East Implode?* Cambridge, UK: Polity.

Bass, Gary J. 2000. *Stay the Hand of Vengeance: The Politics of War Crimes Tribunals*. Princeton, NJ: Princeton University Press.

Brinton, Crane. 1962. *The Anatomy of Revolution*. New York: Prentice Hall.

Bull, Hedley. 1966. "The Grotian Conception of International Society." In *Diplomatic Investigations: Essays in the Theory of International Politics*, edited by H. Butterfield and Martin Wight, 71–94. Oxford University Press.

Falk, Richard. 2004. *The Declining World Order: America's Imperial Geopolitics*. London and New York: Routledge.

Falk, Richard. 2015a. "Saudi Arabia and the Price of Royal Impunity." *Middle East Eye*, October 6.

Falk, Richard. 2015b. *Chaos and Counterrevolution: After the Arab Spring*. Charlottesville, VA: Just World Books.

Falk, Richard. 2016. "Rethinking the Arab Spring: Uprisings, Counterrevolution, Chaos, and Global Reverberations." *Third World Quarterly* 37 (12): 2322–34.

Falk, Richard, Gabriel Kolko, and Robert Jay Lifton, eds. 1971. *Crimes of War*. New York: Random House.

Goldsmith, Jack L., and Eric Posner. 2005. *The Limits of International Law*. New York: Oxford.

Gready, Paul, and Simon Robins. 2014. "From Transitional to Transformative Justice: A New Agenda for Practice." *International Journal of Transitional Justice* 8 (3): 339–61. https://doi.org/10.1093/ijtj/iju013.

Hashemi, Nader, and Danny Postel, eds. 2013. *The Syria Dilemma*. Cambridge, MA: MIT Press.

Hitchens, Christopher. 2001. *The Trial of Henry Kissinger*. London: Verso.

Ikenberry, John G. 2011. *Liberal Leviathan: The Origins, Crisis, and Transformation of the American World Order*. Princeton, NJ: Princeton University Press.

Jaspers, Karl. 1961. *The Question of German Guilt*. New York: Capricorn Books.

Kissinger, Henry. 2001. "The Pitfalls of Universal Jurisdiction." *Foreign Affairs* (July/August): 86–96.

Lynch, Marc. 2012. *The Unfinished Revolutions of the New Middle East*. New York: Public Affairs.

Minear, Richard H. 1971. *Victors' Justice: Tokyo War Crimes Trial*. Princeton, NJ: Princeton University Press.

Ohlin, Jens David. 2015. *The Assault on International Law*. New York: Oxford.

Pal, Radhabinod. 1948. "Judgement." In B. V. A. Roling and C.F. Riter, *Tokyo Judgment: The International Military Tribunal for the Far East, April 29, 1946, to November 12, 1948*. Amsterdam: APA-University Press.

Roth, Kenneth. 2001. "The Case for Universal Jurisdiction." *Foreign Affairs* (September/October): 150–54.

Saikal, Amin. 2016. *Iran at the Crossroads*. Cambridge, UK: Polity.

Taylor, Telford. 1992. *The Anatomy of the Nuremberg Trials: A Personal Memoir*. New York: Knopf.

14

Revisiting the Earth Charter

Ron Engel has articulated a review of the Earth Charter (2014) so thoughtfully, urbanely, and persuasively that our initial temptation was to restrict a response to a single word: "Amen!" Yet we are familiar enough with the academic folkways of gathering diverse voices to explore a topic or to evaluate the scholarship of a distinguished author to proceed more substantively. At the same time, it would be misleading if we did not praise Engel for putting so many elusive issues before us in such a lucid and compelling manner as to make efforts at dialogue feel forced, given the high level of agreement.

This endorsement of Engel's call to action for the realization of the ambitious goals of the Earth Charter does not strike us as particularly dialogic but rather as expressive of the importance of transnational consensus-building at this stage among the like-minded constituency of ecological patriots who are ready to accept the crucial transformative challenges that lie at the heart of making the Earth Charter into a plan of action or, at the very least, a manifesto. In effect, if the Earth Charter presents the vision, a manifesto could implore its implementation by identifying what needs to be done and by whom.

Can we, amid the complexities and contradictions of the historical present, identify agents of change or social forces comparable to the manner in which Marx and Engel interpreted the role of the working classes in mid-nineteenth-century Europe? We wonder how to achieve political traction for a transformative political movement that recognizes as the most formidable obstacles on the path toward planetary peace and justice those ideologies and practices associated with neoliberal capitalism and its strong linkages of mutual dependence with militarized governmental bureaucracies.

In recent years this toxic set of institutional/ideological linkages has been able to divert the peoples of the world and most governing elites from the challenge of restoring preindustrial ecological integrity to such issues as the threats to civilizational coherence posed by transcivilizational migratory flows that expose the fragility of democratic values and practices, climate change, and various forms of globalization that reinforce unacceptable inequalities, alienating and enraging those left behind. In reaction, many populated and affluent societies of the world have perversely placed their trust and their future in the hands and wayward heads of demagogic leaders and ultranationalist political parties that proclaim anti-ecological agendas in spirit and substance.

Given this, it does seem somewhat utopian to situate current hopes on the ecological radicalization of democracy in ways that insist on the implementation of equality norms across the spectrum of human concerns and even extends the boundaries of ethical sensitivity to encompass nonhuman species. Can we, in other words, responsibly rely on the peoples of the world to form a movement powerful enough to bring a Second Axial Age[1] into being—especially at a time when the transcendent values of the First Axial Age are being so widely betrayed? At least we need some exploration of why such a belief in the reinvigoration of democracy is not a mere exercise in wishful thinking that should be put aside if we are to contemplate the future with an appropriate sense of concern in response to a realistic appraisal of present destructive trends.

If a skeptical eye is turned toward the positive potentialities of democracy, we need to ask, "What then?" to escape from falling into a dark pit of despair. Certainly, none of the competing secular ideologies, or their religious analogs, seems capable of successfully taking on such a mission. It could be that we are experiencing nothing more than a democratic pause and that there will be a dialectical renewal of democracy in reaction to the dominant autocratic/populist political trajectories that now seem to be moving social and economic patterns of behavior toward ecological crises, with possible catastrophic outcomes.

We need to remember that the best Athenian minds—including Plato, Aristotle, and Thucydides—all lost faith in democracy due to the capacity of demagogues to turn the citizenry of their city into a frenzied warmongering mob that led Athens to succumb to its own hubris by overreaching its limits. This surrender has often been misunderstood and misapplied by the power-mad realists shaping global governance in its present hybrid mixture of statism and geopolitics, the chaos of interacting sovereign states "disciplined" by the grand strategies and managerial styles of dominant states.

The Melian Dialogue in Thucydides's *The History of the Peloponnesian War* is often cited by writers on international relations to show that in the foreign encounters of states, only power counts, with reliance placed on Thucydides's often-invoked assured words: "Those who have power do what they like, those who do not, do what they must" (1998, 588). A more careful reading of Thucydides's whole narrative shows that this first great historian of warfare was using this apparent whitewash of cruelty and opportunism in war as indicative of Athenian decline, and not as a comment on the way the world works, much less how it should work. Thucydides was suggesting to attentive readers that those who do not respect universal morality in dealing with their weaker adversaries will themselves perish before long. This is a message our militarist political elites refuse to heed or even comprehend and are aided in their mindlessness by think tank realists and power-hungry academics who wrap themselves in the false flag of "realism."

Perhaps the most startling claim in Engel's essay is that the Earth Charter is illuminating the *ontological* essence of human reality. Such a bold assertion sets the agenda of the Second Axial Age as tasked with converting this sense of humanity as consisting of ecological beings into a living historical reality. By invoking ontology, Engel is claiming that Earth Charter perspectives depict "the essential or true structure of reality" that definitively establishes the moral boundaries of human endeavor and grounds hope for a relevant global movement for self-government as necessarily responsive to this understanding.

We share Engel's view that it is crucial to keep focused on what is *necessary* and *desirable*, and not let our views of the future get hijacked by entrenched self-interested entrepreneurs who insist that responses be confined to what is *feasible* or *reasonable*, who continue to exert near-monopoly control over the exercise of political and economic power, as well as shape the public narrative. Among the most insidious of these entrepreneurs are the corporatized media giants that feed our minds with a false confidence in the normalcy of our times, thereby distracting us from an appreciation of the urgent priorities for change that stem from its unprecedented systemic *abnormality*. This media spin on the contemporary world obstructs most efforts to achieve a relevant critical awareness. Without such an awareness, the needed emergent consensus on who we are and how we should behave is situated on a terrain that is out of human reach. Instead of developing an ecologically driven focus, the mainstream media is leading the worthy fight in so many places to protect freedom of expression from statist and corporate encroachments, thereby offering a better understanding of the abuses attributable to autocratic forms of governance operating at the level of the state and beyond.

While this struggle is truly significant and must be waged, it is not as vital or urgent as the struggle to recover an ecological sense of our beingness-in-the-world—a sense that came naturally to many native peoples in the premodern world, whose existence was not only suppressed and exploited, but whose wisdom was discarded by reductionist and hegemonic versions of how human society interacts coercively with its natural surroundings. At the very time when we need to be conditioned by the ecological imperatives of a new global ethics, most societies are in the grips of these earlier struggles to avoid slipping into twenty-first-century versions of the Dark Ages or, at best, making themselves content with being "entertained" while the fires of ecological disarray move ever closer. In this sense, the political struggles being waged are tinkering with the modalities of how human society manipulates nature for its benefit, instead of restoring modalities of mutuality and reciprocity that can produce *structural* resilient changes as well as fight *policy* battles within anachronistic ontological frameworks.

What is possible and necessary, and follows from the coherence of the Earth Charter and our recognition of the truthfulness of its presentation of reality, is altering the sense of citizenship and political participation, at least for those of us who endorse the vision. We regard the call for global citizenship, which Engel affirms, to be somewhat misleading. Citizenship presupposes community and what is lacking at present is any meaningful sense of global political community. For the overwhelming multitude of people, the boundaries of territorial sovereign states exhaust the spatial extension of political community, which also flourishes in a multitude of subnational and local communities. Moving toward an ecological civilization will require the emergence and construction of a genuine and robust global community. This seems a project for the future rather than presenting an existing alternative. It is a challenging task for the future and needs to be identified as such to avoid a purely nominal claim of *global* citizenship in global settings predominantly shaped by nationalist ideologies that inhibit, in the name of traditional patriotism, any real engagement with either species or ecological well-being, especially when these normative strivings place burdens on the pursuit of nationalist priorities. For this reason, the language of "citizen pilgrim" seems preferable as self-identifying those seeking to construct a global community that is organized around global ethics of the sort that flows from an acceptance of the worldview embedded in the Earth Charter. In this imaginary, the citizen pilgrim is embarked on such a journey equipped with maps that locate no fixed destination, but dwell upon the idea—at once spiritual and material—of establishing an ecologically resilient global community by stages as opportunities arise.

In the background of such musings is a problematic sense that the United Nations, as the institutional nerve center of the international legal order, was expected to prefigure such a global community. From a reading of the preamble to the UN Charter, back in 1945 the new institutional framework was dedicated to promoting *human* interests rather than providing an additional vehicle for the realization of *national* interests. Such an idealistic perception of the UN was always doubtful given its structural design and, at most, expressed a vague expectation that might be fulfilled at some distant time in the future. The constitutional makeup of the UN reflected the anarchic workings of existing world order, giving priority to the equality of sovereign states as against the claims of either people or nature and allowing the dominant states to use their right of veto to opt out of their obligations to comply with the UN Charter, as well as their geopolitical entitlement to view international law as discretionary for themselves and their friends while being mandatory for the others.

In this context, it should have been anticipated that over time the UN would become primarily an instrument combining statecraft and geopolitics and only rarely a crucial venue for global policymaking. As the UN has matured, it has not developed like its most ardent supporters had hoped. On the contrary, it has lost much of its earlier relevance to the resolution of international conflicts and seems more marginal than ever on the peace and security challenges of our time. Such a generalization is not meant to withhold credit from the UN—especially from its specialized organs dealing with health, children, culture, human rights, and the environment in ways that improve lives and the habitat—but within frames of thought and action that are almost totally pre-ecological and disconnected from the war prevention priorities that had inspired those that championed the UN's establishment.

At the very outset of his essay, Engel delimits the overriding goal and challenge facing humanity to be one of achieving what he calls "a new era of global governance." It never becomes evident what that would entail by way of institutional and normative renovation. The realization of the Earth Charter's vision would seem to depend upon the existence of institutions having as their primary mandate a mission to serve peace and justice for all peoples of the world—not by implementing the outlook of a growth-oriented developmental economy but by reference to an ecologically infused global ethics. This undertaking is quite revolutionary in its call for reordering the values and practices that have prevailed throughout *modern* human history; it is further extended by a fundamental ecological pedagogy insisting that we, as a species, can only expect to live in a sustainable manner if we also enlarge our moral and political imagination to take into account the well-being of nonhuman species and our natural surroundings, and commit to policy guidelines that are responsive to a resilient worldview.

What that means concretely needs to be worked out in ways that acknowledge the contradictions that exist when it comes to mediating interspecies relations by reference to measures of mutuality. Does it, for instance, require the adoption of a dramatic dietary embrace of vegetarianism by the entire human species, or is it sufficient to treat animals decently and kill them only for subsistence, as native peoples tended to do? Who is there to identify the demographic limits that meet the standards set by an ecologically grounded global ethics and how will such limits be determined and implemented? Engel regards nonviolence as integral to the dynamics of the transformation expected to result from the Second Axial Age, but does that mean that security for communities can dispense with weapons and count on the disappearance of violent crime? Such questions are illustrative of a process that will need to set some fundamental limits on human discretion.

It was noted in a report on a penguin colony in Antarctica that only two penguins survived from a birth cohort of eighteen thousand due to the diminished ecological conditions prevailing in their customary habitat (Sauven 2017). Among the causes of such a doleful incident is industrial fishing, which has greatly diminished the supply of krill on which not only penguins but also giant squid, the blue whale, and seals depend for sustenance. From the perspective of humane ecology, there arise a series of questions about balancing the needs and desires of the human species against the well-being and survival of other species, including whether certain market-driven activities should be prohibited or severely restricted, as well as the question of who decides when the issue concerns life support for various residents of the global commons.

Given the gross disparities that exist in material circumstances and resource endowments in the world as we know it, is it plausible utopianism to insist on *equality* as the measure of a just society, or is it more credible to settle for *equity*, *fairness*, and *material needs* (as already posited in Articles 25 and 28 of the Universal Declaration of Human Rights)? There are many more relevant issues if the design of ecologically oriented global governance is to become—whether by stages or through a revolutionary surge—the signature achievement of the Second Axial Age. One such overarching issue is whether a kind of minimalism could shape early efforts to make the Earth Charter assume the status of being *a credible political project* while holding more ambitious views in abeyance.

There is also the question of time and the related urgency of meeting challenges that cannot wait for the usual rhythms of historical change to work their way into human experience. The pace of technological innovation shortens time horizons in ways that societies seem unable to absorb and thus deny to varying extents. This seems true whether it is the advent of nuclear weaponry, artificial intelligence, or digital lifestyles. We seem to be living with unrealistic calmness amid a consuming global emergency. We cannot hope to achieve the vision of the Earth Charter by waiting for it to happen, and one value of Engel's essay is to impart such feelings of urgency with respect to moving from envisioning to action and engagement. In our terms, can a band of citizen pilgrims be the Paul Reveres of this age, sounding alarm bells that awaken the slumbering masses and tone-deaf elites before it is too late?

Some respected commentators on the global situation insist that we are already too late, for we have crossed vital ecological and biodiversity thresholds of no return. We resist such pessimism—and its twin, technocratic optimism—for the simple reason that the future is unknowable. If unknowable, then we share the responsibility and opportunity to work toward a preferred, and in this case, viable future. We are living in a period when the only politics that meets our needs as a species and our planet as an ecological entity is "a politics of impossibility"—which is another way of saying that mastering the art of the possible has no chance of embodying the vision and values of the Earth Charter, as enhanced by Engel, in an unfolding human future.

Note

1   The term "axial age" refers to a time where important value shifts were occurring in different places simultaneously. According to the philosopher Karl Jaspers (1953) this period was 800 to 200 BCE. A second axial age would link identity to the earth and the species, overcoming modernity's tendency to create benevolent futures based on the sub-species identity and human hegemony over its natural habitat.

References

Engel, J. Ronald. 2014. "Summons to a New Axial Age: The Promise, Limits, and Future of the Earth Charter." In *The Earth Charter, Ecological Integrity and Social Movements*, edited by Laura Westra and Mirian Vilela, 81–98. London: Routledge.

Jaspers, Karl. 1953. *Origin and Goal of History*. London: Routledge.

Thucydides. 1998. *The Landmark Thucydides: A Comprehensive Guide to the Peloponnesian War*. Translated by Richard Crawley. Los Angeles, CA: Free Press.

Sauven, John. 2017. "Penguins Starving to Death Is a Sign that Something's Very Wrong in the Antarctic." *The Guardian*, October 13.

PART THREE

Varieties of Cosmopolitanism

15

Fred Dallmayr's Visionary Cosmopolitanism

In Fred Dallmayr's arresting words, "What is radically new in our time—often called the 'nuclear age'—is that for the first time life itself is under attack, that life as such on the planet can be annihilated without remainder, leaving only 'desert' behind."[1] He makes clear that he has in mind not only climate change and nuclear warfare but also the atomization of selfhood being caused by a capitalist world order that is responsible for grotesque degrees of inequality, while subjugating humanity to a nihilistic technology- and wealth-driven materialism that results in a devastating de-spiritualization of the human condition.

Dallmayr is philosophically erudite and astonishingly eclectic as well as politically attuned to the discordant rhythms of our age and ethically responsive to desperate calls for empathy and ecological sensitivity on a global scale. He is such an extraordinary expositor that unprepared readers may be inclined to overlook the originality and relevance of Dallmayr's own creative and synthetic journey of ideas. Throughout his long and productive career, he has illuminated a progressive way of thinking, acting, and feeling that richly deserves to be widely disseminated, carefully reflected on, and hopefully embraced. Because Dallmayr's work encompasses so much, evolves over time, is historically and culturally contextualized, and is expository, critical, and visionary, it is impossible to categorize or do justice to even a single aspect or fragment of the immense corpus of his scholarly achievement spread over more than six decades. Dallmayr's outlook can be sampled in numerous books that often address similar themes, yet, quite remarkably, each of his academic writings yields an illuminating and fresh encounter between author and reader. Although his concerns abide, reading Dallmayr, book after book, leaves impressions of valuably new thinking rather than a repetitive rendering of well-plowed fields. An appreciation of Dallmayr's unflinching dedication to continuous exploration is the greatest praise that one scholar can give to another!

The effort here is to depict and respond to Dallmayr's recent work that addresses vital issues of human identity, including the acute tensions between attachments by humanity to its component parts versus the affirmation of its encompassing whole, as well as the growing tension between science and secularity, between religious and spiritual worldviews, and the present and past versus the future. We want to consider Dallmayr's contributions to our understanding of these apparent polarities by briefly reviewing the distinct elements of his approach, which, when considered cumulatively, achieve a high degree of coherence and persuasiveness. Overall, Dallmayr developed a compelling approach to the challenges of this historical moment, which, if acted upon on a large enough scale, could have a major emancipatory impact on the human condition. Admittedly, such a prospect would have to overcome the post-truth political inclinations of late modernity.

Having praised his work, this chapter raises questions about whether Dallmayr's envisioned expectations with respect to ethical, spiritual, and ecological intelligence are capable or can be made capable of generating the collective societal dynamics needed to transform such elevated aspirations into a viable political project. Dallmayr's goals can also be regarded as imperatives, given the severity, magnitude, and urgency of the present global challenges facing humanity. The responses needed to give Dallmayr's way of being in the world political relevance depend on species- and habitat-sustaining transformations of values, structures, and behavior. Dallmayr sets forth his version of what has been described elsewhere as "a necessary utopia" without overlooking the formidable obstacles blocking the path to its realization (Falk 2012b).

In this spirit, Dallmayr conveys throughout his habits of conceptual musing a sense of foreboding about the negativity he associates with the materialism and militarism of late capitalist modernity, perhaps epitomized by choosing *Against Apocalypse* as the ominous title of a recent book (2017a). Yet Dallmayr is never content to settle for a gloom and doom view of the human condition and its destiny. This positive dimension of his political sensibility is expressed by this same book's hopeful subtitle, *Recovering Humanity's Wholeness*. Without a careful understanding of this pattern of light and dark that colors Dallmayr's rendering of the world situation, it is easy to read his work as either overly optimistic or excessively pessimistic. It is neither.

Dallmayr is impressively aware of the global *problematique* in all its aspects and fashions his radical remedial program in response, not venturing an opinion as to the outcome, yet insisting on a full engagement in the struggle. This is crucial. Part of the human condition is to be enmeshed in a web of uncertainties, which explains two features of Dallmayr's praxis: first, there is no reason to accept as a fait accompli the future as determined by the darkness of the present; and second, the appropriate ethical and political response is to struggle amid uncertainty and doubt for the future we need and desire if we as a species are to surmount the crisis-riven present.

Sources of Inspiration

Several characteristics of Dallmayr's thought pervade his writing: a wide-ranging reliance on twentieth-century European philosophical thought, enriched by a recognition of the relevance of non-Western, especially Asian, worldviews. Dallmayr is particularly appreciative of the thought and practice of Gandhi. He also expresses his admiration for exemplary moral authority figures who have had inspirational impacts because of their courageous refusal to submit to oppressive structures and unjust practices. Among those mentioned in his various writings and talks are Nelson Mandela, the Dalai Lama, Martin Luther King Jr., Archbishop Desmond Tutu, Mahatma Gandhi, Saint Francis of Assisi, and Pope Francis. The list discloses Dallmayr's range and vectors of orientation.[2]

His moral and political affinities are a deeply considered response to several influential thinkers whom he acknowledges as his "mentors," above all, Martin Heidegger,[3] but also Montesquieu, Confucius, Aristotle, Plato, Raimon Panikkar, Erasmus, John Dewey, Whitehead, Hegel, Hobbes, and Kant; and a bit less centrally, Jonathan Schell, author of *The Unconquerable World* (2003), and John Cobb and Herman Daly, authors of *For the Common Good* (1994).

Schell's last book offers a compelling account of the primacy of people in achieving change for the better and offering resistance to evil. Cobb and Daly adopt an ecological ethics that they believe would enable humanity to live in dynamic harmony with its natural surroundings, rather than in a relationship of dominion that is causing disruptions, devastating backlashes, and trending toward catastrophe.

Martin Heidegger seems crucial in framing Dallmayr's basic quest: diagnosing what is fundamentally wrong about the way the world is organized, giving rise to exploitative and destructive patterns of behavior exhibited in recurrent warfare as abetted by a technologically dominant mentality and with a stultifying materialism taking as its contemporary form neoliberal capitalism. In stark opposition to this diagnosis, Dallmayr affirms the potential of democratic forms of governance by reference to a crucial transformative commitment to what he calls "democracy to come." Dallmayr attributes the substance of this futurist and normative view of democracy to Montesquieu's insistence that the essential trait of embodied democratic values is "the spirit of equality."[4]

This is a timely, seemingly counterintuitive assessment, given recent trends toward ever greater inequality within and between sovereign states, which in turn is principally responsible for producing social responses of rage, alienation, and extremism, producing a terrifying susceptibility to the Kool Aid of demagogic leaders. As past world history illustrates, democracy can go terribly wrong in practice with resounding negative impacts, while not even bothering to alter democratic rhetoric when the modalities of economic, social, and political development exhibit pronounced antidemocratic tendencies toward greater inequality. In this crucial respect, Dallmayr displays an endorsement of what has become the most accepted explanation of disequilibrium dominating the political horizons of the early twenty-first century.

Dallmayr's publications, although not his oral commentary, stop short of directly appraising the Trump presidency (2017–21) and the related global phenomenon of Trumpism. This turn to the populist and oligarchist right in America is not an unexpected development given the effects that growing inequality is having in the United States (see chapter 9 for elaboration). It has made the very rich even richer while the rest of society anxiously treads water or sinks into poverty. Rather than constructively address the problem, Trump provided a demagogic alternative that puts a hostile spin on immigrants as menacing strangers in our midst, as well on "the shithole countries" of Africa and elsewhere who are exporting their most depraved residents to engage in terrorism, disseminate drugs, and steal jobs from "real" Americans. Trump also blamed the dismal economic situation of the growing American underclass on the bad trade deals made by his immediate predecessors in the White House, particularly Obama, and vowed to end or radically revise economic arrangements that have allowed other countries, especially China, to flourish at the expense of the United States. As Dallmayr so well understands, ultranationalist responses are regressive and inherently dysfunctional. They also contribute to massive distress within countries, which facilitates a potentially fatal distraction from the overriding historical challenge of achieving viable political and ecological habitats, which for Dallmayr presuppose operationalizing "humanity's wholeness." To so move means strengthening greatly the sense of human identity in relation to national and other fragmentary identities, which is the direct opposite of this currently prevalent global pattern of revitalizing the nationalist and civilizational agendas at the expense of global, regional, and local priorities.

In some respects, because his principal published work preceded this turn away from democracy, Dallmayr may strike readers as unresponsive to the scary salience of these recent political trends. To write of "democracy to come," which resembles Derrida's focus on what it might mean "to live together, well," does not seem sensitive to the realities of what might be described as the global phenomenon of "de-democratization," or, as some have put it, the rise of "illiberal democracies," or, more negatively, "fascism to come." This regressive set of developments involves the rebalancing of society/state relations by tilting toward autocratic rulership linking security to exaggerated fears of the other and thereby providing rationalizations for harsher police controls over the citizenry. Such a political pattern reinforces nationalism with policies that punish immigrants and construct walls symbolically and substantively designed to keep unwanted strangers out, widening the gaps among the peoples of the world and thereby ripping apart the holistic fabric of humanity that is central to Dallmayr's prescription for a benevolent future.

Although Trump and Trumpism are the most blatant instances of de-democratization, the same and related dynamics are evident in many other contexts, including Brexit in the United Kingdom, the success of right-wing populists and demagogues in China, Russia, Turkey, Japan, India, Israel, East Europe, and the Philippines, as well as the disturbing rise of neofascist political parties in almost all of the world's leading "democracies," especially in Europe. Such commonalities across regions and stages of development imply a structural explanation taking the form of a series of backlashes against the polarizing effects of neoliberal capitalism dominating the global marketplace, privileging capital flows over the well-being of people, and a post–Cold War hostility to any governmental turn that can be cast by its adversaries as "socialist."

In Dallmayr's view, the rationality and instrumentalism of the Enlightenment, privileging the rise of science, excessive reliance on instrumental rationalism, and false connections between technology, progress, ecological resilience, and human happiness lend credence to a radically critical stance for which Heidegger provides the most influential framing. It also makes it understandable why Dallmayr should be drawn to the approaches taken by Raimon Panikkar, the deceased Berkeley professor of comparative religion, for both his emphasis on religion as a means of grasping the universality and true nature of the human condition and the related need to be receptive to the wisdom and insights of non-Western civilizational perspectives.

It may be helpful to formulate this holistic quest as follows: we now live in a world where some of the parts have much greater power and historical agency than the whole, whether the particular part is a state, civilization, religion, ideology, or private sector constituted by corporate/financial entities. By contrast, to achieve sustainability and well-being, the overriding goal is the transformation of this fragmented reality that constitutes contemporary "world order" into a more coherent whole that is greater than the sum of its parts and sufficiently integrated to function effectively to promote global public interests. As a result, the idea of humanity is no longer a vague abstraction with little political traction and, rather, becomes the foundation of what Dallmayr calls "relational praxis," which holistically situates the primary orientation for individual and group identity, thereby shaping the unfolding of individual and collective life.[5]

John Dewey's influence in diagnosing the ills of American democracy has great relevance with respect to Dallmayr's ideas about a "democracy to come." Dallmayr agrees with Dewey's explanation of the decline of American democracy as attributable to the triumph of "a money culture" producing a citizenry of "atomized individualism" (1927). Mainstream procedural conceptions of democracy miss the indispensable realization that democratic legitimacy is about far more than the free elections and elemental civil rights. For Dewey, as for Dallmayr, democracy fails the citizen if it loses its essential character as "an ethical conception" (ibid.). Dewey bemoans the loss of the wildness of the early American experience so well depicted by the lyric intensity of Walt Whitman's celebratory poetry, an outlook unabashedly endorsed by Dallmayr.[6] So far as we know, this celebration of wildness and the Whitmanesque imaginary come with little acknowledgment of the linkages to the subjugation of Native Americans or the exploitation of slave labor.

Choosing the Road of Spiritual Cosmopolitanism

Although Dallmayr's views of the future of existing societies are preoccupied with fulfilling the potential of democracy—ethically, ecologically, and economically—his broader vision is shaped by hopes and fears surrounding the apolitical destiny of the human species as a totality. It is this broader vision that we would describe as one of "spiritual cosmopolitanism," a sense of humanity as a whole achieving transcendence by a spiritualized interpretation of the meaning of life. This understanding should not be confused with a theological metaphysics projecting a hierarchy of divine being(s) shaping human experience from above, much less a readiness to entrust human destiny to the guidance of institutionalized religion. It may be difficult to articulate the various cultural embodiments of spirituality. What can be clearly grasped is Dallmayr's recognition that human destiny is not well served by subscribing to the various secular fundamentalisms that flow from the post-Enlightenment rise of scientific rationalism and its boundless confidence in technological empowerment.

Here also Heidegger's profound interpretations of being-in-the-world exert a strong influence on Dallmayr's outlook, or this may be better considered as a matter of congeniality of these two thinkers, disguised by Dallmayr's overt deference to one of the towering, if highly controversial, philosophical figures of the prior century. Rather than thinking abstractly about the human condition, being-in-the-world is the proper ontological starting point, suggesting that every human experience is embedded in the concreteness of time, place, and consciousness. Beyond this circumstance of "being" is the complementary reality of "becoming," the all-pervasive reality of process and change. In conceiving of the becoming aspects of being-in-the-world, Dallmayr acknowledges Alfred North Whitehead as an inspirational guid, and notes the affinities of his thought with that of "process theology" as developed by John Cobb and David Ray Griffin.

Dallmayr adds to this beingness of humanity, the degree to which our best lens to perceive reality is by way of hermeneutics, that is, our inescapable dependence on interpretation. Such a dependence makes our interpretation of reality contingent on the particularities of observation and the observer, giving plural civilizational perspectives an equal purchase on reality, although some may have more or less relevance to the prime imperative of recovering and constituting the wholeness of humanity without forgetting its dependence on achieving and sustaining ecological stability.

This relational engagement, as combined with time/place/social location/ civilizational differences, creates a natural disposition toward dialogue as vital for mutual respect and an affirming appreciation of difference in ways that do not undermine the specifics of identity. In other words, dialogue is not a race to the bottom, via the downgrading of difference, but its upgrading through building a brighter future by taking advantage of individual and collective diverse civilizational strengths. Such an understanding creates a firm foundation for a normative view of dialogue that is more than engaging in friendly conversations with diverse others. It mimics an approach well-articulated by Michael Sandel, which recommends "reasoning together" toward a respectful acceptance of transnational and transcivilizational diversities, an acceptance of which is posited as an integral dimension of engaged citizenship in a globalizing world.[7] This recognition of the potential role of engaged citizenship in a variety of national settings seems to represent the best means of acquiring political traction for a spiritual agenda and a subversive patriotism for humanity.

Heidegger also provides the parameters of critique that guides Dallmayr. He emphasizes the contemporary loss of spiritual grounding creating disruptions that are severely aggravated by obsessive technological enchantments and their tendency to produce a materialist societal temperament that contrasts unfavorably with the premodern worldview, stressing an organic connectedness of the human species to nature and the cosmos.

For Dallmayr, as well, these fatal shortcomings of modernity point to a postmodern preferred reconfiguration of being-in-the-world that far exceeds in its imaginative and normative sweep the deconstructionist turn of European postmodernism. Dallmayr also derives from Heidegger the relational essence of being-in-the world, which informs his sense of social and political engagement. By accepting the Gandhian embrace of pacifism as a crucial part of the transformational agenda, Dallmayr (2013) challenges liberal critics, such as Richard Beardsworth, who urge the more modest goal of "the possibility of a less violent politics" (ibid. 8m). Dallmayr's diagnosis of the troubles of the world rests on the utter necessity of a more radical and prescriptive political therapy. Making feasible responses to present challenges, however sensible, will not get the job done. Many would dismiss Dallmayr's call for no-violent politics as "utopian," but for him it is a matter of doing what is right as reinforced by what is necessary, taking account, as well, that all visionary solutions are put aside as utopian until they happen. Certainly, Gandhi had this experience in the course of mounting his challenge to British colonial control over India. And yet, Gandhi's experience is instructive in other wars, including the reversion to a conventional political ethos once the utopian movement did its job of getting rid of the British without excessive bloodshed.

Against this background, Dallmayr constructs a vision of an ideal polity whose citizens assume responsibility for acting ethically and prudently with regard to human destiny, including going beyond dialogue toward "loving the other," which reflects the historical circumstance of establishing a human community that incorporates all the fragmented national communities that remain defining characteristics of a state-centric world order. Given the affirmations of spirituality and democratic values, it seems quite natural that Dallmayr would affirm an ecumenical version of cosmopolitanism that departs from the Stoic legacy that fits more easily within the political template of modernist secularism. Dallmayr posits this hoped-for future as a decontextualized preference, offering few insights as to how sufficient political traction is achieved for systemic transitions from here-and-now to there-and-then. Consistent with being-in-the-world, he acknowledges the difficulties of any transition from the troubled present to a desired future: "The obstacles standing in the way of an ecumenical cosmopolitanism, nurtured by democratic equality, are surely staggering and nearly overwhelming. But if we are serious about democracy, they have to be confronted. In a word, democracy means continuous striving and struggle. As the saying goes: la lotta contua."[8]

It would not be misleading to characterize this overview of Dallmayr's approach to human identity as pointing toward "a new realism" attentive to the actualities of the historical situation. Such attentiveness leads to a blending of aspiration and self-doubt, the affirmation of spiritual cosmopolitanism with a lively realization that the transition from here to there now seems nearly impossible. Dallmayr champions a utopian adventure that is rescued from a sense of futility by the recognition that struggle amid uncertainty can produce unexpected emancipatory changes that inform our historical experience. Notable among such recent changes is the collapse of European colonialism, the transformation of apartheid South Africa, and the ending of the Cold War. To some extent, this is the kind of faith that guides the citizen-pilgrim to embark on the long journey to a better future.[9]

Conclusion

The post-9/11 battlefield exhibits the deterritorialization of war, with political extremists striking violently anywhere on the planet, while the United States and its allies in the Global War on Terrorism ignore sovereign rights of foreign countries by sending drone missiles wherever a suspected adversary is found. As suggested, the contradictory phenomenon occurs when border walls are built and security tightened along borders to keep refugees and migrants out. Anti-migrant policies are often coupled with protectionist forms of economic nationalism that resurrect tariffs on imports, mindless of the lessons of the Great Depression in the 1930s that gave rise to mutually destructive trade wars.

These spatially divergent developments lure our policy gaze away from the urgencies associated with global warming and its secondary effects. Also ignored is the precarious character of geopolitical nuclearism, which creates unacceptably high risks of catastrophic warfare. In effect, our surveillance technology allows our leaders to look everywhere except at themselves. It remains surprising how little they see! This is the discouraging irony of a potent technology of destruction interacting with an obsolescent politics of militarized security.

Despite Dallmayr's impressive scholarly achievements and global reputation, he remains the greatest unknown political philosopher of our time. It may be partly Dallmayr's fault, or maybe not a fault, but an expression of his humility and the selfless integrity of carrying out his lifelong frantic search for usable knowledge during a historically problematic time in ways that could enhance the human experience in all its dimensions. This includes the current formidable challenge, which he so well articulates, of multiple threats to the survival and well-being of the human species and its diverse habitats. It should be stressed that Dallmayr is not content to confine his inquiries to domains of rational thought. He is primarily intent on exploring how to make ideas vehicles for political change, what he calls "moral praxis."

With the dedication of a lifetime, Dallmayr has bestowed to humanity a cartography of emancipation and empowerment, with a navigational compass guided by the values and visions associated with the theory and practice of ecumenical cosmopolitanism. This engaged wisdom provides needed guidance, but as the subtitle of one of Dallmayr's books wryly asks, "Who will listen?" Dallmayr's remarkably rich palate of eclecticism, based on the widest exposure to the best thought, past and present, makes him the most accomplished academic listener ever encountered.[10] He has not only constructed his distinct worldview and proposed lines of engagement on the basis of this deep exposure to some of the most demanding texts in the Western philosophical canon, but he also has taken steps to meet and interact with several of these influential European thinkers.

The stunning result is what is labeled here as "cosmopolitan spiritualism," which is strikingly similar to what Dallmayr calls "ecumenical cosmopolitanism." We have done our best to listen to these seminal outpourings, but we still need to pose and heed a variant on Dallmayr's hauntingly ironic question: "will there be enough listeners to make a difference?" And if not, what then?

Notes

1   Asserted with urgency in Dallmayr (2017a). I have made similar assessments with slightly different phrasing, emphasizing the fundamental shift from *civilizational* jeopardy (as discussed in Diamond 2005) to a situation of *species* jeopardy that encompasses nonhuman as well as human forms of life. See Falk (2012a, especially 253–62).

2   All of these individuals acted with courage in the world, but with a motivation rooted in religious faith and conviction. Only Mandela can be regarded as principally secular, although his politics of reconciliation seemed spiritually grounded. I reached this conclusion after a meeting and conversation with this extraordinary person and at the time was struck by Mandela's moral radiance, which seemed a manifestation of an inner spirituality.

3   For reference to the ideas and influences of Martin Heidegger throughout the chapter, see Heidegger (2008, 2010).

4   Dallmayr (2017b, 5–6); Alexis de Tocqueville is also invoked along similar lines, suggesting that challenges to the formalized hierarchy of monarchy be based on the establishment of democracy rested its legitimacy on the opposite principle of equality. That French commentators should choose such an emphasis is not surprising in view of the hierarchical character of the French monarchy in its most absolute forms, as well as providing the national backdrop for the most revolutionary challenge by a mobilized citizenry that gave a modern, more inclusive rebirth to the earlier Greek embrace of democracy.

5   The central political metaphysic of Dallmayr (2017b).

6   For Dewey's views as interpreted in Dallmayr, see Dallmayr (2015), especially the chapter on "Reimagining Social Democracy."

7   Sandel (2009, 19–20, 260–61); see also Sandel (2012), on which Dallmayr also comments favorably.

8   These are the apt final words of *Democracy to Come* (Dallmayr 2017b, 151).

9   For presentation of the citizen pilgrim as the engaged global citizen embarked on a journey to a desired and necessary future—that is, insisting that time, as well as space, be integral to the ideals of twenty-first-century citizenship—see Falk (2012a, 480–87).

10   For elaboration, see the autobiography of Fred Dallmayr (2017c).

References

Cobb, John B., and Herman E. Daly. 1994. *For the Common Good*. London: Penguin.

Dallmayr, Fred. 2013. *Being in the World: Dialogue and Cosmopolis*. Lexington: University Press of Kentucky.

Dallmayr, Fred, 2015. *Freedom and Solidarity: Towards New Beginnings.* Lexington: University Press of Kentucky.

Dallmayr, Fred. 2017a. *Against Apocalypse: Recovering Humanity's Wholeness.* Washington, DC: Lexington Books.

Dallmayr, Fred. 2017b. *Democracy to Come: Politics as Relational Praxis.* Oxford: Oxford University Press.

Dallmayr, Fred. 2017c. *On the Boundary: A Life Remembered.* New York: Hamilton Books.

de Tocqueville, Alexis. 1945. *Democracy in America.* Edited by Phillips Bradley, vol. 1. New York: Vintage Books.

Dewey, John. (1927/1954). *The Public and Its Problems.* Athens, OH: Swallow Press.

Diamond, Jared. 2005. *Collapse: How Societies Choose to Fail or Succeed.* New York: Viking Press.

Falk, Richard. 2012a. *The Writings of Richard Falk: Towards Humane Global Governance.* Delhi, India: Orient Black Swan.

Falk, Richard. 2012b. "Toward a Necessary Utopianism: Democratic Global Governance." In *The Writings of Richard Falk*, by Richard Falk, 430–47. Delhi, India: Orient BlackSwan.

Heidegger, Martin. 2008. *Basic Writings of Martin Heidegger.* New York: Harper Perennial.

Heidegger, Martin. 2010. *Being and Time: A Revised Edition of the Stambaugh Translation.* Albany, NY: SUNY Press.

Sandel, Michael. 2009. *Justice: What's the Right Thing to Do.* New York: Farrar, Straus, and Giroux.

Sandel, Michael. 2012. *What Money Can't Buy.* New York: Farrar, Straus, and Giroux.

Schell, Jonathan. 2003. *Unconquerable World: Power, Nonviolence, and the Will of the People.* New York: Metropolitan Books.

16

Father Miguel d'Escoto's *The Spiritual Sources of Legal Creativity*[1]

Of the many political personalities I have encountered, Father Miguel d'Escoto was among the especially vivid in exhibiting a remarkable quality of moral radiance and spiritual commitment that was immediately apparent to those fortunate enough to cross his path. The only person in my experience who possessed a comparable depth of beingness was Nelson Mandela, whose aura of love and worldly engagement was captivating. Father Miguel, vocationally trained as a priest in the Roman Catholic Church, was a prominent activist in the Sandinista movement that overcame huge obstacles to give Nicaragua progressive political governance after a long period of blood-soaked dictatorship sustained by US support.

Father Miguel d'Escoto became foreign minister in the early years of Sandinista political struggle, and later Nicaragua's ambassador at the United Nations (UN). He served as president of the General Assembly in 2009, the year that Israel launched its first of several massive attacks on Gaza, causing widespread death and destruction, a prelude to the genocidal assault of 2023–24. Miguel d'Escoto was a consistently progressive force whose experience was rooted in his native Nicaragua, but whose vision extended to any struggle of peoples suffering the injustices of Western domination and seeking liberation.

Father Miguel d'Escoto's originality combined an intense spirituality with a deep faith in international law and the UN as potentially liberating aspects of a world order too long dominated by militarism and geopolitics. His political idealism and personal warmth were inspirational to those who were fortunate enough to have contact with Father Miguel d'Escoto, a warrior in the struggle for what Dallmayr had in mind by his call for a "democracy to come."

The point of departure is this: if we believe, which many do not, that if justice is the proper end of law, then we must struggle to overcome the calculative or transactional mentality that dominates our legal culture, restricting our attitudes and endeavors involving law to the domain of the feasible. What is feasible most often favors those that benefit from existing structures of economic and political inequality and mobilizes media and elites to resist significant normative change. We are quite aware that we are endorsing an unconventional outlook by elevating the moral imagination and professing our understanding of "utopian realism." This formulation disregards the conventional understanding of law as essentially offering a suite of techniques for problem-solving that presupposes, at its liberal best, a view of politics as "the art of the possible," and more typically regarded as "the art of stabilizing present social, economic, and political arrangements" without regard to their compatibility with the canons of justice or the international and national standards of human rights.

It is this kind of ethical radicalism that made the life of Father Miguel d'Escoto so exemplary and, in the best sense, "revolutionary," for all those whose lives he affected, whether in ministering to the poor or challenging the high and mighty, whether acting in a pastoral capacity or as a man of the world. It is important to appreciate that Father Miguel was both an ardent Nicaraguan nationalist and a passionate citizen of the world, a model "citizen pilgrim," embarked on his own pilgrimage to a global future that embodies peace with joy and justice.

We preface this inquiry into the spiritual sources of legal creativity with a general remark that pertains particularly to international law. Writing as Richard Falk, I may be almost alone among law professors in believing that international law is the field of law that is most relevant to the ultimate survival of the human species. The sad reality is that international law continues to struggle for academic survival as a field of study, being often denigrated, evaded, and violated by the most powerful governments on the planet whenever law is seen as blocking a preferred policy of strategic importance. There always seem to be numerous apologists among the ranks of legal experts and diplomats ready to offer a comforting rationalization to the macabre machinations of those with power and wealth. And yet viewed from a perspective other than war/peace and security, international law in relation to trade and investment has basically served to protect the interests of the rich and powerful, while shackling the poor and vulnerable. In other words, international law has this dual face: it bends to the geopolitical will of the militarily powerful while often cruelly imposing accountability on the weak. At the founding of the UN, a Mexican diplomat caustically observed that "we have created an organization that regulates the mice while the tigers roam freely." And so it became and remains as such.[2]

It is against this background that Miguel d'Escoto's spiritual wisdom creates a contrast with business as usual in the world of realpolitik. Even for most global reformers, the criterion for constructive action is a realistic appreciation of achievable limits, or *horizons of feasibility* (which quietly incorporated embedded private and public interests in sustaining a privileged status quo). We are living in a world in which there are growing gaps between what is feasible and what is necessary. Adapting to climate change at a time of ultranationalism underscores this menacing gap between feasibility and necessity. As a diplomat, Miguel d'Escoto was almost unconcerned with feasibility as conventionally understood if it stood in the way of necessity or desirability. He was deeply sensitive to the imperatives of necessity, and even more so to the moral and spiritual imperatives of doing what is right under a particular set of circumstances, and for this reason alone, he was most responsive to what we would identify as *horizons of spirituality*.

He was motivated by a belief, undoubtedly reflecting his religious faith, in the potency of right reason, and on this basis conceived of international law as a crucial vehicle for realizing such a vision, embracing with moral enthusiasm a kind of "politics of impossibility" in which considerations of justice outweighed calculations of feasibility or the obstacles associated with geopolitics. It is with his deep experience of the trials and tribulations of Nicaragua and its long-suffering population that Father Miguel turned to law as an imaginative means of empowerment, especially its implicit commitment to treat the weak equally to the strong.

An illustrative reference is the historic case that Nicaragua brought against the United States in the early 1980s at the International Court of Justice (ICJ) in The Hague. It was a daring legal flight of moral fancy to suppose that tiny and beleaguered Nicaragua could shift its struggle from the bloody battlefields of US-armed intervention and a mercenary insurgency against the Sandinista government, of which he was then foreign minister, to the lofty legal terrain that itself had been originally crafted to reflect the values and interests of dominant states. But more than this, it was a brilliant leap of political imagination to envision the soft power of law neutralizing the hard power of high-tech weaponry in an ideological struggle of strategic significance being waged during the Cold War. Such an attempt to shift the balance of forces in an ongoing conflict by recourse to international law and the World Court had never been made in a serious conflict situation. It was a David and Goliath challenge that the World Court as the highest judicial institution in the UN system had yet to face in a war/peace context, and it turned out to be a test of the integrity of the institution. The ICJ has been more recently tested by South Africa's submission of a complaint under the provisions of the Genocide Convention to obtain rulings ordering Israel to cease committing genocide in Gaza.

Let us briefly recall the situation in Nicaragua. The United States was supporting a right-wing insurgency, the counterrevolutionary remnant of the Somoza dictatorship, a single family that had cruelly and corruptly ruled Nicaragua between 1936 and 1974 on behalf of corporate America (the era of "banana republics" in Central America), leaving the country in impoverished ruins when the Somoza dynasty finally collapsed. The

Somoza-oriented insurgents were known as the Contras and were called "freedom fighters" by their American sponsors and paymaster because they were opposing the Sandinista government, which had won a war of national liberation in 1979 but was accused by its detractors of leftist tendencies and Soviet sympathies. This was the right-wing ideological way of obscuring the true affinity of the Sandinista leadership with the teachings of liberation theology rather being subscribers to the secular dogmatics of Marxism. Promoting counterrevolutions was a way of depriving the people of Nicaragua of their inalienable right of self-determination, as well as their historical agency. The United States government via the CIA was training and equipping the Contras and quite overtly committing acts of war by mining and blockading Managua, Nicaragua's main harbor and its lifeline to the world. It was these undertakings, amounting to unlawful interventions in the internal affairs of a sovereign state, that was acting in defiance of the authority of international law and the UN Charter. D'Escoto addressed the UN General Assembly in his capacity as Nicaragua's foreign minister, vividly describing the conflict with some well-chosen provocative words: "It is obvious that the war to which Nicaragua is being subjected is a US war, and the so-called Contras are merely hired hands serving the diabolical objectives of the Reagan Administration" (UNGA 1986). Later in the same speech, he condemned the US government for recently appropriating an additional $100 million "to finance genocide against our people" (ibid.).

This robust language shows that d'Escoto's spiritual nature did not always manifest itself by way of a gentle demeanor or denote the absence of a fighting spirit. As here, when deemed appropriate to the situation, d'Escoto readily relied on undiplomatic candor to get his point across. He was also insistent on using such occasions to talk truth to power and to lay blame and responsibility for the torment of the Nicaraguan people where it belonged, however impolitic it was to point his finger of accusation at the United States, the self-proclaimed guardian of political life in Latin America.

Without going into the details of the case, it was possible for Nicaragua to lodge such a complaint against the United States because the US government had earlier agreed to accept the authority of the ICJ if the other side, in an international conflict, was also similarly committed in advance.[3] With this awareness, Father Miguel, in his role as foreign minister (1979–90), realized two things: that the sovereign rights of Nicaragua were being overridden in a manner in flagrant violation of international law and that the World Court, that is, the ICJ, was supposed to provide countries with a nonviolent option of resolving international legal disputes. This institutional innovation was advocated as an important contribution to the war prevention priorities of the UN. It could be viewed as maintaining world peace that the United States had itself strongly championed throughout most of the twentieth century. It may not seem so unusual for a small country to take advantage of a potential judicial remedy, but in fact it had never happened—no small state had ever gone to the World Court to protect itself against such a military intervention, and to do so on behalf of a progressive government in the third world in the midst of the Cold War seemed to many at the time like a waste of time and money that Nicaragua could ill afford.

It is here where one begins to grasp this potentially revolutionary idea of relying upon the spiritual sources of legal creativity. D'Escoto was convinced that what the US government was doing was legally and morally wrong, and that it was an opportune time for the mice to fight back against a predator tiger. It was a perfect occasion to act by reference to *horizons of spirituality*.

Yet this did not mean that Father Miguel would ignore the pragmatic dimensions of effectiveness. Nicaragua managed to persuade a Harvard law professor, Abram Chayes, to act on their behalf as head legal counsel. This was a brilliant tactical move that I applauded at the time (even though it meant that, as Nicaragua's second choice, I lost out). Aside from being a first-class international lawyer with a high global profile, Chayes had previously served as John F. Kennedy's legal adviser and close confidant at the time of the Cuban Missile Crisis. The symbolism could not have been more pointed, underlining the fact that Chayes was committed to upholding international law rather than being a combatant in the ideological sideshow carried on at the expense of the third world throughout the Cold War. Not surprisingly, the *Wall Street Journal* audaciously and revealingly described Chayes as a traitor for accepting such a role.

I had the opportunity to work with Chayes and Father Miguel in the Irish American Center in Manhattan that was operating under the benign tutelage of none other than Dr. Kevin Cahill. We worked hard for several days as a team developing the arguments both as to the authority of the ICJ to adjudicate, what lawyers call "jurisdiction," to be decided in a separate preliminary decision, as well as on the substance of Nicaragua's allegations, which constituted the second phase of the litigation. What was so impressive to me then, and even now, some forty years later, is that this effort to combine a somewhat utopian motivated legal undertaking with a practical mastery of the technical dimensions of the case illustrated for me the extraordinary blending of spiritually grounded yet worldly wisdom with the down-to-earth skills of legal craft.

The outcome of the Nicaragua legal narrative is too complicated to describe properly, but in short—counsel for Nicaragua persuaded the Court that it had jurisdictional authority, at which point the United States petulantly, yet not unexpectedly, withdrew from the proceedings. It likely realized that if it could not prevail at this jurisdictional phase, it had virtually no chance to have its legal arguments accepted at the merits phase of the case. Further, the US government was displeased with the ICJ that it seized the occasion to renounce its earlier formal acceptance of what is technically referred to as "compulsory jurisdiction," which meant that no state could commence such an action against the US government in the future without its consent, and that the United States was itself permanently foreclosed from proceeding against another state with which it had legal grievances unless that state gave its consent to do so.

This retreat from adjudicating international legal disputes has been an unintended and unfortunate lasting effect of the Nicaragua case. The American stance of viewing international law as only viable when it supports its geopolitical tactics has sent a damaging message to the world that it has strongly reinforced by subsequent refusals to abide by international law. This pattern by such a leading member of the UN has weakened the role and potential of the ICJ and of international judicial authority, in general. In one sense, the US withdrawal was understandable for those who are driven to shape foreign policy by feasibility calculations rather than by certain abiding values, such as here, adhering to the rule of law. It hardly required a legal genius in the State Department to anticipate that if the Court upheld its legal authority to pronounce upon the controversy, then it would almost certainly rule in favor of Nicaragua on the substantive issues revolving around the mining of a foreign harbor at a time of peace between the two countries. Despite some technical issues involving the selection of the applicable legal authority, given the sweeping prohibitions of international law and the UN Charter against nondefensive uses of international force except in situations of self-defense against a prior armed attack, the pro-Nicaragua outcome was entirely predictable.

What was rather intriguing from a jurisprudential point of view was that despite its much-hyped boycott of the ICJ proceedings and accompanying denunciation of the jurisdictional finding, the United States in the end quietly complied with the principal finding in The Hague, namely, that the naval blockade of Nicaragua's harbors was unlawful. As would be expected, it never acknowledged that it was complying, nor did Nicaragua dance in the streets of Managua, but the cause/effect relationship between the judicial decision and compliant behavior was clear to any close observer. There was then some reality to the expression "the force of law," and the US government, even during the Reagan presidency, did not want to stand before the world as openly defying the law, even international law. Such an assessment may have reflected the fact that the US government was in a struggle to win the legitimacy war being waged against the Soviet Union, which partly hinged on the relative reputation of these two dueling superpowers in relation to respect for international law and human rights, which then were signature issues of "the free world." Ironically, since the end of the Cold War, this liberal posture has receded to a point where the United States, for strategic reasons, is complicit with Israel's assault directed at Gaza that many governments and people regard as a textbook instance of genocide.

The Nicaragua experience was a compelling example of Father Miguel's achievements that followed directly from his deep commitment to the horizons of spirituality and decency. It was far from the only instance. Another one of my other connections with Father Miguel was to serve as one of his special advisers during his year as president of the UN General Assembly throughout its sixty-third session, 2008–9. As continues to be the case, life could become difficult for any leading UN official who openly opposed Israel. Father Miguel was deeply aware of the Palestinian ordeal and unabashedly supportive of my contested role as special rapporteur for Occupied Palestine on behalf of the Human Rights Council in Geneva. When I was detained in an Israeli prison and then expelled from Israel at the end of 2008, Father Miguel wanted to organize a press conference in New York City to give me an opportunity to explain what had happened and defend my position. I declined his initiative, perhaps unadvisedly, as I didn't want to place Father Miguel in the line of fire sure to follow.

At the end of 2008, Israel launched a massive attack against Gaza, known as Cast Lead, and Father Miguel sought to have the General Assembly condemn the attack and call for an immediate ceasefire and Israeli withdrawal. It was a difficult moment for Father Miguel, feeling certain that this was the legally and morally the right thing to do, yet as events proceeded and diplomatic positions were disclosed, he was forced to recognize that the logic of geopolitics worked differently—in fact, so starkly differently that even the diplomat representing the Palestinian Authority at the UN intervened to support a milder reaction than what Father Miguel deemed appropriate. Here the backers of feasibility prevailed, but in a manner that Father Miguel could never reconcile himself to accept. I met many diplomats at UN headquarters in New York who said that no one had ever occupied such a high position at the UN with Father Miguel's manifest quality as someone so passionately dedicated to righteous principle.

Pondering this acclaim, it occurred to me that one possible exception was Dag Hammarskjöld, an early outstanding UN secretary general, who died in a plane crash in 1961, apparently assassinated, for his principled, yet geopolitically obstructive dedication to peace and justice. From his private writings, we know that Hammarskjöld's UN efforts also sprung from wellsprings of spirituality that resembled those of Father Miguel but lacked his institutional association with an established religion.

Most General Assembly presidents take the post as an honorific feather in their cap, the symbolic culmination of a public sector career, and spend the year presiding over numerous tedious meetings and hosting an endless series of afternoon receptions, but never make any effort to influence, much less enhance, the role of the General Assembly or otherwise strengthen the UN as a more empowered institution of potential global governance. Father Miguel, in contrast, worked tirelessly to make the UN more effective, more respectful of law, more democratic, and, above all, more sensitive to claims associated with the pursuit of global justice.

Father Miguel took full advantage of his term as president of the General Assembly to provide venues within the organization that offered critiques of, as well as humane alternatives to, neoliberal economic globalization. He sponsored and organized meetings at the UN designed to overcome current patterns of economic injustice, making use of the presence in New York City of less orthodox, more normative economists, including Jeffrey Sachs and Joseph Stiglitz. Here again, Father Miguel demonstrated his grounded spirituality by once more combining the visionary with the practical.

I had the opportunity to work with Father Miguel on several proposals to raise the profile and role of the General Assembly as the most representative and democratic organ of the United Nations. These initiatives were rather strategic and partly meant to counter the US-led campaign to concentrate UN authority in the Security Council to make sure that Global South aspirations and demands would be effectively thwarted and the primacy of geopolitics reestablished after the assault mounted in the 1970s by the briefly bold and ambitious Non-Aligned Movement eager to make the political weight of the Global South felt at the UN.

What this describes is the deep bond in the life and work of Father Miguel between the spirituality of his character and motivations and the practicality of his involvement in what the German philosopher Habermas calls "the lifeworld." It is indicative of Father Miguel's deep spiritual identity that he suffered a punitive response to his life's work from the institution he loved and dedicated his life to serving, being suspended in 1985 by Pope Paul II from the priesthood because of his involvement in the Nicaraguan Revolution. Father Miguel was reinstated twenty-nine years later by Pope Francis, who many view as a kindred spirit to Miguel.

There is an object lesson here for all of us: in a political crisis, the moral imperative of service to people and ideals deserves precedence over blind obedience to even a cherished institution. This kind of dilemma would undoubtedly almost always pose a difficult and painful choice, but it was one that defined Father Miguel d'Escoto at the core of his being, which he expressed over and over by doing the right thing in a spirit of love and humility, but also in a manner that left no one doubting his courage, his affinities and commitments, and his unwavering and abiding convictions.

The daring and creativity that Father Miguel brought to the law and to his work at the UN sprung from spiritual roots that were deeply grounded in both religious tradition and in an unshakable solidarity with those among us who are poor, vulnerable, oppressed, and victimized. For Miguel, spirituality did not primarily equate with peace but, rather, with justice and an accompanying uncompromising and lifelong struggle on behalf of what was right and righteous in every social context, whether personal or global.

There is no assurance that this way of believing and acting will control every development in the world or even control the ultimate destiny of the human species. Humanity retains the freedom to fail, which could mean extinction in the foreseeable future. The happy ending of the Nicaragua case needs to be balanced against the prolonged and tragic ordeal of the

Palestinian people, for which there is still no decent end in sight. Beyond wins and losses, what should be clear is that unless many more of us become attentive to the horizons of spirituality and necessity, the outlook for the human future is bleak.

Father Miguel d'Escoto's disavowal of the domain of the feasible is assuredly not the only way to serve humanity, but it is a most inspiring way and challenges us all to act justly, an orientation that is underrepresented in the operations of governments and other public and private bureaucracies, and most flagrantly in the speculative frenzies on Wall Street and the backrooms of hedge fund offices. Father Miguel d'Escoto was one of the great *citizen pilgrims* of our time. His life was a continuous journey toward what St. Paul called "a better city, a heavenly city" to manage and shape the totality of life on Planet Earth. It was a great privilege and invaluable learning experience to have this extraordinary man as mentor and friend.

Notes

1   In this chapter alone, I take full responsibility because it derives from a talk that I was invited to give in honor of Father Miguel d'Escoto.

2   For an attempt to cage the tigers, see Falk and von Sponeck (2024).

3   Many international treaties governing sensitive subject matter contain a "compromissory clause" that allows either party to submit a legal dispute to the ICJ that obliges the defendant state to participate, provided that both states had accepted such a clause. A compromissory clause of this type is a treaty specific form of what is called "compulsory jurisdiction."

References

Falk, Richard, and von Sponeck. 2024. *Liberating the United Nations: Realism with Hope.* Redwood City, CA: Stanford University Press.
United Nations General Assembly (UNGA). 1986. "Address by Nicaragua's Acting Foreign Minister Miguel d'Escoto." New York, November 3.

17

David Ray Griffin's Postmodern Politics and Spirituality:

Do We Need (or Want) World Government?

Whether in theology, philosophy, or politics, David Griffin has been dedicated to a search for truth reinforced by a strong ethical commitment to human well-being as conceived in biopolitical terms. In this respect, there is an organic consistency that links his explorations of the 9/11 attacks with investigations of the plausibility of life after death and paranormal psychological experience. In all these instances, Griffin's truth-seeking swims against the strong tides of conventional wisdom and societal consensus. It is no different in relation to world order, which Griffin finds ethically intolerable and geopolitically unsustainable.

Moving beyond critique, Griffin believes that the only way to respond to the dual challenge is by the establishment of a *democratic world government*. A satisfactory ethical solution could, in principle, be achieved within a system of global governance without any major centralization of political authority—for instance, by a redistributive global tax and drastic reform of the world trading and investment structure—but given ecological challenges and nuclear war dangers, in Griffin's view, such a world order would not be sustainable over time. Alternatively, it is possible that the American global state, a new form of empire, could impose limits on carbon emissions and control recourse to political violence sufficiently to establish a high probability of a sustainable future, but it would be ethically intolerable due to the need to subjugate most of the people in the world so as to stabilize a regime of radical inequality in material benefits and human rights. On the basis of this rational assessment of world order alternatives, Griffin's advocacy of a democratic world government is a natural sequence to his assessment of global ills.

This chapter depicts Griffin's approach and then questions the viability, and even the desirability, of his proposed solution, while endorsing the values and analysis informing his position. Our view differs from that of Griffin because we believe it essential to think more dialectically about the necessary and desirable forms of future global governance. We aim for decentralization of power and authority to the extent possible while avoiding either empire or world government as preferential images of world order. Ideologically, our preferred image can be summarized on a bumper sticker: "anarchism without anarchy." This puzzling image will be explained and defended in the concluding section.

The first section of this chapter discusses why a democratic world government is needed and desirable in Griffin's understanding. The second section is devoted to Griffin's rationale provided for his conceptions of a preferred plausible future world order. And finally, a brief set of suggestions based on globally constituted democratic values, but without a comparable reliance on world governmentality.

It may be clarifying to ground this inquiry in a rejection of the "realist" frame of reference based on state-centric global governance as the endpoint of world order. As Alexander Wendt observes in a trenchant and influential essay (2003): "If Realists are right that anarchy is programmed for war, then it makes sense to define one's sovereignty in egoistic terms and act on that basis. International law is irrelevant or an impediment to the national interest, and one should pursue a unilateralist policy whenever possible" (529). It seems useful to acknowledge that despite some elements of empathy for the poor and vulnerable, behavior in world politics continues to be driven by policy elites seeking to maximize national or corporate interests in wealth, power, and prestige, with very little deference to policies associated with the realization of global human interests. In an era of neoliberal globalization, corporate and financial orientations may be rather cosmopolitan in their outlook, although without overcoming their egoistic calculus in exerting influence.

Such an acknowledgment helps us understand the limits on rational problem-solving at the global level, accounting for the inability to rid the world of war, or even of nuclear weaponry, and to address the multiple ecological challenges posed by climate change despite the near universal realization that the collective well-being of the humanity requires at this stage of history that such steps be taken. In effect, as long as realist orientations guide the behavior of the most influential political and economic actors, the prevailing mode of global governance will remain catastrophe prone, and the imperatives of realism and rationality will be locked in a dysfunctional embrace with one another.

Why a Democratic World Government Is Necessary

Griffin is very clear about his point of departure with respect to the advocacy of democratic world government:

> If civilization is going to thrive or even survive much longer, I have long been convinced, the present system of global governance, which is based on power and wealth, must be replaced by global democracy, in which laws on all matters affecting the planet as a whole be made by representatives from all the peoples of the world. A transition to global democracy in this sense is necessary, I believe, if we are to have a chance of solving our problems of global scope, such as war, imperialism, terrorism, international crime, global apartheid, climate change, and the threat of nuclear annihilation.
>
> (2011, 101)

Griffin writes of "civilization" as the unit of concern and posits that lawmakers of a global democracy need to be "representatives" of the "peoples" of the world. Such political language completely bypasses the centrality of states and their leaders in shaping laws and policies and implies that the authority structure of a global democracy will be legitimated by the consent of peoples (not people) rather than through delegated representatives appointed by the governments of sovereign states (in the manner that ambassadors are currently designated). Griffin has a long list of global challenges that can only be solved by a global mechanism, although some of these would seem likely to persist, undoubtedly in an altered form, even if such a global democracy came into being: terrorism, crime, apartheid, and civil war have long flourished within states, and might not be easier to address if some sort of global government did indeed come into being. Arguably, unless current levels of inequality were greatly reduced in the process of transition to a global democracy, these kinds of threats to human security could actually become worse as some form of world government was being constituted. It is this widely shared fear of worsening that helps explain the persisting attachment to the sort of global pluralism that is the structural part of the Westphalian heritage.

What gives great force to Griffin's argument for democratic world government is a combination of two empirically grounded historical interpretations: first, that the catastrophic risks of the present form of world order render it unsustainable over time, and something of an unheralded miracle that it has so far avoided apocalyptic events; second, that despite the palpable menace of nuclear weaponry or the scientifically validated warnings about the dire consequences of trends toward global warming, there is little basis for believing that the present way in which global governance operates is capable of providing satisfactory solutions. In general, Griffin believes that after centuries of what he calls "serious talk" about eliminating war, "the globe remains more heavily militarized than ever before" (2004, 174). Indeed, Griffin is convinced that all the world order problems of global scope are getting worse, not better, and that this situation reflects a structural deficiency that can only be solved by the establishment of a unified governmental structure that can create and enforce law and policy globally. His belief in governmentality is asserted in confident language: "Just as no problem of national scope could be solved in a country without a central government, the problems of global scope cannot be solved without a global government" (Griffin 2011).

Griffin does acknowledge that there exists an unacceptable organizational alternative to a democratically constituted world government: empire. He rejects this alternative on both political and religious grounds. Griffin insists that the global structure of anarchy (that is, state-centric world order) is "demonic"—not only is it conducive to ceaseless warfare but necessarily produces domination by the strong of the weak, with resulting patterns of exploitation and waste and the incapability of taking sufficient account of either long run considerations or global public interests.

Even beyond this problem of structure (which is almost synonymous with government in Griffin's formulations) is a fatal flaw embedded in human nature itself and is at the root of most religious understandings of the human condition. In Griffin's words, "[t]here is after all a deep truth in the testimony of the world's religions to the presence of a transcultural proclivity to evil deep within the human heart, which no new paradigm, combined with a new economic order . . . or any social arrangements, will suddenly eliminate" (Griffin et al. 1989, xiv). This view of the reign of the demonic is confirmed for Griffin by the teachings of the major world religions, especially their interpretation of the human condition. He points especially to the life and work of Jesus as expressing the need for a radical repudiation of "demonic control of the planet," which "has continued to increase during the past 2000 years, especially in the past four centuries, what we call the modern age" (Griffin 1993, 223). Despite this long trajectory, Griffin insists that the dangers posed by the demonic have reached a circumstance of historical urgency: "Even if we do avoid nuclear holocaust, furthermore, the present trajectory of civilization, with its increasing population, consumerism, and depleting-and-polluting technologies, promises unprecedented suffering through scarcity and climate change sometime in the 21st century" (ibid.). And these concerns are further magnified by "ethnic and cultural animosities, the proliferation of nuclear weapons, and arms sales" making "any realistic picture of the future based on present trends . . . completely terrifying" (ibid.).

Significantly, Griffin acknowledges that there are influential advocates of an imperial solution to world government in the United States, and not only neoconservative ideologues such as Richard Perle and William Kristol but also liberal internationalists such as Michael Mandelbaum.[1] Perhaps the argument is best understood in its cruder forms as articulated, for instance, by William Kristol and Lawrence Kaplan, as quoted by Griffin: "The alternative to American leadership is a chaotic, Hobbesian world" in which "there is no authority to thwart global aggression, ensure peace and security, and enforce international norms" (2011, 102).[2]

Usually, such advocacy is hidden beneath a language that disguises its imperial character and talks instead of "leadership" and "universal values," but the nature of the solution to the structural problems posed by state-centric anarchy are to be overcome by the projection of American power, a prospect that, according to these thinkers, should be welcomed. Griffin is politely skeptical of such pretensions, concluding that it would be unacceptable to most of the world's peoples and governments, especially given the declining respect for the American global role in many parts of the world and the postcolonial distrust of any world order scheme that is rooted in West-centric control (Griffin 2011).

In this central regard, an American world state would be just one more phase in the long geopolitical narrative of demonic world order, and although responsive to the challenges posed by political fragmentation or anarchy, would not be acceptable politically, morally, or spiritually. It is against such a background of analysis and assessment that Griffin believes that the only ethically acceptable political path for the future is the one that leads to *democratic world government*.

Why a Democratic World Government Is Possible

Griffin's views on the necessity of more centralized global governance seem rather widely shared. There are few careful students of the contemporary global setting who believe that the Westphalian framework can provide humanity with a sustainable future without drastic modification. Unfortunately, this consensus on the need for change is ignored by political leaders and their advisers, who devote their energies and resources to the short-term and somewhat manageable challenges of the present. As far as the underlying challenges depicted by Griffin, and especially the reign of the demonic, is concerned, the current managers of world order are in total denial. There is no hint given that nationalism, statism, and militarism, much less consumerism, patriarchy, and capitalism, exert a tightening stranglehold on human destiny. Although Griffin does not directly address this issue of severe alienation at elite levels, it implicitly shifts his hopes for drastic change away from the enlightenment of governments to a dependence on the activism of people, what has been called throughout the book and elsewhere "globalization-from-below" or "moral globalization" (Falk 1997).

Griffin does not adopt a utopian outlook that dispenses with the prospects for attaining his desired future. Following Hans Küng in affirming that the world religions share a universal adherence to a minimal morality encapsulated in the golden rule, Griffin believes that such a moral commonality is sufficient to provide the basis for a survival-oriented transition to democratic world government. This idea of a moral foundation for universalism is only credible as the basis for political change if it informs the imaginary of ordinary people, and Griffin makes clear that part of his indictment of modernism is that it has detached ethics from its grounds in religion and nature, giving rise to "disenchantment," and in reaction to Whitehead's strong efforts, informing process theology to "reenchant" nature and the reality of the human worldly presence.[3] In Griffin's introduction to his series on Postmodern Constructive Thought, there is written the idea that his reorientation of perspective rests on the awareness that "the continuation of modernity threatens the very survival of life on our planet."[4] Putting this thought in the pre-political terminology that Griffin employed in the 1980s and 1990s, the emergence of a postmodern consciousness involves a set of emancipatory ideas and norms to be encountered in religious and philosophical thought but also in the lived experience informed by such normative ideals. Modernity has suppressed these ideals, but the challenges of the postmodern world are restoring their relevance to a sustainable human future that needs at some point to be translated into responsive political arrangements. Griffin believes, and argues repeatedly to this effect, that responsiveness presupposes democratic world government.

Griffin also finds confirming support for this confidence in a universal foundation for the establishment of a democratic world government even in the thought of such communitarian luminaries as Michael Walzer and Amitai Etzioni, as well as in the wide adherence to the Universal Declaration of Human Rights. There are no claims being made by Griffin of a full-fledged cosmopolitan ethos, and no evasion of the relevance of civilizational and religious differences, but only the minimalist assertion that under the various pressures of necessity and a shared "minimal morality supported by a minimal theism" (Griffin 2011, 122). This allows world government to remain possible provided it is democratic. If political centralization were to come about via unipolarity or imperial expressions of global responsibility, then its establishment would probably be impossible, because it would encounter strong resistance, and it could only be imposed by an extreme reliance on coercion and intimidation, and hence highly undesirable.

Arguably, the imperial possibility is more *probable* that the democratic government alternative, which is already functioning as the vertical dimension of the current form of Westphalian world order. From an ethical perspective, Griffin rejects this merger of American grand strategy on a global scale with hyped claims of providing the world with benign global governance, but the projection of American military, diplomatic, and cultural influence on a global scale does create some of the components of a global state. It is, to be sure, dysfunctional in many respects, and likely to be unsustainable, but is more likely than the emergence of global democracy, for which there is no evidence of sufficient support to allow even an imagined scenario of how to transition from the doomed present to the preferred democratic future.

At present there does not even exist a widespread understanding of what is meant by "global democracy." There is some limited attention given to democratic reforms of specific international institutions by way of making their operations more transparent, giving a wider range of stakeholders' participatory roles, imposing mechanisms of accountability on officials, and de-Westernizing control over policy. The United Nations has been the target of such reformist campaigns, as have been such institutions as the World Bank and the International Monetary Fund. In addition, some speculations have suggested that the development of European institutions under the aegis of the European Union might provide some lessons for comparable developments in other regions, but no attention has been given to whether there is any reason to think of extending this European experience worldwide, and there is a fundamental difference. For states and regions, there is an "outside" that exerts pressure for collective security and provides a basis for shaping an "inside" political identity. As experience in Europe during its period of economic crisis in the last several years has demonstrated, the development of institutional regionalism has not produced a strong enough European identity to overcome divergent national interests and rivalries.

World government, in contrast, is (mis)understood by drawing an implicit analogy to well-governed territorial constitutional democracies, sometimes given greater specificity by taking the shape of a greatly strengthened United Nations or relying on the structure of the United States to provide a model for governing the world according to federalist criteria. Such ideas set forth as proposals have had three features in modern times: emanate from the West, have greatest political traction in the aftermath of major wars, and, so far, seem formulated by members of political and social elites.[5]

Griffin has a different approach to the political plausibility of world government, relying on neither war elites, nor Western leadership. Instead, he pins his hopes on the extraordinary spread of nongovernmental organizations (NGOs) creating movement possibilities in recent decades, that is, a bottom-up form of political action enacted on the new playing field of world order that he and others characterize as "global civil society." Griffin believes that global democracy would provide this multitude of NGOs with the only common cause that makes sense given the various agendas being pursued. Griffin strongly believes that activists will come to understand and agree with his view that without global democracy partial global reform efforts are destined to fail. He has faith that a coalition of NGOs, if organized to exert leverage on powerful political actors to shape a future for humanity, and guided by widely shared universal values, would greatly enhance the potential for benevolent global reform. In the process, he bemoans the passivity of the most influential NGOs when it comes to reforming the existing morally and politically deficient normative order.

So far, nothing that could be called responsive to Griffin's call has taken place. There have been impressive gatherings of NGOs at UN conferences devoted to such global issues as women, human rights, population, and environment, but the emphasis was a particular cause being addressed and networking among likeminded NGOs. The World Social Forum's annual gatherings in Brazil and elsewhere were mainly unified by their hostility to neoliberal globalization and their demands for a more equitable and ecologically responsible world economy, with little focus on restructuring world order around democratic principles. Perhaps closest in spirit to the Griffin recommendation was the 2011 Occupy movement, itself taking inspiration from the Arab Spring, and notable for its stress on democratic empowerment and learning how to act politically by mimicking challenges to the established order in the non-West, symbolized by the call in Occupy London for a "Global Tahrir Square." Unfortunately, while the Occupy movement had a promising moment, it lacked the staying power to become a historical force, and if it did, it likely would have adhered to a locally driven set of priorities and failed to unify around an overarching theme, as Griffin hoped, by dedicating itself to the pursuit of global democracy. What was encouraging from the Griffin perspective was the spontaneous convergence on global democracy as the expression of their affirmative alternative to the status quo, but with little effort to explain what that might mean, if anything, governmentally. In other words, the Occupy movement failed to connect the dots in Griffin's manner of linking global democracy to world government. Whether the Black Lives Matter or the Palestinian solidarity movement will sustain momentum and broaden its agenda to encompass drastic global reform is unknowable, but on the basis of past experience, the odds are strongly against such a Griffin-friendly outcome.

This turn to global civil society as a site of struggle is overtly reinforced by Griffin's assessment of the compatibility of world religions and universal or naturalistic morality with a worldwide movement to promote democratic world government, creating a non-Western foundation for political action that draws upon religion and culture. Griffin makes the same recommendation to the religions of the world as he does to the moral NGOs: "Religions of the world, unite! You have nothing to lose but your impotence." Creatively, Griffin posits a potential synergistic relationship between the domain of religion and that of the moral NGOs, the former benefiting from the knowledge and experience with substantive issues that the latter has accumulated, while the moral NGOs gain leverage by the mobilization of the masses drawn to religion and by the practical wisdom embedded in religious traditions. This religious/secular orientation does lend an element of originality to the Griffin approach, as well as his incorporation of non-Western thought and agency.

As far as the democratic nature of the world government that Griffin favors, not too much detail is provided beyond an insistence that democratic values pervade all governance structures from the local to the global and that the devolution of authority be shaped by deference to the principle of subsidiarity, that is, only as much centralization as is needed, with preference for maximum decentralization consistent with meeting material needs of people and the sustainability needs of the planet. To what extent such arrangements would challenge existing structures of inequality and hierarchy is not specified, nor is the need to moderate the consumerist ethos in this global democracy to come (Derrida 2001).

The Griffin approach to democratic world government seems coherent and comprehensive. Its arguments from necessity and possibility are thoughtful, and its ideal is depicted in a manner that seems responsive to both the survival imperatives of humanity and the justice ideals of religion and morality. It offers a welcome shift of political emphasis away from West-centric top-down proposals and situates its hopes for the future on the mobilization and collective action of popular forces that combine the ongoing emergence of global civil society with the deep-rooted visions of human betterment and solidarity found in the world religions. But Griffin does not make any effort to develop a credible scenario of transition or to assess the kinds of obstacles that would be placed in the path of the sort of movement he recommends, and thus does not take sufficient account of the possible drawbacks of advocating world government within our present historical circumstances.

Why the Advocacy of a Democratic Global Government Is Not Desirable

While sharing Griffin's concerns about the inability of the inherited structures and societal priorities of modernity to overcome the multiple crises confronting contemporary humanity, as well as the relevance of resting hope on the emergence of postmodern consciousness, visions, and initiatives, we remain skeptical, even opposed to, pinning out hopes on the emergence of a democratic global government. At first glance, this skepticism may seem more semantic than substantive, as Griffin actually seeks to minimize the governmental presence at the global level via reliance on the subsidiarity principle_to the extent practical, and we both seek to rely on values of democracy and nonviolence in responding to these challenges. Nevertheless, the divergences are significant both in relation to the goal being pursued and our shared commitment to democratization (Falk 2005 and 1998).

The goal of world government seems ill-conceived, completely lacking in grassroots support throughout global civil society, including among those elements that are seeking to maximize democratization in international society. In addition, there is no support for world government among political elites. If the language of world government is avoided, and the issues are put forth as distinct functional requirements for sustainability, there is removed the teleological concern that arises when "world government" is posited as a postmodern sequel to the modern, politically fragmented system of world order, but this weakens the Griffin tone of urgency in relation to the scope, gravity, and immediacy of the problem. The reason that postwar situations create a temporary willingness to consider centralizing world order alternatives, including world government, for a fraction of the elite is the reality of wartime suffering and hardship, and a realization that, given technological advances in weaponry, the future is likely to be worse. These feelings were sufficient after World War I to establish the League of Nations and after World War II the United Nations, but not enough to give such institutions the capabilities and independence they need to carry out the grandiose mission of war prevention.

The more substantive difficulties with the Griffin approach relate to issues of justice in a world that currently exhibits such drastic inequality among and within existing political communities. The United States is experiencing the hollowing out of democratic political life mainly due to the effects of inequality. In global settings, where the sense of shared nationality is absent, there is even less sense that those who are in privileged positions will be prepared to accept a leveling downward to create humane global governance. When such inequality exists, governmental coercion tends to increase, with negative impacts on freedom and democratic liberties. In this regard, it is highly unlikely that the universalist norms found in "natural religion" or in human rights instruments of international law would be able to offset the political pressures mounted to preserve existing distributions of wealth and income.

Such a posture does not intend to convey a sense of despair or the absence of an engagement with the work of human betterment under the darkening shadows of unresolved and neglected global challenges. There are various signs of potential surges of support for democratizing political movements at various levels of social organization. In this regard, the upheavals associated with the Arab Spring and the widespread enthusiasm that accompanied the globally dispersed Occupy movement reveal a fertile ground for the rise of a democratizing global political current. In such an atmosphere, a condition of radical uncertainty exists that underscores the importance of "the black swan" phenomenon in which our sense of history is limited by our inability to anticipate the emergence of forces that alter trends in radical and unexpected ways.[6]

Our immediate preference would be to promote specific initiatives that move in a democratizing direction, exhibit sensitivity to moral globalization, and avoid any teleological pretension of a world order endpoint. Among those initiatives that seem to have significant democratizing potential we would mention the establishment of a global peoples parliament, the imposition of a tax on international financial transactions or transnational air travel, strengthening of regional institutions along democratic lines, imposition of tax on carbon emissions, and scrapping of the Non-Proliferation Treaty and the establishment of a nuclear disarmament process to establish a world without nuclear weapons.[7]

Notes

1   The least overtly imperialistic, yet self-serving and insensitive to the historical situation is Michael Mandelbaum's elaborate argument that America already provides world government as a global public good (2005).

2   See their original text in Kaplan and Kristol (2003).

3   This perspective is elaborated by the theologian Hans Küng (1997).

4   See Griffin (2011, 107–11), explaining the religious grounding of lived morality.

5   See Ikenberry (2001), Weiss (2009), and Campbell (2011).

6   See Taleb (2007); many important transformative events in recent international history were unanticipated by pundits and experts: collapse of the Berlin Wall; release of Nelson Mandela from jail after twenty-seven years; 9/11 attacks; Arab Spring; the rise of Trumpism; the AI breakthroughs; genocide in Gaza.

7   Falk and Strauss (2011); Falk and Krieger (2012); President Barack Obama Prague speech on nuclear disarmament (White House 2009).

References

Cabrera, Luis, ed. 2011. *Global Governance, Global Government: Institutional Visions for an Evolving World System*. Albany, NY: SUNY Press.

Campbell, Craig. 2011. "Why World Government Failed After World War II: A Historical Lesson for Contemporary Efforts." In *Global Governance, Global Government: Institutional Visions for an Evolving World System*, edited by Luis Cabrera, 77–97. Albany, NY: State University of New York Press.

Falk, Richard. 1997. "Resisting 'Globalization-from-Above' Through 'Globalization-from-Below.'" *New Political Economy* 2 (1): 17–27.

Falk, Richard. 1998. "The United Nations and Cosmopolitan Democracy: Bad Dream, Utopian Fantasy, Political Project." In *Re-Imagining Political Community: Studies in Cosmopolitan Democracy*, edited by Daniele Archibugi, David Held, and Martin Köhler, 309–31. Cambridge, UK: Polity Press.

Falk, Richard. 1999. *Predatory Globalization: A Critique*. Cambridge, UK: Polity Press.

Falk, Richard. 2005. *Governing Globalisation: Issues and Institutions*, edited by Deepak Nayyar, 122–39. Oxford: Oxford University Press.

Falk, Richard, and David Krieger. 2012. *Path to Zero: Dialogues on Nuclear Danger*. London: Routledge.

Falk, Richard, and Andrew Strauss. 2011. *A Global Parliament: Essays and Articles*. Berlin: Committee for a Democratic UN.

Griffin, David Ray. 1993. "Postmodern Theology for the Church." *Lexington Theological Quarterly* 28 (3): 223–39.

Griffin, David Ray. 2004. *The New Pearl Harbor: Disturbing Questions About the Bush Administration and 9/11*. Northampton, MA: Olive Branch Press.

Griffin, David Ray. 2011. "Is a Global Ethic Possible?" In *Global Governance, Global Government: Institutional Visions for an Evolving World System*, edited by Luis Cabrera, 101–26. Albany, NY: State University of New York Press.

Griffin, David Ray. 2021. *Reinhold Niebuhr and the Question of Global Democracy*. Anoka, MN: Process Century Press.

Griffin, David Ray, and Richard Falk. 1993. *Postmodern Politics for a Planet in Crisis: Policy, Process, and Presidential Vision*. Albany, NY: State University of New York.

Griffin, David Ray, William A. Beardslee, and Joe Holland. 1989. *Varieties of Postmodern Theology*. Albany, NY: State University of New York Press.

Griffin, David Ray, John B. Cobb Jr., Richard A. Falk, and Catherine Keller. 2006. *The American Empire and the Commonwealth of God, A Political, Economic, Religious Statement*. Westminster, KY: John Knox Press.

Ikenberry, John G. 2001. *After Victory: Institutions, Strategic Restraint, and the Rebuilding of Order after Major Wars*. Princeton, NJ: Princeton University Press.

Kaplan, Lawrence, and William Kristol. 2003. *The War over Iraq: Saddam's Tyranny and America's Mission*. San Francisco, CA: Encounter Books.

Küng, Hans. 1997. *A Global Ethic for Global Politics and Economics*. Oxford: Oxford University Press.

Mandelbaum, Michael. 2005. *The Case for Goliath: How America Acts as the World Government in the Twenty-First Century*. New York: PublicAffairs.

Murphy, Cornellius F. Jr. 2001. *Theories of World Governance: A Study in the History of Ideas*. Washington, DC: Catholic University of America Press.

Taleb, Nassim. 2007. *Black Swan: The Impact of the Highly Improbable*. New York: Random House.

Weiss, Thomas. 2009. "What Happened to the Idea of World Government?" *International Studies Quarterly* 53 (2): 253–71.

Wendt, Alexander. 2003. "Why a World State Is Inevitable." *European Journal of International Relations* 9: 491–42.

White House. 2009. "Remarks by President Barack Obama in Prague as Delivered." Office of the Press Secretary, April 5, Prague.

18

Edward Demenchonok's Visionary Cosmopolitanism

Edward Demenchonok is an erudite advocate of cosmopolitan thought. His extensive writings are both responsive to humane values that are universally resonant, as well as resonant to the obstructive presence of entrenched political, economic, and cultural structures that fracture human identity and cloud perceptions of the biopolitical crisis of our time. He is fully alert to the urgency of actualizing a worldview that can persuasively discredit lawless violence, militarism, and hegemony, and looks to philosophers, seers, and an assortment of thinkers from a variety of civilizational backgrounds in his search for illuminating truths with transformative potential. By analyzing and drawing from an astonishing range of such intellectual figures, Demenchonok composes a coherent vision of the way forward for human society. This chosen path is dialogic, rational, ideational, ethical, nonviolent, humanistic, ecologically enlightened, spiritual, and radical. It contrasts with the various strands of historicist, positivist, and technocratic thought, and above all with the grand illusions and reprehensible practices of various forms of imperial geopolitics.

A Cosmopolitan Visionary for Our Time

Edward Demenchonok is among the philosophers who are concerned about the situation of individuals and humankind in facing world problems that affect all human beings and future generations. First of all, these are global problems, such as wars in a world threatened by the presence of nuclear and other weapons of mass destruction, poverty in underdeveloped countries, climate change, and pandemics. He identifies wars, militaristic geopolitics, and imperial ambitions as the central political problems of our time. These are the features of present world order, along with nationalistic forms of patriotism, that obstruct the collaboration of nations in jointly working toward solutions to common global problems, the progression of which threatens the future of humanity.

He points to the end of World War II as an important historical turning point, when the horrors of total war and of the Holocaust shocked the consciousness of humanity and prompted humankind to transform world order in accord with the principles of the United Nations Charter. But those hopes and opportunities for change were lost by the continuation of power politics, taking the potentially catastrophic form of the Cold War rivalry. Demenchonok concurs with those scholars who argue that there was no justification for the development of the atomic bombs and even less for their use against the predominantly civilian population of Hiroshima and Nagasaki three months after the capitulation of Germany, when Japan was already arguably on the verge of surrender. These early critics of nuclearism concluded that US president Harry Truman's decision to drop the atomic bomb was primarily an expression of power politics that was motivated by the geopolitical interests of an emerging superpower in possession of a powerful weapon that could be used as a policy instrument in a post-WWII political atmosphere, anticipated to be one of geopolitical rivalry centered on the on the control of Europe. In elite foreign policy circles of the West, it was believed that this new weaponry could be used as a demonstration of both capability and will, a warning to the Soviet Union and to the world (Alperovitz 1985, 290; Bernstein 1995; Hasegawa 2005). Of course, such a belief rested on the monopoly of this weaponry of mass destruction and this rationale was undermined by Soviet acquisition of comparable weapons capabilities within a decade.

Truman's decision marked the beginning of the nuclear age and the Cold War even before its formal declaration and humanity is still living beneath the shadow cast by that fateful act. Albert Camus, Jean-Paul Sartre, Bertrand Russell, and John Dewey are singled out by Demenchonok not only for condemning the atrocity of the act but also for revealing its deeply disturbing implications for the future that were so self-destructive as to imperil the survival of the human species, if not in its totality, surely in the advanced forms achieved in the twenty-first century.

Demenchonok takes serious account of what we should learn from Auschwitz and Nazism, as well as from Hiroshima and Nagasaki. He refers to the writings of Theodor Adorno to underpin an argument that such barbaric behavior represents a failure of philosophy, which at its root reflects the refusal to take proper account of the suffering of other human beings. Without commitments by scholars to challenge gratuitous forms of suffering or cruelty, barbarism eventually erupts, as in Nazi Germany, under conditions of societal stress. Demenchonok reminds us of Emmanuel Lévinas's warning that instrumental reason of the sort that informs and empowers all aspects of modernity, when coupled with the will and incentive to dominate, produces "a type of knowledge which leads to the atomic bomb."[1] In pinpointing the locus of this evil-generating disposition of modernity, Demenchonok reveals his awareness of the "dangerous gap between sophisticated high-tech power and inadequate ethics" and between "the worldwide effects of politico-economic activities and the level of global consciousness" (Demenchonok 2010, 18). In one respect, without directly acknowledging it, Demenchonok seems to have a Hegelian anxiety that the most influential purveyors of ideas are disposing late modernity to a crash landing.

For Demenchonok, meaningful reflection on creating a peaceful world is anchored in the work of Kant, especially *Perpetual Peace* (1795) and his related essay "Idea for a Universal History with a Cosmopolitan Aim" (1748). Kant counterposes to the existing violent "state of nature" a law-governed social organization based on a republican constitution, lawful governance of external relations, and a cosmopolitan right. He rejects a "world republic" modeled on the structures of European sovereign states.

Kant fears that the hegemony of a powerful global state would quickly come to resemble a despotic "universal monarchy" and pose a crippling danger to human freedom. He affirms the idea of a cosmopolitan right that would transform the political and international right into "a universal right of humanity," providing the conditions for lasting peace (Demenchonok 2019, 224–25). An important feature of Kant's thought that also informs Demenchonok's cosmopolitanism is the explicit repudiation of world government as the solution for the torments of hegemony and war. Demenchonok's way forward proceeds through an acceptance of the foundational insight of human rights affirming the human dignity of all persons, combined with a respectful attitude of tolerance toward differences of gender, culture, religion, race, and mode of development. Cosmopolitanism is about universality, not sameness, and its prophetic proponents celebrated in Demenchonok's writings, aside from Kant, include Leo Tolstoy, Mahatma Gandhi, and Martin Luther King Jr.

The Cold War, generating a reckless nuclear arms race, pushed humankind to the precipice of nuclear self-destruction. As Demenchonok notes, many philosophers argued that nuclear war could bring about the end of the human species, and the "extinction" thesis or "omnicide" was broadly discussed in numerous publications by John Somerville, Carl Sagan, Jonathan Schell, Douglas Lackey, Gregory Kavka, Steven Lee, Russell Hardin, William C. Gay, and Andrey D. Sakharov, among others (Demenchonok 2009, 17).

The emergence in the 1980s of "new political thinking" had elements of a cosmopolitan worldview in stressing the priority of universal human values over all others (ideological, class, national, state), peaceful coexistence, and constructive types of mutual cooperation. The rise of global consciousness, which resulted in movements for peace and democratization, as well as inducing the prudence of political leaders, led to an eventual end of the Cold War. Moreover, as Demenchonok emphasizes, the task was much broader and deeper—to remove the root causes of wars in a nuclear age and to proceed toward gradual denuclearization and demilitarization, and by stages over time achieve complete disarmament.

These movements were underpinned by an understanding of the necessity of encouraging the construction of a pluralistic world order of peaceful, collaborative relationships among nations. Solutions for the escalating global problems associated with ecological crises and economic underdevelopment also are needed and must be reinforced by a greater sense of responsibility to the future (an altered time consciousness) and to societal imperatives of empathy. In effect, the short-termism of current political cycles of accountability and the individualist ethos of capitalism not only fracture the commonality of life but have become historically dysfunctional.

After the end of the Cold War, there was another turning point that provided opportunities for the positive transformation of society and international relations within a framework of peaceful coexistence and collaboration in solving global problems, evolving toward a cosmopolitan world order. Demenchonok shows that, since the early 1990s, numerous philosophers and political theorists, including Karl-Otto Apel, Jürgen Habermas, Fred Dallmayr, Seyla Benhabib, Judith Butler, James Bohman, Daniele Archibugi, Ulrich Beck, David Held, and Mary Kaldor have expressed innovative ideas about democratizing relationships among nations in a polycentric world and the possibility of actualizing cosmopolitan democracy.

Demenchonok emphasizes the transformative meanings of cosmopolitanism in the quest to improve humanity's future prospects and describes the 1990s as "a time of a rebirth of the ideals of cosmopolitanism and striving toward their practical implementation" occasioning a tidal wave of stimulating publications and discussions (2017, 188). The predominant view was "moral cosmopolitanism," which asserts that every human being has a global stature as the ultimate unit of moral concern, is entitled to equal respect, and whose well-being must be properly considered in practical deliberations about any lawmaking and policymaking actions that may affect anyone's vital interests" (ibid.). Cosmopolitanism was regarded by its proponents as a benevolent alternative to the war-prone Westphalian state-centric system. It envisioned a long-range democratic transformation of societies and international relations while proclaiming as its ultimate goal the freedom and equality of each human being as a "citizen of the world."

However, the neoconservative "revolution" thwarted this transformative movement and steered US policy toward the pursuit of global hegemonic ambitions, unipolarity, and unilateralism. Furthermore, the global hegemonic project presents itself as the universalized ethnocentrism of the sole superpower, which amounts to a regressive alternative to cosmopolitanism. This claim has been criticized as "imperial cosmopolitanism" (Mendieta 2009), which is ethically and ideologically opposed by the concept of "de-colonial cosmopolitanism" (Mignolo 2010).

The continuation of the existing trend of militarized hegemonism, coupled with the intensification of global problems, threatens the future of humanity and needs to be changed for the sake of species well-being. It may seem counterfactual to talk about cosmopolitanism when facing the hegemonic superpower imposing its domination by using instruments of "soft" and "hard" power. However, for Demenchonok, this is not discouraging but, rather, supportive of the claimed pivotal role of cosmopolitanism in shaping the future of humankind. He does not believe that the current situation is the "end of history" and rather views the current phase of fear and flux within a broad philosophical-historical perspective. He shows that cosmopolitanism has deep roots in the philosophical tradition of thought and is more pertinent than ever. Indeed, he views cosmopolitanism not merely as a moral ideal, but as a highly practical political project. He shows that it is a preferable alternative to both the state-centered international system and the hegemon-centered "world state."

Demenchonok, together with like-minded philosophers, reevaluates the classical conception of cosmopolitanism and develops a "new cosmopolitanism" for a culturally diverse world as a political project that has distinctive characteristics, such as being dialogic, reflexive, rooted, critical, democratic, and transformative (Demenchonok 2017). He refers to Jacques Derrida's idea that, beyond the traditional cosmopolitical ideal, we should see "the coming of a universal alliance or solidarity that extends beyond the internationality of nation states and thus beyond citizenship" (Derrida 2001, 123–24).

Demenchonok outlines the twofold task of a new cosmopolitanism:

In its critical role, cosmopolitan theorizing should clearly distinguish genuine cosmopolitan ideas from the hegemonic pseudo-democratic and pseudo-universal simulacra put forward by "imperial" versions of cosmopolitanism. Adopting a positive role, this theorizing should elaborate the progressive course for the promotion of the cosmopolitan alternative to the hegemonic regression: the struggle for cosmopolitanism in the time of hegemony.

(Demenchonok 2017, 213)

This project is viewed as a process of cosmopolitanization and in perspective as a "cosmopolitanism to come."

Demenchonok also considers the necessary steps of the political transformations required to prepare the conditions for its implementation in a post-hegemonic and polycentric world: establishing the authority of international law and institutions. His programmatic vision includes a properly reformed United Nations, relying on cooperative multilateral mechanisms to address social and global problems, and a gradual transition from an international to a cosmopolitan order.

The richness of thought that Demenchonok offers his readers covers an astonishing range of contemporary deep thinkers, including Jacques Derrida, Hannah Arendt, Judith Butler, Fred Dallmayr, and others, each of whom lends authority to a series of distinctive cosmopolitan syntheses, which exemplifies listening to what others have to say, accompanied by a readiness for dialogue. In the process, Demenchonok also draws on the political theory of kindred liberal/progressive thinkers such as Daniele Archibugi and David Held, especially for their attempts to extend democratic theory and practice beyond sovereign states. In seeking to globalize democracy, respect for a non-hegemonic conception of international law and the UN provides a normative and institutional architecture to underpin his hopes for humane global governance without enduring the tyrannical tendencies of world government.[2]

By creatively drawing on these disparate sources of critical and restorative thought, Demenchonok offers a comprehensive vision of a transformed world order that embodies the wisdom of congenial philosophers together with the practical insights of ecologists and others. To imagine, in the spirit of "possibilism," the emergence of "world citizens," who will make this impossible scenario actually happen, exhibits Demenchonok's extraordinary confidence in the "possibilization of reality" based on the belief that there exists an "excess of the possible over the actual, the proliferation of possibilities rather than their reduction to the mode of actuality" (2009, 33).

One aspect of Demenchonok's vision that is less developed but integral to the unfolding of a cosmopolitan polity is that of "global solidarity," of a quality grounded in functional imperatives and reinforced by a culture of human rights.

In the concluding two chapters, we try to develop a conception of global solidarity that is congruent with Demenchonok's cosmopolitanism. Such a preoccupation with the relevance of global solidarity to the cosmopolitan quest is the current absence of "global community," without which the postulated political ethos of "world citizen" is drained of meaning. Global community remains to-be-created, and until that happens at some future time, if at all, citizenship may extend somewhat beyond state borders through transnationalism, but it will fall short of attempts to overcome the persisting primacy of geopolitics, which continues to rely on violence, hypernationalism, and militarist patterns to retain its bloody hegemonic grip on wellsprings of world order.

Notes

1   See interview with Emmanuel Lévinas in Mortley (1991, 19).

2   See also Falk (1995).

References

Alperovitz, Gar. 1985. *Atomic Diplomacy: Hiroshima and Potsdam*. Chicago: Pluto Press.

Bernstein, Barton. 1995. "The Atomic Bombings Reconsidered." *Foreign Affairs* (January-February): 135–52.

Demenchonok, Edward. 2009. "Philosophy After Hiroshima: From Power Politics to the Ethics of Nonviolence and Co-Responsibility." *American Journal of Economics and Sociology* 68 (1): 9–49.

Demenchonok, Edward. 2010. "From Power Politics to the Ethics of Peace." In *Philosophy After Hiroshima*, edited by Edward Demenchonok, 95–114. Newcastle upon Tyne, UK: Cambridge Scholars Publishing.

Demenchonok, Edward. 2017. "World in Transition: From a Hegemonic Disorder toward a Cosmopolitan Order." In *A World Beyond Global Disorder: The Courage to Hope*, edited by Fred Dallmayr and Edward Demenchonok, 1–22. Newcastle upon Tyne, UK: Cambridge Scholars Publishing.

Demenchonok, Edward. 2019. "Learning from Kant: On Freedom." *Revista Portuguesa de Filosofia* 75 (1): 224–25.

Derrida, Jacques. 2001. *On Cosmopolitanism and Forgiveness*. London and New York: Routledge, 123–24.

Falk, Richard. 1995. *On Humane Governance: Toward a New Global Politics*. Cambridge, UK: Polity Press.

Hasegawa, Tsuyoshi. 2005. *Racing the Enemy: Stalin, Truman, and Japan's Surrender in the Pacific War*. Cambridge, MA: Harvard University Press.

Kant, Immanuel. (1917/1795). *On Perpetual Peace: A Philosophical Sketch*. Translated with introduction and notes by M. Campbell Smith. London: George Allen and Unwin.

Kant, Immanuel. (1963/1748). "Idea for a Universal History from a Cosmopolitan Point of View." In *On History*. Translation by Lewis White Beck, 3–24. Indianapolis, IN: The Bobbs-Merrill Co.

Mendieta, Eduardo. 2009. "From Imperial to Dialogical Cosmopolitanism?" *Ethics and Global Politics* 2 (3): 241–58.

Mignolo, Walter. 2010. "Cosmopolitanism and the De-Colonial Option." *Studies in Philosophy and Education* 29 (2): 111–27.

Mortley, Raoul. 1991. *French Philosophers in Conversation: Lévinas, Schneider, Serres, Irigaray, Le Doeuff, Derrida*. London and New York: Routledge.

19

Global Solidarity:

Toward a Politics of Impossibility

The Imprisoned Imagination

As the COVID-19 pandemic slowly subsides, it is not clear what lessons will be drawn by political leaders and publics around the world. Entrenched power, wealth, and conventional wisdom have demonstrated the overwhelming resilience of hegemonic forms of world order even while the virus continues to ravage many national societies. Despite some notable exceptions revealing extremes of solidarity or discrimination, efficient competence or irresponsible partisanship, this reversion to the status quo occurred at all levels of social organization, from the village to the world, and is especially salient at the level of the sovereign state, which continues to generate the most formidable resistance to the realization of a cosmopolitan alternative.

For the most part, rich and powerful governments used their leverage to corner the vaccine market, allowing a draconian market-driven logic to drive distribution that privileges intellectual property rights and technical know-how, leading to unacceptable disparities in vaccine access between the peoples of the North and those of the South. It has become a truism to observe that no country will be safe from the virus, or its variants, until the entire world is vaccinated, and even then we cannot be sure. Never had the self-interest of the species so vividly and concretely coincided with an ethos of global solidarity. And yet such an ethos did not materialize, and governments were not even embarrassed by their nationalist biases, market-driven priorities, or even their opportunistic resort to "vaccine diplomacy." Geopolitical actors maintained harsh sanctions against governing processes of some states, heedless to widespread suffering and international appeals, including from the World Health Organization (WHO), for a humanitarian pause during the pandemic. We must search for explanations and correctives.

A people-first approach to the global health emergency would have transcended statist and profit-making priorities during all phases of COVID-19 prevention and treatment and situated them within a global commons framework that gestured toward a cosmopolitan future. Such an approach might have dramatically heightened prospects for the social transformation at the heart of the Great Transition Initiative of the Tellus Institute and would at least have restored some confidence that the human species, at least in response to a planetary emergency, is capable of meeting the most acute challenges of the Anthropocene. Instead, the pandemic revealed the resounding strength of statist structures and private sector interests. It seems necessary to acknowledge this tragic interlude as but one more lost opportunity for the human species to awaken from its prolonged slumber before it is too late.

To some extent, the failure has been masked by the newfound pragmatism of some countries as the sense of a world health emergency appeared to recede and virus supplies exceeded national demands in richer countries. In a spirit of philanthropy rather than solidarity, shipments of the vaccine to countries in need were made, recipients often selected on the basis of short-term diplomatic advantage rather than humanitarian urgency. At best, charity toward those less fortunate can be considered a weak form of solidarity, filtered by political leaders motivated by selfish national interests.

More than ever, we must face the question: Can the peoples of Earth, doomed to share a ravaged planet, learn to live together in ways that encourage our species to flourish in an emergent future? Ideas about systemic transition invite us to reimagine such a future by exploring what might be possible, which requires an initial willingness of the imagination to let go of the trappings of the present without engaging in wishful thinking. Such a balancing act is not as straightforward as it sounds. What was science fiction a generation ago is increasingly entering the realm of the possible and even the real. What seemed unimaginable a generation ago, through technocratic ingenuity has already become a feasible goal to be achieved in the near future. It is an opportune time to explore the cosmopolitan seedlings of possibility sprouting around us, inscribing a more hopeful mapping of the human future in the prevailing collective consciousness.

On What Is Possible

Some men [sic] see things as they are and say "why?" I dream of
things that never were and ask "why not?"

—GEORGE BERNARD SHAW

We must start by rejecting conventional foreclosures of the imagination. We cannot accept the idea that politics is "the art of the possible" if the "possible" remains circumscribed by the play of current forces of stasis, confining the idea of change to policy shifts at the margin or—at the most ambitious—elite-driven national revolutions. The structures of state and market remain essentially untouched and continue to run the show, as reinforced internationally by geopolitical maneuvers designed to sustain hegemonic privilege. As long as these features of world order remain unchallenged by popular movements, transitions toward a more humane and ecologically viable future for humanity will be stymied. The first, yet most difficult, challenge is to find effective ways to subvert and transform these primordial structures. Meeting this challenge starts with liberating the mind from ingrained conventions that solidify the ideological biases of modernity, including above all, the sense of its inevitability and the accompanying dismissal of alternative ways of organizing life on the planet to that generated by the European "invention" of statism in the middle of the seventeenth century as an antidote to mutually destructive and "forever" religious wars.

If we carefully consider our own lives, we are likely to appreciate how many epochal public happenings had been previously deemed "impossible," or only seemed possible after the fact. A potent illustration of the tyranny of a status quo bias is Winston Churchill's derisive attitude toward Gandhi during the early stages of the rise of Indian nationalism. Dismissive of any self-determination threat to British colonial rule, Churchill (1974) described Gandhi as a "malignant subversive fanatic" and "a seditious Middle Temple lawyer, now posing as a fakir of a type well known in the East, striding half-naked up the steps of the Viceregal palace." The illustrious British wartime leader (and predatory colonialist) displayed his attachment to a Western understanding of power that had little insight into historical circumstances that would soon reveal the vulnerability of colonial forms of exploitative domination to the mobilized emancipatory energies of anti-colonial nationalism.

Similar patterns of the seemingly impossible happening are evident in contemporary history, such as the peaceful ending of the Cold War followed by the collapse of the Soviet Union; the American defeat in the Vietnam War despite overwhelming military superiority; China's half-century rise from mass impoverishment to prime geopolitical challenger, including threatening

Western mastery of innovative technology such as artificial intelligence (AI), G5 connectivity, robotics, and genetic engineering; and the abandonment of apartheid by South Africa in the face of nonviolent resistance from within and anti-apartheid solidarity from without.

What these examples demonstrate is that our understanding of the scope of the possible has been artificially circumscribed in ways that protect the interests of various elites in the maintenance of the status quo, making it seem reckless and futile to mount structural challenges, however justified they may be morally or bio-politically. Such foreclosures of imagined futures have been key to the protection of institutions like slavery, discrimination, systemic racism, patriarchy, ecocide, and warfare, but often remain limited in scope to specific locales or policy areas.

The uniqueness of the Anthropocene is to be burdened by ideologies that restrict the possible to unsustainable and dysfunctional structures and modes of behavior, while bringing to a head the question of finding more viable ways of organizing life on the planet and living together in a manner that protects future generations. Demenchonok's long engagement with the transformative potential of philosophical thought should be seen as both an enlargement of our sense of the possible and a stirring refutation to the fatalism of Thatcherism with its touchstone mantra of TINA—there is no alternative.

Such foreclosures of the imagination inflict damage both by shortening our temporal vision and by constraining our understanding of useful knowledge. Despite what science and rationality tell us about the future, our leaders—and, indeed, most of us—give scant practical attention to what is needed to preserve and improve the life prospects of future generations. Given the scope and depth of the challenges, responsible anthropocentrism in the twenty-first century should incorporate a sense of urgency to temporal axes of concern besides extending the reach of political aspiration to the natural habitat. We should acknowledge that humanity is now dependent on making happen a "politics of the impossible," a necessary utopianism that stands as an avowal of the attainability of the cosmopolitan quest. We must begin by interrogating the semantics of the possible as a cultural, political, economic, and ideological construct binding humanity to a system that is increasingly bio-politically self-destructive for the species and its natural surroundings.

Closely connected to this foreclosure of our temporal vision has been a scientifically conditioned epistemology asserting the limits of useful knowledge. Within the most influential epistemic communities, an Enlightenment ideology prevails that sets boundaries limiting productive intellectual inquiry. The positive legacies of the Enlightenment in grounding knowledge on scientifically verified evidence rather than cultural superstitions and religiously framed metaphysics and dogma are real and important, but there have been costs as well. Notably, a bias against subjectivity discourages normative inquiry and advocacy, which is dismissed as "non-scientific," distorting the guidance provided by relying upon instrumentalization of knowledge. The noted Confucian scholar Tu Weiming has powerfully criticized the impact of what he calls "instrumental rationalism" on the capacity of Western civilization to appreciate and operationalize the value of empathy, which he views as integral to human dignity and humane governance (Weiming 2017, 20).

We need a moral epistemology to achieve responsible anthropocentrism exploring right and wrong, and to distinguish between desirable and diminished futures, not as matters of opinion but as the underpinnings of "normative knowledge." Universities, split into specialized disciplines and privileging work within the Enlightenment paradigm, are largely oblivious to the need for a holistic understanding of the complexities and solidarities with which we must grapple in order for humanity to extricate itself from present structures that divide and fragment the human experience, strangling possibilities. This paradigm also rejects the relevance of dialogue as essentially a waste of time, given the "truths" of science and reason, which allows predatory patterns to remain embedded and basically unquestioned until challenged by insurrectionary popular opposition. Such is the civilizational price paid by viewing ethics as essentially irrelevant to the management of society, including the workings of the market.

It may be helpful once again to distinguish "the feasible," "the necessary," and "the desirable" to further illuminate "the pursuit of the impossible." In short, "the feasible" from the perspective of the status quo seems incapable, under the best of circumstances, of achieving "the necessary" and "the desirable." We will need to pursue "the desirable" to mobilize the capabilities needed to engage effectively in realizing "the necessary." Science is helpful in identifying the necessary in certain behavioral domains, for example, climate change and biodiversity, while ethics is normative, prescribed in other contexts such as the extensions of democracy to vulnerable people or to transnational and global policy frameworks.

If existing conditions continue, the biopolitical destiny of the human species seems destined for dark times. In the past, before the nuclear age, we could ignore the future and address the material, security, and spiritual needs of bounded communities. Success or failure had no ramifications for larger social systems. Now we must find ways to attend to the whole, or the parts will perish and likely destroy one another in the process. St. Francis found some fitting words for such an emancipatory path: "Start by doing what is necessary, then what is possible, and suddenly you are doing the impossible."

References

Churchill, Winston. 1931/1974. "Speech in the House of Commons." In *Winston S. Churchill: His Complete Speeches 1897–1963*, vol. 5, edited by Robert Rhodes James, 5334–35. New York: Chelsea House Publishers.

Weiming, Tu. 2017. "Spiritual Humanism: An Emerging Global Discourse." In *A World Beyond Global Disorder: The Courage to Hope*, edited by Fred Dallmayr and Edward Demenchonok, 177–82. Cambridge Scholars Publishing.

20

Global Solidarity as the Vital Precondition to Cosmopolitan Transition

When seeking alternative worldviews not defined by states, empires, or markets, many have turned toward the premodern realities and cosmologies of native peoples. Recovering that premodern worldview might be instructive in fundamental respects, but it is not responsive to the practical contours of contemporary liberation. Retreat to the premodern past is not an option, except as forced upon humanity as a result of a planetary calamity.

Instead of the realities of localism and tribal community, our way forward needs to engage globalism and human community, and to affirm such strivings as falling within the realm of possibility. We must reimagine a sense of our place in the cosmos so that it becomes our standpoint: a patriotism for humanity in which the whole becomes greater than the part, and the part is no longer the dominant organizing principle of life on the planet. Understanding the interplay of parts and wholes is a helpful place to begin this transformative journey. Parts are not only enclaves of space on world maps but the separate identities of race, gender, class, belief, and habitat. An ethos of human solidarity would not eliminate differences but would complement them with a sense of commonality or cosmopolitan unity while sustaining their separate and distinctive identities. Such an ethos would generate new modes of being for addressing the challenges of transition. For this to happen, a sense of global solidarity must take over the commanding heights of the imagination rather than continue to inhabit echo chambers hidden in underground places far from the domains of policy formation. Never has the human species more needed the wisdom of philosophers and sages, but not the voices of language philosophers, which has exiled critical thought to obscure academic enclaves unmindful of a darkening sky filled with ominous storm clouds.

Without global solidarity, the structural features of the status quo will remain too deeply entrenched to allow a more cooperative, peaceful, just, and ecologically mindful world to emerge. Such a benevolent future is blocked by the prevailing consciousness in government and corporate board rooms, a paralyzing blend of ignorance, denial, incrementalism, and most of all, an unconscious respect for and deference to fragmenting boundaries that make global solidarity seem "impossible" to achieve. Assuming the paralysis has been overcome by an enhanced conception of the possible, then what?

Global solidarity would benefit humanity functionally, ethically, ecologically, and spiritually. Its functional role is most immediately obvious from a problem-solving perspective. Whether we consider vaccine diplomacy, climate change, or nuclear weapons, it becomes clear that only on the basis of human solidarity will we treat vaccines in the midst of epidemics or pandemics as part of the global commons rather than as a source of national diplomacy, international property rights, and pharmaceutical profits. With climate change, whether we will manage a displacement of national and financial interests on the basis of general global well-being depends on achieving an unprecedented level of global solidarity. Similarly, with nuclear weapons, will we find the courage to live without such weaponry within a security framing that represents the well-being of people rather than the short-sighted hegemony of a few governments and their self-regarding societal elites? And in a postnuclear world, it will seem more plausible to propose comprehensive forms of collective security premised upon demilitarizing processes and global exclusions of violence as instruments of dispute settlement or conflict resolution.

Higher measures of global solidarity would almost certainly enhance the democratic quality and nature of global governance. Even if the defining unit of solidarity remained the sovereign state rather than the human being or humanity as a whole, a sense of world citizenship could underpin a much more robust United Nations, whose membership sought shared goals shaped by ideas of the global public good, as proclaimed by its Charter, rather than the statist competition and geopolitical rivalry that has been its characteristic operating mode up to now, especially on issues of peace and security. The world economy would become much less tied to militarized forms of security, freeing resources for peace building processes of social protection and economic development. From a broadening sense of global identity, we could also expect a more effective approach to biodiversity, preserving or even restoring the ecological viability of the rainforests and polar regions as indispensable aspects of our common heritage. And as heightened empathy would inhere in the manifestations of global solidarity, there would be a greater tendency to take human suffering seriously, including poverty, displacement, and the victimization that follows from natural disasters and political strife.

Perhaps the greatest benefits of global solidarity would be felt ethically, ideationally, and spiritually. We can presume that the collective self of a world exhibiting high levels of global solidarity would enhance cosmopolitan loyalties and identities. The enmities of difference (race, nation, religion, gender, class) would lose their existential and normative relevance, replaced by a radically democratic calibration of "otherness"—perhaps even inclusive with the cosmos regarded as the great other of the earth. It seems reasonable to anticipate the emergence of a less metaphysical religious consciousness inspired by the greater harmonies on earth and a growing experience of cosmic awe as knowledge of this larger realm spreads and is reinforced by mind-broadening experience, such as a greater awareness of life elsewhere in the galaxy and even beyond.

Do We Have the Time?

An ethos of global solidarity led an idealistic group of jurists in 1976 to draft the Declaration of the Rights of People to be implemented by a Permanent Peoples Tribunal, and many inquiries have been carried out since to hold states and their leaders symbolically accountable for violations of international law. People throughout the world have organized numerous civic initiatives organized by social forces in defense of nature and of peace.

Recently, Bolivia and Ecuador enacted a text devoted to the Rights of Mother Nature. New Zealand passed a law recognizing that animals are sentient beings with a legal entitlement to decent treatment. A movement is underway to regard "wild rivers" as subjects of rights, prohibiting the construction of hydro-electric dams. Civil society groups in Europe and South America have formed the International Rights of Nature Tribunal to protect various natural habitats from predatory human behavior.

Within the wider orbit of UN activities, many quiet undertakings involving health, children, food, cultural heritage, and environment proceed in an atmosphere of global solidarity, obstructed by only occasional intrusions from the more conflictual arenas of the Security Council and General Assembly. There are no vetoes, and partisanship is kept at a minimum in these venues within which cosmopolitan ways of engaging-the-world flourish.

Gestating within the cultural bosom of world civilizations and world religions have been subversive ideas of global solidarity. Philosophic and religious affirmations of unity in the ideas and values of "cosmopolitanism," whether so named or not, have garnered increasing numbers of adherents. Growing attachments to nature and humanity proclaimed in many forms gives rise to loyalties that find no place on world maps or within national boundaries. Fears of future catastrophe by way of nuclear war and ecosystem collapse inform a growing awareness that present arrangements are not sustainable, thereby making many persons receptive to creating more inclusive forms of organizing life on the planet. Transition is not off in the distance or only in dreamscapes or science fiction imaginaries; it is happening around us if we only learn to open our eyes and hearts to the rich array of hopeful possibilities now emerging.

We cannot know the future, but we can know that great enhancement of global solidarity would underpin the future we need and desire. Although this enhancement may currently seem impossible, we know that the impossible can happen when the historical moment is conducive. This century of interdependent risks and hopes has been germinating the possibility of human solidarity globalizing. We know what is to be done, the value of struggling on behalf of our beliefs based on species survival and ecological sustainability, and the urgency of the quest. This is the time to dedicate our hopes and indeed our lives to making cosmopolitanism in its protean forms begin to happen globally and locally, which is coincident with learning to live in accord with the ethical, ecological, and spiritual precepts of responsible anthropocentrism.

INDEX

accountability mechanisms, legal 254; conceptual approach to 179–82; generalizations of 182; geopolitical nullification and 182; geopolitical resistance to 198–99; implementation crises and 179; in international law 179–200; after Iraq War 198; after Kosovo War 193, 198; normative determinism and 183–90; nuclear weaponry and 180; universal 200; after Vietnam War 192–93; in Westphalian governance frameworks 181–82. *See also* Nuremberg Tribunals; Tokyo War Crimes Tribunal; *specific courts; specific tribunals*
activism: antiwar 117; in civil society 1, 44–45, 58; transnational contexts for 58
Adorno, Theodor 318
Afghanistan: international interventions in 80; interventionist struggles in 39n9; NATO withdrawal from 36–37; peacebuilding in 75n2; Taliban in 36; U.S. crimes in 199. *See also* First Gulf War
Africa 3, 12. *See also specific countries; specific topics*
Against Apocalypse (Dallmayr), 284
agro-ecology 139
Algeria 35, 78–79
Alliance of Civilizations project 73, 105
American exceptionalism 190
Amnesty International 180
anarchy. *See* global anarchy
Anthropocene 90, 328–29

anti-Apartheid campaign, in South Africa 34–35
anti-colonialism, international law and 149
anti-colonialist nationalism 47, 123–24
antifascist coalitions, during World War II 29
anti-imperialist nationalism 47
anti-nuclearism 131. *See also* deterrence; nuclear apartheid; nuclear disarmament treaties
Anti-Personnel Landmines Treaty 19
anti-Utopianism, cultural dispositions to 21
antiwar activism, international law as goal of 117
Apartheid, as delegitimizing practice 42
Apel, Karl-Otto 320
Appiah, Kwame Anthony 75n3
Aquinas, Thomas 122
Arab Spring protests 108; authoritarianism challenged by 257; failures of 261; legacy of governance structures after 23; as soft power 37; transformational justice and 257; transitional justice and 255–58; Westphalian governance frameworks influenced by 14
Archibugi, Daniele 320, 322
Arendt, Hannah 322
Argentina 221, 237, 255
Aristotle 274, 285
Aron, Raymond 73, 75n6, 77
Asia 3, 6n2, 12, 121. *See also specific countries; specific topics*
Asian Tigers 172, 174n8

atomic bombs, development and use
of: in Japan 124–25; legitimacy
crises and 51; Trinity Test explosion
131
Augustine 122
authoritarian regimes, Arab Spring
protests in 257
autocratic leaders 171
Axial Age 279n1. *See also* First Axial
Age; Second Axial Age

barbarism. *See* global barbarism
Barkan, Elazar 220
al Bashar, Omar 192
Basso Foundation 99, 194
Baxi, Upendra 14, 92
BDS (Boycott, Diversity, Sanction)
Campaign 150, 154
Beardsworth, Richard 289
Beck, Ulrich 320
Beijing Declaration on Ending Division
and Strengthening Palestinian
Authority 265
Ben Ali, Zine El Abidine 267
Benhabib, Seyla 320
Berlin, Germany 31, 38n3
Biden, Joe 5, 198
biodiversity, loss of 57, 126
bio-ethical-ecological crisis 6
Black Lives Matter movement 64, 312
"black swan" events 14, 314
Blair, Tony 211
Blinken, Antony 203n28, 270
Bohman, James 320
Bolivia 333
bottom-up democracy, in post-
Westphalian governance
frameworks 23
Boycott, Diversity, Sanction Campaign.
See BDS Campaign
Brazil 39n8, 85, 212, 237, 255
Bretton Woods institutions 52, 94, 162.
See also International Monetary
Fund; World Bank
BRIC countries: economic rise of 39n8;
hard power in 85; International
Monetary Fund challenged by
139n4; in United Nations 129;

World Bank challenged by 139n4.
See also Brazil; China; India; Russia
Brzezinski, Zbigniew 94–95, 97
Bull, Hedley 70, 77, 181, 254
Bush, George H. W. 32, 55, 202n13
Bush, George W. 39n5, 147, 193, 211
Butler, Judith 320, 322

Cahill, Kevin 299
Camarakis, Helen 2
Cambodia 223
Camus, Albert 318
Capital (Piketty) 175n13
capitalism: crony 172; disaster 201n2;
Marxist critiques of 172n9;
neoliberal 285
Cardoso, Fernando Henrique 255
Catholic Church, delegitimization
practices of 44
CCC. *See* Center for Constitutional
Rights
censorship, political realism and
135–37
Center for Constitutional Rights
(CCC) 211
Chávez, Hugo 268
Chayes, Abram 299
Chechnya 35
Chile 193–94, 237, 255
China: economic rise of 39n8, 128;
geopolitical rivalry with U.S., 20;
Global West and 138; hard power
in 85; as threat to West 56–57;
transformational justice in 268;
transitional justice in 266; in United
Nations 103. *See also* Great Powers
Chomsky, Noam 201n4
Churchill, Winston 190–91, 327
citizen pilgrims 137, 276, 292n9. *See
also* d'Escoto, Father Miguel
citizenship: Earth Charter and 276;
global 276; revisioning of 137–39;
world 19
civil society: activism in 1, 44–45, 58;
cosmopolitanism in 20; global 311–
12; in Global South 44–45; justice
in 211–12; transnational activism
in 58; Treaty on the Prohibition

of Nuclear Weapons and 133–34; United Nations and 141–56

clash of civilization hypothesis 188

classical realism 67, 73

von Clausewitz, Carl 77

climate change: chlorofluorocarbon use and 93; Conference of Parties 107; as global collective goods problem 90; global events from 2; oil and gas energy production and 155; Paris Climate Agreement (2015) 5, 58, 107, 130; scientific consensus on 5; as security threat 57. *See also* global warming

climate denialism 107

climate justice 59

Cobb, John 285, 288

Cold War: European colonialism collapse during 53–54; global governance during 52–54; historical circumstances for 2; legitimacy crises during 52–54; market-based constitutionalism during 2; populist geopolitics during 145–46; reparations mechanisms and 219; Ukraine War as renewal of 65; U.S. leadership after 2, 54; Westphalian governance frameworks influenced by 14. *See also* Nuremberg Tribunal; Tokyo War Crimes Tribunal

collective goods 90–91, 102–3

collective violence: conceptual approach to 117–20; new realism and 118; political realism and 118; state building and 118. *See also* antiwar activism; ethnic cleansing; genocide; warfare

colonialism, colonization and: collapse of 53–54, 97, 111n19; de-development of Asia and 6n2; humanitarian interventions during 241n3; international law and 121; League of Nations' approach to 48; legitimacy and 42; of Palestine 24; settler 79; world orders and 97. *See also* anti-colonialist nationalism; decolonization

commons. *See* global commons; public goods

Conference of Parties (COP) 107

Confucius 66–67, 285

Congressional Act (Hague Invasion Act) 205n54

constitutionalism, constitutions and: during Cold War 2; global governance informed by 87–109; Islamic 259; market-oriented 54; UN Charter and 93

constructivism 68, 72–73, 232, 310

COP. *See* Conference of Parties

corrective justice, reparations mechanisms and 239

cosmic humanism 68

cosmopolitanism: advantages of 74; assessment framework for 68–69; citizen pilgrims 70; in civil society 20; conceptual approach to 68; Declaration of the Rights of People and 333; decolonial 320; definitions of 63–64; ecumenical 291; forms of 69–72; global solidarity for 331–34; hard power and 321; imperial 320; moral 320; new 321–22; new political thinking and 319; new realism of 105; in policy contexts 73; preconditions for 331–34; as process 69–70; responsible 70; scope of 73–74; soft power and 321; spiritual 288–90; theoretical foundations of 283–84; universal aspects of 319; visionary 317–22; world order and 111n21

counter-hegemonies, international law and 139n1

counterterrorism 33; Global War on Terrorism 102, 290–91; Great Power rivalry and 65; against Al Qaeda 35; U.S. war on terror 56, 123

COVID-19 pandemic: as collective goods problem 91; geopolitics during 4; as global health emergency 325–26; in Global North 91; global responses to 46; in Global South 91; nationalism

during 4; statism 4; United Nations
    response to 46–47; World Health
    Organization response to 46–47,
    325–26
crimes of silence 126
criminal accountability. *See*
    accountability mechanisms
*Critical Perspectives on the Crisis of
    Global Governance* (Gill) 71–72
critical realism 69–70, 201n6
critical theory 71–73
crony capitalism 172
Cuba 268
Cuban Missile Crisis 31, 299
cultural evolution 5

Dalai Lama 285
Daley, Herman 285
Dallmayr, Fred 283–91, 320, 322.
    See also cosmopolitanism
Davos World Economic Forum 45
Declaration of the Rights of People
    333
Declaration on the Rights and
    Liberation of Peoples 212
decolonial cosmopolitanism 320
decolonization: in Algeria 78–79;
    ethnic cleansing and 79; hard
    power and 78–80; in India 79; in
    Indochina 78–79; morality of 78;
    soft power and 80; in South Africa
    79; sovereignty and 78; in Tibet
    78–80
de-democratization 286–87
de-development, of Asia 6n2
delegitimization practices: Apartheid as
    42; of Catholic Church 44; ecocide
    as 42; genocide as 42; slave trade
    as 42
Demenchonok, Edward 317–22
democracy: bottom-up 23; illiberal
    286; in post-Westphalian
    governance frameworks 23
democratic world governance: advocacy
    of 313–15; decentralization of
    power and 306, 313; global civil
    society and 311–12; Griffin on
    305–15; necessity for 307–9;

nongovernmental organizations
    and 311–12; possibility of 309–13;
    sovereignty and 306; theoretical
    approach to 305–6; Universal
    Declaration of Human Rights
    and 310
denialist politics 2
Derrida, Jacques 321
desirability, politics of, in Westphalian
    governance frameworks 13
deterrence, doctrines of 31, 127
de-territorialization, of world orders
    20
Dewey, John 285, 287–88, 318
Diamond, Jared 21
discrimination 122
Douglas, William O. 195
Doyle, Michael 70
drone warfare 19

Earth Charter: citizen pilgrims and
    276; coherence of 276; First
    Axial Age 274; global citizenship
    and 276; reviews of 273; Second
    Axial Age 274–75, 277–78,
    279n1
Earth Summit (UN) 55
Eastern Europe 38, 253
ecocide, as delegitimizing practice 42
ecological civilization 74
ecological security 135
economic nationalism 230
economic rights 164–65
Ecuador 333
ecumenical cosmopolitanism 291
Egypt: Arab Spring protests in 256–59;
    autocratic leadership in 171; Morsi
    Brotherhood in 261; Muslim
    Brotherhood in 256–58, 260, 267;
    transitional justice movement in
    258–63, 266–67, 270n8
Einstein, Albert 131–32
Eisenhower, Dwight 35
empathy, politics of, globalization and
    92
Engel, Ron 273–74, 276–77. *See also*
    Earth Charter
Ennahda Movement 267

enslaved people, reparations for
descendants of 235–36, 243n27
epistemology. *See* situated
epistemology
equality, of states, in Westphalian
governance frameworks 11
Erasmus, Desiderius 285
d'Escoto, Father Miguel 295–303
ethnic cleansing: as collective violence
118; decolonization and 79; Kosovo
War and 42–43; in Myanmar 219;
in Sudan 219; UN Security Council
response to 148; use of force
against 59n1. *See also* genocide
Etzioni, Amitai 310
EU. *See* European Union
Europe: international law development
in 121–27; rights of nature
movement in 24n2; Thirty Years'
War 183; Westphalian governance
system in 121–22. *See also*
European Union; *specific countries;
specific topics*
European Convention for the
Protection of Human Rights and
Fundamental Freedoms 225
European Parliament 99, 129
European Union (EU): loss of global
confidence in 12; Ukraine War
and 129; Westphalian governance
frameworks in 129. *See also specific
countries*
evolution, theory of: bio-ethical-
ecological crisis and 6; biological
5; cultural 5; natural selection
privileges 4; species identity in 5
exceptionalism: American 190;
geopolitical 104

Falk, Richard 296
feasible Utopias 66, 109n2
feminist theory 71
Financial Crisis of 2008-2009, 55
First Axial Age 274
First Gulf War 32, 148, 193, 198, 217,
227
For the Common Good (Cobb and
Daley) 285

formal juridical equality 120
Francis (Pope) 104, 285, 302
Francis of Assisi 285
Free Gaza Movement 154
Freire, Paulo 92
French Revolution 111n22, 265
Friedman, Milton 255
fundamentalist religious movements,
rise of 14
futureness 24

Gambia 42
Gandhi, Mahatma 38, 68, 285,
289–90, 319, 327. *See also* India
Gay, William C., 319
Gaza region, in Palestine: BDS
Campaign in 150, 154; Free Gaza
Movement 154; genocide in 79,
120, 139n3, 219, 221; Mavi
Marmara Freedom Flotilla 150;
Operation Cast Lead and 13, 200;
Operation Protective Edge 213. *See
also* Israel-Palestine conflict
Gaza War 153
genocide: as collective violence 118;
as delegitimizing practice 42; in
Gambia 42; in Gaza region 79, 120,
139n3, 219, 221; against Hamas
31; in Myanmar 193; in Palestine
79; in Rwanda 219; UN Genocide
Convention 204n35; UN Security
Council response to 148; use of
force against 59n1; Westphalian
governance frameworks and 49–50
geopolitical crimes 59n2
geopolitics, geopolitical issues and:
during COVID-19 pandemic 4;
enforcement regimes 132–33;
exceptionalism in 104; geopolitical
ambition 5; in Global South 127;
of Global West 79; Great Power
rivalry in 20; hard power and
84; intergovernmental behavior
influenced by 5; law and 27;
modification of expectations in
21–24; populism and 145–46;
situated epistemology and 65;
situated methodology and 65;

United Nations and 148–49;
in Westphalian governance
frameworks 123. *See also*
nonviolent geopolitics; *specific
topics*
Germany: illiberal societies in 124;
legitimacy crises after World War II
49; Pact of Paris and 184; post-
World War I punitive approaches
to 47; reparations mechanisms and
227, 243n21; transformational
justice in 251–52; under Versailles
Treaty 29
Gill, Stephen 71–72
Gini Coefficients, for global inequality
163, 167, 174n5
global anarchy 130
global barbarism 130
global citizenship 276
global civil society 311–12
global commons 135
global governance: during Cold
War 52–54; collapse of
European colonialism during
53–54; constitutional guidelines
for 87–109; decentralization of 52;
failures of 55–57; geopolitics and
41; internationalist approaches to
209–10; judicial dimension of
209–11; new era of 277; new
realism and 95–96; political
legitimacy and 47–52, 54–55; in
twenty-first century 55–57; after
World War I 47–49; after World
War II 49–52
global health emergencies: COVID-19
pandemic as 325–26; Great
Transition Initiative and 326
global humanism 68, 74
global interests, in Westphalian
governance frameworks 17, 24n2
globalization: neoliberal 2, 54–55,
71–72; politics of empathy and 92;
territoriality and 19
globalization-from-above 110n10
globalization-from-below 110n10
global justice movement 74
global norms. *See* norms

Global North: COVID-19 pandemic
in 91; International Criminal
Court and 209; international law
in 143–44; reaction to Israel-
Palestine conflict 214; reparations
mechanisms in 229. *See also*
Europe; European Union; United
States
Global Parliament 98–101
Global Rule of Law 147
global security, international law and
27–28
Global South: civil society activism
in 44–47; COVID-19 pandemic
in 91; economic inequality in
161–63; geopolitical interventions
in 127; historical circumstances
in 3; human rights in 143;
International Criminal Court
and 209; international law in
143; nationalism in 123; New
International Economic Order in
45; Non-Aligned Movement in 302;
reaction to Israel-Palestine conflict
214; reparations mechanisms in
229; transformational justice in
249; World Order Models Project
and 66. *See also* Africa; Latin
America; South America
global warming 2, 54–55, 84
Global War on Terrorism 102, 290–91
Global West 117, 123; China and 138;
geopolitics of 79; international law
manipulated by 156n1; political
imaginary of 136–37; political will
in 143–44
Goldstone Report 200, 202n17
Graeber, David 21, 23
Gramsci, Antonio 14
Great Britain: establishment of
Jewish homeland and 49; Iraq War
Tribunal 212; "Irish Problem" and
34; in Palestine 48–49. *See also*
decolonization
Great Depression 291
Great Powers: diplomacy by 143,
181; as geopolitical actors 42;
international law and 117, 119;

rivalry between 20, 65; United
Nations and 28; in world order
103–4
Great Recession of 2008, 159
Great Transition Initiative 326
green politics 59
Green Revolution 271n9
Griffin, David Ray 39n5, 288,
305–15. *See also* democratic world
governance
Grotius, Hugo 121, 183
gunboat diplomacy 34

Habermas, Jürgen 302, 320
Hague Invasion Act. *See* Congressional
Act
Hamas 31, 264
Hammarskjöld, Dag 301
Hardin, Russell 319
hard power 33; in Brazil 85; in China
85; cosmopolitanism and 321;
decolonization and 78–80; global
geopolitics and 84; global warning
imperatives and 84; in India 85;
international interventions in 81;
after 9/11 terrorist attacks in U.S.
82; post-Westphalian governance
frameworks and 128; in Russia 85;
United Nations and 146; warfare
and 84
Hathaway, Oona 183–86, 201n8
Hegel, Georg Wilhelm Friedrich 285
hegemony, hegemonic dimensions
and: U.S. geopolitical power as
83–84; in Westphalian governance
frameworks 12
Heidegger, Martin 285, 288–89
Held, David 320, 322
vanden Heuvel, William 64
historical circumstances, for global
events: for Cold War 2; in Global
South 3; for neoliberal globalization
2; for political mobilization 3;
scientific consensus and 2; in
Western world 3
The History of the Peloponnesian War
(Thucydides) 274–75
Hitler, Adolf 29, 191

Hobbes, Thomas 70, 77, 285
Holocaust, reparations mechanisms
after 228, 234–35
Holy Roman Empire 44, 108–9, 201n8
Hong Kong, as Asian Tiger 174n8
horizons of spirituality 297
humanism: cosmic 68; global 68, 74
humanity, in international law 122
human rights: Declaration on the
Rights and Liberation of Peoples
212; European Convention for
the Protection of Human Rights
and Fundamental Freedoms
225; European Court of Human
Rights and 225; global economic
inequality and 159–73; in Global
South 143; of Indigenous and
native peoples 143; Inter-American
Convention on Human Rights
224–25; international law
architecture of 141–42, 165,
230–31; justice as responsive to
6; neoliberalism and 173n3; new
realism and 95; nongovernmental
organizations and 165; UN
Declaration on Human Rights
164–65. *See also* Universal
Declaration of Human Rights
Human Rights Council 104, 151–52
Human Rights Watch 180
Hungary, autocratic leadership in
171
Huntington, Samuel 73; clash of
civilization hypothesis 188
Hussein, Saddam 151, 191–93, 211

ICC. *See* International Criminal Court
ICCPR. *See* United Nations
ICESCR. *See* United Nations
ICJ. *See* International Court of Justice
idealism, social 71
ideologies 4; nationalism as 90
Ikenberry, John 70
ILC. *See* International Law
Commission
illiberal democracies 286
illiberal societies 105, 124. *See also*
specific countries; specific states

IMF. *See* International Monetary Fund
imperial cosmopolitanism 320
imperialism: international law and
    121; in Latin America 54, 121.
    See also anti-imperialist nationalism
India 38, 39n8, 79, 85, 171
Indigenous and native peoples, human
    rights of 143
individualism, global inequality and
    160
Indochina 35, 78–79. *See also* Vietnam
    War
inequality, global: in Arab world
    161; Bretton Woods institutions'
    responses to 162; critiques of 162;
    economic 159–73; economic rights
    and 164–65; Gini Coefficient for
    163, 167, 174n5; global reform and
    174n6; in Global South 161–63;
    individualism and 160; meritocracy
    and 163–64; in Middle East region
    162; neoliberal globalization and
    164; Obama on 161, 168, 173n1;
    Occupy Movement 23, 107–8,
    159–60; in OECD countries 161;
    rise of 160; Universal Declaration
    on Human Rights and 169–71;
    in U.S. 161–63. *See also* political
    inequality
instrumental rationalism 329
intellectuals. *See* radical intellectuals
Inter-American Convention on Human
    Rights 224–25
International Commission on Kosovo
    204n41, 240n2
International Court of Justice (ICJ):
    Advisory Opinions of 100;
    compulsory jurisdiction for 303n3;
    Gambia and 42; jurisdiction of 209;
    Nicaragua v. United States 202n22,
    297, 299–300; Non-Proliferation
    Treaty and 110n8; rights of states
    under international law 110n13;
    Thailand and 223
international crimes: geopolitical
    crimes as distinct from 59n2.
    *See also specific courts and
    tribunals*

International Criminal Court (ICC):
    appraisal of 209; claims of selective
    enforcement 13; establishment
    of 19; Global North leaders in
    209; Global South leaders in 209;
    jurisdiction for 187–88; reforms of
    100; reparations mechanisms and
    239; Rome Statute and 214
international criminal law:
    Congressional Act 205n54;
    crimes of silence 126; Putin and
    125; Westphalian governance
    frameworks and 15. *See also*
    international crimes; *specific courts
    and tribunals*
International Criminal Tribunal for
    Rwanda 191–92, 195, 203n32,
    204n36, 204nn45–46
International Criminal Tribunal for the
    Former Yugoslavia 191–92, 195,
    203n32
international interventions, in foreign
    states: in Afghanistan 80; hard
    power and 81; illegitimacy of 81;
    soft power and 80; by Soviet Union
    80; by U.S., 81; in Vietnam 80
internationalism: from below 142–43;
    liberal 57, 137; new 19
The Internationalists (Hathaway and
    Shapiro) 183, 186
international law: accountability
    mechanisms in 179–200; anti-
    colonialism and 149; authority
    of 222–26; colonialism and 121;
    counter-hegemonic reconstruction
    of 139n1; customary norms of 122;
    European development of 121–27;
    geopolitical crimes under 59n2;
    in Global North 143–44; global
    security issues and 27–28; in Global
    South 143; Great Powers and 119;
    historical roles of 119; humanity
    in 122; human rights protections
    under 141–42, 165, 230–31;
    imperialism and 121; instruments
    of 222–26; just war traditions and
    220; margin of appreciation in
    59n3; militarism under 5; necessity

in 122; new realism and 95; outlawing of war under 123–26; political realism and 5; Principles of International Law 139n2; realist consensus on 77–78; reciprocity in 201n5; reparations mechanisms under 218–26, 229, 238–40, 241n4; rights of states under 110n13; state-level deference to 5; Third World Approaches to International Law 143; United Nations' responses to 141–56; U.S. war on terror under 123; war policy contexts for 117. *See also* International Criminal Court; international criminal law; *specific topics*

International Law Commission (ILC) 139n2, 195–96, 242n9; reparations mechanisms and 223–24

International Monetary Fund (IMF) 44, 52, 139n4, 240, 311

International Peace Force (UN) 132

international relations: de-securitization of 54; legitimacy crises and 53; in U.S. after 9/11 terrorist attacks 56

international reparations 227

international rule of law 100–101

IRA. *See* Irish Republican Army

Iran: Islamic constitutionalism in 259; Islamic Revolution in 259–63; Khomeini in 259–62; Nuclear Arms Agreement with Iran 57–58, 130; transitional justice in 266

Iranian Revolution 151, 258–63

Iraq: interventionist struggles in 39n9; nuclear weapons program in 16; peacebuilding in 75n2; reparations mechanisms in 233. *See also* Hussein, Saddam

Iraq War 16, 147–48, 198, 212

Iraq War Tribunal 126, 212

"Irish Problem" 34

Irish Republican Army (IRA) 34

Islamic Revolution 259–63

Israel: genocidal assault in Gaza 79, 120, 139n3; genocidal campaign against Hamas 31; Goldstone Report and 200, 202n17; Human Rights Council and 151–52; legitimacy war against 35; new wars by 152; in Occupied Palestine 31, 149–55; Operation Cast Lead 13, 200; Operation Protective Edge 213; Six Day War 151; suicide bombings in 152–53

Israel-Palestine conflict 212–13; d'Escoto and 295–303; Global North reaction to 214; Global South reaction to 214; transformational justice in 263–64; transitional justice in 261–64

Jackson, Robert 194, 211

Japan: illiberal societies in 124; legitimacy crises after World War II 49; transformational justice in 251–52, 270n3. *See also* Tokyo War Crimes Tribunal

Jaspers, Karl 252, 279n1

JCPOA. *See* Nuclear Arms Agreement with Iran

Jencks, Charles 14

Jervis, Robert 128

Johansen, Robert 17, 93, 105–6

judicial philosophy. *See* justice

justice, judicial philosophy and: in civil society 211–12; corrective 239; human rights and 6; rights of nature and 6. *See also* law; transformational justice; *specific topics*

just war traditions 122, 220

Kaldor, Mary 151–52, 320

Kant, Immanuel 285, 319

Kaplan, Lawrence 309

Kavka, Gregory 319

Kennan, George F. 77, 202n19

Kent, Roman 235

Khomeini (Ayatollah) 259–62

King, Martin Luther, Jr., 285, 319

Kissinger, Henry 67, 73, 77, 97, 192, 202n19, 270n4

Klerk, F. W. de 266

knowledge: normative branches of 88; situated 71

Koskenniemi, Martti 143–44
Kosovo War: criminal accountability
    after 193, 198; ethnic cleansing and
    42–43; International Commission
    on 204n41, 240n2; NATO and
    42–43, 219. *See also* International
    Criminal Tribunal for the Former
    Yugoslavia
Kristol, William 308–9
Krugman, Paul 168
Küng, Hans 310
Kuwait 126, 193, 202n13, 227, 237

Lackey, Douglas 319
Lasswell, Harold 243n22
Latin America 54, 121, 265–66. *See also*
    South America; *specific countries*
Lauterpacht, Hersch 183–84
law, geopolitics and 27
League of Nations 94, 204n35;
    colonialism and 48; establishment
    of 97; limitations of 180–81;
    nonviolent geopolitics and 28–29;
    United Nations and 146–47
Lebanon War 153
Lee, Steven 319
legitimacy, political: atomic bomb
    development and use and
    51; during Cold War 52–54;
    colonialism and 42; dimensions
    of 41; global crises in 49–54,
    58; through global governance
    47–52, 54–55; international
    relations and 53; legality and 41,
    59n1; of Myanmar 42; neoliberal
    globalization and 54–55; in nuclear
    age 51; of Palestine 41–42; Peace
    of Westphalia and 43–44; political
    legitimation as distinct from 41; of
    postwar Germany 49; of postwar
    Japan 49; transformational justice
    and 251; of United Nations 42;
    warmaking and 43; Westphalian
    governance frameworks and 12,
    44; after World War I 47–49; after
    World War II 49–52. *See also*
    delegitimization practices
legitimacy wars 35, 189, 203n30

legitimation, political, legitimacy as
    distinct from 41
Levinas, Emmanuel 318–19
liberal internationalism 57, 137
liberalism 69; realism and 70–71;
    scope of 73. *See also* neoliberalism
Liberia 192
Libya 43, 220, 256–58
Lichtenstein 103
Limits to Growth (study) 88
London Charter 191, 195–96

Machiavelli, Niccolò 77
MAD. *See* mutual assured destruction
Madrid, Spain, terrorist attacks in 33
Major, John 34
Malaysia, withdrawal from UN
    59n4
Mandela, Nelson 38, 266, 285, 292n2,
    295, 315n6. *See also* anti-Apartheid
    campaign; South Africa
Mandelbaum, Michael 22, 309, 315n1
market-based constitutionalism, during
    Cold War 2, 54
market socialism 172
Marshall Plan 253
Marxism, capitalism critiqued by
    172n9
Mavi Marmara Freedom Flotilla 150
Mazower, Mark 11–12
McDougal, Myres 243n22
McNamara, Robert 192
Mearsheimer, John 77
Micklethwait, John 111n22
Middle East region 48, 162. *See also*
    specific countries; specific states
militant popular movements 106
militarism: failures of 203n23; under
    international law 5; U.S. investment
    in 55–56. *See also* warfare
military-industrial complex, in U.S. 35
military Keynesianism, in U.S. 35
Milonova, Sasha 175n12
Milosevic, Slobodan 151, 193, 199,
    211, 219
modernity, political order and 1
Montesquieu, Baron de 285
moral cosmopolitanism 320

morality: cosmopolitanism and 320; of decolonization 78; realist consensus on 77–78
Morgenthau, Hans 77, 202n19
Morocco, inequality in 175n12
Morsi, Mohamed 256, 267
Morsi Brotherhood 261
Moscow Declaration 205n48
Mubarak, Hosni 256–57, 260
Muslim Brotherhood 256–58, 260, 267
mutual assured destruction (MAD) 96
Myanmar 42, 105, 193, 219

nationalism: anti-colonialist 47; anti-imperialist 47; during COVID-19 pandemic 4; economic 230; in Global South 123; intergovernmental behavior and 5; non-Western 123; as political ideology 90
NATO. See North Atlantic Treaty Organization
natural selection, privileges of 4
nature. See rights of nature movement
Nazism 21–22, 318
necessity, politics of: in international law 122; justification of 14–15; in Westphalian governance frameworks 13–14; World War I and 16; World War II and 16
neoliberalism: capitalism and 285; global inequality and 164; globalization of 2, 54–55, 71–72; global warming issues and 54–55; human rights and 173n3; legitimacy and 54–55; "there is no alternative" approach to 21, 255; transformational justice and 249–69
Netanyahu, Benjamin 198
new cosmopolitanism 321–22
New Deal policies, in U.S. 52
New Haven School 243n22
New International Economic Order (NIEO) 45
new internationalism 19
new realism 94, 97, 290; of cosmopolitanism 105; global

governance and 95–96; human rights and 95; international law and 95; Treaty on the Prohibition of Nuclear Weapons and 134; Utopianism and 136, 296
new wars 144, 152
new world order (NWO) 183–84, 186, 188, 202n13
New Zealand 333
NGOs. See nongovernmental organizations
Nicaragua 297–98
Nicaraguan Revolution 302
Nicaragua v. United States 202n22, 297, 299–300
NIEO. See New International Economic Order
9/11 terrorist attacks, in U.S.: Bush, George W., and 39n5, 193; forms of power after 82–83; hard power after 82; re-securitization of international relations after 56; rush to war after 39n5; soft power after 82–83
Nixon, Richard 192
Non-Aligned Movement 302
nongovernmental organizations (NGOs): democratic world governance and 311–12; human rights and 165; in Myanmar 42; Treaty on the Prohibition of Nuclear Weapons and 133. See also specific organizations
Non-Proliferation Treaty (NPT) 16, 96, 132–33, 179; Article VI 110n8; discriminatory implementation of 104; International Court of Justice and 110n8
non-state civil actors, in Westphalian governance frameworks 19
nonviolent geopolitics: alternatives to 37–38; challenges in 37–38; conceptual approach to 27–28; ethical argument for 32–37; Great Depression and 29; League of Nations and 28–29; legalistic approach to 28–31; opportunities in 37–38; patterns in 37–38; political

argument for 32–37; soft power and 34; UN Charter and 28–31; after World War I 28–29; World War II and 28–29

norms, global 4

North Atlantic Treaty Organization (NATO): global security and 129; Kosovo War and 42–43, 219; Libya and 43; non-proliferation regime and 16; strategic interests and 219; withdrawal from Afghanistan 36–37

North Korea 126

NPT. See Non-Proliferation Treaty

nuclear apartheid 96, 133

Nuclear Arms Agreement with Iran (JCPOA) 57–58, 130

nuclear disarmament treaties 38; Treaty on the Prohibition of Nuclear Weapons 19, 105, 133–34, 200, 203n25. See also Non-Proliferation Treaty

nuclearism 67, 131–32, 318. See also anti-nuclearism

nuclear weapons, policies and programs for: as global collective goods problem 90; in Iraq 16; legitimacy crises and 51; No First Use strategies for 134–35; Non-Proliferation Treaty 16, 96, 104, 110n8, 132–33; nuclear apartheid 96; Nuclear Arms Agreement with Iran 57–58, 130; of Obama 13; political realism and 133; as security threat 57; Treaty on the Prohibition of Nuclear Weapons 19, 105, 133–34, 200, 203n25. See also atomic bombs

Nuremberg Tribunals/Nuremberg Trials 49–50, 252; as accountability mechanism 254; Charter of the Nuremberg Tribunal 139n2; global context for 210–11; Jackson and 194, 211; legal legacy of 194–200; London Charter and 191, 195–96; Nuremberg Judgment 125, 185, 188–200, 203n27, 214–15; Nuremberg Principles 125, 195, 199–200; "Nuremberg Promise" 30, 125; secondary 191; as transitional justice 254

NWO. See new world order

Obama, Barack 13, 36, 161, 168, 173n1, 193

Occupied Palestine: Israel in 31, 149–55; U.S. crimes in 199

Occupy Movement 23, 107–8, 159–60, 312, 314

OECD. See Organization for Economic Development and Cooperation

old realism 94–97

old world order (OWO) 183, 185–86, 188, 201n8

Operation Cast Lead 13, 200

Operation Protective Edge 213

Organization for Economic Development and Cooperation (OECD) 161

Oslo Framework of Principles 264

Ottoman Empire 47, 108–9

OWO. See old world order

Pact of Paris 124, 184–85, 187–89, 205n47

Pahlavi, Reza (Shah) 259–60. See also Iranian Revolution

Pal, Radhabinod 270n1

Palestine, Palestinian people and: BDS Campaign in 150, 154; Beijing Declaration on Ending Division and Strengthening Palestinian Authority 265; British authority in 48; colonialism of 24; establishment of Jewish homeland in 49; Free Gaza Movement 154; genocidal assaults in 79; Hamas in 265; Human Rights Council and 151–52; Israel occupation of 31, 149–55; legitimacy of 41–42; legitimacy war by 35; in new wars 152; self-determination of 37, 79. See also Gaza region; Israel-Palestine conflict; Occupied Palestine

Palma, Gabriel 174n5

Panikkar, Raimon 285, 287

Paris Climate Change Agreement (2015) U.S. participation in 5, 58, 107, 130
Parker, Richard 175n18
Paul II (Pope) 302
peace, peacebuilding and: maximal 64; methodological approach to 87–88; minimal 64; realism and 127–28; as regime-changing intervention 75n2; theoretical approaches to 63–64; U.S. policy and 65, 117–18
Peace of Westphalia (Treaty of Westphalia) 11, 43–44, 97, 121
Pedagogy of the Oppressed (Freire) 92
people power movement, in Philippines 38
Perle, Richard 308–9
Permanent Court of International Justice 222
Permanent Peoples Tribunal (PPT) 99–101, 126, 212. *See also specific tribunals*
Perpetual Peace (Kant) 319
Philippines 38, 171
Piketty, Thomas 175n13
Pinochet, Augusto 192–94, 219
Plato 274, 285
plutocratic leadership 174n7
Poland, autocratic leadership in 171
political inequality 120
political legitimacy. *See* legitimacy
political mobilization, historical circumstances for 3
political order, modernity and 1
political realism: censorship and 135–37; international law and 5; limitations of 138; new world order and 186; nuclear weapons policies and 133; in Westphalian governance frameworks 126–27
politics of possibility/impossibility 325–29
politics of spirituality, in Westphalian governance frameworks 13
populism 23–24, 145–46; issue-oriented 108
postmodern constructive thought 310

post-Westphalian governance frameworks: bottom-up democracy in 23; as collective goods challenge 102–3; global anarchy and 130; hard power approach and 128; historical relevance of 11; normative potential of 102; responsibility to protect norms in 103; scope of 110n14; soft power approach and 128
power: realist misunderstandings of 83. *See also* hard power; soft power
PPT. *See* Permanent Peoples Tribunal
Project for a New American Century 39n5
proportionality 122
public goods, in Westphalian governance frameworks 17
public policies, zero-sum 4
Puerto Rico 35
von Pufendorf, Samuel 121
Putin, Vladimir 104, 125

Al Qaeda 35

R2P norms. *See* responsibility to protect norms
radical intellectuals 23
rationalism. *See* instrumental rationalism
Reagan, Ronald 298
realism: critical 201n6; international law and 77–78; liberalism as derivative of 70–71; morality and 77–78; new 94–97, 105, 134, 136, 290, 296; old 94–97; peacebuilding and 127–28; power and 83; scope of 73; in statecraft 75n6; warfare and 127–28; in Westphalian governance frameworks 85. *See also* classical realism; critical realism; political realism; structural realism
Reich, Robert 168
Reisman, Michael 243n22
relational praxis 287
reparations ethos 226
reparations mechanisms: in Argentina 237; in Brazil 237; categories of

claimants 240; in Chile 237; Cold War and 219; confusion over 228; as corrective justice 239; for descendants of enslaved people 235–36, 243n27; extreme selectivity of 238, 243n33; after First Gulf War 227; generality of obligation in 237–38; generational approaches to 234–36; Germany and 227, 243n21; in Global North 229; in Global South 229; after Holocaust 228, 234–35; individuation in 236–37, 242n13; International Criminal Court and 239; international historical context for 218–22; under international law 218–26, 229, 238–40, 241n4; International Law Commission and 223–24; International Monetary Fund and 240; international reparations 227; in Iraq 233; for Japanese-Americans 236; just compensation assessments 240; in Kuwait 227, 237; limiting conditions for 232–33; misunderstandings about 226–27; as punitive 243n23; reliance and 217; remoteness in time and 217, 234–36; sanctions and 227–28; in South Africa 233–34; in transitional societies 228–30; UN Charter and 217; unevenness of 233–34; Universal Declaration of Human Rights and 224, 230–31, 241n6; UN Voluntary Fund for Victims of Torture 240; in U.S. 175n11; Versailles approach 242nn12–13; World Bank and 240
responsibility to protect norms (R2P norms) 219; in Libya 220; non-use of 104; in post-Westphalian governance frameworks 103; United Nations and 43–44, 149–50; Westphalian governance frameworks and 102
re-territorialization 20
rights. See human rights; rights of nature

Rights of Mother Nature 333
rights of nature movement 6, 24n2
Robins, Paul 251
Robins, Simon 251
Rome Statute, International Criminal Court and 214
Roosevelt, Franklin D. 29, 97, 191; New Deal policies 52
Roy, Arundhati 194
rule of law: Global Rule of Law 147; international 100–101
Russell, Bertrand 126, 194, 318
Russell Tribunal 99, 188, 194, 210–11, 212–15
Russia: autocratic leadership in 171; economic rise of 39n8; geopolitical rivalry with U.S. 20; hard power in 85. See also Great Powers; Ukraine War
Russian Revolution 123–24, 252, 265
Rwanda: genocide in 219. See also International Criminal Tribunal for Rwanda

Sachs, Jeffrey 302
Sagan, Carl 319
Saied, Kais 257
Sakharov, Andrey D. 319
Sandel, Michael 289
Sanders, Bernie 159–60, 168
Sands, Philippe 191, 203n27
Sartre, Jean-Paul 318
Saudi Arabia 258
Schell, Jonathan 285, 319
Schoenman, Ralph 126
scientific consensus: on climate change 5; historical circumstances for 2
Second Axial Age 274–75, 277–78, 279n1
security. See global security
"security dilemma" 128
Sen, Amartya 164
settler colonialism 79
Shapiro, Scott 183–86, 201n8
Shaw, George Bernard 327
Singapore, as Asian Tiger 174n8
situated epistemology 65
situated knowledge 71

situated methodology 65
Six Day War 151
slave trade, as delegitimizing practice
    42
smart agriculture 139
social idealism 71
socialism 2–3, 164; market 172
social rights 164–65
soft power: Arab Spring protests
    as 37; cosmopolitanism and
    321; decolonization and 80;
    international interventions in 80;
    after 9/11 terrorist attacks in U.S.,
    82–83; nonviolent geopolitics and
    34; post-Westphalian governance
    frameworks and 128
soft revolutions, in Eastern Europe 38
Somerville, John 319
Somoza, Anastasio 297–98
South Africa: anti-Apartheid campaign
    in 34–35; decolonization in 79;
    reparations mechanisms in 233–34;
    transitional justice in 265–66
South America, rights of nature
    movement in 24n2
South Korea 126, 174n8
sovereignty, sovereign rights and:
    decolonization and 78; democratic
    world governance and 306;
    intergovernmental behavior
    and 5; for Kuwait 193. See also
    territoriality
Soviet Union: collapse of 3; Cuban
    Missile Crisis 31; international
    interventions by 80; socialism and
    2–3; UN Security Council concerns
    50
Soviet Union collapse, Westphalian
    governance frameworks influenced
    by 14
Spain, Madrid terrorist attacks 33
spiritual cosmopolitanism 288–90
Sri Lanka 105
Stalin, Joseph 190–91
Stalinism, false label as Utopian
    21–22
statism, statehood and: during
    COVID-19 pandemic 4; Hobbes on

70; realism and 75n6; Westphalian
    governance frameworks and 65
Stiglitz, Joseph 302
Stoics 290
Stone, Harlan Fiske 194–95
Strategic Vision (Brzezinski) 94–95
structural realism 67
sub-system dominance 4
Sudan, ethnic cleansing in 219
Suez Operation 126
Sweden 105
Syria 31, 43, 203n24, 258
systems theory 4

Taiwan, as Asian Tiger 174n8
Taleb, Nassim 14
Taliban, in Afghanistan 36
Taylor, Charles 192
territoriality, territorial borders
    and: after collapse of Ottoman
    Empire 47; globalization and
    19; in Westphalian governance
    frameworks 18–20
Thailand 223
Thatcher, Margaret 21, 92, 255
"there is no alternative" approach
    (TINA approach), to neoliberalism
    21, 255
Third World Approaches to
    International Law (TWAIL) 143,
    156n1
Thirty Years' War 183
Thomas Aquinas 122
Thucydides 77, 274–75
Thunberg, Greta 1, 58
Tibet 35, 78–80
TINA approach. See "there is no
    alternative" approach
Tobin Tax 99
Tocqueville, Alexis de 160, 292n4
Tokyo War Crimes Tribunal 49–50,
    205n50, 252; as accountability
    mechanism 254; "comfort women"
    issue 212; global context for
    210–11; Tokyo Judgment 125,
    195, 203n33; as transitional
    justice 254
Tolstoy, Leo 21, 319

TPNW. *See* Treaty on the Prohibition
of Nuclear Weapons
transformational justice: Arab Spring
protests and 256; assessment of
268–69; in China 268; conceptual
approach to 249–51; in Eastern
Europe 253; in Germany 252–54;
in Global South 249; goals of 250;
in Israel-Palestine conflict 263–64;
in Japan 252, 270n3; legitimacy
and 250; Marshall Plan and 253;
neoliberalism and 249–69; Russian
Revolution and 252; world orders
and 249–69; after World War II
252–54
transitional justice: Arab Spring
protests and 256–58; in Argentina
255; assessment of 268–69; in
Brazil 255; in Chile 255; in China
265; in Egypt 258–63, 266–67,
270n8; in Iran 266; in Israel-
Palestine conflict 263–64; in Latin
America 265; liberal bias toward
265–68; Nuremberg Tribunals as
254; in South Africa 265–66; Tokyo
War Crimes Tribunal and 254; in
Tunisia 256–58, 266–67; world
order constraints on 254–55. *See
also* transformational justice
transnational civil society activism 58
Treaty on the Prohibition of Nuclear
Weapons (TPNW) 19, 105, 133–34,
200, 203n25
Trilateral Commission 45
Truman, Harry 318
Trump, Donald: climate denialism
by 107; criminality of 197–98;
defunding of WHO 47; on
economic inequality 159–60; legal
accountability for 197; nuclear age
under 318; Paris Climate Agreement
withdrawal by 5, 107, 130; 2016
election of 162, 168
Trumpism 286–87
Tunisia 256–58, 266–67
Turkey: autocratic leadership in 171;
Islam in 260; Kurdish rights in 154

Tutu, Desmond 285
Tu Weiming 66, 92, 329
TWAIL. *See* Third World Approaches
to International Law

UDHR. *See* Universal Declaration of
Human Rights
Ukraine War: EU and 129; geopolitical
rivalry as foundation of 20; nuclear
threats as result of 91, 106; renewal
of Cold War and 65
UN. *See* United Nations
UN Charter: constitutional framework
in 93; doctrines of deterrence and
31; internal sovereignty principles
31; nonintervention commitments
of 30; nonviolent geopolitics and
28–31; "Nuremberg promise"
and 30; Preamble to 63, 276;
principles of 29–30; prohibition of
force in 125–26; reform of 22, 71;
reparations mechanisms and 217;
retreat from universalism 50; Syria
and 31; use of force principle in
142; World War II and 29, 38n2
The Unconquerable World (Schell),
285
UNESCO. *See* United Nations
unipolarity 136, 155
United Nations (UN): Alliance of
Civilizations project 73, 105; BRIC
countries' influence within 129; civil
society and 141–56; Conference
on Environment and Development
60n7; constitutional framework
for 98; Convention Against
Torture 225, 241n6; Declaration
on Human Rights 164–65; as
dysfunctional structure 4; Earth
Summit 55; Educational, Scientific,
and Cultural Organization 42,
163; Emergency Force 98–101;
establishment and founding of 63;
formal juridical equality and 120;
General Assembly 103, 169–70,
174n6; Genocide Convention
204n35, 213; geopolitics and

148–49; Great Powers and 29; hard power states and 146; International Convention on the Elimination of All Forms of Racial Discrimination 241n6; International Covenant on Civil and Political Rights 24n5, 241n6; International Covenant on Economic, Social, and Cultural Rights 24n5, 170; international law and 141–56; International Peace Force 132; Israel/Palestine conflict and 149–55; Law of the Sea Treaty and 204n35; League of Nations and 146–47; loss of legitimacy for 42; Malaysia withdrawal from 59n4; military ascendancy and 144–45; political ascendancy and 144–45; response to COVID-19 pandemic 46–47; responsibility to protect norms and 43–44, 149–50; statist framework for 103; Sustainable Development Goals 175n10; in Syria 43; Thunberg at 1; Treaty on the Prohibition of Nuclear Weapons 19, 105–33–134, 133–34, 200, 203n25; Voluntary Fund for Victims of Torture 240; Westphalian governance frameworks and 145–49. *See also* d'Escoto, Father Miguel; UN Charter; UN Security Council

United States (U.S.): American exceptionalism 190; autocratic leadership in 171; Cuban Missile Crisis 31, 299; geopolitical rivalry with China 20; geopolitical rivalry with Russia 20; gunboat diplomacy and 34; as hegemonic geopolitical power 83–84; international interventions by 81; investment in militarism 55–56; Iraq War and 16; Iraq War Tribunal 212; Marshall Plan 253; military-industrial complex in 35; military Keynesianism in 35; New Deal policies in 52; as non-territorial global state 18–19; Nuclear Arms

Agreement with Iran 57–58, 130; participation in Paris Climate Change Agreement 5, 58, 107, 130; peacebuilding policies 65, 117–18; reparations mechanisms in 175n11; "Vietnam syndrome," 32, 81–82; war on terror 56, 123; Washington Consensus 255. *See also* First Gulf War; Great Powers; Ukraine War; Vietnam War; *specific people; specific topics*

Universal Declaration of Human Rights (UDHR) 22–23, 141, 165–68; Article 25, 278; Article 28, 278; democratic world governance and 310; inequalities of income and wealth and 169–71; instruments of 174n4; reparations mechanisms and 224, 230–31, 241n6

universalism, UN Charter and 50

UN Security Council: Iraq War and 147–48; permanent members of 31, 98, 129–30, 146; reform of composition of 12–13; response to ethnic cleansing/genocide 148; Soviet Union concerns about 50

U.S. *See* United States

use of force: in UN Charter 125–26, 142; UN prohibitions on 125–26

Utopianism 89; feasible 66, 109n2; Nazism and 21–22; new realism and 136, 296; Stalinism and 21–22

Vattel, Emer de 121
Venezuela 268
Versailles Treaty, Germany under 29
Vietnam, international interventions in 80
"Vietnam syndrome," 32, 81–82
Vietnam War: criminal prosecutions after 192–93; as doctrinal failure 80; Russell Tribunal and 99, 188, 194, 210–15; U.S. role in 32, 136, 187

Walt, Stephen 77
Waltz, Kenneth 67, 77

Walzer, Michael 310
war crimes trials and tribunals. *See*
    Nuremberg Tribunal; Tokyo War
    Crimes Tribunal
warfare, war policies and: chemical
    weapons use 201n7; crisis
    management for 96; deterrence
    strategies 96; drone warfare 19;
    under international law 117,
    123–26; just war traditions 122;
    legitimacy as justification for
    43; mutual assured destruction
    philosophy and 96; new wars 144;
    after 9/11 terrorist attacks 39n5;
    realism and 127–28; Westphalian
    governance frameworks and 106.
    See also antiwar activism
war on terror, as U.S. foreign policy
    56, 123. *See also* Global War on
    Terrorism
Warren, Elizabeth 168
Washington Consensus 255
Wendt, Alexander 306
Westphalian governance frameworks:
    accountability mechanisms in
    181–82; Arab Spring protests
    and 14; Cold War influenced by
    14; equality of states in 11; in
    EU 129; in Europe 121–22; as
    European regional arrangement
    44; exclusion of non-state civil
    actors in 19; expectations of 13;
    genocide documentation and
    49–50; geopolitics of 123; global
    interests in 17, 24n2; Great Power
    diplomacy and 181; hegemonic
    dimensions of 12; hierarchical
    dimensions of 12; Holy Roman
    Empire and 44; international
    criminal law and 15; just war
    traditions 122; legitimacy and
    12, 44; legitimating logic of 12;
    paradigm shift in 126–27; Peace
    of Westphalia and 11, 97; political
    realism in 126–27; politics of
    desirability in 13; politics of
    necessity in 13–14; politics of

spirituality in 13; prioritization
    of national interests in 17–18;
    public goods in 17; realism in 85;
    responsibility to protect norms
    102; rethinking of 97–98; Soviet
    Union collapse influenced by 14;
    statehood and 65; structural reform
    in 129–30; subversion of 101–9;
    territorial borders ands territoriality
    in 18–20; United Nations and
    145–49; vertical dimensions of 12;
    war dangers and 106; world orders
    influenced by 15, 97–98, 129. *See
    also* democratic world governance;
    post-Westphalian governance
    frameworks
Whitehead, Alfred North 285, 288, 310
Whitman, Walt 288
WHO. *See* World Health Organization
Wilson, Woodrow 29, 123
WOMP. *See* World Order Models
    Project
Woolridge, Adrian 111n22
World Bank 44, 52, 139n4, 240, 311
world citizenship 19
World Economic Forum 172, 176n22
World Health Organization (WHO),
    46–47, 325–26
world order complacency 108
World Order Models Project (WOMP),
    66–67, 109n2
world orders: collapse of colonialism
    and 97; de-territorialization of
    20; fragmented forms of 1; Great
    Powers in 103–4; new 183–84, 186,
    188, 202n13; old 183, 185–86,
    188, 201n8; transformational
    justice and 249–69; transitional
    justice and 254–55; Universal
    Declaration of Human Rights and
    22–23; Westphalian governance
    frameworks as influence on 15,
    97–98, 129; after World War II 28,
    38n2. *See also* post-Westphalian
    governance frameworks;
    Westphalian governance
    frameworks

World Trade Organization (WTO), 52, 162

World War I: anti-colonialist nationalism after 47; anti-imperialist nationalism after 47; global governance after 47–49; horizons of necessity and 16; legitimacy after 47–49; nonviolent geopolitics after 28–29; peace arrangements after 217; Permanent Court of International Justice after 222. *See also* League of Nations

World War II: antifascist coalition during 29; global economy during 51–52; horizons of necessity and 16; legitimacy crises after 49–52; Marshall Plan after 253; nonviolent geopolitics and 28–29; transformational justice after 251–54; UN Charter and 28; world order after 28. *See also* atomic bombs; Nuremberg Tribunal; Tokyo War Crimes Tribunal

Wright, Martin 70

WTO. *See* World Trade Organization

Yemen 256–58

zero-sum policymaking 4

ABOUT THE AUTHORS

Richard Falk is Albert G. Milbank Professor Emeritus of International Law at Princeton University, where he was an active member of the faculty for forty years (1961–2001). He is also chair of global law at Queen Mary University's Faculty of Law in London (2021), as well as co-director of the Centre of Environmental Justice and Crime. He is research associate the Orfalea Center of Global Studies at the University of California, Santa Barbara (UCSB), and fellow of the Tellus Institute. He directed the project on Global Climate Change, Human Security, and Democracy at UCSB and formerly served as director of the North American group in the World Order Models Project. Between 2008 and 2014, Falk served as UN special rapporteur on human rights in Occupied Palestine. His memoir, *Public Intellectual: The Life of a Citizen Pilgrim*, received an award from Global Policy Institute at Loyola Marymount University as "the best book of 2021." Other recent books include *On Nuclear Weapons: Denuclearization, Demilitarization and Disarmament* (2019), *Liberating the UN: Realism with Hope* (2017), *Power Shift* (2017), and *Revisiting the Vietnam War* (2017). His book *This Endangered Planet* (1972) was selected by the journal *Foreign Affairs* as one of the six most influential books published in the last century to address global issues. In 2016, Falk published a book of poems under the title of *Waiting for Rainbows*. He has been nominated for the Nobel Peace Prize several times since 2008. He currently serves as president of the Gaza Tribunal Project.

Sasha Milonova is a researcher, writer, and activist. She is a research assistant to Richard Falk at Queen Mary University School of Law, as well as the Rapporteur of the Gaza Tribunal. She is pursuing a PhD in the Centre for Research Architecture at Goldsmiths University in London, where she is investigating state crimes against migrants.